New Proofs for the Existence of God

New Proofs for the Existence of God

Contributions of Contemporary Physics and Philosophy

Robert J. Spitzer, S.J., Ph.D.

WILLIAM B. EERDMANS PUBLISHING COMPANY
GRAND RAPIDS, MICHIGAN / CAMBRIDGE, U.K.

Published 2010 by

Wm. B. Eerdmans Publishing Co.

2140 Oak Industrial Drive N.E., Grand Rapids, Michigan 49505 /

P.O. Box 163, Cambridge CB3 9PU U.K.

Printed in the United States of America

16 15 14 13 12   7 6

Library of Congress Cataloging-in-Publication Data

Spitzer, Robert J., 1952-

New proofs for the existence of God: contributions of contemporary physics
and philosophy / Robert J. Spitzer.

p.   cm.

Includes bibliographical references and index.

ISBN 978-0-8028-6383-6 (pbk.: alk. paper)

1. God (Christianity) 2. God — Proof. 3. Physics — Religious aspects —
Christianity. 4. Philosophical theology.   I. Title.

BT103.S687   2010

212′.1 — dc22

2010013887

www.eerdmans.com

In memory of my mother,
whose faith has inspired me from childhood to this day;

and my father,
whose love of learning stirred the spirit of inquiry within me.

And in memory of Paul Weiss,
whose freedom and discipline in metaphysical creativity
made a lifelong impression.

Contents

Contents

Contents

Acknowledgments

I owe a sincere debt of gratitude to Camille De Blasi Pauley, without whom this book would have never seen the light of day. She has not only typed multiple drafts of this manuscript, but also has played a crucial role in transferring the material from my head to the computer. She has spent countless hours interacting with me and formatting and fine-tuning this text. Her many editorial suggestions have made this volume clearer and more accessible.

I would also like to thank *International Philosophical Quarterly* for permission to use my published materials from the June 2001 and September 2001 issues; Pachart Publishing and the Vatican Observatory for permission to use my published materials from the 2003 issue of *Philosophy in Science;* and the *Journal of Ultimate Reality and Meaning* (Toronto) for permission to use my published materials from the December 2004 issue.

I am grateful to the many people who have supported and influenced me intellectually throughout the last fifteen years, particularly Dr. Paul Weiss, Dr. James Collins, Dr. Vernon Bourke, William Wallace, O.P., Dr. Timothy Eastman, Thomas King, S.J., Joseph Koterski, S.J., and William Stoeger, S.J. I am also grateful to Theodore Wolf, S.J., and William Carney, S.J., who got me started in the philosophical enterprise at Gonzaga University in 1972-73.

I would also like to express my sincere appreciation to Joan Jacoby for her invaluable help in preparing the final manuscript and to those who have helped me indirectly, including the Jesuit Community, my staff, and the professors and students at Gonzaga University, Seattle University, and Georgetown University.

Introduction

The last few years have seen several books championing agnosticism or atheism making their way into the popular press. These books leave most informed readers quite baffled, because they ignore the vast majority (if not the entirety) of the considerable evidence for theism provided by physics and philosophy during the last few decades. This evidence is capable of grounding reasonable and responsible belief in a super-intelligent, transcendent, creative power that stands at the origins of our universe or any hypothetically postulated multiverse. The main purpose of this book is to give a brief synopsis of this evidence to readers who are interested in exploring the strongest rational foundation for faith that has come to light in human history.

The great physicist Sir Arthur Eddington remarked in his classic work *The Nature of the Physical World:*

> We all know that there are regions of the human spirit untrammeled by the world of physics. In the mystic sense of the creation around us, in the expression of art, in a yearning towards God, the soul grows upward and finds the fulfillment of something implanted in its nature. The sanction for this development is within us, a striving born with our consciousness or an Inner Light proceeding from a greater power than ours. Science can scarcely question this sanction, for the pursuit of science springs from a striving which the mind is impelled to follow, a questioning that will not be suppressed. Whether in the intellectual pursuits of science or in the mystical pursuits of the spirit, the light beckons ahead and the purpose surging in our nature responds.[1]

1. Eddington 1928, pp. 327-28.

1

Perhaps this light is responsible for the persistent rational pursuit of ultimate grounds and causation which has been frequently associated with God since the time of Plato[2] and Aristotle.[3] Though there have been centuries of controversy about the legitimacy of these proofs (particularly from the late eighteenth to early twentieth centuries), contemporary developments in physics, philosophy, and mathematics have led to a rekindled interest and an expanded pursuit of them.[4]

In the twentieth century, David Hilbert (the father of finite mathematics) has given new probative force and depth to the argument for the intrinsic finitude of past time (implying a timeless Creator) in his article "On the Infinite."[5] Quantum Theory has expanded the horizons of ontology by obliging it to contend with non-location and information fields, which, in their turn, have given new evidence for non-materialistic (information-like) dimensions of physical reality. The General Theory of Relativity has forced us to re-envision the universe as a dynamically integrated finite whole in contradistinction to Newton's infinite universe of mass points in empty space.

---

2. Incipient proofs for the existence of God may be found in "the argument for participation in perfect Goodness" (in Books VI and VII of the *Republic,* Plato 1961); in the intimations of an eternal Creator from which all else is a fleeting image (in the *Timaeus,* Plato 1961, p. 1167; 37d-39e): "Wherefore [the eternal Creator] resolved to have a moving image of eternity, and when he set in order the heavens, he made this image eternal but moving according to number, while eternity itself rests in unity; and this image we call time." See also Being, one of the five greatest forms, in the *Sophist* (Plato 1961, pp. 999-1007; 254c-259e).

3. Aristotle formulates the first *a posteriori* proofs for the existence of God, arguing to a first *efficient* Cause of all reality in Book VIII of the *Physics,* and a first *final* Cause of reality in Book XII of the *Metaphysics.* He initiates his proof for a first efficient Cause as follows: ". . . the fact that there must exist something which is immovable and exempt from all external change, both unqualified and accidental, and which can move another, is clear from the following considerations" (Aristotle 1991, *Physics,* Book VIII — 252b10ff.). In *Metaphysics,* Aristotle articulates his solution to the problem of how the first Mover can move without being in motion, namely, by drawing (as a final Cause) all subsidiary movers into locomotion: "That the final cause exists in immovable things is clear by distinguishing the two meanings of 'final cause.' . . . and it [the final cause] causes motion as something which is loved, and that which is moved moves the others. If, then, something is moved, it can be otherwise with respect to place, even if not with respect to its substance. And since there is some mover which causes motion but is itself immovable and exists as actuality, this can in no way be otherwise than as it is" (Aristotle 1991, *Metaphysics,* Book XII — 1072b1-9).

4. Adler 1980, Craig 1979 and 1993, Lonergan 1992, Plantinga 1964, and Ross 1969, to name just a few.

5. See, for example, Hilbert 1964. This is discussed extensively in Chapter 5 of this book.

Big Bang cosmology has introduced the probability of the finitude of the observable universe and contemporary universal inflationary theory has shown the strong probability of an initial singularity, implying a causative power transcending universal space and time. When these and other discoveries are allowed to complement traditional proofs for the existence of God, they provide a remarkable rational foundation for the existence of a unique, unconditioned, unrestricted, absolutely simple, super-intelligent, continuous Creator of all else that is.

I. The Contemporary Theistic Scene

Parts of this book could not have been written before 2003 when Borde, Guth, and Vilenkin established the requirement for a singularity in all inflationary model universes,[6] and when the data of the MAP satellite helped to verify the inflationary universe and the age of the universe — 13.7 billion years; other parts could not have been written before 1989 when Roger Penrose calculated the odds *against* an anthropic universe compatible with the second law of thermodynamics emerging from the big bang.[7] The *classical* Big Bang model could not have been addressed before 1964 when evidence indicated the likelihood of finite space and time in our *observable* universe, and quantum cosmology could not have been addressed prior to that time.

These developments not only have an important effect on Chapters 1 and 2 of this book, but also on the philosophical proofs given in Chapters 3-5, because they give greater credence to classical and medieval philosophical ideas that lost credibility during the era of Newtonian mechanics (which affected philosophy all the way through the early twentieth century). Today, concepts like "ontological simplicity," "conditioned and unconditioned realities," and "formal cause" (particularly in the "information fields" intrinsic to quantum fields) enjoy a veracity and significance beyond that of their classical and medieval origins. These discoveries provide experimentally verifiable examples of concepts used to prove the existence of God in Chapters 3-5.

In view of this, I here offer my rendition of a "state-of-the-art" formulation of the proofs. I hope to provide a staging area to assemble the work of

---

6. Borde, Guth, and Vilenkin 2003, pp. 3-4.
7. Penrose 1989(a), pp. 344-45.

great astrophysicists, cosmologists, and philosophers who have contributed so much to this field, and to bring their thoughts together in a single, comprehensive volume.

II. Why Are These Proofs New?
A Brief History of the Five Approaches

Significant updates in rational approaches to God have been achieved in five major areas over the last seventy years:

1) evidence from physics and cosmology about an initial singularity (implying a creation event transcending universal space-time asymmetry — Chapter 1),
2) evidence of the extremely high improbability of an anthropic universe (one that will allow the emergence of *any* life form), implying the possibility of supernatural design (Chapter 2),
3) development of the notions, and corroboration of the reality, of causation and simplicity in quantum theory and cosmology, which can be applied to what was traditionally conceived as the "uncaused Cause argument" (Chapter 3),
4) an ontological grounding for Bernard Lonergan's proof for the existence of God in *Insight: A Study of Human Understanding* (Chapter 4), and
5) contemporary developments in the ontological explanation of time and the Hilbertian prohibition of "infinities hypothesized within finite structures," which has led to a credible contemporary formulation of the long-discarded proof of the impossibility of infinite past time (Chapter 5).

A brief history of each of these developments and their effect on the rational approach to God will be discussed below.

Chapter 1 begins with a brief account of the general elements of *classical* Big Bang cosmology, and shows how those combined elements ground the contemporary position that our observable universe is approximately 13.7 billion years old and 13.7 billion light years in radius (from its theoretical originative center). The chapter then gives a brief account of developments in the *contemporary* Big Bang model that allow for an initial state that may be conceived in terms of quantum cosmology and/or string theory, and universal inflation (a hyper-accelerating phase of expansion in the early universe, seemingly caused by "vacuum energy" or "dark energy").

The *classical* Big Bang model seemed to indicate a beginning of the universe at a Hawking-Penrose singularity, but this was mitigated by the *contemporary* Big Bang model, which opened up the possibility of an early quantum cosmological era and an inflationary dynamic (allowing our universe to be but one amidst a multiplicity of possible universes within a theoretical multiverse). This mitigating view was itself subsequently mitigated by the discovery of Borde, Guth, and Vilenkin that every inflationary model universe (and/or multiverse) must have a beginning. Since this indicates an edge of time (prior to which there is no time), the conclusions of Borde, Guth, and Vilenkin point strongly to a creation of the universe (from no previously existing *physical* matter-energy). The cause of such a creation would then have to transcend our universe (and any multiverse in which it may be situated).

Chapter 2 considers the so-called teleological argument (the argument from design) from the vantage point of contemporary Big Bang cosmology. Prior to the time of Newton, the argument from design had an intuitive appeal because it was grounded in the idea that the number of *higher-order complexes* (producing higher-order activities such as self-motion, eyesight, intelligence, etc.) which could be produced by the interaction of simpler constituents is extremely remote by comparison to the number of *non-productive combinations* of those simpler constituents. From the vantage point of both physics and probability theory, this is not an erroneous idea.

However, when Newton theorized that space, time, and mass points were infinite (and his theories were virtually dogmatically accepted), philosophers began to reason that even though "higher-order complexes giving rise to higher-order activities" were extremely improbable, literally *any* highly improbable event could occur in an infinite amount of time, in an infinite amount of space, with an infinite amount of mass. Once an infinite number of possibilities is inserted into the probability equations, improbability disappears — and literally anything becomes possible. Thus, the teleological argument slipped from the horizon for nearly 270 years.

But then came two remarkable developments in cosmology: (1) the classical and then later contemporary models of Big Bang cosmology, and (2) the discovery of additional universal constants. (A universal constant is a fixed quantity that mathematically governs the fundamental equations of physics throughout the observable universe during its duration, such as the speed of light constant, Planck's constant, the gravitational constant, weak force constant, strong force constant, mass of a proton, mass of an electron, charge of an electron/proton, etc.)

As noted above, Big Bang cosmology put an end to the Newtonian assumptions of infinite time and mass in our *observable* universe. Now the universe was thought to be only 13.7 billion years old and to have 10^{53} kg of visible mass, and a finite amount of dark matter and vacuum (dark) energy. It was all quite finite, and that meant that the probability equations would once again have to be taken seriously. When this eventuality was combined with the discovery of additional universal constants, a host of exceedingly improbable "cosmic coincidences" were discovered.

Essentially, our universe should *not* be anthropic (capable of sustaining *any* kind of life form), because the range of anthropic values for our universe's constants is exceedingly small by comparison to the immense range of non-anthropic values. This meant that a random occurrence of the anthropic values of our universe's constants is so remote as to be virtually impossible. As a result, physicists began to advocate that it might be just as reasonable, if not more reasonable, to believe in a super-Intellect "setting the values of the constants at the inception of the universe," as to believe in their random occurrence. Even persistent atheists like Fred Hoyle changed their minds and openly declared their belief in such a "super-Intellect."

Chapter 2 will set out seven of these cosmological coincidences so that readers might be able to verify for themselves the unbelievably high improbability of an anthropic universe emerging from the big bang by pure chance. Notice that we are not talking about the emergence of life *as we know it,* but about the very conditions necessary for the possibility of *any* life form. It is this universality that makes the teleological argument more powerful than it ever could have been in any previous age.

I am not responsible for the research set out in Chapters 1 and 2, and so I am deeply indebted to the fine work of Roger Penrose, Arvind Borde, Alan Guth, Alexander Vilenkin, Brandon Carter, Walter Bradley, Fred Hoyle, Paul Davies, and many others whose insight and research have contributed so much to unveiling the mystery behind our anthropic universe.

I include a Postscript to Chapters 1 and 2 written by Dr. Bruce Gordon, who analyzes and criticizes some recent attempts by physicists to wriggle out of the preponderance of evidence for intelligent, transcendent, universal design. His incisive response to Steinhardt's and Turok's cyclic ekpyrotic hypothesis, Gasperini's and Veneziano's string perturbative vacuum phase within inflationary cosmology, and Susskind's, Polchinski's,

Bousso's, and Linde's inflationary string landscape theory reveals the strength and probative force of the conclusion that our universe had its origin in an intelligent transcendent cause. He concludes with the words of the string landscape theory's key proponent, Leonard Susskind, who worries out loud that if his theory proves to be inconsistent, physicists will be left without any alternative to intelligent design.

Chapter 3 initiates our philosophical arguments, and reconsiders what has come to be known as Saint Thomas Aquinas's uncaused Cause argument (which has its roots in Aristotle's unmoved Mover argument). This argument suffered greatly from the seventeenth- and eighteenth-century view of causation, which was concerned more with "bodies and forces" than with Aristotle's four causes. The early twentieth century completely transformed the view of the physical universe from Newton's "mechanics of bodies" to the "activity of fields" (quantum fields, electromagnetic fields, space-time fields, plasma fields, etc.), which changed the view of both physical reality and causation.

These new views of causation and physical reality shed new light on the metaphysical argument (the uncaused Cause argument) given in Chapter 3. I begin that chapter by dropping the terminology of "causation," which carries an enormous amount of historical baggage, and turn instead to an ontological use of the concepts "conditioned reality," "conditions," and "unconditioned Reality," which I have borrowed from Bernard Lonergan's *Insight: A Study of Human Understanding*. The result is that these concepts do *not* exclude *any* of the kinds of causation discovered by contemporary physics and cosmology (such as causation within and through space-time fields, quantum fields, strings, plasmas, etc.). The inclusivity, universality, and versatility of these concepts allow a truly *meta*physical argument to be developed that will not be discounted by future developments in causation. This is explained in Chapter 3 (Section I) and Chapter 6 (Section I.C).

Moreover, contemporary developments in physics and cosmology reinvigorated the notion of ontological "simplicity." Ancient and medieval philosophers used the notion of "simplicity" to explain higher and higher levels on the "tree of being" (i.e., higher and higher levels of activity such as cognition and self-consciousness, which arise out of "less intrinsic and extrinsic restrictions within a power or substance").

When science and philosophy turned to a more mechanistic viewpoint beginning in the seventeenth century, this idea of simplicity seemed superfluous because it was thought that higher-order activities could be explained through aggregates and complexity *alone*. Thus, if one wanted to explain higher-order activities, one only needed to explain the complex of lower-order bodies or activities that produced them. This approach seemed to be valid for a while, until electromagnetic fields became an inescapable datum. Then the world of physics experienced a proliferation of fields. Quantum theory revealed quantum fields. General Relativity Theory revealed that space was not a vacuum or emptiness, but a dynamic field that could interact with mass energy. Plasma physics revealed plasma fields with non-aggregative unities. These fields could not be explained by aggregations of bodies and Newtonian forces, because they were more like unities (organic mediums) than aggregates (collections of things).

The notion of "simplicity" is very capable of explaining fields because it puts unity before aggregate, manifold (continuum) before body (self-enclosed, discrete entity), and activity before "thing." Therefore, a complexity of bodies was not the only way of explaining higher-order activities. They could also be explained by a lack of intrinsic or extrinsic restrictions in powers or activities (simplicity). This gave physics and philosophy a new way of explaining not only higher-order activities, but also fields, unities, space-time, etc.

This notion of simplicity is useful not only in physics, but also in metaphysics; for as will be seen in Chapter 3, one can use this notion to explain the highest level of power or activity, namely, an unconditioned Reality (which does not depend on anything for its existence). As will be proved, an unconditioned Reality must be absolutely simple, and that absolute simplicity must be unique (one and only one) and unrestricted. This requires that it also be the continuous Creator of all else that exists.

Chapter 4 presents a Lonerganian argument for the existence of God. As many readers may know, Bernard Lonergan was a twentieth-century philosopher, and his proof for the existence of God has been written about extensively.[8] So, why call this a *new* proof? Because it grounds his premises in an ontological rather than an epistemological starting point. It is well known that Lonergan's cognitional theory gives rise to his epistemology; his epistemology to his ontology; and his ontology to his metaphysics and philosophy of God. Thus, the grounding premises of his argument for the existence of God are traced back to his epistemology (particularly his self-affirmation of the knower and his pure, unrestricted desire to know). Though these epistemological underpinnings do not in any way undermine his ontology,

8. Lonergan 1992, Chapter 19.

metaphysics, or proof for God's existence, I thought it might be helpful to present a version of Lonergan's proof with what I hope to show is an unassailable ontological foundation, namely, the proof of at least one unconditioned reality.

Lonergan's argument is so versatile that one can begin with this proof of an unconditioned Reality (the denial of which requires that there be absolutely nothing in reality), and then prove that this unconditioned Reality must be unrestrictedly intelligible, and then that unrestricted intelligibility must be unique (one and only one), and finally that this unique, unrestrictedly intelligible, unconditioned Reality must be an unrestricted act of understanding — understanding Itself.

Why begin with an ontological starting point? Because, first and foremost, it can be done; second, it complements and reinforces Lonergan's proof; and third, it will make the proof accessible to readers who prefer an initial ontological (rather than epistemological) foundation. I am deeply grateful to Bernard Lonergan and to his many interpreters for the epistemological insights, the ontological analysis of intelligibility, and the intricate reasoning leading toward the unrestricted act of understanding — understanding Itself.

Chapter 5 reconsiders the long-rejected proof for a creator of past time which entails proving the impossibility of *infinite* past time. Aristotle and Saint Thomas Aquinas did not consider such a proof to be truly probative because their view of time and mathematics was not sufficiently developed to see contradictions in the application of infinity to past time (a finite structure). Newton and other classical physicists followed this Aristotelian assumption.

However, developments in contemporary physics (particularly Relativity Theory) showed that the Aristotelian notion of "time" (as the "number/measure of motion") was not adequate. In General Relativity Theory, time was not merely a measure, it was *something* which could have an effect on the emission and interaction of various forms of energy. There not only seemed to be a minimum interval of time (duration), but also a minimum unit of space, and even a minimum unit of energy emission. These natural minimums have predictable physical effects, and so it became more and more difficult to relegate time (and its real interaction with space and energy) to the realm of mere measure. This development led a host of philosophers (including myself) to write books on the ontological status of time. Most of these volumes affirm that ontological status.

When this reality of time was combined with an important development in mathematics (i.e., the Hilbertian prohibition of "infinities hypothesized to be actual within finite or aggregative structures"), the impossibility of infinite past time in any standard universe manifested itself. (The famous mathematician David Hilbert and other contemporary mathematicians have shown that the hypothesis of an infinity within finite or aggregative structures not only undermines the axioms of finite mathematics, but even the realities to which finite mathematics can be applied, making such infinities inapplicable to a standard universe.) Now, if time is real, and the axioms of finite mathematics apply to it (particularly its distensive manifold), then Hilbert's prohibition must also apply to the hypothesis of infinite past time, making infinite past time impossible. This makes the argument for a Creator of past time quite probative.

III. The Rest of the Book

The new evidence for creation and design (from physics and cosmology) and the more complete and probative formulations of the three philosophical proofs require a fresh look at eight issues that have been associated with the philosophy of God throughout the centuries:

1) the distinct methodologies of physics and metaphysics (Chapter 6, Section I.A),
2) the non-use of an infinite regression argument (Chapter 6, Section I.B),
3) causation in light of the new proofs (Chapter 6, Section I.C),
4) how to *comprehend* the infinite Being — the *via negativa,* the hyperphatic way, and analogy (Chapter 6, Section II),
5) the impossibility of disproving the existence of God (Chapter 6, Section III),
6) the dubious rationality of atheism (Chapter 6, Section IV),
7) the unity of the five transcendentals: perfect Being/Unity, perfect Truth, perfect Love, perfect Goodness/Justice, and perfect Beauty (Chapter 7), and
8) the human mystery: the desire for perfect Truth, Love, Goodness/Justice, Beauty, and Home (Chapter 8).

If even half of these topics are taken seriously, they cannot help but transform our view of the universe, transcendence, our destiny, and the meaning of life. I think we are fortunate to have such an abundance of evidence for theism today. Robert Jastrow, founder and former director of NASA's Goddard Institute of Space Studies, provides a suitable conclusion in his book *God and the Astronomers:*

> [The scientist who has lived by his faith in the power of reason] has scaled the mountains of ignorance; he is about to conquer the highest peak; as he pulls himself over the final rock, he is greeted by a band of theologians who have been sitting there for centuries.[9]

9. Jastrow 1978, p. 116.

Indications of Creation and Supernatural Design in Big Bang Cosmology

INTRODUCTION TO PART ONE

Contemporary cosmology has opened the way to a remarkably deep insight into the creation of the universe. Both standard and revised Big Bang models imply a beginning of the universe (a point before which there is no physical reality). This, in turn, provides a rational basis for a supernatural cause (Chapter One) which coincides with evidence of supernatural design of the universe (Chapter Two). This gives remarkable credibility to the words of the Nobel-prize-winning physicist Arno Penzias:

> Astronomy leads us to a unique event, a universe which was created out of nothing, and delicately balanced to provide exactly the conditions required to support life. In the absence of an absurdly improbable accident, the observations of modern science seem to suggest an underlying, one might say, supernatural plan.[1]

The following two chapters and Postscript will show Penzias's contention to be quite reasonable and responsible.

---

1. Brock 1992, cited in Bradley 1998, p. 40.

CHAPTER ONE

Indications of Creation in Big Bang Cosmology

Introduction

The General Theory of Relativity, Hubble's redshifts, Penzias's and Wilson's universal background radiation, black holes, quantum cosmology, inflationary theory, and a host of other ideas and discoveries have led to a grand scheme of universal origins called the "Big Bang theory." In the view of many physicists, this remarkable cosmological theory points to a creation event as well as an ordered unfolding of the universe.

I. The Big Bang Theory

What the Big Bang theory says is that everything in the "observable universe" is the remnant of a huge explosion called the big bang that took place about 13.7 billion years ago. (The term "observable universe" is used to refer to that portion of the universe that can be observed at the present time from earth. There is a "horizon" beyond which we cannot see, no matter how powerful the telescopes we use, because light has simply not had time since the big bang to reach us from more distant places. As time goes on,

---

I would like to express my sincere appreciation to Dr. Stephen Barr of the Department of Physics and Astronomy at the University of Delaware for his extensive and helpful comments to this chapter. His contribution has made the text more lucid, contemporary, and accessible.

more and more of the universe will be observable to us. In a billion years from now, if we are still here, we shall be able to see a billion light-years further). While people still talk of the Big Bang "theory," it is no longer doubted by cosmologists that the big bang actually happened, i.e., that it is a historical fact. In science the word "theory" does not necessarily imply that an idea is merely a hypothesis. Often it means a very solidly established and well-tested explanation of a body of phenomena, in which case it is regarded as "*the* theory," the correct theoretical explanation of the experimental and observational data. (One talks about the "BCS theory" of superconductivity, for example, despite its having been completely confirmed as correct). Moreover, cosmologists think they have a fairly good overall picture of the history of the observable universe since the big bang. What, if anything, may have happened *before* the big bang and what may exist *beyond* the bounds of the observable universe (i.e., beyond the "horizon" of what can be seen from our place in the universe) is the subject of much speculation, some of it reasonable and some of it pretty wild. The generally agreed-upon "overall picture" of what has happened *within* the observable universe *since* the Big Bang is sometimes called the "standard" model of cosmology.

In the standard model of cosmology, space-time is described by Einstein's theory of gravity, which is called General Relativity.[1] According to Einstein's theory, space-time is a four-dimensional manifold, which acts somewhat like an elastic medium. It can stretch, warp, and vibrate.[2] When cosmologists say that the universe is expanding, they do not simply mean that objects within the universe are flying away from each other *through* space, they mean that *space itself* is stretching. Galaxies that are very distant from each other are getting farther apart, not because they are moving through space (which is a relatively small effect), but because the space in between them is getting stretched out. In an analogy that is often used to explain this expansion, the universe is likened to the surface of an expanding balloon with all of the galactic clusters like little spots painted on the surface of the balloon. As the universe (balloon) expands, the galactic clusters (paint spots) all move away from one another. So, it is not that the paint spots are sliding over the balloon's surface (though they are a bit), but instead the balloon has more area (or in the case of the universe, volume).

1. See Einstein 1945 and 1961.
2. See Steinmetz 1967.

15

All of this stretching of space is described by Einstein's theory. How space-time stretches and warps is determined by the matter and energy filling the space and how it is distributed. In the vicinity of a massive object like the earth, for instance, space-time is warped in such a way that objects moving near the earth have their trajectories affected, and they seem to be attracted to it by the "force" of gravity. In the Big Bang theory, the fact that the galaxies are flying apart from each other is explained by the space of the universe expanding. As one looks back in time, the galaxies were closer together, because there was actually less space! The farther back one looks, the smaller the distance between galaxies was. Extrapolating back, one can deduce that all the matter in our observable universe would have been in the same place about 13.7 billion years ago. In fact, they had to be in the same place, because the volume of space of our presently observable universe was — 13.7 billion years ago — either zero or very close to zero. At that point, all the matter we see in the universe today (i.e., that is now within our horizon) was compressed into a fantastically dense, hot mass, which flew apart with inconceivable speed — an explosion.

Fr. Georges Lemaitre, the Belgian physicist (and priest) who proposed the Big Bang theory, called this dense hot mass the "primeval atom." We now call it, and the explosion which emanated from it, the big bang. Lemaitre was one of the first people to realize that Einstein's theory of gravity implied an expansion of space, and he combined this idea with the fact that galaxies were observed to be receding from each other to come up with the Big Bang theory. The recession of the galaxies from each other was discovered in 1929 by the American astronomers Hubble[3] and Humason, following up on earlier work of Slipher. This is now called the "Hubble expansion."

There was a lot of skepticism about Lemaitre's Big Bang theory at first. The idea of a beginning of the universe was unpalatable to not a few scientists, because it seemed too much like a religious idea. But also, there was for a time some evidence that didn't seem to square with it. In particular, the age of the universe (deduced from the recession of the galaxies in the Big Bang theory) came out less than the age of stars and planets (deduced in other ways). It was then discovered that the calculation of the recession speeds had been in error by a significant factor, and this objection went away. The breakthrough happened with the discovery by Penzias and Wilson in the 1960s of the so-called Cosmic Microwave Background Radiation (CMB or

3. See Hubble 1929.

CBR for short), whose characteristics were consistent with its being the light from the Big Bang explosion, once very intense, but now made very faint (and red-shifted into microwaves) by billions of years of cosmic expansion.[4] Very precise measurements and refined mathematical analyses of this radiation (and, in particular, of the tiny fluctuations in its intensity in different parts of the sky) show a complex structure that is in remarkable agreement with the predictions of the Big Bang theory. Also, calculations based on the Big Bang theory correctly account for the relative amounts of the smaller elements (especially hydrogen and helium) in the universe. There are other pieces of confirmatory evidence, so that by now there is no serious doubt that the big bang happened.

The details of the Big Bang theory have undergone refinement from the time Lemaitre proposed it to the present. One refinement was the idea of a brief period in the first moments after the big bang when the universe suddenly underwent a huge increase in size. We shall mention this "inflationary era" again shortly. There are several powerful theoretical reasons to believe that such an inflationary period occurred (that we needn't get into), and there are now several predictions of this idea that have been confirmed. Another refinement is the discovery of dark matter. Several pieces of evidence point to the fact that about a quarter of the mass in the universe is in the form of particles that do not emit or absorb light. This is called "dark matter." It is not yet known what these particles are — they cannot be any of the kinds we already have seen in the laboratory.

A third refinement has been the discovery of dark energy, not to be confused with dark matter. For most of the history of the universe (at least the history of the part we can now observe), the expansion of the universe slowed with time. Basically that is because all the matter of the universe is mutually attracting by gravity, and that tends to oppose matter flying apart. In 1998, it was discovered that several billion years ago the expanding universe actually started to speed up! This implied the existence of some matter in the universe which gravitates differently from ordinary matter. This dark energy is not made up of particles, but is more like a "field."

Further refinements will undoubtedly be required to describe the very first moments of the big bang for the following reason. Almost all the history of the observable universe after the big bang can be described using Einstein's theory of gravity — General Relativity — in its "classical"

4. See Penzias and Wilson 1965.

(meaning "non-quantum") form. For an exceedingly brief era right at the big bang, however, within a so-called "Planck time" of the big bang, it is known that a classical description of gravity does not suffice. (A Planck time is 10^{-43} seconds.) The mass densities during this "Planck era" would have been so large that quantum gravity effects would have been important and the mathematics of classical General Relativity would therefore not be adequate to describe them. What is needed to describe physics in the Planck era is a theory of gravity that fully incorporates the principles of quantum mechanics. At the moment, only one such theory is known, and it is called "superstring theory." But people do not yet understand how to calculate in superstring theory well enough to handle the Planck era. In any event, all these refinements — post–Big Bang inflation, dark energy, dark matter, and quantum effects in the Planck era — are now part of the standard Big Bang model of cosmology.

A common misconception is that the big bang says that the universe has a finite size. People think this because they reason that if the universe started at zero size and has been in existence for only a finite time, then it can only have gotten to a finite size. But the standard Big Bang model allows for both the possibility that the universe is finite in size (the so-called "closed universe" case) and the possibility that it is infinite in size (the so-called "open universe" case). In the closed universe case, space-time curves around on itself, analogous to the way the surface of a balloon curves around on itself, and just as the balloon's surface is finite in area but has no edges, the closed universe has a finite volume but no edges. In the open universe, space curves but goes on forever in every direction. How then can an infinite "open" universe be said to expand? Think of a closed universe as being not a balloon but an infinite sheet of rubber. Again, the clusters of galaxies are painted on the rubber. Imagine now the whole sheet of rubber being uniformly stretched in every direction — the sheet is still infinite, but now all the little spots of paint are stretched farther apart from each other. No one knows if the universe is open or closed. What determines this is a parameter called Ω (omega) that is related to the average energy density in the universe and also to how curved three-dimensional space is at some time after the Big Bang. If $\Omega > 1$, the universe is closed. If $\Omega < 1$ it is open. In fact, Ω is observed to be very close to 1. Moreover, there are theoretical arguments that suggest that it is so close to 1 that we shall never be able to measure it accurately enough to tell if it is just a bit less or a bit more than 1. Whether the universe is open or closed will be a hard thing to find out — maybe impossible. But whether it is open or closed, the same arguments that tell us that Ω is very close to 1 also imply that the universe is probably vastly bigger than the part we can see, i.e., the part within our horizon.

The simplest version of the standard model of cosmology assumes that it describes the *whole* universe. In other words, it assumes (a) that there was no universe "before" the big bang, and (b) that the part of the universe beyond the "horizon" looks essentially the same as the part within the horizon. It is important to emphasize that there is at the moment not a shred of empirical evidence that these two assumptions are wrong. The simple version of standard cosmology, which makes these assumptions, we shall call the Standard Big Bang Model (SBBM). In the Standard Big Bang Model, the big bang was actually the beginning of the universe in a very strong sense: it was the beginning of time itself (and of space too). Thus, in the Standard Big Bang Model it is quite meaningless to ask what went on "before" the "big bang" — there was no "before." This is a very difficult concept to grasp. How can there not be a "before" the big bang? The physicist answers this as follows: Time is a feature of the physical universe. It is something physical, just like atoms or light. Time and space form a manifold that, as we noted, can stretch, warp, and vibrate. Since time is just a physical part of our physical universe, it follows that if the physical universe had a beginning, then time and space themselves began then too.

Interestingly, the first person to understand this was not a physicist, but a bishop: St. Augustine of Hippo (A.D. 354-430). Ancient pagans had taunted Christians and Jews for believing that the universe had a "Beginning." What, they asked, was God doing for the infinite time preceding this Beginning? Why did he wait so long — infinitely long — to get things started? St. Augustine gave an answer that deeply impresses modern cosmologists. He said that there was no time "before" the Beginning. His argument was theological, but parallels the argument of the modern cosmologists. Time, noted Augustine, is something created — it is not God, so it must be something created by God. Therefore, if the created world had a beginning, then time had a beginning too. There could not have been time passing before the Beginning, since if time was passing, that meant something (namely time) had already been created. He said that it was meaningless to ask what God was doing "before" the beginning because there was no "before": "Do not ask what [God] was doing 'then', there was no 'then' where there was no time." As the physicist Steven Weinberg noted, it is common in research papers on quantum cosmology to quote the very prescient comments made by St. Augustine in his famous discussions of time.

In any event, in the Standard Big Bang Model, time itself has a beginning at the big bang.

However, a variety of modifications and extensions of the SBBM have been proposed over the years that postulate things happening before the big bang. In one extension, it is supposed that the universe has undergone many cycles of expansion and contraction and will undergo many more — perhaps *ad infinitum* — with the big bang having been just the beginning of the latest cycle. This is usually called the "bouncing universe" scenario.

Another speculative scenario supposes that the observable universe is a part of an island, as it were, that is one of many islands within a much vaster universe. In each of these islands, space is expanding in a relatively slow and sedate way. For example, in our island, it takes billions of years for the universe to appreciably increase its size. But between these islands, the universe is supposed to be doing something very different: it is undergoing an extremely rapid "exponential expansion" — in fact, doubling in size every 10^{-40} seconds, in a typical version of this scenario. When the universe, or some part of it, is undergoing exponential expansion, it is said to be "inflating." Such exponential expansion is described by a solution to Einstein's equations of gravity that was found in the 1920's by a physicist named Willem de Sitter. Thus, a universe, or part of one, that is inflating exponentially is said to be in a de Sitter phase. The speculative scenario we are talking about is called the "eternal inflation" scenario. In this scenario, the big bang was not the beginning of the whole universe, but only the formation of our "island."

One point that should be emphasized is that even in the Standard Big Bang Model, an *extremely* brief period of inflation — lasting only a tiny fraction of a second — is now assumed to have happened shortly after the big bang. This brief inflationary era, for which there is very strong evidence, is not to be confused with the much more speculative "eternal inflation" idea that says that inflation is *always* happening except in scattered regions of the universe such as the part our observable universe sits in. To avoid confusion, when we refer to the generally accepted idea of a brief, post–Big Bang era of inflation, we shall talk about it as "the inflationary era," or as "post–Big Bang inflation." Most of the time when cosmologists talk about "inflation," they are talking about this brief era. When they mean the eternal inflation idea, they usually say "eternal inflation."

A third kind of speculative scenario supposes that our four-dimensional universe (three space dimensions plus one time dimension) is just a slice of a universe with more dimensions. There are many speculative theories in particle physics that posit the existence of higher dimensions, for a variety of reasons: Kaluza-Klein theories, supergravity theories, superstring theory, Randall-Sundrum theories, and so on. Einstein worked on theories with extra dimensions for a while. One of the main reasons for taking the possibility of higher dimensions seriously is that the only way that is known to unify Einstein's theory of gravity with quantum mechanics in a mathematically consistent manner (and to unify it also with the other forces of nature) — called superstring theory — requires that there be several "extra" space dimensions.

In one class of higher-dimensional scenarios, our four-dimensional universe can be viewed as one "membrane" (called "brane" for short in the technical literature) moving around within a higher-dimensional space-time, where there may be other branes. In the so-called "ekpyrotic" scenario of Steinhardt and Turok, our universe is one of two such branes that are parallel to each other and repeatedly collide, move apart, and collide again. The big bang is supposed to have been one of these collisions. They have suggested that this cycle of collisions may have been going on forever.

In the three speculative scenarios just mentioned (bouncing universe, eternal inflation, and ekpyrotic) something is supposed to have happened before the big bang, and so the big bang is not in these scenarios the "beginning of the universe" and the "beginning of time" as it is in the Standard Big Bang Model. We will call speculative scenarios that posit something happening before the big bang "Past-extended Big Bang Models" or PBBMs. It is important to realize that many speculative scenarios are being proposed all the time in theoretical cosmology. Many are rather short-lived or attract little attention from theorists. We will focus mainly on the three we have just outlined, because they have received the most attention over the years and they typify certain basic approaches. What we shall see later is that there are certain arguments that strongly suggest that even in Past-extended Big Bang Models, the universe and time itself had to have had a beginning at some point, even if that point was not the big bang itself. In some specific scenarios this can be proven. So far, no one has found a completely consistent and satisfactory PBBM in which time had no beginning, and there is reason to believe that such a scenario is unlikely to be found in the future.

II. Can Science Indicate Creation?

We should begin by clarifying what science can really tell us about a beginning of the universe and supernatural causation. First, unlike philosophy and metaphysics, science cannot *deductively* prove a creation or God. This is because natural science deals with the physical universe and with the regularities which we call "laws of nature" that are obeyed by the phenomena within that universe. But God is not an object or phenomenon or regularity within the physical universe; so science cannot not say anything about God. Moreover, science is an empirical and inductive discipline (see Chapter Six, Section I). As such, science cannot be certain that it has considered all possible data that would be relevant to a complete explanation of particular physical phenomena or the universe itself. It is always open to new data and discoveries which could alter its explanation of particular phenomena and the universe. This can be seen quite clearly in revisions made to the Big Bang model (see below, Section III).

So what *can* science tell us? It can identify, aggregate, and synthesize evidence indicating that the finitude of past time in the universe as we currently know it to be or and conceive it could be. Science can also identify the exceedingly high improbability of the random occurrence of conditions necessary to sustain life in the universe as we currently know it to be or and conceive it could be.

Even though scientific conclusions are subject to change in the light of new data, we should not let this possibility cause us to unnecessarily discount the validity of long-standing, persistent, rigorously established theories. If we did this, we might discount the majority of our scientific theories. Thus, it is reasonable and responsible to attribute qualified truth value to such theories until such time as new data requires them to be changed.

The arguments that suggest the finitude of past time, i.e., that time had a beginning, are basically of two types: (a) arguments about the possible geometries of space-time and (b) arguments based on the Second Law of Thermodynamics. Though the arguments we shall give may conceivably have loopholes in the sense that cosmological models or scenarios may be found in the future to which these arguments don't apply, their persistence and applicability to a large number of existing cosmological models give them respectable probative force. Until such time as they are shown to be invalid or inapplicable to empirically verifiable characteristics of our universe, they should be considered as justifying the conclusion that it is at least highly probable that the universe had a beginning.

When we speak of a beginning (a point prior to which there is no physical reality), we stand at the threshold of physics and metaphysics (beyond physics). Even though science cannot be validly used to prove a metaphysical claim (such as, "a Creator or God exists"), it can be used (with the qualifications mentioned above) to maintain as highly probable a limit to physical reality (such as a beginning). This *scientific* evidence for a beginning can be combined with a *metaphysical* premise (such as "from nothing, only nothing comes") to render a *metaphysical* conclusion that there must be *something* beyond physical reality which caused physical reality to exist (i.e., a transcendent cause — see below, Section V).

There are other indications of supernatural causation arising out of contemporary cosmology besides the implications of a beginning — namely, the occurrence of several cosmological conditions essential for the development and sustenance of any life form — that seem at least prima facie to be highly improbable. These seemingly highly improbable conditions (which are sometimes called "cosmic coincidences" or "anthropic coincidences") can imply an element of supernatural fine-tuning if no satisfactory naturalistic explanation can be found for them. This evidence is discussed in Chapter Two.

The existence of a Creator does not rest on scientific cosmological evidence alone, of course. There would be sufficient rational grounds to affirm the existence of a Creator without modern science. Chapters Three through Five present three different philosophical proofs for the existence of a Creator. But the purely philosophical and metaphysical arguments and the arguments based on the findings of modern science can be seen to complement and corroborate each other. This complementarity and corroboration constitute a network of evidence.

John Henry Newman termed such a network of evidence an "informal inference," i.e, reaching a conclusion by considering the accumulation of converging antecedent probabilities. For Newman, truth claims did not have to be grounded in an infallible source of evidence or in a strictly formal deduction. They could be grounded in the convergence (complementarity and corroboration) of a multiplicity of *probabilistic* evidential bases. Certitude is not grounded in one base alone, but in a multiplicity of likely or probable evidential *bases*. Thus, even if one (or more) of these bases undergoes modification, the certitude intrinsic to the convergence remains intact (though it may be lessened). The purpose of this book is to set out the specific evidential bases for this convergent probability in which science plays an integral role.

Therefore, certitude about a beginning of physical reality will not depend upon a particular anthropic coincidence or a particular scientific basis for a beginning. In this way, the changes to our understanding of science and the universe that may arise out of new discoveries will not significantly undermine the general conclusion about the likelihood of a beginning of physical reality.

III. Arguments for a Beginning of the Universe in Big Bang Cosmology

In the Standard Big Bang Model, the big bang is the beginning of time. The question of whether time has a beginning or stretches infinitely into the past is therefore only a question for the speculative extensions of the big bang model that we are calling Past-extended Big Bang Models, such as the bouncing universe model, the eternal inflation model, and the ekpyrotic universe model. There are several arguments that suggest that even in Past-extended Big Bang Models the universe and time had a beginning — though that beginning would then have been some point prior to the big bang. These arguments, as mentioned earlier, are generally of two types: arguments based on possible space-time geometries, and arguments based on the Second Law of Thermodynamics.

III.A. The Second Law of Thermodynamics

The Second Law of Thermodynamics says, basically, that certain kinds of processes happen only in one direction. Suppose, for example, one opens a bottle in which there is gas at high pressure (like a soda bottle that has been shaken). The gas will rush out of the bottle until the gas that is left in the bottle has the same pressure as the surrounding air. The gas, in other words, will come into "equilibrium" with its surroundings. We never see the opposite happen. We don't see air rushing *into* an open bottle until the air in the bottle comes to a much higher pressure than its surroundings. What happens when a bottle of gas at high pressure is opened and the gas rushes out is called a "thermodynamically irreversible process."

To take another example, a cup of hot coffee will gradually cool off until it has the same temperature as its surroundings. This happens by the flow of heat from the hot coffee to the cooler air (as well as by other effects such as radiation and evaporation). One does not see the reverse happen: heat flowing from the cooler air into the coffee and making the coffee hotter and hotter. Again, the cooling of the coffee is an "irreversible process." Of course, we see irreversible processes all around us. We don't grow younger, for example. Ashes in the fireplace don't turn into logs. Broken dishes don't spontaneously reassemble. In fact, most processes we see around us are "irreversible." They happen only one way. That is one reason why time seems to "flow" from past to future.

What causes this irreversibility? It is basically a question of probabilities. Consider a pool table with its fifteen pool balls "racked up," i.e., arranged in a nice triangular array. The cue ball strikes the array and scatters the fifteen balls every which way. Suppose we took a film of that process and ran it backwards at the same speed. We would see sixteen balls rolling around aimlessly and then suddenly come together, arrange themselves into a motionless triangle, and spit the cue ball out. Anyone looking at that film both ways would have no difficulty deciding which was the "correct" way to run the film: which is the beginning and which the end, i.e., which way time should be "flowing" in the film. From the point of view of physics, what makes one way correct and the other way wrong? It is not that in one way the laws of physics are satisfied and the other way they are broken. Actually, either way one runs the film, one would see a process that is *possible* according to the laws of physics. The film run "backwards" isn't showing something that is "physically impossible"; rather, it is showing something that is simply incredibly *improbable*. The reason it is improbable is not hard to understand. There are, relatively speaking, a huge number of ways for the balls to be rolling around in a scattered and disorganized manner, but very, very few ways for the balls to be arranged neatly in an organized manner. So, left to chance, balls are vastly more likely to be in a disorganized configuration than an organized one. If they start disorganized, they are incredibly unlikely to become organized. But if (somehow) they start organized, it is very probable that they will become disorganized if anything causes them to change their configuration.

This is the idea of "entropy" in physics. Entropy is a technical concept that, basically, measures the degree of "disorder" or disorganization of a system. For purely probabilistic reasons, systems left to their own devices ("isolated systems") tend to evolve in a way that keeps the level of disorganization (entropy) constant or increases it. Almost never does the entropy of an isolated system decrease. Systems do not spontaneously get more organized. To make a system more organized takes something coming in from outside and expending energy. (I can make the coffee in a cup hotter than its surroundings, for instance, by using a "heat pump" — the opposite of a refrigerator — to pump thermal energy from the cooler air into the hotter coffee. But that would require the expenditure of energy to run the heat pump.)

The famous Second Law of Thermodynamics says that in isolated systems, entropy always increases or stays the same, and never goes down. That is why some processes are irreversible. If a process changes the entropy, then it can go only one way — the way that entropy (disorganization) increases. That is why dead bodies decompose, but do not recompose! Of course, these are, ultimately, probabilistic statements. Entropy can have random fluctuations downward, but these are usually very tiny decreases, and the larger the decrease in entropy, the more unlikely it is to happen.

The result of the Second Law of Thermodynamics is that systems tend to "run down," "wear out," "decompose," and so on. Consider a ball rolling on a level floor. As it rolls, friction with the floor stirs up motion in the molecules of the ball and the floor (i.e., the ball and floor get slightly warmer — just as when you rub your hands together the friction makes them warmer). So the relatively organized energy of the ball's rolling motion gets converted into the disorganized motion of thermally agitated molecules in the floor and ball. As a consequence, the ball slows down and eventually stops. To keep it rolling requires energy to be expended. Maybe a battery-powered motor, for example. But that won't last forever. The battery has only a finite supply of energy, and that first gets converted by the motor into the energy of the ball's rolling, which in turn gets converted into heat by friction. Eventually, all the battery's (organized) energy has been turned into (disorganized) heat energy. The battery dies and the ball stops rolling.

This is a universal phenomenon. It is why physicists regard "perpetual motion machines" as impossible. And here is the relevance to the question of whether the universe had a beginning. If the universe did not have a beginning, then it has been around for an infinite time. In a sense, the universe is then itself a "perpetual motion machine," a system that never "runs down" or "wears out."

Now, what we have just said is not a proof that the universe had a beginning. It is not rigorous enough to be a proof. But some cosmological models can be rigorously proven to have a beginning. And when one looks at the proofs, one sees that many of them are based on the Second Law of Thermodynamics. A good example is the case of the bouncing universe scenario. It can be shown that even a bouncing universe must have had a beginning, and the argument is based on the Second Law, as we will now see.

III.B. Why a Bouncing Universe Cannot Have Been Bouncing Forever

In the Standard Big Bang Model the universe started with the big bang and started to expand. The universe might expand forever, or the expansion might slow and eventually reverse and turn into a collapse that ends in what is called a "big crunch." It used to be thought that the expansion of the universe has been slowing ever since the big bang until now. That made either possibility seem equally likely: either the universe expands forever but ever slower, or it eventually slows to a stop and starts collapsing. And people wondered what would happen at the big crunch. In the Standard Big Bang Model, it is assumed that the big crunch is the end of the universe and of time, just as the big bang is the beginning of the universe and of time. But some people suggested that when the universe collapses down to a crunch, it may "bounce" and start getting bigger again. That leads to the idea that the universe just keeps on bouncing: each big crunch is a Bounce that is also the big bang for the next cycle.

The question naturally arose whether this could have been going on forever. Maybe before "our" big bang there was an infinite succession of bounces: an endless cycle of expansion and contraction. A major problem with this idea is that we now know that our universe's expansion is no longer slowing down. It was slowing down for several billion years, but then it started to speed up! The universe for the last several billion years has been expanding faster and faster. This is the evidence for what is called "dark energy." (Recall that dark energy is a form of energy that would cause the expansion of the universe to speed up — see above, Section I.) If that speeding up of the expansion were to continue into the future, then there will be no big crunch — and no bounce. That puts a big crimp into the notion of a universe that is endlessly bouncing.

But let us ignore that "inconvenient truth," and suppose that the universe will slow down, collapse, and re-expand. Is it possible that the universe has been bouncing like this forever? There are three indications that this is not likely: (1) the radiation paradox, (2) the entropy paradox, and (3) an increase in cyclic expansion. All of them are related to the Second Law of Thermodynamics.

In every cycle of the bouncing universe, irreversible processes go on. For example, stars shine. That is, because they are much hotter than their surroundings, they release energy into their surroundings in the form of light. And, just as in the case of a hot cup of coffee releasing energy into its environment, this is a "thermodynamically irreversible process" — it increases the entropy of the universe. It also increases the amount of radiation filling the universe.

III.B.1. The Radiation Paradox

There are two kinds of light (i.e., electromagnetic radiation) in the universe right now: (a) the famous Cosmic Background Radiation (CBR) left over from the big bang (and discovered by Penzias and Wilson), which has a rather featureless spectrum called a "blackbody spectrum," and (b) light from various other sources, primarily stars, which has a very complicated spectrum. Right now, in our universe, about 99 percent of the light is in the cosmic radiation and 1 percent is in starlight. In every cycle of the universe, during the expansion phase, stars are formed and emit light. If the universe then enters a collapsing phase, this starlight gets scattered, reabsorbed by matter, and re-emitted many times. This basically homogenizes it into a blackbody spectrum, and it gets folded into the cosmic radiation. If the collapse ends in a bounce, the cosmic radiation is still there and is released in the big bang of the next cycle, whereupon it becomes the cosmic radiation of the next cycle. So, in each cycle the cosmic radiation includes all the starlight emitted *in all previous cycles,* whereas in each cycle the only starlight present is that produced by stars *during that cycle.*

Therefore, if there have been, say, a thousand cycles before now, there should be at least a thousand times more light in cosmic radiation than in starlight. If there have been a million cycles, there should be at least a million times more light in the cosmic radiation than in starlight. As we have seen, however, observations show that in fact there is only about a hundred times as much light in the cosmic radiation as in starlight. So there cannot have been many more than a hundred cycles in the past, which implies that the universe has not been cycling forever, and that (in the bouncing universe scenario) the universe must have had a beginning.

One might ask, what if the universe keeps undergoing cycles in the future? The ratio of cosmic radiation to starlight would keep growing without limit. But that would not be because the amount of cosmic radiation would keep growing without limit. Rather, at some point, the amount of starlight being produced would go to zero. The universe would not keep making stars forever. At some point, the fuel available for stars would have been used up, so to speak. The universe would have "run down" to such an extent that stars would no longer be formed. This is the Second Law in action. The fact that stars are still forming even today tells us that the universe has not run down completely — and that puts a *limit* on how long it has been around.[5]

III.B.2. The Entropy Paradox

As we have seen, entropy keeps getting released as stars burn. So the amount of entropy should grow with each cycle. But as we shall see later, the entropy of our universe at the time of "our" big bang 13.7 billion years ago was fantastically small. In fact, the entropy in our universe at the time of the big bang was so small that it constitutes one of the small-number/fine-tuning puzzles that theorists have been grappling with for a long time. How, after a huge number of cycles, in which entropy was being generated, can our cycle have started with tiny entropy? Here again we see the Second Law at work.

III.B.3. Increase in Cyclic Expansion

The third piece of evidence militating against an infinitely oscillating universe is related to the first. It stems from Richard Tolman's discovery of the cumulative effects of radiation on cyclic expansion.[6] If each cycle inevitably leads to increased radiation, then that radiation will cause increased pressure. This increased pressure, in turn, will make each cycle longer, giving rise to more volume of the universe before a collapse. Quentin Smith assesses the consequences as follows:

> Radiation from previous cycles accumulates in each new cycle, and the accompanying increase in pressure causes the new cycle to be longer than the last one; the universe expands to a greater radius and takes a longer time to complete the cycle. This disallows an infinite regress into the past, for a regress will eventually arrive at a cycle that is infinitely short and a radius that is infinitely small; this cycle, or the beginning of some cycle with values approaching the values of this cycle, will count as the beginning of the oscillating universe.[7]

5. This is basically the argument that one cannot have a perpetual motion machine.
6. See Tolman 1987 [1934].
7. Smith 1993(a) p. 112.

This "beginning" of cycling will hereafter be termed "Tolman's Limit." Once again, the number of universal oscillations seems to be inherently limited in the Standard Big Bang Model, which points strongly to a beginning of the universe in a finite proper time.

There are other speculative scenarios, such as the ekpyrotic universe model proposed by Steinhardt and Turok,[8] in which some of these problems with endless cycling are resolved. In Steinhardt and Turok's model, the universe is infinite in extent, and in each cycle the universe space-time gets stretched out and the density of entropy is thinned out by this expansion. So, it is claimed that the entropy *density* is reset to a small value in each cycle. This wouldn't violate the Second Law of Thermodynamics: entropy still gets generated and is still increasing in the ekpyrotic model. However, because of the stretching of space (the cosmic expansion), entropy gets spread out over a larger and larger volume and the *density* of entropy remains the same from one cycle to the next. Nevertheless, as we shall see, the ekpyrotic scenario has other problems, and, in fact, it also has problems of consistency with the Second Law of Thermodynamics.

III. C. Space-Time Geometry Arguments for a Beginning of Time

The Hawking-Penrose Singularity theorems were considered to be one of the most probative pieces of physical evidence for a limit to past time in the universe according to the *Standard* Big Bang Model. In 1980, Hawking wrote, "a curvature singularity that will intersect every world line . . . [makes] general relativity predict a beginning of time."[9] A "singularity" is a place where something becomes infinite.

In the Standard Big Bang Model, if one uses a "classical" (i.e., non-quantum) description of gravity, one finds that at some finite time in the past one reaches a singularity where energy density, temperature, and the curvature of space-time become infinite. That singularity is the big bang. "World lines" (i.e., paths through space-time) when traced back through time will eventually have to hit this singularity and come to an end. That singularity is the "edge" or beginning of time. Some people wondered whether one could find solutions of Einstein's equations of gravity where this Big Bang singularity could be avoided, and world lines could be traced back infinitely into the past. Hawking and Penrose proved otherwise.

8. See Steinhardt and Turok 2002(a) and 2002(b). See also Steinhardt 2004.
9. Hawking 1980, p. 149.

Quentin Smith summarized the consequences of this by noting:

> . . . The definition of a singularity that is employed in the singularity theorems entails that it is impossible to extend the space-time manifold beyond the singularity. The definition in question is based on the concept of inextendible curves [which must avoid implying infinite curvature and other similar mathematical paradoxes]. . . . This effectively rules out the idea that the singularity is an effect of some prior natural process.[10]

Hawking and Penrose set out five conditions in their proof of a singularity. Prior to the discovery of evidence for an inflationary era (and the vacuum energy which likely produced it), all five of these conditions were thought to be met, including the third, "the mass density and pressure of matter never become negative."

There is now a great deal of evidence that a very brief period of inflation happened shortly after the big bang, evidence that has convinced most cosmologists, and this is now part of what we are calling the Standard Big Bang Model. It is thought to be most likely that something called "vacuum energy" caused this brief era of inflation to occur. If so, then it undermines the third condition elucidated by Hawking and Penrose in their list of five conditions (the mass density and pressure of matter never become negative), because vacuum energy entails a very strong pressure which is equal to *minus* its energy density. Vacuum energy is different from mass energy, which is why it tends to cause the universe's expansion to speed up rather than slow down. The presence of this vacuum energy would then exert a very strong negative pressure, violating Hawking's and Penrose's third condition.

The violation of this third condition undermined the Hawking-Penrose proof of a singularity which weakened the evidence for a beginning of the universe. However, as will be shown below, the Borde-Vilenkin-Guth Theorem predicts a boundary to past time in any universe where the average rate of Hubble expansion is greater than zero ($H_{av} > 0$). This result is practically independent of the physics of any hypothetical universe, and applies to quantum cosmology, higher dimensional cosmologies, multiverses, and bouncing universes.

10. Smith 1993(a), p. 120.

III.D. Quantum Cosmology

Another factor that complicates proving a beginning of time is the importance of quantum gravity effects when space-time has extreme curvature and matter has high density, as it was, for example, in the "Planck era" within 10^{-43} seconds of the big bang. Even ignoring the vacuum energy issue that we mentioned above, the Hawking-Penrose Theorems were derived using classical (i.e., non-quantum) gravity. These theorems say that under certain assumptions space-time has singularities. But it is precisely near such singularities that the classical description of gravity is no longer valid! Therefore various possibilities open up, and many scenarios that go beyond the Standard Big Bang Model have been proposed that invoke quantum gravity effects. In many of these scenarios the big bang no longer has a singularity associated with it. There are basically two types of such scenarios:

(a) scenarios in which the big bang is still the beginning of the universe, but it is no longer "singular,"
(b) scenarios in which the big bang is no longer the beginning, but rather a gateway or portal, if you will, to an era that preceded the big bang.

A famous example of *type (a)* is the Hartle-Hawking "no-boundary" model. The idea of it can be partially illustrated with a simple analogy. Consider a piece of wood in the shape of a cone that is perfectly sharp at the end. The curvature of the surface of the cone is finite — except at one point: the sharp end. The sharp end can be said to have infinite curvature, and is in fact a singularity. If one thinks of "time" as running down the length of the cone from the narrower (the "past") to the wider (the "future"), then this singularity at the sharp tip is the "beginning of time." Call that point, then, t = 0. One can then say two things about "time" on that cone: (1) Measured "back" from any place on the cone the "past" is finite (it is only a finite distance to the tip). (2) There is a unique and well-defined "first instant of time" (the singular point at the tip). Now, imagine that the sharp tip of the cone is rounded off slightly with sandpaper. (In fact, if one looks at even the sharpest needle under a powerful microscope, it is found to be rounded off.) Then, while the point may still be *very* sharp, it won't be infinitely sharp. It won't be singular anymore. In this case, (1) is still true: i.e., measured back from any place on the cone, the "past" is finite. One cannot travel unlimited distance back toward the tip; one comes to the end after a finite distance. But (2) is no longer necessarily true. It may no longer be possible to identify "the" point at the tip, i.e., pinpoint "the" first instant of "time."

This is what, basically, the Hartle-Hawking "no-boundary" model does. Formulated in the context of certain ideas about quantum gravity, it smoothes out the Big Bang singularity so that it is no longer singular. It does this by assuming that in the "Planck era" the time direction in four-dimensional space-time becomes just like the three space directions — in fact four dimensional space-time becomes a four-dimensional *space*. This makes it even harder to pick out the "first" moment of time, because there is no one direction that is the time direction anymore. Nevertheless, in this scenario, the past of the universe is finite.

Some people imagine that the "no-boundary" proposal, if true, would mean there is no "beginning." In one sense that is true: one cannot identify a particular "first moment" of the universe. But that is somewhat of a pedantic point. The universe still began, but not at a uniquely identifiable point. It has a finite past. To say that it has no beginning in the no-boundary scenario is as misleading as to say that the cone has no end, just because the end is not sharp.

More important for the issues discussed in this book are the scenarios of *type (b)*, where the big bang is not a singularity, but rather a gateway to an earlier era that may have had an infinite past. These are examples of what we called the Past-extended Big Bang Models. To take one example, it is likely that for a bouncing universe to even bounce at all, it would require that the bounce be caused by quantum gravity effects.

One lesson in all this is that the real issue is whether there is a beginning, not whether the beginning is singular. Of course, if there is an "initial singularity," then there is a beginning. But the lack of a singularity may still mean there is a beginning.

III.E. The Borde-Vilenkin-Guth Theorem's Boundary to Past-Time

In light of such things as quantum gravity effects and vacuum energy, it may seem that theorems like those of Hawking and Penrose — that is, arguments based on the possible geometry of space-time — cannot get us very far in answering the question of whether time had a beginning. To take a very important example, the "eternal inflation scenario" supposes that the universe as a whole is perpetually undergoing inflation, except for regions such as ours where ordinary expansion is going on. Since that inflation is presumably caused by "vacuum energy," which does not satisfy the assumptions that go into the Hawking-Penrose theorems, it seems that the geometrical arguments for an "initial singularity" and beginning of time in the Standard Big Bang Model simply don't apply to the eternal inflation scenario. Indeed, Linde, who originated the eternal inflation idea, has suggested that it allows the universe to be infinite into the past, and time to have no beginning.

However, soon after the developments that cast doubt on the applicability of the Hawking-Penrose singularity theorems to certain newer cosmological scenarios, such as eternal inflation, Arvind Borde and Alexander Vilenkin devised a proof for a singularity (and beginning of the universe) with respect to *inflationary* cosmology — i.e., even assuming vacuum energy (1994).[11] However, they found an exception to their proof in 1997 with regard to the weak energy condition. Even though this exception was highly unlikely in our universe, it reopened the possibility of an eternal universe (in the past).[12] During the same period, Alan Guth tried to show that all known mathematical configurations of inflationary model cosmologies required a beginning.[13] Though Guth's study was comprehensive, it did not constitute a proof of a beginning in all inflationary cosmologies.

In 2003, all three joined together to formulate an elegant proof of a boundary to past time in all cosmologies where the average Hubble expansion is greater than zero. This proof is not dependent on the weak energy condition which allowed for possible exceptions. They formulated their findings as follows:

> Our argument shows that null and time like geodesics are, in general, past-incomplete [requiring a boundary to past time] in inflationary models, whether or not energy conditions hold, provided only that the averaged expansion condition $H_{av} > 0$ hold along these past-directed geodesics. This is a stronger conclusion than the one arrived at in previous work in that we have shown under reasonable assumptions that al-

11. Borde and Vilenkin 1994, pp. 3305-8.
12. Borde and Vilenkin 1997, p. 720.
13. Guth states: "In my own opinion, it looks like eternally inflating models *necessarily* have a beginning. I believe this for two reasons. The first is the fact that, as hard as physicists have worked to try to construct an alternative, so far all the models that we construct have a beginning; they are eternal into the future, but not into the past. The second reason is that the technical assumption questioned in the 1997 Borde-Vilenkin paper does not seem important enough to me to change the *conclusion*" (Guth 1999), p. 13.

most all causal geodesics, when extended to the past of an arbitrary point, reach the boundary of the inflating region of space-time in a *finite* proper time.[14]

This simple, elegant, and extensively applicable proof is grounded in the effect of expansion on relative velocity in *any* universe or multiverse with an average Hubble expansion greater than zero. Alexander Vilenkin gives the following illustrative example:

> Suppose, for example, that [a] space traveler has just zoomed by the earth at the speed of 100,000 kilometers per second and is now headed toward a distant galaxy, about a billion light-years away. That galaxy is moving away from us at a speed of 20,000 kilometers per second, so when the space traveler catches up with it, the observers there will see him moving at 80,000 kilometers per second. If the velocity of the space traveler relative to the spectators gets smaller and smaller into the future, then it follows that his velocity should get larger and larger as we follow his history into the past. In the limit, his velocity should get arbitrarily close to the speed of light.[15]

Remarkably, this proof has extensive general applicability — i.e., to *any universe* with an average Hubble expansion greater than zero. In particular, it applies to the eternal inflation scenario. Vilenkin states it as follows:

> We made no assumptions about the material content of the universe. We did not even assume that gravity is described by Einstein's equations. So, if Einstein's gravity requires some modification, our conclusion will still hold. The only assumption that we made was that the expansion rate of the universe never gets below some nonzero value, no matter how small. This assumption should certainly be satisfied in the inflating false vacuum. The conclusion is that past-eternal inflation without a beginning is impossible.[16]

14. Borde, Guth, and Vilenkin 2003, p. 3.
15. Vilenkin 2006, p. 173. Alan Guth, at the University of California Santa Barbara's Kavli Institute, noted: "If we follow the observer backwards in an expanding universe, she speeds up. But the calculation shows that if $H_{average} > 0$ in the past, then she will reach the speed of light in a finite proper time."
16. Vilenkin 2006, p. 175.

The implications of Vilenkin's statement should not be underestimated, for he is claiming that the proof is valid practically *independently of the physics* of any universe, and he is further claiming that such a universe without a beginning is *impossible*.

There is one caveat. The BVG theorem establishes a boundary. To the extent that classical gravity is operative near that boundary, the boundary is a singularity and therefore a beginning of time. However, if quantum gravity effects are important near that boundary (which would be the case in some scenarios) the boundary could merely be a gateway to another earlier region of space-time.[17] If the boundary represents only a transition to a new kind of physics, then the question arises as to whether that new physics is subject to a BVG boundary that is fundamental (such as a singularity or an absolute boundary to past time).

This is where the extensive general applicability of the BVG theorem comes into play, for inasmuch as the theorem applies to *any* universe with an average Hubble expansion greater than zero (practically independent of the physics of that universe), then the BVG theorem implies that a past-time boundary be present; and if that boundary is not another transition to new physics, then it would be an *absolute* boundary to past time (a beginning).

Borde, Vilenkin, and Guth consider two such possibilities in their seminal article, both of which come from theories with higher-dimensional space: (1) a particular string-theory-inspired scenario and (2) the Steinhardt-Turok ekpyrotic scenario.[18]

> Our argument can be straightforwardly extended to cosmology in higher dimensions. For example, [1] in the model of Ref. [19] brane worlds are created in collisions of bubbles nucleating in an inflating higher-dimensional bulk space-time. Our analysis implies that the inflating bulk cannot be past-complete [i.e., must have a boundary to past time]. [2] We finally comment on the cyclic Universe model in which a bulk of four spatial dimensions is sandwiched between two three-dimensional branes. . . . In some versions of the cyclic model the brane space-times are everywhere expanding, so our theorem immediately implies the existence of a past boundary at which boundary conditions must be imposed. In other versions, there are brief periods of contrac-

17. See Borde, Guth, and Vilenkin 2003, p. 4. See also Craig and Sinclair 2009, p. 142 (n. 41).

18. See Steinhardt and Turok 2002(a) and 2002(b), and also Steinhardt 2004.

tion, but the net result of each cycle is an expansion. . . . Thus, as long as $H_{av} > 0$ for a null geodesic when averaged over one cycle, then $H_{av} > 0$ for any number of cycles, and our theorem would imply that the geodesic is incomplete [i.e., must have a boundary to past time].[19]

Notice that the extensive general applicability of the BVG theorem allows it to establish a past-time boundary for quite diverse models where quantum gravity effects play important roles. Notice also that the BVG theorem applies to the ekpyrotic hypothesis even though it has a contracting phase, because all that is required for the applicability of BVG is that the *average* Hubble expansion be greater than zero (no matter how small the positive non-zero average might be). Since the ekpyrotic universe has an *average* Hubble expansion greater than zero (amidst its many expansions and contractions), it must have a boundary to its past time.

If the BVG boundary of the ekpyrotic universe is not another transition to a new physics, then the BVG boundary would constitute an *absolute* beginning of the universe and its higher-dimensional space.

Does the BVG theorem apply also to Linde's eternal inflation scenario? According to Borde, Guth, and Vilenkin, it does. Linde originally suggested that each bubble universe begins with a singularity and further suggested that these regional singularities might mitigate the need for a singularity of the multiverse itself.[20] Craig and Sinclair explain why this does not escape the theorem of Borde, Vilenkin, and Guth:

> Andre Linde has offered a critique, suggesting that BVG implies that all the individual parts of the universe have a beginning, but perhaps the WHOLE does not. This seems misconstrued, however, since BVG are not claiming that each past inextendible geodesic is related to a regional singularity. Rather, they claim that Linde's universe description contains an internal contradiction. As we look backward along the geodesic, it must extend to the infinite past if the universe is to be past-eternal. But it does not (for the observer commoving with the expansion).[21]

The extensive general applicability of the BVG theorem (whose only condition is an average Hubble expansion greater than zero) makes possible

19. Borde, Guth, and Vilenkin 2003, p. 4.
20. See Linde 1998, p. 105.
21. Craig and Sinclair 2009, p. 169.

exceptions that fall within a very narrow range. A possible exception will either (1) have to postulate a universal model with an average Hubble expansion *less* than zero (i.e., where average contraction is greater than expansion) or (2) postulate a universal model where the average Hubble expansion is *equal* to zero (what is termed an "asymptotically static universe"). One other alternative would be (3) to deconstruct time in inflationary cosmology (i.e., to get the arrow of time to reverse itself). The general acceptance of the BVG theorem has incited several theorists to creatively attempt all three exceptions to the BVG theorem. These three possible exceptions will be briefly examined.

Let us turn to the first exception. Theories postulating *average contraction* (instead of average expansion) necessarily entail a bounce, and as we have seen above (Section II.B), bouncing universe hypotheses have several problems. These problems are further elucidated below in this section. The other two exceptions to the BVG theorem require less explanation and can be briefly addressed here.

With respect to the asymptotically static universe hypothesis,[22] Craig and Sinclair sum up the fundamental (and seemingly insurmountable) problem as follows:

> [The asymptotically static hypothesis] has the dilemma that it must begin static and then transition to an expansion. Hence, the static phase is metastable, which implies that it is finite in lifetime. The universe begins to exist.[23]

It is difficult to see how any asymptotically static universe hypothesis can escape this problem, and so it does not present a significant alternative to the BVG theorem's implication of a beginning.

The other hypothesized non-bouncing alternative to the BVG theorem comes from a reinterpretation of time proposed by Aguirre and Gratton. To understand their proposal, one must understand a curious fact about inflating universes, which are described by a solution of Einstein's equations called "the de Sitter solution." As often described in the de Sitter solution,

---

22. There is another version of the hypothesis that the average Hubble expansion *equals* zero — namely a universe with infinite oscillations in which every expansion is exactly cancelled by every contraction. This option falls along with the Bouncing universe hypothesis.

23. Craig and Sinclair 2009, p. 158.

space is continually expanding in an exponential way. This means, basically, that the universe keeps doubling in size every Hubble time t_H — or, more precisely, every 0.69 t_H. One would think then that as one travels back in time the universe would just get smaller and smaller — but never get to zero size, and as one traveled forward in time the universe would always expand. In that case, the theorem of BVG would certainly apply since the universe is always expanding.

The actual exact de Sitter solution to Einstein's equations, however, does something quite different. In the exact de Sitter solution, space actually contracts approximately exponentially from t = minus infinity until some particular time (let's call it t = 0, for simplicity) at which it starts expanding exponentially to t = plus infinity. In other words, it has an infinitely long contracting phase followed by an infinitely long expanding phase. Most physicists would say that a universe that behaved as the exact de Sitter solution describes is "physically unrealistic" or "unphysical."

To take an analogy, if one solves the equations for sound waves associated with a sudden disturbance such as two hands clapping together, one gets two solutions: (a) an outgoing wave, consisting of a spherical shell of sound that spreads outward from the disturbance getting larger and larger, and (b) an ingoing wave, which consists of a spherical shell of sound coming in from far away and converging upon the disturbance. One is the time-reverse of the other. Physicists normally and unhesitatingly "throw away" the incoming wave as an "unphysical" solution that has no relevance to the real world. Such an incoming wave would indeed satisfy the laws of physics, but where would such a wave come from? Why would there be this wave coming in from infinity from all directions simultaneously, just carefully arranged to meet up at the right place and time of the disturbance? The same unphysical "solutions" to equations appear in many contexts in physics. Basically, these solutions are regarded as unphysical because they get the arrow of time wrong. The sound should come after the clap, not before it.

This is where we get to the proposal of Aguirre and Gratton. They suggest that the universe is really described by this "full" de Sitter solution, but they switch around the arrow of time for the "contracting" phase of the universe, so that from t = minus infinity to t = 0 time is considered to pass in the reverse direction, so the presumed contracting phase is really also an expanding phase! In other words, the universe is Janus like: at t = 0, where the universe has its minimum size, it looks to the "future" in both directions. That is, time "flows" from past to future *both* as one goes from t = 0 to t =

plus infinity *and* as one goes from t = 0 to t = minus infinity.[24] Even though this amounts to what Craig and Sinclair call a "gross deconstruction of the notion of time" (which is questionable in itself), they criticize it from the standpoint of physics:

> ... The Aguirre-Gratton scenario denies the evolutionary continuity of the universe which is topologically prior to *t* and our universe. *The other side of the de Sitter space is not our past.* For the moments of that time are not earlier than *t* or any of the moments later than *t* in our universe. There is no connection or temporal relation whatsoever of our universe to that other reality. Efforts to deconstruct time thus fundamentally reject the evolutionary paradigm.[25]

In any event, few physicists would take this idea as being at all plausible. They would dismiss it as utterly "unphysical."

Many other scenarios for a universe with no beginning have been proposed. There is no point in trying to do an exhaustive survey. They all (so far) run afoul of the kinds of arguments we have been discussing, based on either geometrical considerations such as the BVG theorem or the Second Law of Thermodynamics. Just to take one more example, there is a proposal by a physicist named Bojowald for a universe with no beginning.[26] It is based on a theory of quantum gravity called Loop Quantum Gravity (which some uphold as a more promising way than string theory to make Einstein's theory of gravity quantum mechanical). The details of Bojowald's proposal are not important for our purposes. What is instructive, however, are the comments on it by Sean Carroll, a leading cosmologist:

> Bojowald uses some ideas from Loop Quantum Gravity to try to resolve the initial singularity and follow the quantum state of the universe past the [Big] Bang back into a pre-existing universe. If you try to invent a cosmology in which you straightforwardly replace the singular Big Bang by a smooth Big Bounce continuation into a previous space-time, you have one of two choices: either the entropy continues to decrease as we travel backwards in time through the Bang, or it changes direction and begins to increase. Sadly, neither makes any sense. If you are imagining

24. Aguirre and Gratton 2002.
25. Craig and Sinclair 2009, p. 157.
26. See Bojowald 2007 and 2008.

that the arrow of time is continuous as you travel back through the Bounce, then you are positing a very strange universe indeed on the other side. It's one in which the infinite past has an extremely tiny entropy, which increases only very slightly as the universe collapses, so that it can come out the other side in our observed low-entropy state. That requires the state at t = minus infinity state of the universe to be infinitely finely tuned, for no apparent reason (the same holds true for the Steinhardt-Turok cyclic universe). On the other hand, if you imagine that the arrow of time reverses direction at the Bounce, you've moved your extremely-finely-tuned-for-no-good-reason condition to the Bounce itself. In models where the Big Bang is really the beginning of the universe, one could in principle imagine that some unknown law of physics makes the boundary conditions there very special, and explains the low entropy (a possibility that Roger Penrose, for example, has taken seriously). But if it's not a boundary, why are the conditions there [at the Bounce] so special?[27]

Carroll is referring to the fact that the entropy of our universe just after the big bang was fantastically low. It was so low that the odds of it being so low, if it was just a matter of chance, have been estimated to be a mere 1 in $10^{10^{123}}$ by Roger Penrose. Penrose has offered as one conceivable explanation of this fantastically low entropy the idea that there might be something special about the beginning of a universe. Perhaps some as-yet-unknown law or fundamental principle of physics implies that at the beginning of a universe the entropy has to be low. The point Carroll is making in the above passage is that if the big bang was *not* the beginning of the universe, but a transition (e.g., a bounce) from an earlier era of the universe that had no beginning, then it becomes even harder to explain the low entropy just after the big bang. He notes that as one goes from t = minus infinity up to the point of the transition/bounce, the entropy should have been increasing, and yet it could not have been increasing very much at all, since we know that just after the transition/bounce (i.e., what we see as the big bang) the entropy was fantastically small.

He further notes that one can try to get around this by the somewhat desperate assumption that entropy was actually decreasing from t = minus infinity up to the transition/bounce (this is the idea adopted by Aguirre and Gratton, for instance). This is equivalent to saying that the arrow of time was

27. Carroll 2007, p. 1.

opposite in the "pre"–Big Bang era. In other words, one might say that entropy decreased from t = minus infinity until t = 0 (the transition/bounce/ big bang), at which point it was very low, and then started increasing again. But then, Carroll notes, one has to explain why the entropy was so absurdly small just at the time of the transition/bounce. After all, that point in time is not a beginning or boundary of a universe, so there is nothing fundamentally special about it. One cannot, therefore, even hope for an explanation along the lines suggested by Penrose.

In fact things are probably even worse for models in which the big bang was a bounce preceded by a phase in which the universe was collapsing. It has been argued by the particle physicists Banks and Fischler that during such a collapse the rapidly changing space-time would have excited and amplified random "quantum fluctuations" in such a way that entropy would have been driven to very *large* values, rather than small ones. This makes it even more difficult to account for the fantastically low entropy just after the big bang. In Banks's words,

> I have a problem with ALL cyclic cosmologies. . . . The collapsing phase of these models always have a time-dependent Hamiltonian for the quantum field fluctuations around the classical background. Furthermore the classical backgrounds are becoming singular. This means that the field theories will be excited to higher and higher energy states. . . . High energy states in field theory have the ergodic property — they thermalize rapidly, in the sense that the system explores all of its states. Willy Fischler and I proposed that in this situation you would again tend to maximize the entropy. We called this a Black Crunch and suggested the equation of state of matter would again tend toward $p = \rho$. It seems silly to imagine that, even if this is followed by a re-expansion, that one would start that expansion with a low entropy initial state, or that one had any control over the initial state at all.[28]

We shall come back to the question of why the entropy at the time of the Big Bang was so low in Chapter Two, Section II. It is one of the "fine-tuning" problems discussed there. Carroll's use of "fine-tuning" refers to a set of conditions which is highly improbable and quite unlikely to occur by pure chance. If there is no natural explanation for this, and pure chance is

28. Banks 2007 from a private communication to James Sinclair, October 12, 2007, in Craig and Sinclair 2009, p. 156.

virtually out of the question, then an element of nonnatural causation might be necessary to explain this phenomenon.

In view of the above, the infinite Bouncing universe hypothesis appears to be untenable in realistic classical and quantum configurations of the universe. In addition to the radiation paradox, entropy paradox, and Tolman's Limit (see above II.B), it also faces Carroll's paradox of "extreme fine-tuning for no apparent reason." The combination is quite confounding.

IV. Conclusion

One important linguistic point should be made. There is much loose talk, even among physicists and philosophers, of "many universes." In all the theories we have been talking about, there is really just one universe, if we mean by universe the entirety of physical reality that is in any way physically connected to the world we experience. In "multiverse" models, the universe has many "domains," but they are all parts of the same structure that is governed, ultimately, by one set of fundamental laws. Those fundamental laws may be realized in different ways in different domains, but the fundamental laws are the same in every domain, and the domains physically interact with each other in ways governed by those laws. Similarly, in bouncing or cyclic universe scenarios, there may be different cycles, but all those cycles are all part of a single process governed by one set of fundamental laws. In scenarios with many "branes" in a higher-dimensional universe, those "branes" are not really other universes, but all parts of one physical reality.

The discussions in the foregoing sections show that the preponderance of cosmological evidence favors a beginning of the universe (prior to which there was no physical reality whatsoever). This beginning of physical reality marks the point at which our universe came into existence. There are currently no truly satisfactory alternatives to this beginning of physical reality. If theorists are to construct a cosmological model which *does* present an alternative to a beginning, they will have to meet at least *four* major conditions which have been presented in various places above:

1. Assure that the model avoids the first fundamental problem — inconsistency with cosmological observation.
2. Assure that the model avoids the second fundamental problem — internal inconsistency and nonworkability.

3. Assure that the model is not subject to the BVG theorem (does not have an average Hubble expansion greater than zero).
4. With respect to a bouncing proposal, assure that the model avoids the buildup of entropy, Tolman's Limit, and Carroll's paradox of "extreme fine-tuning for no apparent reason."

So far, no models have succeeded in doing all these things. Accomplishing them in the future will be quite difficult because of the extensive general applicability of the BVG theorem and the Second Law of Thermodynamics.[29]

Perhaps one day physicists will be able to construct a model which meets all these conditions. Yet accomplishing this does not mean that this model will resemble (or even remotely resemble) reality. Just because a hypothetical proposal meets the above conditions does not mean that it corresponds to the past and present nature of the universe. Therefore, the hypothesis may only be a testimony to human ingenuity. This means that the model will have to be verified, which will likely entail probing the domain of quantum gravity, higher-dimensional space, or even beyond. This will be quite difficult.

In view of the extensive applicability and preponderance of evidence for a beginning of the universe (and the narrow and tenuous path which must be taken to get around it), it can be concluded that the evidence currently supports a *reasonable likelihood* of a beginning — a point at which the universe came into existence.

V. Metaphysical Implications

Given the likelihood of a beginning of the universe, we find ourselves at the threshold of metaphysics. Though physics cannot prove a metaphysical conclusion, it can provide probative evidence for the *first premise* of an argument leading to a metaphysical conclusion. This first premise provides evi-

---

29. Furthermore, "beginningless hypotheses" (which try to get around the BVG theorem and the Second Law of Thermodynamics) are likely to be exceedingly complex and esoteric (judging from past attempts to do this). Such hypotheses tend to violate the canon of parsimony (Ockham's razor — which suggests that nature favors a simple and elegant description rather than a complex and esoteric one). Though this canon is not a test of validity, it suggests that any successful attempt to formulate a beginningless hypothesis is likely to go against "nature's tendency."

dence for a beginning of the universe and combines with a second premise coming specifically from the domain of metaphysics.

This second metaphysical premise dates back to the time of Parmenides. It may be summed up as follows: "From nothing, only nothing comes." If we don't put any content into "nothing" (such as continuity, dimensionality, or orientability, as might be found in a spatial continuum), then "nothing" will not mistakenly refer to "something"; it will not mistakenly be thought to have characteristics, do something, or be somewhere, etc. Nothing is nothing. There is no such thing as "nothing." To say anything else argues the most fundamental of contradictions.

We may now proceed to our conclusion — combining a first premise from physics and a second premise from metaphysics. (1) If there is a reasonable likelihood of a beginning of the universe (prior to which there was no physical reality whatsoever), and (2) if it is apriori true that "from nothing, only nothing comes," then it is reasonably likely that the universe came from *something* which is *not* physical reality. This is commonly referred to as a "transcendent cause of the universe (physical reality)" or "a creator of the universe."

This transcendent cause of the universe may also be the cause of time itself. Of course we cannot demonstrate this from the physical universe, because the most we can show from cosmological evidence is the reasonable likelihood of a beginning of the universe. Furthermore, we would have no way of understanding such a transtemporal condition from the vantage point of physical modeling. It would probably be impossible to imagine. In Chapter Five, we will consider the transtemporality of the creator of past time from a *philosophical* point of view.

This leads to our final topic, which revisits our starting point. Recall John Henry Newman's idea of "an informal inference," namely, reaching a conclusion by considering the accumulation of converging antecedent probabilities. We have shown in this chapter that the preponderance of cosmological evidence points to a beginning of the universe, which, when combined with a metaphysical premise, implies a transcendent cause of the universe. This probable conclusion combines with an argument given in Chapter Five from the philosophy of mathematics (David Hilbert) which demonstrates the same conclusion.

These two conclusions, in turn, converge with the conclusion of Chapter Two, which shows the exceedingly high improbability of explaining our low-entropy universe and the anthropic values of our cosmological constants by pure chance. This conclusion corroborates either *belief* in a nonnatural/supernatural cause of fine-tuning or *belief* in a virtual infinity of hypothetical universes.

Can we judge which of these two beliefs is more probative? If we take seriously the convergence of probabilistic data from Chapters One, Five, and Two, then belief in a supernatural cause of fine-tuning emerges as more probative, because a transcendent cause of physical reality (manifest in a beginning) can also be the cause of the apparent fine-tuning of our low-entropy universe and our anthropic constants. This convergence of data is not only mutually corroborative, but also revelatory, because it suggests that the cause of the universe is not only transcendent, but also "super intelligent." This will be discussed in the next chapter.

CHAPTER TWO

Indications of Supernatural Design
in Contemporary Big Bang Cosmology

Introduction

Since the time of Aristotle,[1] philosophers have given considerable thought to purpose in nature. Saint Thomas Aquinas used this notion of purpose (final cause) as the basis of a proof for God's existence (an intelligent Designer).[2] This insight was considered seriously in post-Renaissance thought by philosophers such as William Paley.[3] Despite a long period of criticism from Des-

---

1. "So what should prevent the parts in nature, too, from coming to be of necessity in this manner, for example, the front teeth of necessity coming out sharp and so fit for tearing but the molars broad and useful for grinding food, not however for the sake of this but by coincidence? . . . [A]ll things by nature come to be either always or for the most part, but none of those by luck or chance do so likewise. . . . There is, then, final cause in things which come to be or exist by nature" (Aristotle 1980, p. 38 — 198b23-199a8).

2. St. Thomas Aquinas, in his "Fifth Way," expressed this insight as follows: "The fifth way is taken from the governance of the world. We see that things which lack intelligence, such as natural bodies, act for an end, and this is evident from their acting always, or nearly always, in the same way, so as to obtain the best result. Hence it is plain that not fortuitously, but designedly, do they achieve their end. Now whatever lacks intelligence cannot move towards an end, unless it be directed by some being endowed with knowledge and intelligence; as the arrow is shot to its mark by the archer. Therefore some intelligent being exists by whom all natural things are directed to their end; and this being we call God" (Aquinas 1947, vol. 1, p. 14; ST I.Q2.A3).

3. "But suppose I had found a watch upon the ground, and it should be inquired how the watch happened to be in that place; I should hardly think of the answer which I had before given, that for any thing I knew, the watch might have always been there. Yet why should not this answer serve for the watch as well as for the stone? . . . [Nor] would any man in his senses think the existence of the watch, with its various machinery, accounted for, by being told that it was one out of possible combinations of material forms; that whatever he

47

cartes to Nietzsche, the intuition of design worked its way back into both philosophical and scientific thought in the mid-twentieth century as evidence began to accumulate for the finitude of our universe in both mass and time.[4]

Prior to the development of revised Big Bang cosmology, Albert Einstein intuited the extreme improbability of an anthropic universe (i.e., a universe having enough intrinsic orderliness to sustain a life form):

> You find it strange that I consider the comprehensibility of the world to the degree that we may speak of such comprehensibility as a miracle or an eternal mystery. Well, a priori one should expect a chaotic world which cannot be in any way grasped through thought. . . . The kind of order created, for example, by Newton's theory of gravity is of quite a different kind. Even if the axioms of the theory are posited by a human being, the success of such an enterprise presupposes an order in the objective world of a high degree which one has no a-priori right to expect. That is the "miracle" which grows increasingly persuasive with the increasing development of knowledge.[5]

Since that time, developments in astrophysics have substantiated Einstein's intuition in remarkable ways:

1) determination of the age of the observable universe (13.7 billion years),
2) determination of the distribution of matter and energy in the universe: visible matter (4.6%), dark matter (23%), and dark energy (72.4%),
3) determination of the visible mass of the observable universe (10^{53} kg), and
4) the identification of most universal constants (discussed below in Section I).

These developments reflect the universe's intrinsic parameters, which were not recognized by Newton and the modern philosophers who were heavily dependent upon him (e.g., Hume, Kant, Nietzsche, etc.). Prior to Einstein's

---

had found in the place where he found the watch, must have contained some internal configuration or other; and that this configuration might be the structure now exhibited, viz. of the works of a watch, as well as a different structure" (Paley 1831, Chapter 1).

4. See Chapter 1, particularly the necessity for an initial singularity in both classical and contemporary Big Bang cosmology.

5. Einstein 1956.

publication of the General Theory of Relativity, one could have thought that supernatural design was completely unnecessary because it was believed (in accordance with Newton's postulates) that the universe existed for an infinite amount of time with an infinite amount of space and an infinite amount of interacting content. Therefore, there would have been an infinite number of "tries" to bring about virtually any degree of complexity.

Standard Big Bang cosmology totally changed these postulates, and reduced the total number of "tries" in the observable universe to a very finite number; that is: 13.7 billion years (age of the observable universe) × 365 days × 24 hours × 60 minutes × 60 seconds × 10^{43} (reduction to minimum units of time — Planck time) × 10^{53} kg of visible mass in the observable universe × 10^8 (reduction to minimum units of mass). This is approximately equal to 10^{120} total possibilities for interaction of mass energy expressed in minimum units of mass and time. This is a large, but very finite number. When it is compared with the enormous odds against a low-energy universe emerging from the big bang ($10^{10^{123}}$ to one — the Penrose number), it is absolutely minuscule. This comparatively small number of "total possible mass energy interactions in the universe for all time" revealed the extreme improbability of high degrees of complexity arising out of the universe by pure chance.

This produced a remarkable openness on the part of some physicists to the prospect of supernatural design. Contemporary physicists such as Arno Penzias,[6] Roger Penrose,[7] Owen Gingerich,[8] John Polkinghorne,[9] Fred Hoyle,[10] and Paul Davies[11] have since adduced the plausibility of a designing intelligence from the evidence of contemporary physics. In *God and the New Physics,* Paul Davies notes:

> . . . the numerical coincidences [necessary for an anthropic universe] could be regarded as evidence of design. The delicate fine-tuning in the

6. See the quotation on p. 13 (from Brock 1992, cited in Bradley 1998, p. 40).

7. See the quotation on pp. 13-14 (from Penrose 1989(a)).

8. See the end of this chapter (p. 73).

9. "Freeman Dyson says, 'The more I examine the universe and the details of its architecture, the more evidence I find that the universe in some sense must have known we were coming.' I cannot see what sense that could be other than the will of a Creator. I reject the strange claim of the Participatory Anthropic Principle, that somehow observers bring about the grounds for their own existence, as being scientifically incredible" (Polkinghorne 1996, p. 76).

10. See the end of this chapter (pp. 72-73).

11. See p. 50 (Davies 1983, p. 189).

values of the constants, necessary so that the various different branches of physics can dovetail so felicitously, might be attributed to God. It is hard to resist the impression that the present structure of the universe, apparently so sensitive to minor alterations in the numbers, has been rather carefully thought out. Such a conclusion can, of course, only be subjective. In the end it boils down to a question of belief. Is it easier to believe in a cosmic designer than the multiplicity of universes necessary for the weak anthropic principle to work? . . . Perhaps future developments in science will lead to more direct evidence for other universes, but until then, the seemingly miraculous concurrence of numerical values that nature has assigned to her fundamental constants must remain the most compelling evidence for an element of cosmic design.[12]

This chapter will summarize some of the results upon which physicists base their belief in design by supernatural intelligence. It will then respond to the major alternative to supernatural design forwarded by some contemporary physicists (a multiplicity of hypothetical universes grounding the weak anthropic principle — see below, Section III).

The general form of the argument used by some physicists to justify belief in a supernatural designing intelligence may be set out as follows:

1) The values of the universal constants controlling the interrelationship among space, time, and energy in the universe must fall within a very *narrow, closed* range in order to allow any life form to develop.

2) But the possible values that these universal constants *could* have had that would have *disallowed* any life form from developing are astronomically higher (falling within a virtually *open* range).

3) Therefore, the odds against an anthropic condition occurring are astronomically high, making any life form (or universal condition allowing a life form) exceedingly improbable. This makes it highly, highly unlikely that the conditions for life in the universe occurred by pure chance, which begs for an explanation (cause) — physical or metaphysical.

In contemporary astrophysics, this explanation (cause) has been described in two major ways: (1) a supernatural designing Intellect, and (2) a

12. Davies 1983, p. 189.

multiplicity of universes allowing the weak anthropic principle to work (a naturalistic explanation). There are serious weaknesses in the multiple universe postulate of the weak anthropic principle; and so there is considerable room for the evidence of contemporary astrophysics to ground reasonable and responsible belief in a supernatural designing Intellect. This will be discussed below, in Section III.

As can be seen, this argument turns on the values of *universal* constants, and is therefore different from the arguments constructed by the Intelligent Design Movement. The latter *presume* an anthropic universe and seek an explanation for how highly complex integrated biochemical and biological systems could arise from far less complex ones. Pure chance (random occurrence) does not seem to be reasonable, because a random emergence of a highly complex system from a far less complex one is highly improbable.

The argument for supernatural design in *this chapter* does not address these biochemical and biological "leaps" in complexification. It focuses solely on the incredibly high improbability of an anthropic condition of the *universe itself.* It therefore does not focus on the *process* of evolution so much as on the initial underlying conditions (in the universe) that make such anthropic processes possible. It focuses almost exclusively on physics (particularly the physics of the early universe) and leaves the explanation of highly improbable leaps in biochemical and biological complexification to other domains of inquiry.

The inquiry into design from the vantage point of physics is quantifiable because the constants that form the foundation of this inquiry have very precise numeric values, and the consequences of these numeric values for the underlying structure of the universe can be precisely known. So also can the consequences of alternative values of the constants. This allows for accurate quantification of the range any constant can have to produce an anthropic condition, which, in turn, enables an assessment of the probability (or improbability) of an anthropic universe. This quantification has lent considerable probative force to the argument for supernatural design within the astrophysical community.

In view of the centrality and quantifiability of universal constants in this argument, we will begin with an explanation of how constants operate in our universe (Section I), and then show the extreme improbability of our anthropic universe arising by random occurrence (Section II). We can then select the most reasonable and responsible explanation (cause) for the universe's anthropic condition (Section III). Ironically, a supernatural explanation may well be more reasonable and responsible than the most recognized naturalistic one.

I. Universal Constants

By now it will be apparent that an anthropic universe is one in which a life form can be developed and maintained. A non-anthropic universe is one that is hostile to *any* life form. As will be shown, there are far more non-anthropic possibilities for our universe than anthropic ones. Such non-anthropic possibilities would include a universe of black holes, a high-entropy universe, a universe that changes its underlying structure with great frequency (disallowing any form of complexification or evolution), a universe with minimal energetic interaction among its constituents, a universe that disperses so quickly it cannot gather into interacting clusters, etc.

If a universe is not to be random and chaotic (disallowing schemes of recurrence necessary for the emergence of complex structures such as life forms), the interactions and interrelationships among space, time, and the different kinds and emissions of energy would have to occur through *fixed,* or virtually fixed, long-term *parameters* (called "*universal constants*"). These quantitative parameters control virtually every interaction in the universe, and they are integral to the equations of physics.

The equations of physics are quite different from those of mathematics. The latter show the *necessary* intrinsic relationship among axiomatically defined properties. The former describe a relationship among different kinds and emissions of energy, space, and time within a universe.

In mathematics, for example, given the Euclidean axioms, and given that A represents one side of a right triangle, and B represents another side, and C the hypotenuse, then it *must* follow for *any* right triangle that $A^2 + B^2 = C^2$. This can be demonstrated by proof such that a denial of the equation will result in a contradiction of its axioms.

In contrast to this, the equations of physics are not concerned with either necessity or axiomatic definitions. They *describe* empirically discovered consistent interactions and interrelationships among energy, space, and time within a universe. Hence, the equations of physics (unlike mathematics) could be other than they are.

As noted above, universal constants fix the parameters of interaction and interrelationship among space, time, and different kinds and emissions of energy. They therefore have very precise values in all places and times. In our universe, these constants come in a variety of forms, including minimums (such as Planck's constant), maximums (such as the speed of light constant), fixed quantities (such as M_u — the total visible mass of the universe), ratios (such as cosmic photon/proton ratio), units of individuation (such as the rest mass of a proton or the unit charge of a proton), or fixed parameters of transformation.

The values of these constants (within the determinate schemes of interaction — represented by the fundamental equations of physics) determine the precise structure and dynamics of the universe. As will be explained below, if the values of these constants were a little higher or lower, the universe could have been constituted by multiple black holes, by a single black hole, by diffuse non-interacting particles, etc. All these scenarios would prohibit the development of any life form. In Section II, it will be shown that the probability of these non-anthropic conditions is far greater than anthropic ones, leading to doubts about our anthropic conditions occurring by pure chance.

Our universe is governed by five kinds of constants: A) constants of space and time, B) energy constants, C) individuating constants, D) large-scale constants, and E) fine-structure constants. Each group will be considered in turn.

I.A. Constants of Space and Time

There must be certain finitely small natural minimums of space, time, and energy emission within any universe, because these natural minimums prevent space and time from being reduced to infinitesimals (e.g., Euclidean points having position but no divisible magnitude).

No real continuum can be constituted by infinitesimals (which have no magnitude, interval, or "Delta") because an infinite accumulation of such infinitesimals is still equal to zero magnitude. Now, if no real continuum can be constituted by infinitesimals, it must be constituted by some non-zero magnitude that is only finitely divisible. The point beyond which divisibility cannot proceed marks the *finitely* small (non-zero) natural minimum of space and time. One should therefore expect to find finitely small minimum units of space and time (where no further divisibility can really occur) in the universe. This is explained in greater detail in Chapter 5 (Section II.C.5).

The so-called "Planck minimums" of space and time seem to resemble these finitely small natural minimums in our universe.[13] The minimum interval of space in our universe would therefore seem to be:

[1] $l_p = 1.62 \times 10^{-33}$ cm

and the minimum unit of time would seem to be:

[2] $t_p = 5.39 \times 10^{-44}$ sec

and the minimum unit of energy emission would seem to be determined by Planck's constant for any given frequency of light (E=hν), where Planck's constant is equal to:

[3] $\hbar = 6.6 \times 10^{-34}$ joule seconds.

If any universe is to be anthropic, then these three natural minimums would have to be virtually constant over the long-range age and expanse of that universe. If they were not, the universe would change in its small-scale and large-scale structure, throwing its elementary constituents into chaos and interrupting any process of evolution or complexification.

There is another constant related to the natural minimums of space and time, namely, maximum velocity. A minimum interval of time predicts a maximum possible velocity, because no specific distance could be traversed in any less time than that minimum possible interval. In our universe, this maximum seems to be identifiable with the invariant velocity of light (in any reference frame), which is equal to:

[4] $c = 300,000$ km/sec.

---

13. There could be other more fundamental natural minimums of space and time, but the Planck intervals consistent with the gravitational constant seem to be the most fundamental minimums discovered in the post–big-bang era. There may have been a unified era prior to the big bang, having scales equal to or less than the Planck minimum of length and time. Quantum gravity could well be applicable here and the structures of interaction could be considerably smaller than the Planck minimums. Hence, one cannot generalize, even for the history of *our* universe, that the values of the Planck minimums were applicable to the earliest epochs. Nevertheless, there would have to have been some non-zero minimum interval of space and time in the Planck era. Such minimums would have to apply not only to quantum gravity configurations of the unified era, but also to string and other theoretical configurations.

I.B. Energy Constants

Energy may manifest itself in different ways. In our universe, energy is manifest through four fundamental forces: gravitational, electromagnetic, strong nuclear, and weak.

If *any* universe is to be anthropic, then each kind and emission of energy would have to have virtually fixed parameters over its long-range age and expanse. If they did not, then their interaction among each other and with space and time would be random and chaotic, which would virtually preclude patterns and schemes of recurrence, and therefore complex structures necessary for life. Therefore, *any* anthropic universe would require constants (fixed parameters) of the emission of each fundamental kind of energy. Not surprisingly, then, our anthropic universe has constants for each of the four fundamental forces:

[5] Gravitational attraction constant G = 6.67×10^{-11}

[6] Weak force coupling constant g_w = 1.43×10^{-62}

[7] Strong nuclear force coupling constant g_s = 15

The electromagnetic force (discussed immediately below) has three constants, because it is individuated and charged.

I.C. Individuating Constants

Since the electromagnetic force is constituted by *individuated* protons[14] and electrons, there are three constants associated with it:

[8] Rest mass of a proton m_p = 1.67×10^{-27} kg

[9] Rest mass of an electron m_e = 9.11×10^{-31} kg

[10] The electron or proton unit charge e = 1.6×10^{-19} coulombs

---

14. It may be thought that the charge and rest mass of a proton are not fundamental since they are composed of quarks, but as Davies notes: "the masses of the individual quarks (believed to come in at least six varieties) are quite uncertain. . . . A further complication is that most quark theories treat the quark union as completely unbreakable; isolated quarks are regarded as impossible. ¶ If quarks are permanently confined inside particles such as protons, it makes more sense to regard the proton mass, rather than the quark masses, as a fundamental unit" (Davies 1982, p. 38).

The electromagnetic force has *individuated* constituents (protons and electrons), which can act as discrete units within an electromagnetic field. These discrete units have opposed charges of the same magnitude. Hence, the unit charge of the proton and electron, though opposed to one another, are the same.

One other constant is likely to be present in a universe constituted by space, time, and energy: namely, minimum mass. If there are individuated (discrete) emissions of energy in a particular universe, then it would be subject to the minimums of length, time, and energy emission. In our universe, this individuating characteristic (termed "rest mass") is a function of gravity, and is convertible into energy through the maximum velocity constant (c) squared ($E=mc^2$). The minimum mass in our universe is:

[11] $(hc/G)^{1/2} = 2.18 \times 10^{-8}$ kg.

I.D. Large-Scale and Fine-Structure Constants

In any given universe at any given time, there must be a total amount of energy and a total amount of rest mass related to it. In our observable universe, the total visible rest mass is currently thought to be:

[12] 10^{53} kg.

Our observable universe is also determined by an additional eight large-scale and fine-structure constants that further refine large- and small-scale interactions among the above twelve:

[13] Boltzmann's constant $k = 1.38 \times 10^{-23}$ J/°K
[14] Hubble constant $H = 2 \times 10^{-18}$ (SI units)
[15] Cosmological constant $\Lambda < 10^{-53}$ (SI units)
[16] Cosmic photon/proton ratio $S = 10^9$ (SI units)
[17] Permittivity of free space $\varepsilon = 8.85 \times 10^{-12}$ (SI units)
[18] Electromagnetic fine-structure constant $\alpha = 7.30 \times 10^{-3}$ (SI units)
[19] Weak fine-structure constant $\alpha_w = 3.05 \times 10^{-12}$ (SI units)
[20] Gravitational fine-structure constant $\alpha_G = 5.90 \times 10^{-39}$ (SI units)

The operation of these constants within the universe gives rise to a variety of quantitatively determinate interactions and interrelationships from which the equations of physics are derived. The gradual unfolding of the total mass energy and vacuum (dark) energy in the post-big-bang GTR (space-time) universe (according to these determinate interactions and interrelationships, as well as random and indeterminate quantum and spontaneous occurrences) *could* give rise to complex structures (even highly complex structures such as life forms), *if* the values of the above constants coalesce to avoid non-anthropic states (such as a universe filled with black holes).

Now, it so happens that this coalescence did occur in our universe. Yet, as will be seen, the odds of this happening are extremely remote in view of the fact that there are so many more non-anthropic values of constants (i.e., a virtually open range) than anthropic ones (i.e., a narrow, closed range). This will be shown in the following section.

II. The Extreme Improbability of Our Anthropic Universe

Roger Penrose, Owen Gingerich, Fred Hoyle, Walter Bradley, Brandon Carter, Paul Davies, and others have assembled an immense amount of data to show the very narrow, *closed* range of values required for our universe's energetic, individuating, large-scale, and fine-structure constants allowing for anthropic conditions. This narrow range of constants is necessary for both an *initial state* and *gradual unfolding* of the universe toward an anthropic condition. The following are seven instances of this narrow range of constant values necessary for our anthropic universe.[15]

(1) The first instance is given by Roger Penrose, who shows the exceedingly high improbability of a low-entropy condition (which is compatible with the Second Law of Thermodynamics and essential for our anthropic universe) arising out of the big bang. Note that a low entropy condition occupies a very small volume of the total phase space of possible universes which could have arisen out of our big bang (explained below), while high-entropy conditions occupy a much larger volume of the phase space of possible universes. Therefore, Penrose can determine the improbability of this essential low-entropy condition by calculating the ratio of the *total* phase-space volume of possible universes for a creation event *and* the phase-space volume of *our* anthropic universe (compatible with the second law of thermodynamics — low entropy).

A phase space is a space in which all possible states of a system are represented, with each possible state of the system corresponding to one unique

---

15. In Davies' work, *The Accidental Universe,* and Fred Hoyle's work, *The Intelligent Universe,* many other examples of the requirement for a narrow, closed range of values for the constants are given.

point in the phase space. The phase space of a single particle can be represented by three position coordinates (x_1, x_2, x_3) and three momentum coordinates (p_1, p_2, p_3) so that the phase space is a six-dimensional representation of that single particle.[16]

Penrose begins by calculating the total entropy of our universe, which represents the logarithm of the total phase-space volume of possible universes in a creation event. The total entropy of our universe is equal to the total number of baryons (protons and neutrons) in the universe (10^{80}) × the entropy per baryon (10^{43}), which yields a total entropy of 10^{123}. Since 10^{123} (total entropy) is the logarithm of the total phase-space volume, the total phase-space volume of possible universes for a creation event (**V**) is the exponential of 10^{123}, namely, $10^{10^{123}}$.

Now Penrose calculates the phase-space volume of *our* anthropic universe (**W**) and then finds the ratio between the *total* phase-space volume of possible universes calculated above (**V**) *and* the phase-space volume of our anthropic universe (**W**). He does this as follows:

> How big was the original phase-space volume **W** that the Creator had to aim for in order to provide a universe compatible with the second law of thermodynamics and with what we now observe? It does not much matter whether we take the value $\mathbf{W} = 10^{10^{101}}$ or $\mathbf{W} = 10^{10^{88}}$, given by the galactic black holes or by the background radiation, respectively, or a much smaller (and, in fact, more appropriate) figure which would have been the *actual* figure at the big bang. Either way, the ratio of **V** to **W** will be closely $\mathbf{V/W} = 10^{10^{123}}$.
>
> This now tells us how precise the Creator's aim must have been: namely to an accuracy of one part in $10^{10^{123}}$.[17]

He summarizes as follows:

> In order to produce a universe resembling the one in which we live, the Creator would have to aim for an absurdly tiny volume of the phase space of possible universes — about $\frac{1}{10}^{10^{123}}$ of the entire volume, for the situation under consideration.[18]

16. Though three dimensions is the maximum number of spatial dimensions, six dimensions is allowable in mathematics to represent the position-momentum of any given individual particle.

17. Penrose 1989(a), p. 343.

18. Penrose 1989(a), p. 343.

The odds of our anthropic universe arising amidst the total phase-space volume of possible universes for a creation event is so exceedingly, exceedingly, exceedingly remote that its notation in regular exponential form is one part in: $10^{10000000000000000000000000000000000000000000000000000000000000000000000000000000000000000000000000000000000000000000000000000000000000000000}$. This number is so large that if we were to write it out in ordinary notation (with every zero being, say, ten point type), it would fill up a large portion of the universe!

In the absence of natural explanation for this highly improbable occurrence, many physicists have concluded that our universe was influenced by a supernatural designing intelligence.

Yet other physicists find such a metaphysical explanation quite difficult and even disheartening, leading them to postulate some new "naturalistic" explanations which go far beyond our universe and our methods of empirical verification. These so-called naturalistic explanations postulate limitless numbers of unseen, unverified actual or potential universes which provide the conditions for the weak anthropic principle. As will be seen below, these naturalistic explanations not only violate the canon of parsimony (Ockham's razor), but also are scientifically questionable if not dubious.[19]

If we find these dubious naturalistic alternatives to be unsatisfying or even "over the top," we are left with the stark reality of supernatural intelligent design staring at us through the specter of the Penrose number. In 1989 Penrose himself called this Intelligence behind the number — "the Creator."

(2) The second instance concerns the interrelationship among the gravitational constant (G), weak force constant (g_w), and the cosmological constant (Λ) with respect to the rate of acceleration (and possible collapse) of the universe as a whole. As Davies notes:

> If G, or g_w, differed from their actual values by even *one part in 10^{50}*, the precise balance against Λ_{bare} would be upset, and the structure of the universe would be drastically altered.[20]

He later explains this by noting:

19. See Section III of this chapter for a critique of the "many universes" of the weak anthropic principle, and Section V of the Postscript following this chapter (authored by Bruce Gordon) for a critique of the string landscape theory.

20. Davies 1982, p. 107. Italics mine.

[I]f Λ were several orders of magnitude greater, the expansion of the universe would be explosive, and it is doubtful if galaxies could ever have formed against such a disruptive force. If Λ were negative, the explosion would be replaced by a catastrophic collapse of the universe. It is truly extraordinary that such dramatic effects would result from changes in the strength of either gravity, or the weak force, of less than one part in 10^{40}.[21]

If the universe's constituents had not formed into clusters, there would be virtually no interaction allowing for complexification, and therefore no development of *any* life form. Similarly, a catastrophic collapse of the universe would be very deleterious to the development of *any* life form. Thus, outside the very narrow permissible range of the values of the weak force and gravitational constants (which cannot differ from their current values by any more than one part in 10^{50}!), the universe would not be able to support *any* life form.

Again, it should be noted that the virtually open range of *non*-anthropic values of G and g_w in their relationship to Λ far exceeds the narrow closed range of anthropic values. This narrow closed range of anthropic confluence (in contradistinction to the virtually open range of *non*-anthropic confluence) reveals the extreme improbability of our universe's anthropic condition.

(3) A third instance of improbable anthropic conditions concerns the strong force constant (especially in its relationship to the electromagnetic constant). This constant cannot vary more or less than 2 percent from its current value ($g_s = 15$) without rendering impossible the formation of either hydrogen or any other element heavier than hydrogen. Either one of these two scenarios would have disallowed a life form (composed of elements from our periodic table) from developing within our universe. Walter Bradley sums up Brandon Carter's research on this topic by noting:

Brandon Carter in 1970 showed that a 2 percent reduction in the strong force and its associated constant would preclude the formation of nuclei with larger numbers of protons, making the formation of elements heavier than hydrogen impossible. On the other hand, if the strong force and associated constant were just 2 percent greater than it is, then all hydrogen would be converted to helium and heavier elements from the beginning, leaving the universe no water and no long-term fuel for the stars. The absolute value of the strong force constant, and more importantly, its value relative to the electromagnetic force constant is not "pre-

21. Davies 1982, p. 108.

scribed" by any physical theories, but it is certainly a critical *requirement* for a universe suitable for life.[22]

A 2 percent variance on either side of the real value of the strong force constant would have been disastrous for the development of life in the universe. If the strong force constant had been > 15.3, there would have been no hydrogen in the universe (only heavier elements), which would have precluded life (due to an absence of stellar heat and water); and if the strong force constant had been < 14.7, there would have been no elements heavier than hydrogen (e.g., carbon — the building block of life), which, once again, would have precluded life (arising out of our periodic table) in the universe.

Notice, again, that the *non*-anthropic values of the strong force constant (relative to the electromagnetic constant) are a virtually *open* range by comparison with the narrow, closed range of anthropic values for g_s (which are restricted to plus or minus 2 percent of its real value). Life arising out of the elements of the periodic table in our universe is once again shown to be highly improbable.

(4) A fourth instance of the improbability of anthropic conditions in our universe concerns the relationship between the gravitational and weak force constants on the one hand, and the neutron-proton mass and electron mass on the other. The value of the weak force constant in its relationship to the value of the gravitational constant guarantees a sufficient amount of hydrogen for solar power and water. Slight variations from this would have given rise to a universe inhospitable to life. As Davies notes:

> It is at this stage that an extraordinary coincidence is discovered. First, it so happens that the neutron-proton mass difference is only a little greater than the electron mass: $\Delta m \simeq m_e$. Second, the strength of the weak interaction is, apparently accidentally, related to the strength of gravity through the following numerical concurrence: $(Gm_e^2/\hbar c)^{1/4} \simeq g_w m_e^2 c/\hbar^3 \sim 10^{-11}$. When these two numerical accidents are used in Eq. (3.4), one obtains $kT_F \simeq \Delta mc^2$.[23]

If kT_F had been either greater than or less than Δmc^2, either hydrogen would have been absent from the universe (because the proton content would be completely used in helium atoms), or diverse heavier elements would have

---

22. Bradley 1998, p. 39. Italics mine. See also Breuer 1991, p. 183.
23. Davies 1982, pp. 63-64.

been substantially limited. In either case, the universe would have been quite inhospitable to life. Again, it should be noted that the non-anthropic values of these constants form a virtually open range by comparison with a narrow closed range of anthropic values.

(5) A fifth instance of the improbability of anthropic conditions concerns the gravitational constant in its relation to the electromagnetic constant and the ratio of electron to proton mass. These constants must have their precise actual values in order for stars with sufficiently stable energy to develop. Without these precise values the vast majority of stars would have been blue giants or red dwarfs (unable to sustain a life form). Davies outlines this coincidence as follows:

> What is remarkable is that this typical mass M_* just happens to lie in the narrow range between the blue giants and red dwarfs. This circumstance is in turn a consequence of an apparently accidental relation between the relative strengths of gravity and electromagnetism, as will be shown. . . . The product of the penetration and Maxwell-Boltzmann factors peaks around $E = (bkT)^{2/3}$. It follows that the protons that are most effective in nuclear burning are those with energy close to this value. Prolific reactions will occur if this optimum value is not far from the average value; say $kT_c \sim 10^{-2}b^2 \simeq 10^{-2}m_p e^4/16\pi^2\varepsilon^2\hbar^2$. The temperature need not rise far above this to maintain a good supply of energy.
>
> For the star to avoid convective instability, kT_s must exceed the ionization energy $\sim 0.1 e^4 m_e/16\pi^2\varepsilon^2\hbar^2$, so . . . $k^4T_s^4 \sim 10^{-4}m_p^3 m_e^2 e^4 G^{1/2}c^{11/2} / 16\pi^2\varepsilon^2\hbar^{5/2} / 10^{-4} e^{16}m_e^4/(4\pi\varepsilon)^8\hbar^8$, which reduces to $\alpha_G / \alpha^{12}(m_e/m_p)^4$, where α is the electromagnetic fine structure constant. This remarkable relation compares the strength of gravity (on the left) with the strength of electromagnetism, and the ratio of electron to proton mass. Moreover, α is raised to the twelfth power, so the inequality is very sensitive to the value of e.[24]

Davies concludes by remarking on the incredibly small variance that is permissible in the constants of gravity, electromagnetism, and "electron mass relative to proton mass," in order to avoid red dwarfs or blue giants (incapable of sustaining life forms). He notes that this coincidence is truly astonishing:

> Putting in the numbers, one obtains 5.9×10^{-39} for the left hand, and 2.0×10^{-39} for the right hand side. Nature has evidently picked the values of the

24. Davies 1982, pp. 71-73.

fundamental constants in such a way that typical stars lie very close indeed to the boundary of convective instability. The fact that the two sides of the inequality are such enormous numbers, and yet lie so close to one another [10^{-39}], *is truly astonishing.* If gravity were *very* slightly weaker, or electromagnetism *very* slightly stronger, (or the electron slightly less massive relative to the proton), all stars would be *red dwarfs.* A correspondingly tiny change the other way, and they would all be *blue giants.*[25]

Once again, the anthropic values of these four constants have a very narrow closed range while the non-anthropic values have an open, almost indefinite range, making the emergence of stable stars necessary for the development of life forms exceedingly improbable.

(6) A sixth instance of the improbability of anthropic conditions concerns the weak force constant and its relationship to the carbon atom. This constant must have a value similar to that in our universe if carbon (the building block of life) is to be operative. Sufficient heat is required for carbon bonding to occur; the kind of heat that can only be provided by a supernova explosion. This same heat is also required for the production of iron and uranium atoms. As Davies notes, if the weak force had varied ever so slightly, supernovae would never have occurred, thereby depriving carbon atoms of the heat necessary for their production:

> We owe the presence of the carbon in our bodies, the iron core of our planet and the uranium in our nuclear reactors to supernovae that occurred before the solar system formed. Without supernovae, Earth-like planets would not exist.
>
> If the weak interaction were much weaker, the neutrinos would not be able to exert enough pressure on the outer envelope of the star to cause the supernova explosion. On the other hand, if it were much stronger, the neutrinos would be trapped inside the core, and rendered impotent. Either way, the chemical organization of the universe would be very different.[26]

A slight variation in the weak force constant above *or* below its current value would have prohibited supernovae explosions, which would, in turn, have prohibited the generation of carbon necessary for the development of life

---

25. Davies 1982, pp. 71-73. Italics mine.
26. Davies 1982, p. 68.

forms in our universe. Once again, the range of non-anthropic constant values is virtually open, while the range of anthropic constant values is narrow and closed, making our anthropic universe exceedingly improbable.

(7) A seventh instance can be adduced from the resonances of atomic nuclei. These resonances are dependent upon the precise values of fundamental constants as well as the generation of atomic nuclei through universal and stellar evolution. One of the most remarkable examples of this (which moved Fred Hoyle from atheism to a belief in a "supercalculating Intellect"[27]) is the resonance of the carbon nucleus.

Owen Gingerich shows that the precise resonance of the carbon atom necessary for its multiple bonding properties happens to coincide perfectly with the resonance of beryllium, helium, and oxygen. If this *extremely remote coincidence* had not occurred, then carbon would be extremely rare, and carbon-based life forms would not have emerged:

> ... here the internal details of the carbon nucleus become interesting: it turns out that there is precisely the right resonance within the carbon to help this process along. ... The specific resonances within atomic nuclei are something like [a sound wave which can shatter a glass at a very precise frequency], except in this case the particular energy enables the parts to stick together rather than to fly apart. In the carbon atom, the resonance just happens to match the combined energy of the beryllium atom and a colliding helium nucleus. Without it, there would be relatively few carbon atoms. Similarly, the internal details of the oxygen nucleus play a critical role. Oxygen can be formed by combining helium and carbon nuclei, but the corresponding resonance level in the oxygen nucleus is half a percent too low for the combination to stay together easily. Had the resonance level in the carbon been 4 percent lower, there would be essentially no carbon. Had that level in the oxygen been only half a percent higher, virtually all of the carbon would have been converted to oxygen. Without that carbon abundance, none of us would be here now.
>
> I am told that Fred Hoyle, who together with William Fowler first noticed the remarkable arrangement of carbon and oxygen nuclear resonances, has said that nothing has shaken his atheism as much as this discovery.[28]

27. See Hoyle 1983.
28. Gingerich 2000, pp. 524-25.

The non-anthropic values of the resonance levels of carbon and oxygen (a virtually open range) far exceed their anthropic values (a narrow, closed range), making the occurrence of bondable carbon exceedingly improbable. Once again, the conditions of the universe have managed (astonishingly) to find their way to this exceedingly improbable anthropic condition.

Though many other examples could be given, the above seven are sufficient to show that slight variations in the actual values of our universal constants would have given rise to a universe incapable of sustaining *any* life form. If the values of these constants had not been built into the initial conditions of the universe, the universe would have very probably emerged as a collection of black holes, or a universal black hole, a universe of high entropy, or a dispersion of weakly interacting particles, or a universe without hydrogen, or a universe without heavier elements, or a universe without carbon or iron, or a universe of blue giants or red dwarfs . . . all of which would have meant a universe incapable of sustaining any life form.

The above examples show that the values of our universal constants must fit within a narrow closed range in order to be hospitable to life. The range is even narrower than might be implied by any one of the above seven examples, for the gravitational constant, for example, must not only conform to a narrow range in its relationship to the weak force constant, but also to the electromagnetic constant and to the ratio of electron to proton mass while it is conforming to the weak force constant. Furthermore, the gravitational constant must conform to the weak force constant while the weak force constant is conforming to the electromagnetic constant and the strong force constant. Furthermore, it must be conforming to the cosmological constant while it is conforming to all the other constants . . . etc. As can be seen, this makes the range of anthropic values of our universal constants extremely narrow by comparison with the virtually open range of non-anthropic values of these constants. Inasmuch as the values of these constants could have fallen within a huge, virtually open, non-anthropic range (*above or below* those required for an anthropic universe), it follows that the odds of our universe being anthropic are exceedingly, exceedingly, exceedingly remote.

Are we to believe that this occurred by pure chance? Since it is difficult to quantify a virtually open range of non-anthropic values in their relationship to a narrow closed range of anthropic values, we may do well to express the contrast in terms of a simple but enlightening analogy.

The enormity of the differential between non-anthropic and anthropic values of our universe's constants may be likened to a monkey typing out *Hamlet* (without any recourse to the play) by random tapping on the keys of a typewriter. Needless to say, it requires *belief* to explain this occurrence by pure chance.

If one were to come into a room where such a monkey had been typing randomly for a month, and were to discover twelve sheets of perfect Shakespearean prose, one could reasonably and responsibly *believe* that someone intelligent (and possessing a fine knowledge of Shakespeare) had snuck into the room and helped the monkey. Alternatively, one might *believe* that the monkey had a random stroke of luck that allowed a conspiracy of coincidences unimaginably remote to occur by pure chance. In one case, one *believes* in an intellect that one did not see. In the other case, one *believes* that an unbelievably improbable occurrence took place by pure chance.

Thus, the teleological argument makes belief inescapable. I leave it to the reader to ascertain which kind of belief is more reasonable and responsible. If one cannot force oneself to believe that such an exceedingly improbable event took place by pure chance, then one will want to return to the two options given by Davies with which we started:

> . . . the numerical coincidences [necessary for an anthropic universe] could be regarded as evidence of design. The delicate fine-tuning in the values of the constants, necessary so that the various different branches of physics can dovetail so felicitously, might be attributed to God. It is hard to resist the impression that the present structure of the universe, apparently so sensitive to minor alterations in the numbers, has been rather carefully thought out. Such a conclusion can, of course, only be subjective. In the end it boils down to a question of belief. Is it easier to believe in a cosmic designer than the multiplicity of universes necessary for the weak anthropic principle to work? . . . Perhaps future developments in science will lead to more direct evidence for other universes, but until then, the seemingly miraculous concurrence of numerical values that nature has assigned to her fundamental constants must remain the most compelling evidence for an element of cosmic design.[29]

Davies' contention about the "universes necessary for the weak anthropic principle" will be taken up below (Section III). If, for the moment, we disre-

29. Davies 1983, p. 189.

gard the possibility of a large number of alternative universes, it would seem that the immensity of the difference between anthropic and non-anthropic values of our universal constants provides reasonable and responsible rationale, for belief in supernatural design.

III. Many Universes or Supernatural Design?

The extreme improbability of our anthropic universe begs for an explanation beyond mere "chance occurrence." The idea that the universal constants assumed the *narrow* closed range of anthropic values instead of the virtually open range of non-anthropic values by pure chance is so improbable that many highly regarded physicists reject its occurrence. They do this out of respect for the equations of probability and the need for sufficient explanation. For this reason, the same physicists would also reject a pure chance "non-explanation" of a monkey randomly typing twelve pages of Shakespearean prose.

Nevertheless, it would not be surprising to find a group of agnostic physicists attempting to give a super-extensive naturalistic *explanation* for the extreme improbability of our anthropic universe. This explanation makes recourse to a myriad of hypothetical universes instead of a supernatural Designer. Though this *might* seem more natural, it still appeals to an explanation beyond our observable universe that currently cannot be verified through evidence in this universe. Further investigation of the multiple universes hypothesis will be necessary in order to make an intelligent choice between these two explanations.

The idea behind the weak anthropic principle is to lessen the extreme improbability of our anthropic universe by situating it within a larger context of other universes having different conditions and constants. The odds of having an anthropic universe amidst trillions upon trillions upon trillions of other non-anthropic universes would seem to diminish the improbability of its occurrence.

It is like having a die with $10^{10^{123}}$ sides, and having to roll the die onto one particular side (say the side with number nine on it). The odds of accomplishing this in one roll are exceedingly low, and if this were to happen, one might strongly suspect that the die was loaded (designed for this outcome). But if one were given $10^{10^{123}}$ tries to roll a "nine" one could say that this highly unusual outcome would be expected to occur (though this may take a while).

If there really are $10^{10^{123}}$ universes (or regions of a multiverse) then our low-entropy anthropic universe would not be exceedingly improbable. The improbability of its occurrence would be cancelled by the enormous number of opportunities to achieve the improbable outcome.

Do such an enormous number of universes really exist? Can they be known to exist? Are they physically realistic or are they only theoretical? The plausibility of the weak anthropic ("many universes") hypothesis depends on the answers to these questions.

If a *naturalistic* (many universes) explanation of our low-entropy anthropic universe is to be as plausible as a *transcendent* explanation, it must be based on comparable evidence. As we saw in the previous chapter, cosmological evidence currently supports a reasonable likelihood of a beginning of our universe (implying a reasonable likelihood of a non-natural/supernatural cause of that beginning). This lends probative force to the supernatural explanation of our low-entropy universe and its anthropic constants (assuming the supernatural cause of the universe is also the cause of its fine-tuning). Therefore, if the many universes explanation is to have as much probative force as the supernatural explanation, there should be sufficient evidence to establish a *reasonable likelihood* of the other universes.

There have been three major proposals for the many universes hypothesis over the last four decades:

1. The Everett-DeWitt Quantum "Many Worlds" Hypothesis
2. Linde's Chaotic Inflationary Multiverse
3. The String Theory Landscape

These proposals are subject to two or more of the following three problems which mitigate their reasonable likelihood:

a. Running counter to the *canon of parsimony* or "Ockham's razor."
b. Being *highly theoretical* (and likely to remain so in the indefinite future).
c. Having significant problems of workability and consistency with cosmological observation.

The first proposal is the grandfather of them all. Hugh Everett's quantum multiple universe conjecture (1957, updated by DeWitt in 1970). Davies describes it as follows:

[A]ll the possible alternative quantum worlds are equally real, and exist in parallel with one another. Whenever a measurement is performed to determine, for example, whether the cat is alive or dead, the universe divides into two, one containing a live cat, the other a dead one. Both worlds are equally real, and both contain human observers. Each set of inhabitants, however, perceives only their own branch of the universe.... The splitting [of universes] is repeated again and again as every atom, and all the subatomic particles, cavort about. Countless times each second the universe is replicated. Nor is it necessary for an actual measurement to be performed in order that the replication occur. It suffices that a single microscopic particle merely interacts in some way with a macroscopic system.[30]

The Everett-DeWitt hypothesis encountered some problems with its workability (problems of circularity) which necessitated an updating from Deutsch, Wallace, and Saunders. Though this updating may have recovered the workability of the hypothesis, it is still subject to two major problems: (1) its violation of the canon of parsimony and (2) its *highly* theoretical character.

Let us begin with the first difficulty, the canon of parsimony. This scientific canon is popularly known as "Ockham's razor" and holds that, *in general,* nature seems to prefer simple and elegant causal systems (instead of esoteric, complex, and convoluted ones). Though this is a general norm, it does not constitute a proof of a theory's validity. Simple and elegant causal systems could be false, and complex, esoteric, and convoluted causal systems could be true. Nevertheless, in general, nature *does* tend toward simple and elegant causal systems, and this tendency provides a clue about the potential tenability of a particular explanation.

As Davies notes, the Everett-DeWitt quantum many universes proposal violates the canon of parsimony on a rather grand scale:

Another weakness of the anthropic argument is that it seems the very antithesis of Ockham's razor, according to which the most plausible of a possible set of explanations is that which contains the simplest ideas and least number of assumptions. To invoke an infinity of other universes just to explain one is surely carrying excess baggage to cosmic extremes, not to mention the fact that all but a minute proportion of these other universes go unobserved (except by God perhaps).... It is

---

30. Davies 1983, p. 116.

hard to see how such a purely theoretical construct can ever be used as an *explanation,* in the scientific sense, of a feature of nature. Of course, one might find it easier to believe in an infinite array of universes than in an infinite Deity, but such a belief must rest on faith rather than observation.[31]

Davies final observation points to the second major difficulty with the quantum mini universes hypothesis, namely, that it is a *"purely theoretical construct"* which is exceedingly difficult to use "as an *explanation* in the scientific sense of a feature of nature." Indeed, the "purely theoretical" nature of this hypothesis is likely to persist into the future because visiting those universes is prohibited by quantum theory. Davies notes in this regard:

> . . . the many-universe theorists concede that the 'other worlds' of their theory can never, even in principle, be inspected. Travel between quantum 'branches' is forbidden.[32]

If the quantum mini universe theory remains highly theoretical, it will not provide a more probative alternative to the transcendent explanation of our low-entropy, anthropic universe, because the evidence of a beginning will be more probative than the evidence for the speculative and unverifiable "other universes."

This leads us to the second major proposal for multiple universes (or regions of a multiverse), namely Linde's chaotic inflationary multiverse.[33] This proposal has more explanatory depth than the quantum "many worlds" proposal and is therefore less theoretical. Nevertheless, it is still highly speculative.

This proposal postulates that our universe is a bubble universe amidst other bubble universes within a multiverse. The number of bubble universes increases as the multiverse expands. It arises out of a vacuum which has not decayed to its ground state. The peaks in the evolution of the scalar field determine the energy of the vacuum and correspond to regions ("bubbles") of rapid inflation, having different qualities and dimensions.

The original formulation of inflation led to a significant problem — the collision of bubbles. Linde (along with Albrecht and Steinhardt) revised the original theory to resolve the problem by postulating a "slow roll." This

---

31. Davies 1983, pp. 173-74.
32. Davies 1983, p. 173.
33. See Linde 1998, p. 102. See also Wikipedia "inflation (cosmology)."

new inflationary theory entails considerable fine-tuning of the initial conditions of inflation to produce the slow roll.[34]

This proposal finds itself caught between a workability problem and fine-tuning of initial conditions. As noted in Chapter One, "fine-tuning" refers to a set of initial conditions that are exceedingly improbable; in the absence of a natural explanation they imply nonnatural or supernatural design. This is ironic, because it is the precise result that Linde's chaotic multiverse was intended to avoid. Yet avoiding the result will lead to significant difficulties (collisions of bubbles). This leads to a further irony, namely, that the fine-tuning of initial conditions would seem to occur at the universe's absolute beginning, because Linde's chaotic multiverse is subject to the BVG theorem (see Chapter One, Section III.E). This would associate the initial fine-tuning with the implicit supernatural cause of the universe's absolute beginning.

Perhaps another formulation of the Linde multiverse will be able to avoid this dilemma, but for the moment, its workability seems to lead inevitably to the fine-tuning of initial conditions (seemingly by a transcendent cause). As such, it does not seem to avoid supernatural design.

We may now consider the third major proposal for a multiverse, namely, the string theory landscape. This theory was formulated by Susskind, Bousso, and Linde.[35] It is based on the large number of possible false vacua in string theory (in some views, 10^{500}). Each vacuum theoretically has the potential to generate a universe (within a multiverse) having arbitrarily different dimensions, values of constants, etc. It also attempts to include the anthropic principle (favoring conditions allowing for life) within the expanding multiverse. This may allow for the possibility of a low-entropy universe with anthropic constants (like our own).

Two problems with this proposal have emerged. First, as Michael Dine and others imply, it may run into inconsistencies with cosmological observation, because it predicts low energy supersymmetry, but "many features of low energy physics are not anthropic and as currently understood, the landscape picture will get them wrong."[36] Susskind's attempt to respond to Dine's criticism is not particularly strong. Secondly, the merging of string theory

34. See Alabidi and Lyth 2006.

35. Bousso and Polchinski 2000; Kachru, Kallosh, Linde, and Trivedi 2003; Kachru, Kallosh, Linde, Maldecena, McAllister, and Trivedi 2003; Susskind 2003; Susskind 2004; Freivogel and Susskind 2004; Bousso and Polchinski 2004, pp. 60-69.

36. Dine 2004, p. 1.

with the anthropic principle is highly controversial because many scientists believe that the anthropic principle is unscientific and nonfalsifiable.

Aside from the problems of consistency with cosmological observation, the string theory landscape, like Linde's chaotic inflationary multiverse, seems to require fine-tuning (Bruce Gordon presents a thorough analysis of this in the Postscript following this chapter — Section V). In view of the fact that the string theory landscape is subject to the BVG theorem (see Chapter One, Section III.E), it gives rise to the same ironic result as Linde's chaotic inflationary multiverse, namely, that the fine-tuning of the landscape seems to be associated with the transcendent cause of an absolute beginning of the landscape.

Bruce Gordon concludes, "it is clear that the string landscape hypothesis is a highly speculative construction built on shaky assumptions and . . . requires meta-level fine-tuning itself." In view of this, and the apparent absolute beginning of the landscape, it does not seem to escape the implication of nonnatural or supernatural design.

Conclusion

The Everett-DeWitt quantum many worlds proposal (even with contemporary adaptations by Deutsch, Wallace, and Saunders) is highly theoretical and is not grounded in evidence comparable to the evidence for a beginning. It is unlikely that this evidence will ever be forthcoming, because access to the other universes is strictly limited by quantum theory. The Linde chaotic inflationary multiverse and the string theory landscape run into problems of workability and consistency with cosmological observation. Furthermore, they require fine-tuning (which is associated with a transcendent cause because both proposals are subject to the BVG theorem and are therefore likely to have an absolute beginning). The above problems mitigate the probative force of these proposals, and show their inability to avoid transcendent design. This gives an evidential advantage to the supernatural explanation.

Could another "many universes" proposal be generated that avoids the above problems? It *may* be possible to avoid the problems of workability and consistency with cosmological observation. However, it is difficult to see how future proposals can successfully avoid: (1) non-conformity with the canon of parsimony, (2) a high degree of speculation, and (3) fine-tuning. First, any new proposal would have to run counter to the canon of parsimony because it will have to explain the generation of enough universes to lower the exceedingly high improbability of our low-entropy universe and its anthropic constants. Such a large number of additional universes inevitably runs counter to parsimony. Secondly, future proposals will run into the problem of being speculative (highly theoretical) because it will be difficult to obtain empirical access to the other postulated universes. Thirdly, if new multiverse proposals resemble Linde's and Susskind's (et al.), they are likely to entail fine-tuning. The persistence of these problems (and the likelihood of fine-tuning) manifests an inherent weakness in the multiverse hypothesis (in general) which makes the supernatural explanation (based on the evidence of a beginning of the universe) *more likely* than the naturalistic alternative.

This leads us to Fred Hoyle's observation (which moved him out of atheism):

> . . . A common sense interpretation of the facts suggests that a superintellect has monkeyed with physics, as well as with chemistry and biology, and that there are no blind forces worth speaking about in nature. The numbers one calculates from the facts seem to me so overwhelming as to put this conclusion almost beyond question.[37]

The current state of cosmological evidence makes it difficult to believe otherwise.

CONCLUSION TO PART ONE

In Chapter One (Section II), it was noted that science, unlike philosophy and metaphysics, cannot *deductively* prove a creation or God. Science is an empirical and inductive discipline, meaning that it cannot be certain that it has considered all possible data that would be relevant to a complete explanation of particular physical phenomena or the universe itself. Nevertheless, it is reasonable and responsible to attribute qualified truth value to long-standing, rigorously established theories until such time as new data requires them to be changed. This is what enables science to (1) identify, aggregate, and synthesize evidence indicating the finitude of past time in the universe, and (2) to identify the exceedingly high improbability of the random occurrence of conditions necessary to sustain life in the universe.

In Chapter One, we showed the current state of cosmological evidence

37. Hoyle 1981, pp. 8-12.

indicating a beginning of the universe, set out the conditions that would be necessary to get around this evidence, and evaluated the current state of alternative proposals. We concluded the following: in view of the extensive applicability and preponderance of evidence for a beginning of the universe (and the narrow and tenuous path which must be taken to get around it), it can be concluded that the evidence currently supports a *reasonable likelihood* of a beginning — a point at which the universe came into existence. This led to the further conclusion (when combined with the metaphysical proposition "from nothing, only nothing comes") that there is a reasonable likelihood of a transcendent cause of our universe.

In Chapter Two, we set out the evidence for the exceedingly high improbability of our low-entropy universe and its anthropic constants. We then indicated that it would not be reasonable or responsible to conclude that our universe arose by pure chance, and therefore, there would have to be some natural or supernatural cause for its occurrence. After evaluating the three major proposals for a naturalistic (many universes) cause (as well as the tenability of future proposals), we concluded the following: the persistence of three problems (and the likelihood of fine-tuning) manifests an inherent weakness in the multiverse hypothesis (in general) which makes the supernatural explanation (based on the evidence of a beginning of the universe) *more likely* than the naturalistic alternative.

Using John Henry Newman's informal inference (synthesizing probabilistic evidence from multiple sources of data), we concluded, with Fred Hoyle and others, to the reasonable likelihood of a transcendent cause which is a Superintellect capable of remarkable fine-tuning.

Bruce Gordon probes this conclusion more deeply in the Postscript following this chapter, and comes to a similar conclusion:

> When the logical and metaphysical necessity of an efficient cause, the demonstrable absence of a material one, and the proof that there was an absolute beginning to any universe or multiverse are all conjoined with the fact that our universe exists and its conditions are fine-tuned immeasurably beyond the capacity of any mindless process, the scientific evidence points inexorably toward transcendent intelligent agency as the most plausible, if not the only reasonable explanation.

Inflationary Cosmology and the String Multiverse

Bruce L. Gordon, Ph.D.

Introduction

We have embarked on an examination of inflationary cosmology and its metaphysical significance; let us extend our journey a bit further, to the reaches of current theory. We begin by noting that the Borde-Vilenkin past-incompleteness theorem for inflationary universes has been strengthened, and will discuss the significance of this fact for various pre-big-bang inflationary scenarios in string cosmology, including landscape and cyclic ekpyrotic models. We then undertake a general critique of inflationary cosmology in respect of its stated goals and conclude with a critical discussion of the string-theoretic multiverse as a "solution" to the problem of cosmological fine-tuning.

I. *All* Inflationary Cosmologies Must Have a Beginning and a Transcendent Cause

The theorem that inflationary models are past-incomplete, which earlier depended on a weak-energy condition that allowed for exceptions,[1] can be es-

---

1. Borde and Vilenkin 1994, pp. 3305-9; Borde and Vilenkin 1997, pp. 717-23.

I thank Fr. Robert Spitzer for his generous invitation to contribute this Postscript to the first two chapters of his book and for discussion of these issues. My thanks also to David Berlinski, Arthur Fine, Robin Collins, and *most especially* Gerald Cleaver and James Sinclair for comments on an earlier draft of this essay. I am solely responsible for any problems that remain.

tablished instead by an argument that needs no energy condition.[2] This stronger proof, put forward in 2003 by Arvind Borde, Alan Guth, and Alexander Vilenkin (henceforth BGV), considers space-times satisfying the condition that the average Hubble expansion in the past is greater than zero, i.e., $H_{av} > 0$. They show that a suitable construction of the Hubble parameter, H, permits it to be defined for arbitrary (inhomogeneous, anisotropic) cosmological models in a way that reduces to its standard definition in simple models. With this generalized Hubble parameter in hand, they demonstrate that its integral along any null or timelike geodesic is bounded, so that any backward-going null or timelike geodesic with $H_{av} > 0$ must have finite length, i.e., be past-incomplete. In other words, the BGV result demonstrates that all inflationary space-times have a beginning in the finite past, presumably in some sort of quantum nucleation event[3] that mitigates the breakdown of physics accompanying a classical singularity. Apart from such physical considerations on expanding space-times, other arguments against an *actual* infinity of time before the present are exceedingly strong: considered in terms of *real* events or instants of time an actual infinity is nonsensical and incapable of coherent positive construction; mathematically, an infinite past is a theoretical limit that is never reached, an extrapolation that, quite apart from its metaphysical impossibility, founders on the necessary *meta*-stability of the primordial state in cosmological models generating universes, like our own, that are *not static*. By the impeccable logic of the *kalām* argument,[4] the BGV theorem implies that space-times expanding on average throughout their histories are *caused* — they are caused because they began to exist, and everything that begins to exist *requires* a cause.[5] Furthermore, this cause must be *transcendent* in nature because space-time *can-*

---

2. Borde, Guth, and Vilenkin 2003.

3. Vilenkin 1982, pp. 25-28.

4. Craig 1979(b); Copan and Craig 2004, pp. 147-266.

5. Some have argued that quantum theory provides an exception to this principle, but I strongly disagree. The failure of local causality in quantum-mechanical description by *no* means leads to the conclusion that some things come into existence *without* a cause; however, the metaphysical resolution of this quantum-mechanical "paradox" is beyond the scope of our present discussion.

One might also argue that *contingent* entities, like our universe, even if there were no time at which they began to exist, would still require an explanation of their existence in virtue of their contingent character. In respect of the universe as a whole especially, this explanation would presumably have to be given in terms of something that existed *necessarily* and *transcendently*. Since, as we shall see, current cosmology does not really lead us in this direction, we will not pursue this argument any further here.

not be self-caused: prior to the existence of all space, time, matter, and energy there was no universe to describe and there were no physical laws or initial conditions that could have played a role in its genesis; rather, all these things came into existence out of *nothing*, so a transcendent immaterial cause must necessarily have acted.[6]

I.A. String Cosmologies Entail a Beginning and a Transcendent Cause

The class of cosmologies satisfying the assumption that the Hubble parameter has a positive value when averaged over the affine parameter of a past-directed null or non-comoving timelike geodesic also includes cosmologies of higher dimensions, and can be extended to Steinhardt and Turok's cyclic ekpyrotic model[7] in string cosmology. A brief primer on string theory will help to facilitate discussion.

I.A.1. A Primer on String Theory

String theory was initially proposed in the mid-1960s as a description of the strong nuclear force generating mesons and baryons, but lapsed into obscurity after the success of quantum chromodynamics. The fundamental con-

6. Some in the physics community try to escape this conclusion by arguing that a "different physics" is required at the past boundary. What is meant by this, for good reason, is not always clear, but usually involves some form of quantum cosmology like the Vilenkin 1982 tunneling model or the Hartle and Hawking 1983 no boundary proposal. Aside from making a variety of questionable assumptions, the Vilenkin "tunneling from nothing" model *does* have a *beginning*, and therefore requires transcendent activation if it is to be anything more than an inert mathematical description. The Hartle-Hawking proposal also involves a variety of unwarranted assumptions, not least of which is retaining in the model's solution the computational expedient of a Euclidean rather than a Lorentzian space-time metric for the precise purpose of avoiding an initial singularity; once the reverse transformation is effected, as it *must* be if the model is to be a potential description of our universe, the singularity/absolute beginning reappears (see Section II.C of Chapter 1 in Fr. Spitzer's text for a slightly more extensive discussion). Other quantum cosmological/gravitational proposals that entail metaphysical pictures of even more questionable coherence are the subject of ongoing research, but evaluating them is beyond the scope of our present concerns.

7. Khoury, Ovrut, Steinhardt, and Turok 2001(a); Steinhardt and Turok 2002(a); Steinhardt and Turok 2002(b); Khoury, Ovrut, Seiberg, Steinhardt, and Turok 2002; Turok, Perry, and Steinhardt 2004; McFadden, Turok, and Steinhardt 2007; Steinhardt and Turok 2007.

stituents of string theory are one-dimensional filaments existing as open strings or closed loops on the scale of the Planck length (10^{-33} cm). The theory was revived in the late 1970s when John Schwarz and other researchers discovered that the spin-2 particle that had thwarted its nuclear ambitions could be reinterpreted as the quantum of the gravitational field, producing a theory that, when the demands of quantum-theoretic consistency were satisfied, reconciled gravity with quantum mechanics in a 10-dimensional space-time. The extra six spatial dimensions of string theory require compactification into Planck-scale Calabi-Yau manifolds to suggest any connection with reality as we know it, and this division of the spatial dimensions (into three large and six small) transforms some of the N=1 SUSY gravitational modes in nine large dimensions into a variety of non-gravitational bosonic and fermionic vibrations.[8]

Just what *kind* of non-gravitational forces (spin-1 bosons) and matter (fermions and supersymmetric scalar partners) are produced by this transformation depends on the size and shape of the compactified dimensions[9] and, alas, there are an *unlimited* number of ways of doing this. This embarrassment of riches was once regarded as a vice, but increasing appreciation of the degree to which the laws and constants of our universe are fine-tuned for life has led some to extol it as a virtue, speaking instead of the "landscape" of string vacua.[10] We will examine the string landscape hypothesis in more detail presently, but for now, note that the BGV theorem applies to it because on average it is continually expanding, and therefore past-incomplete. Thus, if the landscape existed, it too would have a beginning.

One of the most recalcitrant technical problems in the early stages of the

8. Since even when compactified, bosons remain bosons and fermions remain fermions, it takes compactification of the gravitino to produce space-time fermionic matter. I thank Gerald Cleaver for this clarification.

9. Green, Schwarz, and Witten 1987.

10. Bousso and Polchinski 2000; Kachru, Kallosh, Linde, and Trivedi 2003; Kachru, Kallosh, Linde, Maldecena, McAllister, and Trivedi 2003; Susskind 2003; Susskind 2004; Freivogel and Susskind 2004; Bousso and Polchinski 2004, pp. 60-69; Ashok and Douglas 2004; Douglas 2004(a); Kobakhidze and Mersini-Houghton 2004, pp. 869-73; Ooguri and Vafa 2006; Riddle and Urena-Lopez 2006; Barvinsky and Kamenshchik 2006; Susskind 2006; Vanchurin and Vilenkin 2006; Denef and Douglas 2006; Kumar 2006, pp. 3441-72; Polchinski 2006; Cleaver 2006.

Indeed, the embarrassment of riches is so extreme that, were cosmological fine-tuning not so *incredibly* stringent, one might be inclined to modify William Unruh's remark that he could fit any dog's leg you handed him with inflation (Unruh 1996) to say "I'll fit any dog's leg that you hand me with string theory"!

string revival was solved in 1984 by John Schwarz and Michael Green.[11] Ten-dimensional string theory exhibited a quantum anomaly resulting from unphysical longitudinal modes that were shown to be eliminable if the strings obeyed a specific gauge symmetry, SO(32). It was then shown in fairly quick order that there were actually *five* anomaly-free classes of 10-dimensional string theories characterized by different gauge symmetries: Type I, Type IIA, Type IIB, $E_8 \times E_8$ heterotic, and SO(32) heterotic, all Calabi-Yau compactifiable in the six extra spatial dimensions and each with countless numbers of models.

In the 1990s, evidence began to collect that these five classes of string theories were not, in fact, independent of each other. This suspicion was given life in 1995 when Edward Witten demonstrated the equivalence of heterotic SO(32) string theories with low-energy-effective string field theories of Type I.[12] Subsequently, the community of string theorists found dualities expressing the equivalence of all five classes of string theories, along with 11-dimensional supergravity. The key to these equivalences proved to be a string with finite width in addition to its length — in essence a two-dimensional membrane — existing in eleven rather than ten dimensions. Thus was born 11-dimensional "M-theory."

The additional spatial direction in M-theory potentially plays a different role than the others. The ten-dimensional space-time of string theory is a slice of the 11-dimensional bulk of M-theory. Since the new spatial dimension is orthogonal everywhere to the other nine, it can be regarded as a line segment connecting two 10-dimensional string universes (9-branes), each hidden from the other and having only the gravitational force in common.[13] Since six of the extra ten spatial dimensions are compactified throughout the 11-dimensional bulk, the effective picture is that of a 5-dimensional space-time bulk with two 4-dimensional universes (3-branes) at the ends of a line segment. Since gravity would vary as the inverse cube of the distance in four spatial dimensions and the inverse square law has been tested down to 55 micrometers,[14] if this M-theoretic model had any basis in reality, this minuscule distance would provide the current maximum separation between our universe and its twin. Additional tests of this *highly speculative* scenario have been proposed and are being pursued.[15]

11. Green and Schwarz 1985, pp. 93-114; Green, Schwarz, and Witten 1987.

12. Witten 1995.

13. Arkani-Hamed, Dimopoulos, and Dvali 1998, pp. 263-72.

14. Adelberger, Heckel, and Nelson 2003, pp. 87-100; Kapner, Cook, Adelberger, Gundlach, Heckel, Hoyle, and Swanson 2007.

15. Adelberger, Heckel, and Hoyle 2005; Giddings and Thomas 2002.

I.A.2. Steinhardt-Turok Cyclic Ekpyrotic Universes
Require a Beginning and a Transcendent Cause

M-theory also permits the possibility of freely moving universes (branes); it is this possibility that is explored in the cyclic ekpyrotic models[16] of string cosmology. In this scenario, a bulk of four spatial dimensions exists between two 3-branes. The collisions between these branes, which happen on average once every trillion years, release sufficient energy to catalyze the hot big-bang stage of new universes.[17] The effective (3+1)-dimensional geometry in this model describes an expanding and contracting universe with nucleation events that separate each cycle. Because of Planck-scale quantum fluctuations, neither 3-brane remains perfectly flat, and energy release is therefore greatest at points of first contact. Steinhardt and Turok estimate that on each cycle such brane-brane collisions have the potential to produce staggering numbers of new big-bang regions (10^{100} to 10^{500}) that are causally isolated from each other.

Of course, each such universe has a beginning in a quantum string nucleation event induced by a brane-brane collision, and so has a finite past. The original brane space-times were non-singular, however, and this served to ground the claim that the cyclic ekpyrotic scenario does not require initial conditions and can be past-eternal.[18] This turns out *not* to be the case, however, as Borde, Guth, and Vilenkin[19] make clear and Steinhardt has now acknowledged.[20] An essential feature of the ekpyrotic model, which enables it to deal with the thermodynamic objection that defeats conventional cyclic cosmologies,[21] is that the volume of the universe increases with each cycle while the energy released into the branes by each collision is renewed each cycle by the inexhaustible resource of gravitational potential energy. This means that on average the cyclic universe is expanding, i.e., $H_{av} > 0$, and so the BGV theorem implies its geodesic incompleteness[22] — in short, it has a beginning in the finite past.

16. Khoury, Ovrut, Steinhardt, and Turok 2001(a); Steinhardt and Turok 2002(a); Steinhardt and Turok 2002(b); Khoury, Ovrut, Seiberg, Steinhardt, and Turok 2002; Turok, Perry, and Steinhardt 2004; McFadden, Turok, and Steinhardt 2007; Steinhardt and Turok 2007.
17. Khoury, Ovrut, Steinhardt, and Turok 2001(a).
18. Steinhardt and Turok 2002(a).
19. Borde, Guth, and Vilenkin 2003; Vilenkin 2006(a).
20. Steinhardt and Turok 2005, pp. 43-47; Steinhardt 2004.
21. Steinhardt and Turok 2007; Vilenkin 2006(a); Steinhardt 2004.
22. Borde, Guth, and Vilenkin 2003; Vilenkin 2006(a); Steinhardt and Turok 2005; Steinhardt 2004.

I.A.3. Gasperini-Veneziano Pre-Big-Bang Scenarios Require a Beginning and a Transcendent Cause

Before we examine the generic credentials of inflationary cosmology, there is another pre-big-bang scenario in string cosmology we should discuss, the one proposed by Maurizio Gasperini and Gabriele Veneziano.[23] Anachronistically speaking, it sidesteps the $H_{av} > 0$ condition governing the BGV result and, from a *purely* mathematical standpoint, can be geodesically extended into the infinite past. The Gasperini-Veneziano pre-big-bang inflationary (PBBI) model proposes that the universe started its evolution from the simplest string-theoretic initial state possible, namely, its perturbative vacuum, corresponding to a universe that, for all practical purposes, is empty, cold, and flat. This string perturbative vacuum (SPV) phase is neither expanding nor contracting in whole or in part; in this sense, it is static. Since the space-time manifold of this state has models in which timelike and null geodesics can be past-extended for infinite values of their affine parameter, it is proposed that this phase could have been of infinite duration, which would mean that the universe did *not* have a beginning.

Assuming that the primordial universe is a string perturbative vacuum means that the dilaton field[24] started very large and negative, which allows the early history of the universe to be treated classically.[25] The assumption of virtual flatness also enables employment of the low-energy approximation

23. Gasperini and Veneziano 2003, pp. 1-212; Veneziano 1998; Hawking and Penrose 1970, pp. 529-48; Veneziano 1995; Veneziano 1997, pp. 297-303; Feinstein, Lazkoz, and Vazquez-Mozo 1997; Barrow and Dabrowski 1998; Saygili 1999, pp. 225-40; Buonanno, Meissner, Ungarelli, and Veneziano 1998; Barrow and Kunze 1997; Gasperini 1999; Turner and Weinberg 1997, pp. 4604-9; Maggiore and Sturani 1997, pp. 335-43; Kaloper, Linde, and Bousso 1999; Brustein and Veneziano 1994, pp. 429-34; Gasperini, Maharana, and Veneziano 1996, pp. 349-60; Rey 1996, pp. 1929-32; Gasperini, Maggiore, and Veneziano 1997, pp. 315-30; Gasperini 2000; Brandenberger, Easther, and Maia 1998; Foffa 2003; Gasperini 2007; Gasperini 2008. I am grateful to James Sinclair for drawing my attention to this literature and for discussion of this and related subjects.

24. In string theory, *dilatons* (radions, graviscalars) are quanta of a massless scalar field φ that obeys a generalized Klein-Gordon equation and is always linked with gravity. Perturbative string theories automatically contain dilatons in 10-dimensions, but M-theory doesn't include them in its spectrum unless it's compactified. The dilatonic coupling constant is a dynamical variable in string theory. If supersymmetry is *unbroken*, these scalar fields can take arbitrary values (they are *moduli*); supersymmetry breaking, however, creates a potential energy for scalar fields that localizes near a minimum value that is, at least in principle, calculable.

25. Veneziano 1998.

to string theory. This means the evolution of the universe can be described using classical field equations for the low-energy effective action,[26] from which, under the assumptions of homogeneity and flatness, inflationary behavior automatically follows from the hypothesis that the primordial universe was a string perturbative vacuum.[27] Of course, homogeneity and flatness are *fine-tuning* conditions. If the assumption of homogeneity is relaxed and replaced with generic initial conditions *approximating* the perturbative vacuum, it can be shown that it is possible for a chaotic version of the pre-big-bang scenario to arise through dilaton-driven inflation in patches of the primordial SPV[28] *as long as* the kinetic energy in the dilaton is a non-negligible fraction of the critical density.[29] One of the controversial features of this latter scenario is that in order to have sufficient inflation in a patch, dilaton-driven inflation *has to last long enough* to reach a hot big bang nucleation event. Since PBBI is limited in the past by the initial value of spatial curvature, it has to be *extremely small* in string units if sufficient inflation is to be achieved.[30] In other words, no matter which approach to PBBI one takes, *considerable fine-tuning is necessary.*[31]

A word is in order about a feature of PBBI that some may find puzzling: How is it that an inflationary phase leads to a big bang rather than following from it? This result is a consequence of one of the peculiar features of string theory called *T-duality,* which relates small- and large-distance scales. T-duality implies that, at some deep level, the separation between large- and small-distance scales in physics is fluid. In the "inflationary phase" of the PBBI model, spatial expansion is taking place in the string frame coordinates while, in the classical Einstein frame coordinates, matter is collapsing into trapped surfaces, i.e., black holes.[32] At the conclusion of this dilaton-driven inflationary phase, a transition is supposed to take place to a

---

26. Hawking and Penrose 1970, pp. 529-48.

27. Veneziano 1995.

28. Veneziano 1997, pp. 297-303; Feinstein, Lazkoz, and Vazquez-Mozo 1997; Barrow and Dabrowski 1998, pp. 7204-22; Saygili 1999, pp. 225-40.

29. Veneziano 1998; Veneziano 1997, pp. 297-303; Feinstein, Lazkoz, and Vazquez-Mozo 1997; Barrow and Dabrowski 1998, pp. 7204-22; Saygili 1999, pp. 225-40.

30. Turner and Weinberg 1997, pp. 4604-9.

31. Turner and Weinberg 1997, pp. 4604-9; Maggiore and Sturani 1997, pp. 335-43; Kaloper, Linde, and Bousso 1999; Brustein and Veneziano 1994, pp. 429-34; Gasperini, Maharana, and Veneziano 1996, pp. 349-60; Rey 1996, pp. 1929-32; Gasperini, Maggiore, and Veneziano 1997, pp. 315-30; Gasperini 1999, pp. 1059-66.

32. Gasperini and Veneziano 2003, pp. 1-212.

Friedmann-Lemaître-Robertson-Walker (FLRW) phase typical of the standard hot Big Bang model — though models for *how* this happens are *not* well understood.[33]

What shall we say, then: Does the PBBI do an end run around the BGV theorem and provide a viable picture of a universe with no beginning? *Not really.* While the null and timelike geodesics of the SPV phase can in theory be extended into the infinite past, asymptotically approaching exact equilibrium, the fact remains that the string perturbative vacuum is *unstable.*[34] Quantum fluctuations of the background fields, particularly the dilaton, move the SPV from equilibrium, so that at *any* given finite physical time, the system is in a *non*-equilibrium state. Since *each* patch of the SPV has a non-zero probability of decaying into dilaton-driven inflation, quite apart from issues of metaphysical incoherence stemming from the non-traversability of an infinite past, a realistic interpretation of the model, however implausible in itself, requires acknowledging that the SPV phase has *finite* duration. Since the other two phases of the model (inflationary and FLRW) are *also* finite in duration, the universe has a beginning. So, even in Gasperini-Veneziano PBBI scenarios, the universe begins to exist — and since it begins to exist, it has a transcendent cause.

I.B. Deflationary Intermezzo for Strings

So far we have taken inflationary models as a starting point. We have seen that theists have nothing to fear from inflationary cosmology or the string-theoretic multiverse. Indeed, every known version of these models requires that the universe/multiverse begin to exist, and thus have a transcendent cause. We now turn to an examination of the assumptions governing inflationary and/or string multiverse cosmologies and an evaluation of their effectiveness as explanations of cosmological fine-tuning.

33. Veneziano 1998; Brustein and Veneziano 1994, pp. 429-34; Gasperini, Maharana, and Veneziano 1996, pp. 346-60; Rey 1996, pp. 1929-32; Gasperini, Maggiore, and Veneziano 1997, pp. 315-30; Gasperini 2000; Brandenberger, Easther, and Maia 1998; Foffa 2003; Gasperini 2007.

34. Veneziano 1998; Veneziano 1995; Veneziano 1997, pp. 297-303; Feinstein, Lazkoz, and Vazquez-Mozo 1997; Barrow and Dabrowski 1998, pp. 7204-22; Saygili 1999, pp. 225-40; Buonanno, Meissner, Ungarelli, and Veneziano 1998, pp. 2543-56; Barrow and Kunze 1997.

II. A Preliminary Assessment of Inflationary Cosmology[35]

We should now ask a propaedeutic question: Is inflationary cosmology as currently practiced free from arbitrary assumptions? It is not. Inflation was initially proposed for the purpose of solving three problems: the horizon problem constituted by the uniformity of the cosmic microwave background (CMB) radiation, the flatness problem constituted by the precision with which the universe's actual mass density approximates its critical mass density, and the absence of the magnetic monopoles predicted by favorably regarded grand unified theories (GUTs). Yet these three problems do *not* have to be addressed by the assumptions of the contemporary inflationary model.

First, the scalar fields postulated by inflation (and the multiple scalar fields required by the chaotic inflationary multiverse) are *arbitrary*. They constitute false vacua that bear *no* relation to *any* other known fields in physics and that have properties invented *solely* for the purpose of making inflation work. In short, the explanation they offer is *ad hoc*.

Second, Hawking and Page[36] have shown that when an inflaton field is grafted onto standard FLRW cosmology, while the measure of the set of models that inflate is infinite, so is the set of models that do *not* inflate. This is not an inconsequential observation. As Earman and Mosterin[37] have observed, even when inflation is restricted to the class of homogeneous and isotropic cosmologies, inflationary cosmologists have not been able to show, without invoking highly speculative hypotheses, that inflationary mechanisms actually resolve the fine-tuning issues associated with the hot big bang model that prompted their invention.

Third, and this is related to the previous point, inflation may not be an adequate solution to the flatness problem. The matter density (ordinary and dark) in the universe plus the cosmological constant are very close to the critical density that would imply a perfectly flat universe. Exceedingly precise measurements in 1998 demonstrating a very small *positive* vacuum energy led cosmologists to conclude that the universe will expand forever, though recent calculations based on WMAP (Wilkinson Microwave Anisotropy Probe) data seem to indicate very slight positive curvature, which

35. For further discussion of the shortcomings of inflationary cosmology see: Hawking and Page 1987, pp. 789-809; Penrose 1989(b), pp. 249-64; Rees 1997; Earman and Mosterin 1999, pp. 1-49; Martin and Brandenberger 2001; Hollands and Wald 2002, pp. 2043-55; Holder 2004, pp. 130-43; Penrose 2005, pp. 746-57, 762-65; van Elst 2008.

36. Hawking and Page 1987, pp. 789-809.

37. Earman and Mosterin 1999, pp. 1-49.

would imply a closed universe. No one knows for sure — it's that close — but the general bet is for a flat universe. Inflation is put forward as an explanation for this flatness, but so far serious attempts to calculate inflationary consequences for flatness have assumed an FLRW metric and have not addressed what would happen in the generic case. As Penrose points out,[38] expansion from a generic singularity can become *whatever* type of irregular universe we please, *independent* of whether there is an inflationary phase. As a consequence, without a special metric and special assumptions in view, inflation is not an adequate explanation of flatness.

Fourth, as Thomas Banks explains, any suggestion that inflation resolves the problems created by applying the second law of thermodynamics to cosmology — primarily, the recognition that the universe had to be created in a state of very low entropy — is mistaken.[39] The initial inflationary patch has a very small number of degrees of freedom that can be described by effective field theory; most of the degrees of freedom in the observable universe are *not* capable of description using quantum field theory until a large number of e-folds[40] have occurred. To handle this deficiency, the standard discussion of these degrees of freedom, in its most sophisticated form, begins with the *assumption* that they were in the ground state of some slowly varying Hamiltonian that approaches the conventional field-theoretic Hamiltonian in the inflationary background, co-moving mode by mode, as the physical size of each mode crosses the Planck scale. As Banks notes, this approach involves many *ad hoc* assumptions, including a low-entropy initial condition that is smuggled in by assuming the system was in its ground state. Furthermore, the excited states of *every* known large quantum system are highly degenerate and the adiabatic theorem[41] does *not* apply to generic initial conditions chosen as a linear combination of highly degenerate states.

38. Penrose 1989(b), pp. 249-64; Penrose 2005, pp. 746-57.

39. Banks 2007, p. 4. I thank James Sinclair for drawing my attention to Banks's paper.

40. Standard quantification of the inflaton field is given by the number of its "e-foldings," N, which provide a way of measuring the inflationary expansion. If standard slow-roll inflation is operative, $N = \ln(a_f / a_i)$, where "i" and "f" denote the initial and final values of the scale factor of the universe (the global multiplier to universe size). For other cases, such as oscillating inflation, this definition must be modified. See section III of Liddle and Mazumdar 1998 for a brief discussion.

41. The adiabatic theorem states that a quantum mechanical system, subjected to *gradually* changing external conditions, can adapt its functional form; in the case of *rapidly* varying conditions, though, there is no time for the functional form of the state to adapt, so its probability density remains unchanged. See Messiah 1999, pp. 739-50.

What this means is that the standard assumption in inflation of a very special state for a huge number of degrees of freedom is completely *unjustified*, because we do not have a reliable dynamical description of these variables. As Banks concludes, therefore, inflationary cosmology does *not* in this sense solve the problem of the homogeneity and isotropy of the early universe.[42]

Fifth, inflation is regarded as explaining why the monopoles predicted by various favorably regarded grand unified theories have yet to be observed by effectively diluting their density in the observable universe. Invoking inflation in this context, however, is using it as an *ad hoc* measure to spare other favored yet unconfirmed theories from disconfirming evidence. That inflation can be used in this way is not evidence of its *own* merit. If the GUTs do not stand the test of time and additional empirical evidence, then there will be no need to explain why magnetic monopoles have not been detected by appealing to inflation — or any other rescue strategy for that matter.[43]

Finally, while inflationary cosmology has made some predictions about the distribution of the CMB at various wavelengths that are independent of its original motivations in terms of a "solution" to the horizon and flatness problems, and while some of these predictions seem to hold, there are also some anomalies that haven't been resolved. Inflation predicts an isotropic distribution of the CMB at all frequencies on a large scale, yet analysis of WMAP data has yielded a preferred direction for *large-scale modes* of the CMB that disagrees with such a prediction.[44] This issue is still being resolved and looks as if it may have been mitigated,[45] but if anisotropy holds up, not only will inflation's theoretical basis remain insufficient, it may well fail experimental tests in its primary area of empirical testability.

III. All Inflationary and Non-Inflationary Cosmologies Appear to Require a Beginning and Transcendent Cause

Where does this leave us? If inflation is ultimately upheld as a theoretically viable and empirically verifiable explanation of our cosmos, then a begin-

---

42. See also Martin and Brandenberger 2001.

43. Rees 1997, p. 185; Earman and Mosterin 1999, pp. 1-49; Holder 2004, pp. 130-43.

44. Land and Magueijo 2005.

45. Land and Magueijo 2007. The worry is that the anisotropies are the result of insufficient subtraction of Milky Way polar-aligned contributions, since the preferred direction seems to be aligned with the Milky Way pole. Further research should shed definitive light on this issue, especially data from the Planck satellite launched in May 2009.

ning and a transcendent cause are required in all models subject to the BGV theorem. This result applies to all higher-dimensional cosmologies, including those of string theory like the cyclic ekpyrotic and landscape models, that involve space-times satisfying the condition that the average Hubble expansion in the past is greater than zero, i.e., $H_{av} > 0$.

Furthermore, inflationary models such as the one proposed by Gasperini and Veneziano to which the BGV result does not apply, do not end up avoiding the need for a beginning because a realistic interpretation of the model, implausible though it may be, *still* requires acknowledging that the string perturbative vacuum phase has *finite* duration. Since the other two phases of the model (inflationary and FLRW) are *also* of finite duration, the universe has a beginning in this case as well.

On the other hand, if inflation is *not* upheld as a viable explanation, then (apart from non-inflationary cyclic ekpyrosis) we revert from multiverse scenarios to a single universe again. In this context, the singularity theorems of classical general relativity regain their traction, qualified by relevant considerations from quantum gravity and/or quantum cosmology that are physically and metaphysically reasonable, and lead to the conclusion that our universe has a beginning and the concomitant necessity of a transcendent cause for space-time, energy, and matter.

It appears, therefore, that a beginning and a transcendent cause of the universe (or multiverse) are unavoidable.

IV. Inflation and Cosmological Fine-Tuning

Inflation has also been used by some as a strategy for explaining the cosmological fine-tuning of our universe. The irony of this is that the inflaton field, which was invented as a reservoir of virtually unlimited energy for the "explanation" of horizon and flatness fine-tuning in the bubble universes it spawns through the decay of its false vacuum, requires exquisite fine-tuning itself.

The mechanism for bubble formation is Einstein's equation in general relativity, which, even though there is no intrinsic connection between the theories, is assumed to constrain the process of inflation in such a way that bubbles will form from local decay of the inflaton field while the field itself continues to expand. In the creation of these bubbles, however, the inflaton field must be shut off and "converted" to normal mass energy. This shut-off point is *delicate,* operating in the first 10^{-37} to 10^{-35} seconds of the universe's existence, while causing space to expand by a factor of around 10^{60}. The conversion from the inflation to the preheating era necessary to bring about particle production in an initially cold and empty universe involves a variety of highly speculative models with inflaton-preheating coupling parameters that have to be finessed to produce the right results.[46] Furthermore, depending on the inflationary model under consideration, the initial energy of the inflaton field is anywhere from 10^{53} to 10^{123} times the maximum vacuum energy consistent with our universe having the properties it does. This means that the energy decay of the inflaton field also has to be fine-tuned to *at least* one part in 10^{53} and possibly as much as one part in 10^{123}.[47] In short, the decay of the shut-off energy needs to be fine-tuned at a *minimum* to one part in ten thousand trillion trillion trillion trillion. Compared to such levels of precision, the fine-tuning of the big bang inherent in the so-called horizon and flatness problems, like an unruly friend, seems rather manageable.

There is another massive fine-tuning problem that turns out to be affected by inflation: the incredibly precise value of universal entropy needed at the big bang to produce a universe consistent with current observation. As Roger Penrose points out,[48] inflation solves the horizon problem only by increasing the fine-tuning of the already far *more* precise character of the big bang.

How precise was the big bang? In the observable universe there are about 10^{80} baryons (protons and neutrons). The *observed* statistical entropy per baryon in the universe can be estimated by supposing that the universe consists of galaxies populated mainly by ordinary stars, where each galaxy has a million-solar-mass black hole at its center.[49] Under such conditions, the entropy per baryon (a dimensionless number that includes the entropy per baryon of 10^8 in the cosmic background radiation) is calculated to be 10^{21}, yielding an *observed* universal entropy on the order of 10^{101}. If, most likely contrary to fact, our universe were eventually to re-collapse, the en-

---

46. For a *small* sample of these discussions see: Kofman 1996; Boyanovsky, Cormier, de Vega, Holman, Singh, and Srednicki 1997; Bassett 1997; Boyanovsky, Cormier, de Vega, Holman, and Kumar 1998; Bassett and Viniegra 2000; Tsujikawa, Bassett, and Viniegra 2000; Felder, García-Bellido, Greene, Kofman, Linde, and Tkachev 2000; Felder, Kofman, and Linde 2001; Green and Malik 2002; Watanabe and Komatsu 2008; and Brandenberger, Frey, and Lorenz 2008.

47. Collins 2003, pp. 178-99; Cohn 1998; Sahni and Starobinsky 2000, pp. 373-444.

48. Penrose 1989(b), pp. 249-64; Penrose 2005, pp. 746-57.

49. Penrose 1981, pp. 245-72; Penrose 1989(a), pp. 423-47; Penrose 2005, pp. 726-32.

tropy per baryon near the resulting "big crunch" is calculable from the Bekenstein-Hawking formula for black-hole entropy by considering the whole universe to have formed a black hole. Performing this calculation leads to a value of 10^{43} for the entropy per baryon, and thus a total value of 10^{123} ($10^{43} \times 10^{80}$) for *universal* entropy. Since this number also indicates the possible entropy for a universe our size *emerging* from a big bang singularity, we can compare it with what we now observe to estimate how fine-tuned the big bang had to be to give us a universe compatible with the second law of thermodynamics and what we now observe. Since 10^{123} is the natural logarithm of the volume of the position-momentum (phase) space associated with *all* of the baryons in the universe, the volume itself is given by the exponential: $V = e^{10\exp(123)}$; similarly, the *observed* total entropy is $W = e^{10\exp(101)}$. For numbers this size, it makes little difference if we substitute base 10 for the natural logarithm, so Penrose does that. Following his lead, the required precision in the big bang is therefore given by:

$$W/V = 10^{10\exp(101)} / 10^{10\exp(123)} = 10\exp[10^{101} - 10^{123}] \approx 10\exp(-10^{123}).$$

In other words, to satisfy the observed entropy of *our* universe, the big bang had to be fine-tuned to *one* part in $10\exp(10^{123})$. This latter number is difficult to grasp; suffice it to say that the universe would run out of elementary particles long before this number ran out of zeros that could be attached to them![50]

So how is this result affected by inflation's "resolution" of the horizon problem? Again, the fundamental strategy is for inflation to push beyond the observable universe the particle horizons that would preclude explaining the uniformity of the CMB on the basis of thermalization. But, as Penrose has observed, if thermalization serves the role of driving background temperatures to equilibrium in the inflationary context, then it represents a definite *increase* in universal entropy that requires the big bang to be even more finely tuned to account for its current observed value. On the other hand, if thermalization plays *no* role in explaining the horizon problem, then inflationary cosmology is completely *irrelevant* to its solution.

---

50. Penrose 2005, pp. 762-65, offers another quite powerful entropy-based argument against the anthropic inflationary universe. I will not discuss it here, but I commend it to the reader's consideration.

V. Fine-Tuning and String Cosmology

Let's revisit the string multiverse, this time as a resource for addressing cosmological fine-tuning. Khoury, Steinhardt, and Turok[51] have shown that the phenomenological constraints on the scalar field potential in cyclic ekpyrotic models necessitate a degree of fine-tuning comparable to that of inflationary models — the number of degrees of freedom, the number of tunings, and the quantitative degree of tuning are similar.[52] While the claim to be just as good as inflationary models might be received with favor in some quarters, we have established grounds for a somewhat less complimentary view. Kallosh, Kofman, Linde, and others[53] take an even less sanguine view, arguing that the ekpyrotic model faces additional problems. For instance, they argue that the Horava-Witten version of string theory on which the ekpyrotic scenario is based requires the 3-brane of our universe to have positive tension, but the ekpyrotic model requires negative tension. To make the ekpyrotic scenario workable, therefore, they contend that the problem of the negative cosmological constant on the visible brane must be solved and the bulk brane potential fine-tuned with an accuracy of 10^{-50}. Furthermore, they argue that the mechanism for the generation of density perturbations is not brane-specific; rather, it is a particular limiting case of the mechanism of tachyonic preheating, which exponentially amplifies not only quantum fluctuations, but any initial inhomogeneities.[54] As a result, to solve the homogeneity problem the ekpyrotic scenario would require the branes to be parallel to each other with an accuracy of better than 10^{-60} on a scale 10^{30} times greater than the distance between the branes. With some gerrymandering assumptions, Steinhardt and Turok have managed to ameliorate some of these difficulties,[55] but significant technical problems and fine-tuning issues

51. Khoury, Steinhardt, and Turok 2004.

52. Khoury, Steinhardt, and Turok 2004; Khoury, Steinhardt, and Turok 2003; Gratton, Khoury, Steinhardt, and Turok 2004.

53. Kallosh, Kofman, and Linde 2001; Linde 2001, pp. 89-104; Felder, Frolov, Kofman, and Linde 2002; Lyth 2002, pp. 1-4; Räsänen 2002, pp. 183-206; Heyl and Loeb 2002.

54. Felder, García-Bellido, Greene, Kofman, Linde, and Tkachev 2000; Felder, Kofman, and Linde 2001.

55. Turok, Perry, and Steinhardt 2004; Khoury, Ovrut, Steinhardt, and Turok 2001(b); Donagi, Khoury, Ovrut, Steinhardt, and Turok 2001; Steinhardt and Turok 2002(c); Khoury, Ovrut, Steinhardt, and Turok 2002; Tolley, Turok, and Steinhardt 2004; Erickson, Gratton, Steinhardt, and Turok 2006.

remain — in particular, Veneziano and Bozza[56] have shown that a smooth bounce cannot generate a scale-invariant density perturbation spectrum via the mode-mixing mechanism advocated by Steinhardt, Turok, and others;[57] and Kim and Hwang[58] have argued that it is *not* possible to obtain the requisite near Harrison-Zel'dovich scale-invariant density spectrum through a bouncing world model as long as the seed fluctuations were generated from quantum fluctuations of the curvature perturbation in the collapsing phase — rather, the spectrum is significantly blue-shifted in comparison with what is needed.

It is worthwhile considering whether the cyclic ekpyrotic scenario has the probabilistic resources to address the one in $10\exp(10^{123})$ fine-tuning of the big bang entropy of our universe.[59] It does not. It is *not* an inflationary model — though it does involve dark energy — so it does not invoke an unending chaotic cascade of string vacua.[60] Rather, each trillion-year cycle produces 10^{100} to 10^{500} big bang events with opportunities for finely tuned entropy. This means that with each new cycle there is *at best* a *one* in

$$\{10^{500}/10\exp(10^{123})\} = 10\exp(500 - 10^{123}) \approx 10\exp(-10^{123})$$

chance that the requisite entropy condition will be met. In short, the ekpyrotic universe would have to go through a significant fraction of $10\exp(10^{123})$ trillion-year cycles for there to be any reasonable probability of getting a universe like ours! But we have already seen that cyclic models are geodesically incomplete and, as Steinhardt and Turok admit,[61] the most likely story is that the cycling stage was preceded by a singular beginning. Furthermore, even if this picture were true, there is, in principle, no measurement that could be made to determine how many cycles have taken place. It would be a highly unwarranted assumption, therefore, to presume that the model has the probabilistic resources necessary to resolve the prob-

---

56. Bozza and Veneziano 2005(a), pp. 177-83; Bozza and Veneziano 2005(b); Bozza 2005.

57. Gratton, Khoury, Steinhardt, and Turok 2004; Khoury, Ovrut, Steinhardt, and Turok 2002; Tolley, Turok, and Steinhardt 2004; Erickson, Gratton, Steinhardt, and Turok 2006.

58. Kim and Hwang 2007.

59. Not that Steinhardt and Turok would recommend this course of action, since they deplore anthropic arguments. See Steinhardt and Turok 2007, pp. 231-36.

60. Steinhardt and Turok 2002(c).

61. Steinhardt and Turok 2005, pp. 43-47.

lem of universal entropy; in fact, the incomprehensibly large number of trillion-year cycles required inspires deep skepticism, especially when the logico-metaphysical necessity of a transcendent cause for the singular beginning of any ekpyrotic universe brings with it the far more plausible scenario of intelligently directed fine-tuning.

While the ekpyrotic model confronts some extraordinary fine-tuning issues of its own, we may nonetheless reasonably ask whether it resolves any. Steinhardt and Turok[62] have recently claimed that it does — most specifically, that it offers a credible explanation for why the cosmological constant (vacuum energy) is small and positive. What they essentially do is engineer a "relaxation mechanism" that can be incorporated into the cyclic model that slowly decreases the value of the cosmological constant over time while taking account of contributions to the vacuum density over all energy scales. The mechanism works by allowing the relaxation time to grow exponentially as vacuum density decreases, generating asymptotic behavior in which every volume of space spends the majority of time at a stage when the cosmological constant is small and positive — just as it is observed to be today. Again, the solution is *ad hoc*: a mechanism was *invented* to produce the desired behavior and then declared to be a virtue of the model simply because a way was found to make it work. Furthermore, there is no reason intrinsic to the ekpyrotic scenario, which as we have seen is subject to the BGV theorem, explaining why it must start off with a vacuum energy greater than what we observe today, yet the relaxation mechanism assumes that it does, so it can "explain" the value it now has.[63]

As a last consideration, Alexander Vilenkin[64] argues that the cyclic relaxation mechanism provides no explanation for the fact that the vacuum density, which is fine-tuned to 120 decimal places, is roughly twice the average energy density of matter in the universe. These two densities behave very differently with cosmic expansion — the former stays constant while the latter decreases — so why do we live in an epoch when the values are close? This is known as the "cosmic coincidence" problem. The ekpyrotic model provides no answer to it, but Vilenkin contends that standard inflationary cosmology conjoined with the string landscape does: the universe on the largest scale is *postulated* to be in a state of high-energy expansion that is spawning low-energy bubble universes like our own, having, in virtue

62. Steinhardt and Turok 2006, pp. 1180-82.
63. For a slight qualification of this assertion, see footnote 76.
64. Vilenkin 2006(a).

of the string landscape, all possible values for a wide variety of "universal" constants. Since galaxies and observers exist in those rare bubbles only where the vacuum energy is small and a variety of other parameters are appropriately adjusted (the anthropic principle), and since analysis reveals that during the epoch of galaxy formation — which includes our present time — most galaxies will form in regions where vacuum and matter densities are about the same, he contends this cosmic coincidence is thereby "explained."

Before we evaluate the explanatory power of the inflationary string landscape, it is worthwhile revisiting the previously mentioned fine-tuning of the Gasperini-Veneziano PBBI model. Turner and Weinberg[65] have shown that pre-big-bang dilaton-driven inflation of an SPV patch has to last long enough to reach a hot big bang nucleation event, but since the PBBI period is tightly constrained by the initial value of spatial curvature, this curvature has to be *extremely small* in string units if sufficient inflation is to be achieved to "solve" the flatness and horizon problems. It is not completely obvious on this account, however, just how strong this fine-tuning has to be, and others have argued that it may be possible to mitigate this conclusion if the universe is open[66] or if the pre-big-bang conditions are restricted in just the right way.[67]

More tellingly, Kaloper, Linde, and Bousso[68] have shown that PBB dilaton-driven inflation can address the horizon and flatness problems only if the primordial SPV is extremely large and homogeneous from the outset — in short, the fine-tuning of our universe is "explained" by pushing all the fine-tuning into the SPV era. Let me elaborate. The authors show that if our universe appeared as the result of PBBI then it had to originate from a homogeneous domain of exponentially large initial size, with enormously large initial mass and entropy at the onset of inflation. Furthermore, if this PBB universe is *closed,* then at the time the SPV becomes describable by the low-energy effective action, it can be shown that it must consist of *at least* 10^{24} causally disconnected regions of nearly equal density. Needless to say, this is extremely improbable and is a re-expression of the horizon problem with a vengeance — one of the very problems the PBBI scenario was intended to solve!

65. Turner and Weinberg 1997.

66. Veneziano 1998; Buonanno, Meissner, Ungarelli, and Veneziano 1998, pp. 2543-56.

67. Maggiore and Sturani 1997, pp. 335-43.

68. Kaloper, Linde, and Bousso 1999.

On the other hand, if the universe in the SPV era is *open,* then in order to account for the homogeneity of our part of the universe, it must start as a Milne universe (roughly, an *infinitely* large patch of Minkowski space) in the distant past with an *infinitesimally* small and *spatially homogeneous* dilaton kinetic energy density of *infinite* extent. In order for the PBB era to be of infinite duration, it would be necessary for the SPV universe to shrink uniformly for an infinitely long time until the dilaton density grows sufficiently large to cause the scale factor to bounce and undergo super-inflation. Of course, the SPV state is *highly unstable* and can be *completely* destroyed by quantum fluctuations of the dilaton field, which is why, as we saw earlier, the PBBI universe cannot be of infinite duration and must have a beginning. Nonetheless, even if the exquisitely fine-tuned homogeneity required of an open PBB universe were explainable, Kaloper, Linde, and Bousso demonstrate that the possibility of resolving the flatness problem depends on being able to explain the unlikely existence and value of two very large dimensionless parameters on which this flatness depends: $g_0^{-2} > 10^{53}$ and B $> 10^{38} g_0^{-2} > 10^{91}$.

Finally, Kaloper, Linde, and Bousso demonstrate that the dynamics of PBB cosmology preclude the possibility of self-reproduction and hence do not lead to a period of eternal inflation because quantum fluctuations during the inflationary stage are never large enough to overtake the rolling of the dilaton-field. As a consequence of this, the PBBI scenario has no means of alleviating the fine-tuning of its own initial conditions, let alone resources for addressing the one in $10\exp(10^{123})$ fine-tuning of the big bang entropy of our universe.[69]

To draw our discussion to a close, let's evaluate the explanatory power

69. Veneziano 1999 suggests that gravitational contraction is a scale-free phenomenon in that regional patches of perturbed SPV of all different sizes will contract to create big bang events. He then argues that an anthropic explanation of entropic fine-tuning is possible on the basis of a multiverse created by regional contractions. There are two responses to be made here. The first is that the fine-tuning considerations that make the contraction of any SPV patch unlikely make the contraction of multiple patches to create a multiverse hyperexponentially unlikely. It seems to me that the hyper-exponential unlikelihood of multiple contractions far outruns any probabilistic resources that multiple contractions might generate to address entropic fine-tuning, especially when the metastability of the SPV guarantees an origin in the finite past. The second is that Gasperini and Veneziano often talk (and rightly so) as if they regard an infinite past to the SPV phase in the PBBI model as an idealization that has no real existence. If it has no real existence, however, as we have just argued, it cannot provide the resources to explain away entropic or other kinds of cosmological fine-tuning.

of the string landscape[70] to account for cosmological fine-tuning. The "landscape" of string theory is the brainchild of Leonard Susskind, Joseph Polchinski, Raphael Bousso, and Andrei Linde.[71] It aims to turn the vice of the countless moduli associated with the Calabi-Yau compactification of the higher dimensions in string/M-theory into the virtue of a probabilistic resource for anthropic explanations of cosmological fine-tuning. As we observed earlier, the laws and constants of string-theoretic universes are determined respectively by the shape and size of the compactified dimensions. If there were a mechanism for navigating around the "landscape" of these moduli, each combination describing a different string "vacuum," there would be a way to generate universes with different laws and constants — at least 10^{500} of them, in fact, if we restrict ourselves to versions of string theory having a positive-valued cosmological constant like our own universe.

Bousso, Kachru, Kallosh, Linde, Maldecena, McAllister, Polchinski, Susskind, and Trivedi[72] all contributed to devising a mechanism that might do this by finding a way to combine inflationary cosmology with the string landscape: bubbles of lower-energy string vacua nucleate when moduli decay at random locations throughout higher-energy string vacua that continue to inflate forever, so the whole landscape (they contend) gets explored as a series of nested bubble universes. Interior bubbles inflate at a slower rate than their parent universes, and bubbles of still lower energy nucleate inside of them, while all of the vacua so-created inflate eternally. According to this picture, we live in one such bubble universe. Since only the tiniest fraction of such bubbles exemplify laws and constants hospitable to life, and observer selection (the weak anthropic principle) places us in such a bubble, the *anthropic principle* becomes the fundamental "explanation" for cosmological fine-tuning, that is, for why our universe has the laws and constants that it does.

---

70. Bousso and Polchinski 2000; Kachru, Kallosh, Linde, and Trivedi 2003; Kachru, Kallosh, Linde, Maldecena, McAllister, and Trivedi 2003; Susskind 2003; Susskind 2004; Freivogel and Susskind 2004; Bousso and Polchinski 2004, pp. 60-69; Ashok and Douglas 2004; Douglas 2004(a); Kobakhidze and Mersini-Houghton 2004, pp. 869-73; Ooguri and Vafa 2006; Riddle and Urena-Lopez 2006; Barvinsky and Kamenshchik 2006; Susskind 2006; Vanchurin and Vilenkin 2006; Denef and Douglas 2006; Kumar 2006, pp. 3441-72; Polchinski 2006; Cleaver 2006.

71. Bousso and Polchinski 2000; Kachru, Kallosh, Linde, and Trivedi 2003; Kachru, Kallosh, Linde, Maldecena, McAllister, and Trivedi 2003; Susskind 2003; Susskind 2004; Freivogel and Susskind 2004; Bousso and Polchinski 2004, pp. 60-69.

72. Bousso and Polchinski 2000; Kachru, Kallosh, Linde, and Trivedi 2003; Kachru, Kallosh, Linde, Maldecena, McAllister, and Trivedi 2003; Susskind 2003; Susskind 2004; Freivogel and Susskind 2004; Bousso and Polchinski 2004, pp. 60-69.

Setting the debatable legitimacy of anthropic explanations aside, what should we make of the string landscape as an entity, and of the proposed mechanism for exploring it? Just as with inflationary cosmology, there are some very serious reasons to doubt the tenability of string theory;[73] conjoining the two in one picture would seem to provide twice the ground for skepticism. There is no question that string theory has produced some beautiful and interesting mathematics, but there are some very good reasons to question whether it has told us anything about the universe. First of all, string theory does not make any *unique* predictions that are testable by current experiments (the hypothesis of extra dimensions to reality is separable from its string-theoretic embodiment). Second, if models with *non*-positive values for the cosmological constant are also included, string theory comes in a virtually *unlimited* number of versions. With an appreciative nod toward the cleverness of string phenomenologists who have found a set of models consistent with the minimal supersymmetric standard model (MSSM),[74] we still have no idea whether any of these match our reality, and there remains an impossibly large number of them.[75] Third, it is also the case that nobody knows whether 11-dimensional M-theory, which provides the necessary connection among the five anomaly-free classes of 10-dimensional string theory, is itself mathematically *consistent*, that is, whether it avoids assigning infinite values to physical quantities. Finally, since we don't really have a clue what the underlying M-theory *is*, we don't even know whether a complete and coherent framework exists that would justify calling the web of conjectures and approximations about strings a unified "theory." This assessment is not the isolated view of a few cranks; it is the considered judgment of a healthy portion of the physics community, and it deserves serious consideration.

Setting our doubts to one side again, we should still ask whether the proposed inflationary mechanism for actualizing the exploration of the mathematical abstraction known as the landscape is sufficient to the task. As we know, the landscape is subject to the BGV theorem and has an absolute beginning in the finite past. It therefore has a transcendent cause. But in which string false vacuum state did it begin? Scattered throughout the landscape are 10^{500} or more relative minima constitutive of metastable false vacuums in which the string moduli can get stuck for a very long time. There is no reason intrinsic to the landscape that *necessitates* that it begin with a false

73. Krauss 2005; Smolin 2006; Woit 2006.
74. Cleaver, Faraggi, and Nanopoulos 1999, pp. 135-46; Cleaver 2008.
75. Kumar 2006.

vacuum energy greater than what we observe today — indeed, there is no necessity to the supposition that the universe started off in an inflationary state at all, save the convenience of such an assumption.[76] Furthermore, the quantum tunneling mechanism by which modulus decay leads to the nucleation of bubble universes of different vacuum energy is exponentially suppressed for transitions to higher energies (and can only occur in the presence of gravity); it is vastly more likely in the landscape scenario that higher inflationary energy states cascade to lower ones.[77] The assumption of such a cascade is theoretically expedient for the purpose of anthropic explanations, but not guaranteed; there is, in principle, no way of knowing whether it is true. Furthermore, with the exponential suppression of transitions to higher energy states, the only way to ensure that the entirety of the landscape gets explored is either to assume it starts in its highest possible energy state, or if in a low energy state, to assume that the first string vacuum that came into existence is exponentially older than today's Hubble time. If it started off in a state of low enough energy, however, the hypothesized landscape would have no relevance to the explanation of our finely tuned cosmological constant. So even if some version of string/M-theory were true and reification of the landscape were legitimate — an overly generous concession by any measure — there is no way, even in principle, to determine what proportion of space lands in vacua of each type and hence no reason to think that the whole landscape could or would be explored by such means.

It is worth observing too that a cosmological model that randomly varied the laws and constants of nature in the universes it generated *would itself have to be subject to lawful constraints were it not to break down*. This lawful constraint, presumably, is provided by string/M-theory functioning as a "meta-theory" that governs which laws and constants, and hence which vacua, are possible. In other words, the principles governing the string/M-theoretic process of variation (whatever they may be) would have to remain

76. Some would suggest that it is "natural" to start off with an order 1 cosmological constant since the most straightforward calculation of the vacuum energy in quantum field theory comes to roughly one Planck mass per cubic Planck length, which exceeds the actual value by 120 orders of magnitude — the worst prediction in the entire history of physics! Others argue that, given the probability distribution of cosmological constants of *possible* universes over the *whole* landscape, an order 1 cosmological constant is not an unreasonable assumption. My basic point, however, is that the landscape hypothesis *needs* this condition to generate anthropic explanations and it is *not* guaranteed by the model.

77. See Linde 2007; also Coleman and De Luccia 1980 and Guth and Weinberg 1983. I thank James Sinclair for discussions of this subject.

stable for the description to be coherent. Of course, were an explicit meta-theoretic construction to prove consistently realizable, the carefully structured variation process it exemplified would be subject to non-negotiable meta-laws and meta-parameters indicative of design at this higher level — unless, of course, we entertain the absurd notion of an infinite regress of meta-theoretical constructions.[78]

We may also note, with some irony, that 10^{500} universes with different laws and constants *may not be enough* for anthropic explanation of the fine-tuning of the universe in which we live. The cosmological constant (vacuum energy) of our universe is fine-tuned to 120 decimal places; the gravitational constant — considered in relation to the range of coupling strengths shown possible in nature — is fine-tuned to 40 decimal places; the weak force is fine-tuned to 9 decimal places; the proton/neutron mass difference is fine-tuned to 5 decimal places; and, as the main text discusses, there are at least seventeen other independent constants and factors that are fine-tuned to a high degree of precision, some of them requiring a cooperative assignment of values to achieve effects necessary for the existence of life that would be unattainable separately. The cumulative effect of all of these fine-tunings significantly erodes the probabilistic resources inherent in the landscape. A precise calculation of cumulative fine-tuning on the basis of current theory has not yet been made, though significant work continues to be done.[79]

This leaves us with a consideration of the fine-tuning of universal entropy. Unfortunately, the one-in-$10\exp(10^{123})$ probability — rendered even smaller by the inflationary mechanism — that would swamp the resources of 10^{500} or more string vacua is not a fine-tuning of the laws and constants characteristic of the vacua themselves, but rather a fine-tuning of the *initial conditions* of each bubble nucleation.[80] In the inflationary picture, *assuming* a cascade down the string landscape from an initial vacuum with an energy higher than our own and inflationary bubbles that decay at random locations while continuing an eternal expansion, the landscape advocate will

---

78. This point has also been made quite powerfully by both Robin Collins and John Polkinghorne.

79. See, for example: Collins 2003, pp. 178-99; Carter 1967; Carr and Rees 1979, pp. 605-12; Davies 1982; Barrow and Tipler 1986; Leslie 1989; Hogan 2000, pp. 1149-61; Oberhummer, Csótó, and Schlattl 2000, pp. 88-90; Rees 2000; Gonzalez and Richards 2004; Carr 2007; Collins 2007; Collins (forthcoming) *The Well-Tempered Universe*.

80. That this is the case was a nagging concern lurking in the background of my early evaluations of the string landscape; I thank James Sinclair for bringing it to the foreground and turning it into a genuine headache: we all need friends to keep us honest!

contend that there are an unbounded number of instantiations of every possible string vacuum.[81] Given an unbounded number of instantiations of the vacuum characteristic of our universe, so the argument goes, we would expect the one in $10\exp(10^{123})$ initial entropic condition it exemplifies to be instantiated an unbounded number of times. So it is that we encounter the standard but startling claim from practitioners of inflationary cosmology that there are "infinitely many" universes just like our own. A typical example is Alexander Vilenkin,[82] who contends that "(i)n the worldview that has emerged from eternal inflation, our Earth and our civilization are anything but unique. Instead, countless *identical* civilizations are scattered in the infinite expanse of the cosmos." Indeed, clones of each of us are endlessly reproduced throughout the inflationary universe, for "the existence of clones is . . . an inevitable consequence of the theory."

The less enthusiastic among us might be inclined to remark that if it is a consequence of the theory that endless copies of ourselves exist, holding every conceivable opinion and involved in every conceivable activity, then *so much the worse* for inflationary (string) cosmology: it has successfully reduced itself to an absurdity. Nonetheless, it is worthwhile to ask what the consequences of embracing this theory would be for science itself. A fundamental implication of the theory is that every possible event, no matter *how* improbable (say, one in $10\exp[10^{123}]$, just to pick a number), will happen countlessly many times. Indeed, this conclusion has led to a flurry of articles by cosmologists discussing the string landscape in relation to "Boltzmann brains" and the question of our universe's "typicality"[83] — a discussion so fantastical that it drew the incredulous attention of *The New York Times*.[84]

If, as inflation standardly assumes, the de Sitter (dS) space in which

81. As we discussed earlier, this assumption is not *mandated* by the landscape hypothesis and, even though the exponentially suppressed transitions to higher energy states render an uphill climb possible in a timespan exponentially longer than today's Hubble time, a sufficiently low-energy genesis to the landscape would completely vitiate the landscape's utility for anthropic explanations. Even on the unlikely assumption that the landscape exists, therefore, we have no way of knowing what happened and there is no principled way to tell what proportion of space lands in vacua of which type, and hence no reason to think that the whole landscape could or would be explored.

82. Vilenkin 2006(a).

83. Dyson, Kleban, and Susskind 2002; Albrecht and Sorbo 2004, pp. 1345-70; Page 2006; Ceresole, Dall'Agata, Giryavets, Kallosh, and Linde 2006; Linde 2006; Bousso and Freivogel 2006; Carlip 2007; Hartle and Srednicki 2007; Giddings and Marolf 2007; Page 2007(a); Page 2007(b), pp. 411-30.

84. Overbye 2008.

our universe began is a thermal system,[85] then a free-floating "Boltzmann brain" (BB) can spontaneously appear in dS space due to thermal fluctuations.[86] Under standard conditions for bubble universe generation in the landscape,[87] the problem formulated by Dyson, Kleban, and Susskind[88] giving rise to the BB phenomenon becomes quite serious.[89] In fact, some calculations lead to free-floating BBs infinitely outnumbering normal brains,[90] in which case it becomes infinitely more likely that we ourselves are free-floating BBs rather than persons with a history living in an orderly universe several billion years old! In short, the BB issue suggests that the multiverse is falsified because the persons we take ourselves to be are not typical observers within it.

Needless to say, multiverse cosmologists find this conclusion rather disturbing[91] and are trying to preclude it, but they cannot agree on how or whether progress is being made on the problem.[92] One dominant approach is to find some measure by which our actual existence is "typical" in the multiverse and the superabundance of BBs is not,[93] often by finagling the decay time of the inflaton fields so that bubble universes don't get large enough to make BBs more likely than ordinary observers. While there is a sense in which *anything* with a non-zero probability of happening *will* happen — and an *unbounded* number of times at that — in an eternally inflating multiverse, a viable typicality condition would nonetheless have to *privilege* events that we take to be preconditions of *our* existence. It is perhaps unsurprising then that we recently find the inflationary multiverse being invoked by a prominent molecular biologist as an "explanation" for the highly improbable origin of life.[94] It is not hard to see that such a strategy, were it to become a standard means of explaining improbable occurrences, would spell the end of science as a rational enterprise. By providing an all-too-easy

85. Dyson, Kleban, and Susskind 2002.

86. Linde 2006; Bousso and Freivogel 2006; Page 2006.

87. Kachru, Kallosh, Linde, and Trivedi 2003.

88. Dyson, Kleban, and Susskind 2002; Albrecht and Sorbo 2004, pp. 1345-70; Page 2006.

89. Bousso and Freivogel 2006.

90. Dyson, Kleban, and Susskind 2002.

91. Dyson, Kleban, and Susskind 2002.

92. Bousso and Freivogel 2006; Page 2006; Carlip 2007; Hartle and Srednicki 2007; Giddings and Marolf 2007; Page 2007(a); Page 2007(b).

93. Page 2006; Page 2007(a); Page 2007(b).

94. Koonin 2007.

explanation for *anything* that has happened or may happen, the multiverse ends up explaining *nothing* at all.[95]

Finally, there are reasons internal to string theory itself that cast doubt on the tenability of the landscape.[96] Michael Dine[97] argues that if a string landscape of metastable ground states exists, it is likely to lead to a prediction of low-energy supersymmetry. But in the discretuum of the landscape, he argues, the parameters of low-energy physics seem to be *random* numbers, and if this is true, the landscape is *not* a correct description of physics as we know it and so must be rejected. Alternatively, there might be *some* set of principles in the landscape that explain those laws of nature that do *not* seem to be anthropically constrained, but it is far from obvious what such principles might be, so even *if* the landscape were coherent, we would have no key that would enable us to interpret it properly.

Susskind[98] and Douglas[99] think this criticism is very serious and do their best to counter it. Susskind argues, somewhat weakly, that the string landscape is unexplored territory and it is possible that the gauge hierarchy does *not* favor low-energy supersymmetry. Douglas's argument is stronger. Building on earlier work,[100] he argues that the vast majority of string vacua do not produce exponentially small symmetry-breaking scales and that, given many supersymmetry-breaking parameters, adding together the positive breaking terms will produce a distribution weighted toward high scales. It is true that models of supersymmetry breaking driven by a single parameter favor low-scale breaking, but models involving more than one independently distributed parameter lead to an expectation of high-scale breaking. Nonetheless, the idea of "favoring" one type of vacuum over another is not a strong result. Since we do not yet have the mathematical wherewithal to provide a definitive answer to how the SUSY-breaking scale is distributed in a complete ensemble of phenomenologically viable vacua,[101] the observations of Banks, Dine, and Gorbatov[102] remain solid, casting doubt on the tenability of the landscape.

Whatever else may be said, it is clear that the string landscape hypoth-

95. A more rigorous treatment of this issue is forthcoming in Collins 2009.
96. Banks, Dine, and Gorbatov 2003; Dine 2004; Robbins and Sethi 2005.
97. Dine 2004.
98. Susskind 2004.
99. Douglas 2004(b).
100. Denef and Douglas 2004.
101. Kumar 2006.
102. Banks, Dine, and Gorbatov 2003; Dine 2004.

esis is a highly speculative construction built on shaky assumptions and, even if taken seriously, requires meta-level fine-tuning itself, may be unequal to the task it is intended to perform, may ultimately prove phenomenologically untenable, and seems to contain the seeds for destroying science as a rational enterprise. Its prospects, therefore, are not promising.

Given this sobering assessment, one wonders why the string landscape has provoked so much enthusiasm among cosmologists. Leonard Susskind[103] provides a revealing answer:

> If, for some unforeseen reason, the landscape turns out to be inconsistent — maybe for mathematical reasons, or because it disagrees with observation . . . [then] as things stand now we will be in a very awkward position. Without any explanation of nature's fine-tunings we will be hard pressed to answer the ID critics.

Just so.

VI. Conclusion

A closing reflection on the nature of mathematical physics is appropriate. Stephen Hawking[104] has asked, somewhat poetically, "What is it that breathes fire into the equations and makes a universe for them to describe?" This question deserves a genuine answer. As a matter of logic, mathematical descriptions may have ontological implications, but they do *not* function as efficient causes, either metaphysically or materially: *they are causally inert.* When inflationary cosmology describes string vacua as tunneling into existence from absolute nothingness or from another vacuum state, or even when relativistic quantum field theory describes matter as popping out of the quantum vacuum, neither mathematical construction provides an *explanation,* let alone an *efficient cause,* for these events. The belief that a mathematical description shows that the universe does not have and does not need a cause is both a *non sequitur* — it does not follow from the descriptions themselves — and an ontological category mistake. When landscape theorists like Leonard Susskind assert the existence of a landscape of possibilities

---

103. Susskind, as quoted in *New Scientist* magazine, December 17, 2005.
104. Hawking 1988, pp. 174.

giving rise to a megaverse of actualities and suggest that this provides a mindless solution to the problem of fine-tuning,[105] they completely ignore the fact that a virtually unlimited arena of mathematical possibilities *cannot generate even one actual universe*. The mindless multiverse "solution" to the problem of fine-tuning is, quite literally, a metaphysical non-starter. What the absence of efficient material causality in fundamental physics and cosmology reveals instead is the limit of scientific explanations and the need for a deeper understanding.

When the logical and metaphysical *necessity* of an efficient cause, the demonstrable *absence* of a material one, and the proof that there was an *absolute beginning* to any universe or multiverse are all conjoined with the fact that our universe exists and its conditions are fine-tuned immeasurably beyond the capacity of any mindless process, the scientific evidence points inexorably toward *transcendent intelligent agency* as the most plausible, if not the *only* reasonable explanation.

105. Susskind 2006.

Three Philosophical Proofs
for the Existence of God

INTRODUCTION TO PART TWO

Methodological Presuppositions of Philosophical Proof:
Reasonable and Responsible Belief

At the end of Chapters 1 and 2, I noted that it would be necessary to make recourse to metaphysical method in order to unpack two conclusions of contemporary Big Bang cosmology, namely, (1) the high likelihood of an initial singularity implying a creative power transcending universal space-time asymmetry, and (2) the reasonable and responsible belief that this transcendent creative power possesses a "super-Intellect" capable of cosmological design on a grand scale.

As will be explained in Chapter 6 (Section I.A-I.C), there are three fundamental components of philosophical method that go beyond formal scientific method (experimentally and quantitatively grounded hypothetico-deductive method):

1) the use of complete disjunctions whose parts refer to real (or potentially real) conditions or attributes (e.g., finite or infinite; not neither, not both),
2) the use of infinities, and
3) the definition of causation itself (beyond specific kinds of causation).

After teaching metaphysics for twenty years, I have come to learn that it is easier to explain these three dimensions of philosophical method after presenting one or two philosophical proofs, because the proofs give all the examples that might be needed to comprehend the method. Hence, I have delayed the formal explanation of philosophical method to Chapter 6.

However, I cannot delay the consideration of the three fundamental grounds of evidence that are used in *both* the physical sciences and philosophy, because their use in the philosophical proofs begs for an explanation. These three grounds of evidence serve as the foundation for reasonable and responsible belief, and will be discussed immediately below.

Every philosophy professor has had the experience of students who have taken skepticism to the ultimate extreme: "Prove everything," or "Prove the principle of non-contradiction," or "Prove that there really are other people in this room," or "How can I truly know that I am not dreaming right now?" etc., etc., etc. Obviously, when a professor opens students' minds to critical questioning and to critical method, she does not want to shut the door when students take that questioning to its logical conclusion. Thus, she may attempt to show that the very denial of the principle of non-contradiction requires its use, or that public corroboration of sensorial evidence reveals the improbability that two or more people could have exactly the same phantasm within their own completely autonomous "thought worlds." But these arguments are met with further arguments that maybe our minds are controlled by some super agency and that the self-refutational character of denying the principle of non-contradiction is still not a proof. Where does one stop? Perhaps at what might be considered reasonable and responsible belief.

Twenty-four hundred years ago, Aristotle showed that all human knowledge is based on certain first principles which are necessary for the functioning of any proof, and therefore cannot be proved without themselves being used. He implied that it was reasonable to believe in the validity of these first principles since they had shown themselves to be reliable in countless individual circumstances, and responsible to believe in them because their denial would require a virtual cessation of thought.[1]

---

1. *Metaphysics*, Book IV,3 (1005b5-1011b23), and Book VI,3 (1061b34-1063b35). Aristotle sums up his reasoning here as follows: "It would seem also that in saying the man is not a horse we should be either more or not less right than in saying he is not a man, so that we shall be right in saying that the same person *is* a horse; for it was assumed to be possible to make opposite statements equally truly. It follows then that the same person is a man and a horse, or any other animal. While, then, there is no proof of the axiom [the principle of non-contradiction] without qualification, there is a proof relatively to anyone who will make these suppositions. And perhaps if we had questioned Heraclitus himself in this way we

A belief may be considered reasonable and responsible if:

1) it can be affirmed by rigorous public corroboration, *or*
2) its denial leads to an intrinsic contradiction, *or*
3) its denial leads to a contradiction of publicly corroborated fact.

One of these forms of evidence is sufficient to ground the truth of a proposition. More than one would provide additional corroboration, but is not necessary. Standards for the reasonable and responsible definition of terms will be given below.

With respect to (1), rigorous corroboration means an agreed-upon criterion for corroboration that is sufficient to make a preponderance of reasonable and responsible people believe that a denial of the claim is far more unreasonable and irresponsible than an affirmation of it. In the domain of sense description (e.g., Bob Spitzer is coming into his office) this corroboration could occur through agreement on sensorial apparitions from multiple persons having multiple perspectives. In science, rigorous corroboration could occur through different kinds of experimentation, repetitions of experiments, different kinds of measuring devices, etc. In social sciences, this might come from multiple approaches to a single problem or statistical analysis (using correlation coefficients, T tables, etc.).

With respect to (2), I will consider it reasonable and responsible to claim that intrinsic contradictions (e.g., "a square-circle of the same area in the same respect at the same place and time," "an object that acts like both a proton and an electron in the same respect at the same place and time," or "an infinite-finite in the same respect at the same place and time") are impossible states of affairs. Therefore, all such intrinsic contradictions could not be reasonably and responsibly held to be true for real states of affairs.

Furthermore, any hypothetical state of affairs that inevitably and logically *leads to* an intrinsic contradiction will also be held to be an impossible state of affairs. For example, if the claim "past time is infinite" (which, on its surface, may not appear to be contradictory) can be *shown to be* an intrinsic and ontological contradiction, then the statement "past time is infinite" must also be considered an impossible state of affairs.

Furthermore, I will consider it reasonable and responsible to assert that

---

might have forced him to confess that opposite statements can never be true of the same subjects" (Aristotle 1984(a), p. 1678, Book VI,3, 1062a25-31). See also *Posterior Analytics*, Book I,2 (72a12).

the opposite of an intrinsically contradictory proposition is true. With respect to the above example, if the proposition "past time is infinite" results in an intrinsic and ontological contradiction, then the opposite of that proposition *must* be true, that is, "past time is finite." The expression "it is not the case that past time is infinite" is equivalent to "past time is finite," or "not (past time is not finite)" equals "past time is finite." The "nots" cancel each other out.

I will also consider it reasonable and responsible to hold that impossible states of affairs are *universally* false. For example, square-circles of the same area in the same respect at the same place and time will not be able to exist in another universe any more than this one. They will not be able to inhere in steel any more than wood. They will not exist tomorrow any more than they can exist today, and they could not have existed a thousand years ago any more than they can exist today.

With respect to (3), I will consider any hypothetical state of affairs that contradicts a rigorously corroborated fact (such as well-corroborated experimental evidence) to be false. (By the way, this is the ground of scientific method.)

I will consider terms to be reasonably and responsibly defined when those definitions adequately allow for public corroboration, demonstrate non-contradiction, or demonstrate that a hypothetical state of affairs contradicts a rigorously corroborated fact. Terms need not be *perfectly* defined with respect to all possible states of affairs or all possible hypothetical conditions in order to achieve the above objective. They do not even have to be comprehensive. Terms need only have sufficient meaning to successfully complete corroboration or demonstration.

For example, I do not need to know everything about the strong nuclear force constant in order to demonstrate that a 2 percent change in that constant would either prohibit the generation of hydrogen atoms or prohibit the generation of atoms heavier than hydrogen. I only need to know the ways in which the strong nuclear force interacts with the electromagnetic force in order to demonstrate the bonding peculiarities that would prohibit either hydrogen or elements heavier than hydrogen from being generated (see pp. 60-61).

If you, the reader, accept these three grounds of reasonable and responsible belief, as well as the requirements for adequate definition, you will likely also accept the three elements of metaphysical method mentioned above, for these flow directly from the three grounds of reasonable and responsible belief. As noted above, I will delay the explanation of this connection until Chapter 6.

Conversely, if you do not accept the three grounds of reasonable and responsible belief, you will not only have trouble with metaphysics and proofs for God's existence, but also with every form of logical demonstration, scientific method, and application of mathematical principles to reality, for all four of these intellectual enterprises depend equally on the three grounds for reasonable and responsible belief. Metaphysics and proofs for God's existence do not require any more belief or force of will than an application of mathematics or logic to the world.

Introduction to the Forthcoming Philosophical Proofs

Three philosophical proofs for God's existence will be presented in the next three chapters. Each one will help to unpack the metaphysical implications of Big Bang cosmology.

Chapter 3 presents a metaphysical argument for God's existence, and will show that the creative power implied in Chapter 1 is transtemporal (as Davies suggests), and that it is an unconditioned reality which is absolutely simple and unrestricted in its power. It must be absolutely unique and the continuous creator of all else that is.

Chapter 4 presents a Lonerganian argument for God's existence (inspired by the twentieth-century philosopher Bernard J. F. Lonergan). It will show not only the necessity for an unconditioned reality, but also that such a reality must be unrestrictedly intelligible, implying that it is an absolutely unique unrestricted act of understanding — understanding itself. Hence, it further corroborates and clarifies the conclusion of Chapter 2 — namely, the involvement of a "super-Intellect, capable of a grand cosmological design" in the creation of the universe.

Chapter 5 presents an ontological argument for the creation of all past time. It is inspired by contemporary physics, ontology of time, and the famous contemporary mathematician David Hilbert. It extends the conclusion of Chapter 1 (that inflationary model universes must have an initial singularity implying a creative power transcending space-time asymmetry) to *all* universes conditioned by temporality.

Chapter 6 returns to the topic of philosophical method and explicates the three dimensions of that method mentioned above (complete disjunction, the use of infinities, and the definition of causation itself).

We now proceed to the metaphysical argument for God's existence.

CHAPTER THREE

A Metaphysical Argument for God's Existence

Introduction

Many metaphysical arguments for God's existence have been offered since the time of Plato and Aristotle.[2] This one attempts to incorporate two insights from twentieth-century thought into the seminal insights of Plato, Aristotle, St. Augustine, St. Thomas Aquinas, and their interpreters. The first insight comes from Bernard Lonergan, who uses the notion of ontological conditions to interpret causal schemes of recurrence.[3] This view of causation can be applied to the whole range of causal connections (from the simple extrinsic collision of billiard balls, to very subtle and indeterminate information transfers in quantum systems). The second insight comes from quantum theory, which gives very lucid examples of the traditional notion of ontological simplicity. These two insights strengthen and clarify not only the proof of an unconditioned reality, but also the proofs for the absolutely simple, infinite, and unique nature of this unconditioned reality.

This version of the metaphysical argument consists of five steps:

I. Proof of at least one unconditioned reality.
II. Proof that unconditioned reality itself is the simplest possible reality.
III. Proof that unconditioned reality itself is absolutely unique.
IV. Proof that unconditioned reality itself is unrestricted.

2. See the Introduction to this book.
3. Lonergan 1992, pp. 141-43.

V. Proof that the one Unconditioned Reality is the continuous Creator of all else that is.

I. Step One: Proof of the Existence of at Least One Unconditioned Reality

This proof will consist of three substeps:

A) A complete disjunction elucidating the whole range of possible options for all reality.
B) Proof that a finite number of conditioned realities cannot ground the existence of any conditioned reality.
C) Proof that an infinite number of conditioned realities cannot ground the existence of any conditioned reality.

I.A. Complete Disjunction Elucidating the Whole Range of Possibilities for All Reality

In all reality (R), R could have either no unconditioned reality ("Hypothesis ~UR"), *or* one or more unconditioned realities ("Hypothesis UR"), not neither, not both (complete disjunction). Both options cannot be false because the whole range of possibilities for R is covered by these two options. Both options cannot be true because this would violate the principle of non-contradiction. Therefore, one and only one option can be and must be true.

I.A.1. Definitions

"Conditioned reality" means any reality (e.g., individual, particle, field, wave, structure, spatio-temporal continuum, spatio-temporal position, physical laws — e.g., $E = MC^2$) that is *dependent* upon another reality for its existence or occurrence. For example, a cat is a conditioned reality because it *depends* on cells and structures of cells for its existence. Without such cells and their specific structure, the cat would simply not exist. Similarly, cells are conditioned realities because they depend on molecules and specific structures of molecules for their existence. Likewise, molecules are conditioned realities because they depend on atoms and structures of atoms. Atoms are dependent on quarks and structures of quarks, and so forth.

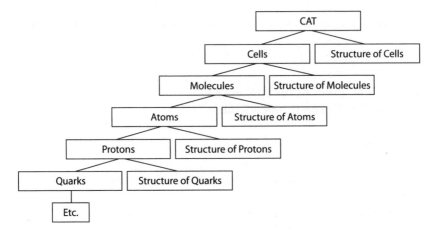

"Conditions" means any reality (e.g., individual, particle, field, wave, structure, spatio-temporal continuum, spatio-temporal position, physical laws — e.g., $E=MC^2$) upon which a conditioned reality[4] depends for its existence or occurrence. For example, cells are the conditions of cats, molecules the conditions of cells, etc.

"Unconditioned reality" means a reality that does not depend on any other reality of any kind for its existence or occurrence.

I.A.2. Consequences of the Complete Disjunction

Notice that the first option in the above disjunction (Hypothesis ~UR — "There are no unconditioned realities in all reality") can be restated as: "In all reality (R), there are *only conditioned realities.*" For it is equivalent to say, "There are no unconditioned realities in all reality" as to say, "There are only conditioned realities in all reality."

---

4. The reader may be accustomed to seeing the word "conditioned" used in an epistemological sense (e.g., in the works of Kant, or with respect to scientific judgments). I am using it in a definitively *ontological* sense here. This usage reflects the contemporary scientific understanding of physical laws and other forms of ontological dependency. A rather poignant example of this ontological use of "conditioned" with respect to physical schemes of recurrence may be found in Lonergan 1992, pp. 141-43.

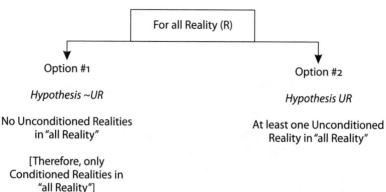

Note that if option #1 is false, then option #2 *must be* true, because one, and only one, of these two disjunctive options can be, and must be true. The remainder of Section I will be concerned with showing that option #1 must be false for all reality. This will prove, by disjunctive syllogism, that option #2 must be true, and therefore, there must exist at least one unconditioned reality in all reality.

For *any* conditioned reality (CR), CR can depend either on a finite number of conditions or an infinite number of conditions, not neither, not both (complete disjunction). Both options cannot be false because all possibilities are covered by these two options. Both options cannot be true because that would violate the principle of non-contradiction. Let us call option 1 "Hypothesis F" and option 2 "Hypothesis ~F." Section I.B (below) will show that "Hypothesis F" must always be false for any conditioned reality. Section I.C will show that "Hypothesis ~F" must also be false for any conditioned reality. Therefore, no conditioned reality can exist under "Hypothesis F" or "Hypothesis ~F." If these two hypotheses cover the whole range of possibilities for any conditioned reality, then no conditioned reality could exist in all reality if there are only conditioned realities in all reality. Therefore, at least one unconditioned reality must exist.

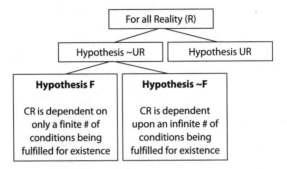

I.B. Proof That "Hypothesis F" Must Be False for Any Conditioned Reality (CR)

1. If any conditioned reality (CR) is dependent on *only* a finite number of conditions for its existence ("Hypothesis F"), then there would have to be a most fundamental condition ("last condition") upon which the CR depends. For example, a quark or some other more fundamental conditioned reality would have to be the most fundamental condition ("last condition") upon which a CR — say, a cat — depends. This temporarily ignores the possibility of a circular set of conditions which will be disproved in Section I.D below.

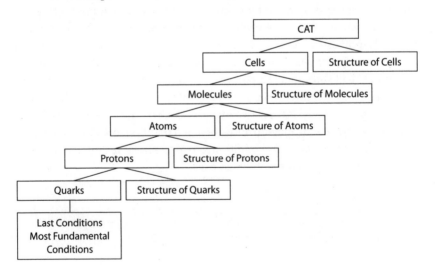

2. "Hypothesis ~UR" (under which "Hypothesis F" is being considered) asserts that there are no unconditioned realities in all reality. This is equivalent to asserting that there are *only* conditioned realities. Therefore, the most fundamental condition for any conditioned reality (CR) would have to be a conditioned reality (since we have hypothesized in "Hypothesis ~UR" that there are *only* conditioned realities in all reality).

3. If we ignore the possibility of a circular set of conditions for the moment, then the most fundamental condition (last condition) must be *a conditioned reality whose conditions are not fulfilled.* The last condition must have conditions because it is a conditioned reality (according to "Hypothesis ~UR"), and its conditions cannot be fulfilled because it is the last, or terminating condition (according to "Hypothesis F"). Therefore, the combination of "Hypothesis F" and "Hypothesis ~UR" requires that the last condition be a conditioned reality whose conditions are not fulfilled. But "a conditioned reality whose conditions are not fulfilled" is literally *nothing.*

4. If the combination of "Hypothesis ~UR" and "Hypothesis F" requires that the most fundamental condition be nonexistent (nothing), then all conditioned realities hypothetically dependent on it would also have to be nonexistent, in which case the conditioned reality would never exist.

Therefore, no conditioned reality can exist under both hypotheses "~UR" and "F." Therefore, "Hypothesis F" under "Hypothesis ~UR" must be false for any conditioned reality in all reality.

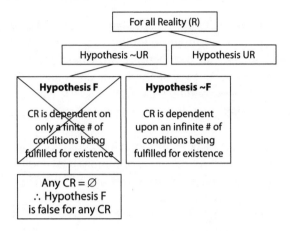

I.C. Proof That "Hypothesis ~F" Must Be False for Any Conditioned Reality (CR)

1. According to "Hypothesis ~F," any conditioned reality is dependent on an infinite number of conditions being fulfilled for its existence. This means there is *no* "most fundamental condition" ("last condition").

2. If there is no "most fundamental condition," then the number of conditions upon which CR depends is always 1+ more than can ever be achieved, and is therefore *unachievable*.

3. If CR depends on an unachievable number of conditions being fulfilled for its existence, it will never exist (*a priori*). In other words, if CR (say, a cat) is dependent upon a dependent upon a dependent upon a dependent, *ad infinitum,* in order to come into existence, it will never come into existence. Its conditions will never be fulfilled.

4. Therefore, no conditioned reality can exist under "Hypothesis ~F." Therefore, "Hypothesis ~F" is false for any conditioned reality.[5]

---

5. There is an obvious similarity here to the uncaused cause argument — the second way of St. Thomas Aquinas (Aquinas 1947, I., Question 2, Art. 3 i). But I have refrained from using the word "cause" in the proof here because "cause" has been interpreted by various philosophers in very narrow ways. It would not be useful, for example, to view "cause" simply as one billiard ball striking another, or an "aggregation of mass points." If it is useful to interpret the concepts in this chapter in causal terms, I could define "proximate cause" as "a proximate fulfillment of a conditioned reality's conditions." "First cause" could be defined as "the ultimate fulfillment of a conditioned reality's conditions by an unconditioned reality." These definitions are not restricted to pre-twentieth-century views of physics and philosophy. By using the vocabulary of this chapter, "proximate cause" could refer to "the collapse of

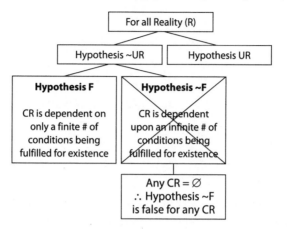

I.D. Proof That a Circular Set of Conditions Is False for Any CR

It may at first seem that a circular set of conditions is an intermediate or alternative position to hypotheses F and ~F. As will be shown in a moment, it is not. **"Circular set of conditions"** means reciprocal conditionality, where CR_a depends upon CR_b for its existence, *while* CR_b depends on CR_a for its existence. It can be shown that "CR_a's dependence on CR_b's dependence on CR_a's dependence ... etc.," would not allow either to exist; but in order to show the fallacy of circular conditionality within the context of hypotheses F and ~F, I have chosen the following argument.

1. Let us suppose there is a circular arrangement of conditioned realities, where CR_a is dependent on CR_b, which is, in turn, dependent on CR_c, which is, in turn, dependent on CR_a.

---

a wave function to an eigen state," "the orientation of motion arising out of irregular geometries of space-time," "plasma interactions, and even the creation of the entire universe by a reality outside of space-time asymmetry."

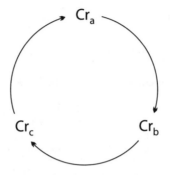

One may postulate any number of CRs in the circle that one wishes (even an infinity). The question is not how many *conditioned realities* are in the circle, but rather how many *conditions* each conditioned reality is *dependent* on in the circle. There are, again, two disjunctive options to respond to this question: (a) each conditioned reality is dependent on a *finite number of conditions* (implying a last condition), or (b) each conditioned reality is dependent on an *infinite number of conditions* (implying no last or terminating condition). This is completely disjunctive; therefore, if the circularity hypothesis is to be tenable, then one of these hypotheses must be true. If neither of the hypotheses is true, then the circularity hypothesis cannot be tenable.

2. If it is postulated that the circle corresponds to "Hypothesis F" (that each CR in the circle is dependent on a finite number of conditions), then there must be a last condition in the circle. Let us say that the last condition is CR_c (though it could be any CR one wishes on any rotation through the circle). The last condition would have to be a "*conditioned reality whose conditions are not fulfilled,*" in which case it would not exist (because inasmuch as it is the last condition, its conditions will not be fulfilled). All other conditioned realities in the circle that depend on CR_c (which would be all CRs in the circle) would likewise not exist. The circle would therefore not be able to come into existence. Notice that this is simply a restatement of the disproof of "Hypothesis F" in Section I.B above.

3. Let us hypothetically entertain the other side of the disjunction, namely that every CR in the circle is dependent on every other CR an infinite number of times (because there is no last condition). This means that every CR in the circle is dependent upon an infinite number of conditions being fulfilled. Since an infinite dependence is unachievable, every CR in the circle would have to be dependent on an

unachievable number of conditions being fulfilled. Again, the circle would not be able to come into existence. Notice that this is simply a restatement of the disproof of "Hypothesis ~F" given in Section I.C above.

4. Inasmuch as a circle must imply either that each conditioned reality is dependent on a finite number of conditions (having a last condition) *or* that each conditioned reality is dependent on an infinite number of conditions (because there is no last condition), and since both sides of this disjunction are false (i.e., will not allow any of the conditioned realities within the circle to exist), then a circle of dependent conditions cannot explain the existence of any of its constituents, and therefore, cannot represent a real state of affairs.

I.E. Conclusion: There Must Exist at Least One Unconditioned Reality in All Reality

1. If hypotheses F and ~F are both false for any conditioned reality, and if hypotheses F and ~F represent the whole range of possibilities for any conditioned reality, and if a circle is not an alternative position to hypotheses F and ~F (it is merely a restatement of either of them) then no CR can exist under either or both hypotheses.

2. If no CR can exist under either or both hypotheses, then there can*not* be *only* conditioned realities in "all Reality."

3. *Therefore, by disjunctive syllogism, there must be at least one unconditioned reality in all Reality.* To deny this would require affirming either hypothesis F or ~F, or both; but such an affirmation is absurd, for nothing, not even this writer, would then be able to exist.

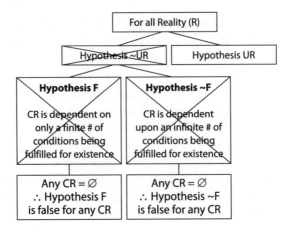

I.F. Another Refutation of Hypothesis ~UR

There is an even more fundamental ontological problem with Hypothesis ~UR than the one stated above, namely, that an infinite number of conditioned realities without an unconditioned reality is equivalent to absolutely nothing. Recalling that Hypothesis ~UR means that there are only CRs in reality, then CR_1 would have to depend on some other conditioned reality, say, CR_2, in order to exist. Hence, it is nothing until CR_2 exists and fulfills its conditions. Similarly, CR_2 would also have to depend on some other conditioned reality, say, CR_3, for its existence, and it would likewise be nothing until CR_3 exists and fulfills *its* conditions. And so forth, *ad infinitum*. Since every hypothetical conditioned reality is dependent upon other *nonexistent* conditioned realities for its existence, it will never come into existence. It does not matter whether one posits an infinite number of them; for each one in the series of dependence is still equal to nothing without the reality of the others. But if the "others" are nothing without others, and those "others" are nothing without still others, it does not matter if one postulates an infinite number of others (or arranges the infinite number of others in a circle). They are all still nothing in their dependence upon nonexistent conditions. Therefore, Hypothesis ~UR will always result in all reality being *nothing*, which readers will hopefully view as false, since they are reading this proof. Once again, we see the necessity for the existence of at least one unconditioned reality in all reality, and recognize that an unconditioned reality will have to be the ultimate fulfillment of all conditioned realities' conditions.

II. Step Two: Proof That Unconditioned Reality Itself Is the Simplest Possible Reality

In Step One (above) it was proved that at least one unconditioned reality must exist. Thus, there must be at least one reality completely free of conditions. The question now arises as to what such a reality is — considered in itself. What, then, is "unconditioned reality itself" ("pure unconditioned reality") without admixture of anything else? In order to assure that I do not sneak anything into the notion of "unconditioned reality" which is distinct from unconditionedness, I will restrict this analysis to consideration of "unconditioned reality *itself*" ("pure unconditioned reality"). The exploration of elements distinct from unconditioned reality (which might be combined with it) is irrelevant to the proof.

The upcoming investigation seeks an understanding of reality which can *exist through itself,* and not a reality which is the *cause of itself.* Notice that the former (a reality which exists through itself) does not exist through a fulfillment of its conditions, but rather through having no conditions of existence whatsoever. However, the latter option (a reality which is the cause of itself) can never exist because it is grounded in a vicious circle. This fallacy of asserting that a reality fulfills its own conditions was traditionally called "*causa sui*" (a reality causing itself to exist). *Causa sui* is self-evidently fallacious because it entails a reality existing before it existed in order to make itself exist (fulfill the conditions of its own existence). Therefore, the first option (a reality existing through itself) is the only one that can explain unconditioned reality itself (pure unconditioned reality).[6]

The notion of simplicity can help us to understand "unconditioned reality itself" (a being which can exist through itself). As will be seen, such a being must be *absolutely* simple. In the next chapter (a Lonerganian argument), unconditioned reality itself will be shown to be unrestricted intelligibility,

---

6. St. Thomas Aquinas tried to elaborate the notion of "a reality existing through itself" through a pure extrapolation of the Aristotelian category of "act," which he called "pure act." He defines this as follows: "Though a being that is sometime in potency and sometime in act is in time in potency before being in act, absolutely speaking act is prior to potency. For potency does not raise itself to act; it must be raised to act by something that is in act. Hence, whatever is in some way in potency has something prior to it. But, as is evident from what was said above, God is the first being and the first cause. Hence, He has no admixture of potency in Himself" (Aquinas 1955, Book One, Chapter 16, paragraph 3, p. 100). Thus, for Saint Thomas Aquinas, unconditioned reality itself (which would have to be a first cause — that is, the ultimate fulfillment of conditioned realities' conditions) must be pure act.

which will, in turn, be shown to be "an unrestricted act of understanding — understanding itself." The former approach emphasizes the power and unity of unconditioned reality itself, while the latter emphasizes the intelligence of unconditioned reality itself. When the two proofs are combined, they show the functional equivalence of absolute simplicity, absolute power, absolute unity, and unrestricted intellection (see Chapter 7, Section I).

For the moment, we will consider the principle of simplicity (Section II.A) and then prove that unconditioned reality itself must be absolutely simple (Section II.B).

II.A. The Principle of Simplicity

"Absolute simplicity" may be defined as "the complete absence of intrinsic and extrinsic boundaries, finitude, or restriction in a reality." The simpler a reality is, the fewer intrinsic and/or extrinsic boundaries it has. As we shall see momentarily, boundaries cause exclusion, that is, limit interaction and interrelation within a reality and with other realities. Hence, "greater simplicity" means "less intrinsic and extrinsic boundaries," which entails "less exclusion within itself and with other realities," which further entails "greater possibility for interaction and interrelationship within itself and with other realities."

This notion may be somewhat counterintuitive to a mindset that associates "higher orders of reality" with complexity. However, as contemporary quantum mechanics and field theory make clear, higher-order reality can be attributable to simplicity as well as complexity.

Let us begin with a simple postulate which can be clarified with a series of examples: *boundaries, finitude, or restrictedness causes exclusion or incompatible states.* The greater the number of intrinsic or extrinsic boundaries or restrictions in a reality, the greater the exclusion of that reality from other realities. This point might be clarified by a thought experiment using simple geometrical configurations. The boundaries of square (four inscribed right angles with four equal sides) *exclude* the boundaries of circle (no inscribed angles and no sides), so that one cannot have a square-circle of the same area, in the same respect at the same place and time. It does not matter whether the boundaries of square and circle inhere in a block of wood, a block of metal, or even in my mind; the *boundaries* of square exclude the *boundaries* of circle (in the same respect) in whatever substance they might inhere at any given place and time.

Another example of how finitude, boundaries, or restrictedness excludes can be seen in elementary particles. A proton (which attracts electrons) cannot act like an electron (which repels other electrons) in the same respect at the same place and time. The *restricted* way in which protons act (i.e., attracting electrons) is *incompatible* with the *restricted* way in which electrons act (i.e., repelling other electrons).

A third illustration of finites producing incompatibilities may serve as an introduction to the principle of simplicity. It is taken from contemporary quantum theory. Waves are incompatible with particles. Waves diffuse themselves (spread out) while particles are self-enclosed. Particles collide with each other (and conserve momentum); waves do not, they simply mesh with one another and form interference patterns. A myriad of other incompatibilities between waves and particles lead to the conclusion that a particular reality cannot possess the boundaries of wave and the boundaries of particle in the same respect at the same place and time.

However, recent quantum experimentation (i.e., the Aspect experiment,[7] the single photon double-slit experiment,[8] and a variety of other experiments) reveals that the same physical phenomenon can give rise to both wave-like and particle-like effects. In the single photon double-slit experiment, for example, a photon behaves like a particle (a self-enclosed entity capable of colliding with other particles at a discrete position), at the beginning and end of the experiment but not in the middle. In the middle of the experiment, the photon displays interference patterns that can only be explained if the phenomenon were a wave in between its beginning and ending manifestations.[9] How is this possible if a single reality cannot have the boundaries of wave and the boundaries of particle simultaneously?

The answer lies in the principle of simplicity. There must exist a simpler quantum state that does not possess the boundaries of either waves or particles, and therefore does not combine mutually incompatible boundaries. The simpler state of the quantum system has fewer boundaries, and therefore has fewer incompatibilities (exclusionary properties) than waves or particles.

Notice that light is *not* a "wavicle" (a combination of incompatible boundaries in the same respect at the same place and time). This would be

---

7. See, for example, Aspect et al. 1982, p. 1804; Davies 1986, pp. 17-19; and Gribbin 1984, pp. 226-27.

8. See, for example, Feynman 1967, pp. 130; Davies 1986, pp. 6-9; and Gribbin 1984, pp. 163-70.

9. Gribbin 1984, pp. 6-9; Davies 1986, pp. 163-70.

tantamount to a square-circle, or a proton-electron. Rather, light is a simpler reality which can, in certain circumstances, take on particle-like boundaries (and therefore behave in particle-like ways); and, in other circumstances, take on wave-like boundaries (and behave in wave-like ways). Therefore, our simpler reality could be a particle as it moves into the black box, become a wave while in the black box (thereby forming interference patterns when both slits are open), and then emerge as a particle when interacting with the photographic plate. This would explain how a single photon acts like both a wave and a particle in different parts of the same experiment.[10]

Before proceeding to an explanation of field theory, it may be well to briefly describe a metaphor which I will use throughout the course of this chapter — the tree of being.[11] This informal concept can be translated into the formal concept of "simplicity." "Tree of being" refers to levels of simplicity. To say that a reality has a "higher place on the tree of being," means that it has less intrinsic and extrinsic boundaries, or is conditioned by fewer restrictions or magnitudes than the realities below it on the tree of being. This higher reality, then, excludes less from itself both intrinsically and extrinsically. Therefore, it is more inclusive than realities below it on the tree of being, making it compatible with those realities.

We may now proceed to an exploration of fields (i.e., mediums through which incompatible states interact) that also display the characteristics of simplicity. Electromagnetic fields, for example, allow for the interaction of protons and electrons (positive and negative charges). Though protons are incompatible with electrons in the same respect at the same place and time, they do interact with each other in an electromagnetic field. These

10. Contemporary quantum theorists have referred to this "simpler" reality as "an information field," "a field of quantum potential," "a quantum superposition," etc. They have called this simpler reality "mind-like," "implicate order," "pre-field," etc. They have endowed it with properties such as "non-location," "immediate transposition," and so forth. All such namings are attempts to deal with the paradox of two incompatible behaviors arising out of the same phenomenon. Plato and Aquinas (who lived before the Newtonian era, which viewed reality in terms of extrinsic bodies and forces) had a virtually pure insight into the notion of simplicity (higher-order activities coming from less intrinsic and extrinsic restrictions in power). See below, note 14.

11. The concept of "tree of being" has proven to be a useful pedagogical device for both graduate and undergraduate students. The proof of the uniqueness of unconditioned reality itself integrates three difficult concepts: simplicity, instantiation of unconditioned reality itself, and the real distinction between unconditioned reality itself and an instantiation of it. The "tree of being" helps students to visualize, and therefore appropriate, the intrinsic intelligibility of these concepts.

field states can be viewed as simpler than particle states, allowing opposite states to interact with one another instead of excluding one another. If an electromagnetic field was not simpler than either a proton or an electron, then it would have the boundaries (restrictions) of one of them to the exclusion of the other. We might view the electromagnetic field's greater simplicity as a higher level on the tree of being.

Electromagnetic forces also interact with space-time (the space-time continuum as described in the General Theory of Relativity[12]). The field through which these seeming incompatibles interact (a unified field?) would have to be simpler than the opposed constituents. Such a unified field could again be viewed as "higher on the tree of being."

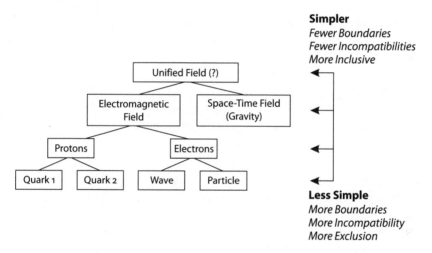

To reiterate, "simplicity" in a reality may be defined as "a lesser degree of intrinsic or extrinsic boundary or restriction giving rise to fewer incompatible states." Simpler states of being can take on additional boundaries. When they do, they take on the exclusionary properties of those boundaries, but they can always revert back to their less exclusionary (i.e., more inclusive) states. In a word, "simplicity" is synonymous with "ontological compatibility and inclusivity."

Two further clarifications may now be made: (1) simplicity in potency versus simplicity in act, and (2) extrinsic simplicity versus intrinsic simplicity.

12. Einstein 1961, pp. 136-37 and 154-57; Steinmetz 1967, pp. 67-68. See the explanation in Chapter 1 of this book.

With respect to the first clarification, medieval philosophers recognized two ways in which greater simplicity could occur: (A) greater potency, and (B) greater act. The epitome of the first mode of simplicity was termed "pure potency" or "prime matter." Here, the absence of restrictions really means the absence of restricted *act* or restricted *being*. The greater the potency, the *less* the act or being. One might compare this to "zero" in mathematics. Zero has no boundaries because it signifies "the absence of reality in which boundaries can inhere." "Simplicity in potency" (referring to an absence of restricted *act*) functions as a unifying substrate, such as space (which contemporaneously unifies excluding entities) or time (which non-contemporaneously unifies opposing — changing — states within the same or different entities).[13] Notice that space conceived as pure potency (as Newton viewed it) does not *do* anything (it does not act). It merely contemporaneously unifies separated or opposed energetic states. This distinguishes it from "simplicity in act" where less restriction does not entail less act.

"Simplicity in act" refers to a decrease of parameters, restrictions, or boundaries *within* act or being (i.e., the non-restrictedness *of* act). As such, a decrease in restriction does not entail a decrease in act (as was the case with "simplicity in potency"), but rather, an *increase* in act. The more simple a reality is, the less restrictions there are to its act or being, and the less restrictions to its act or being, the more it can do. Thus, "simplicity in act" entails *both* greater *act or being* and greater *inclusivity* (i.e., less exclusion arising out of boundaries or restrictions).

As will be seen, if unconditioned reality is found to be absolutely simple, it would have to be "simple in act," because an unconditioned reality must ground the fulfillment of all the conditioned realities that depend on it, that is, it must *do* something. Indeed, it must be an "ultimate doer," because it is an ultimate ground of act or being.

"*Absolute* simplicity in act" would then refer to act or being without *any* intrinsic or extrinsic parameters, boundaries, or restrictions, that is, a being capable of unrestrictedly acting in any and all non-contradictory ways. It would simultaneously refer to a purely *inclusive* reality, that is, a reality which does not exclude anything from itself.

When an absolutely simple reality unifies restricted realities, it is distinct from them in virtue of the *restricted realities'* boundaries. Nevertheless, it can unify them because it is simpler than they are (i.e., does not have ex-

13. See Chapter 5, Section II.

cluding boundaries). Therefore, an absolutely simple reality can interact with *any* restricted reality.

A simple analogy of this might be our act of thinking versus the content of our thoughts. Our act of thinking does not possess the boundaries of the content of our thoughts. Thus, even though the boundaries of square exclude the boundaries of circle in the same respect at the same place and time, I can hold them together — unify them — in a single act of thinking. Of course, I cannot unify them in the same respect at the same place and time, because *their* boundaries exclude one another. Nevertheless, I can hold the two thoughts together, side by side, so that I can observe similarities and differences between them. This unifying capacity is what creates understanding, for understanding is not picture-thinking (imagining single objects), but rather grasping the relationship among the content of thoughts (e.g., seeing similarities and differences), which requires holding multiple thoughts in a unity.

In sum, an absolutely simple reality (in act) is at once pure power and pure simplicity, pure act and pure inclusivity, pure being and pure capacity to unify all beings.

We may now proceed to the second clarification, namely, the difference between extrinsic and intrinsic boundaries. The lack of *extrinsic* boundaries and restrictions allows for unification with and among restricted (excluding) beings. For example, an electromagnetic field can unify protons and electrons (opposite electromagnetic charges).

The lack of *intrinsic* boundaries and restrictions (such as spatial or temporal magnitudes) allows for self-transparency like self-consciousness. Acts of self-consciousness (awareness of awareness) are difficult to explain through regular space-time models (one act of awareness capturing itself, as it were). However, an absence of *intrinsic* boundaries or parameters (e.g., an absence of spatial and temporal magnitude) makes it unnecessary for one act of awareness to "double back upon itself and get itself in space and time," because there is no spatio-temporal separation. The intrinsically simple act is simply transparent to itself. A *pure* act of self-transparency would be a perfect act of self-consciousness, where the content of the known would be absolutely identical with the knower's act of knowing. Subject and object would be differentiable only in their relationship to one another, but not in substance.

II.B. Unconditioned Reality Itself Must Be the Simplest Possible Reality

Recall from the introduction to Section II that we are seeking to understand unconditioned reality considered in itself, that is, unconditioned reality itself (or pure unconditioned reality) without admixture of anything else. The argument for the absolute simplicity of unconditioned reality itself will be given in two substeps.

Substep 1

Unconditioned reality itself cannot be incompatible with any conditioned reality, because it must ground the fulfillment of every conditioned reality's conditions. If unconditioned reality itself were incompatible with a conditioned reality, the conditioned reality would exclude "unconditioned reality itself" from itself (much like proton behavior excluding electron behavior from itself). If a conditioned reality excluded "unconditioned reality itself" from itself, it could not have its conditions fulfilled, in which case it could never exist. No conditioned reality, therefore, can be incompatible with unconditioned reality itself, meaning that unconditioned reality itself must be on a *higher level of simplicity* than any conditioned reality. Were it not on such higher level, it would exclude conditioned realities from itself, for whatever is on the same level of simplicity, excludes.

Substep 2

There is a further ramification of unconditioned reality itself and simplicity, namely, that unconditioned reality itself must be on the high*est* level of simplicity, that is, it must be so simple that it cannot have any incompatible states from itself. Let us explore this contention further, beginning with the bottom of the tree of being (the lowest known level of simplicity — waves and particles) and working our way up to the top of the tree of being (the highest level of simplicity).

Unconditioned reality itself cannot be a wave because the boundaries of waves exclude the boundaries of particles. Therefore, if unconditioned reality itself has the boundaries of waves, and the boundaries of waves exclude the boundaries of particles, then particles could not exist. The same would be true if unconditioned reality itself had the boundaries of particles. In this case, since the boundaries of particles exclude the boundaries of waves, waves could not exist. Thus, unconditioned reality itself cannot have the boundaries of either wave or particle. It must be *simpler* (higher on the tree of being) than both of them.

Could unconditioned reality itself be like an electron (which is one level higher on the tree of being — that is, simple enough to have both wave-like and particle-like states)? The answer, again, is no, because electrons also have incompatible states, namely, protons. If unconditioned reality itself were equivalent to electrons, protons would not exist; and if unconditioned reality itself were equivalent to protons, electrons would not exist.

Well then, could we go one level higher on the tree of being and equate unconditioned reality itself with an electromagnetic field (which is simple enough to unify its electron and proton constituents)? Not if electromagnetic fields have incompatible states. And indeed they do — space-time or gravitational fields.

We now arrive at the most important question. Could unconditioned reality itself be any X which has any real or really possible incompatible state (i.e., a ~X which could be real, or really possible)?

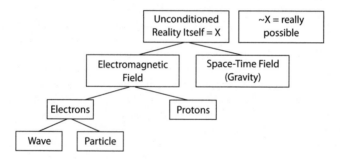

The answer is "no" for the following reason — unconditioned reality itself cannot be any reality X if that reality has an incompatible state (~X) which is or could be real, for if unconditioned reality itself were X, then its incompatible state (~X) would not be able to have its conditions fulfilled. ~X would exclude from itself unconditioned reality itself (the fulfillment of its conditions), and therefore, could not be real or even really possible.[14]

14. This argument goes back to Plato's most profound metaphysical dialogue, the *Sophist.* In it, he is trying to define "the real," that is, "Reality Itself." He gives an argument sometimes termed the "*tertium quid* — third thing" argument, which demonstrates that Reality Itself cannot be identical with anything that could have a real incompatible state. Using the example of hot and cold (hot always having an incompatible state of cold), he argues as follows: ". . . You who say that hot and cold or some such pair really are all

To argue the contrary (that there could be a real or really possible state of affairs incompatible with unconditioned reality itself) is a most fundamental ontological contradiction. Why? Because, if this hypothetical state of affairs is truly incompatible with (excludes from itself) unconditioned reality itself (which must ultimately fulfill the conditions of its existence), then it *could not* in principle be real or really possible. Thus, the very hypothesis of a real or really possible state of affairs incompatible with unconditioned re-

---

things, what exactly does this expression convey that you apply to both when you say that they both are 'real' or each of them is 'real'? How are we to understand this 'reality' you speak of? Are we to suppose it is a third thing alongside the other two and that the all is no longer, as you say, two things, but three? For surely you do not give the name 'reality' to one of the two and then say that both alike are real, for then there will be only one thing, whichever of the two it may be, and not two. . . . Well then, do you intend to give the name 'reality' to the pair of them? . . . 'But that again,' we shall object, 'will clearly be speaking of your two things as one . . .'" (Plato 1961[c], p. 987, 243e). Plato discovered that Reality Itself had to be compatible with both hot and cold, yet It could not be identified with either in the pair (because that would exclude the other part of the pair from reality) or both of the pair at the same time (because that would be a contradiction — hot-cold). He therefore concludes later that Reality Itself must be *neither* hot nor cold, but a third thing which is compatible with both. This is precisely what is meant by "simplicity." Later in the dialogue, Plato tries to describe the nature of this "third thing which is compatible with all real oppositions," and he identifies it with "unity," making the poignant observation: ". . . surely unity in the true sense and rightly defined must be altogether without parts. . . . Whereas a thing such as we described, consisting of several parts, will not answer to that definition. . . . Then, is 'the real' one and a whole in the sense that it has the property of unity, or are we to say that 'the real' is not a whole at all?" (Plato 1961[c], 245a-245b). Reality Itself, it turns out, is not a whole of parts. In order to be compatible and in unity with all real oppositions, it cannot have any intrinsic boundaries or magnitudes which would make it incompatible with anything that could be real. Plato has not only discovered here a conceptual apparatus for defining "Reality Itself," but also for explaining the seeming unity of opposites manifested in quantum mechanics. Plato's "unity" is interpreted as simplicity by St. Thomas Aquinas and other scholastic philosophers. In essence, simplicity refers to "a reality having fewer intrinsic boundaries which could give rise to exclusion and incompatibility." Hence, *absolute* simplicity would have absolutely no intrinsic boundary or magnitude which could give rise to incompatible states. It would not exclude restricted realities from itself, but it would not be identifiable with any of them. Thus, St. Thomas Aquinas describes God (the simplest possible Reality) in this way: "The absolute simplicity of God may be shown in many ways. First, from the previous articles of this question. For there is neither composition of quantitative parts in God, since He is not a body; nor composition of form and matter; nor does His nature differ from His *suppositum;* nor His essence from His existence; neither is there in Him composition of genus and difference, nor of subject and accident. Therefore, it is clear that God is nowise composite, but is altogether simple" (Aquinas 1947, p. 19, Q.3, Art. 7).

ality itself (which makes that state of affairs real or really possible) is an *intrinsic contradiction*.

Therefore, unconditioned reality itself must be the highest level of simplicity (the top of the tree of being), because every real and really possible state of affairs must be compatible with it (lower than it on the tree of being), and there can be no real or really possible alternative state of affairs on the same level of simplicity (the same level of the tree of being); for such an alternative state of affairs would have to exclude unconditional reality itself from itself (because it is on the same level of simplicity), meaning that it could not exist.

Inasmuch as unconditioned reality itself is absolutely simple, it is also a purely inclusive reality. Note that this pure inclusion does not mean that unconditioned reality itself *absorbs* everything into itself (as in Monism). Rather, it means only that unconditioned reality itself can interact with any less simple reality on any level. It does not destroy or absorb the less simple reality, it simply transcends the less simple reality's boundaries.

Note also that the differentiation between unconditioned reality itself and less simple realities occurs because of the boundaries of the *less simple* reality. There is nothing about unconditioned reality itself that excludes. The boundaries of the *less* simple reality *differentiate* the less simple reality from unconditioned reality itself *without excluding it*.

Note, from the above, that there are two kinds of differentiation (and therefore, two ways of producing plurality):

a) Differentiation through *exclusion or incompatibility* (e.g., the boundaries of wave exclude the boundaries of particle). This kind of differentiation is on the *same* level of simplicity. Inasmuch as particles and waves are on the same level of simplicity, they exclude (and are therefore incompatible with) one another.

b) Differentiation through *simplicity.* For example, electromagnetic fields are different from electrons because electromagnetic fields are simpler than (do not have the boundaries of) electrons. Hence, even though electromagnetic fields are different from electrons, they do not exclude electrons from themselves (they are not incompatible with them). Notice that differentiation here occurs on *different* levels of simplicity. That is why the differentiation does not produce exclusion or incompatibility. This kind of differentiation applies to unconditioned reality itself because unconditioned reality itself is the *simplest reality,* that is, *simpler* (on a higher level of simplicity) than *every* reality having an excluding state which could be real or really possible (e.g., electrons have excluding states such as protons, neutrons, positrons, etc., which can be real or really possible). The boundaries of the less simple realities *differentiate* them from unconditioned reality itself, but they do not *exclude* it from themselves, that is, they are not incompatible with it. Indeed, if they were, they could never exist (as was noted above).

III. Step Three: Proof of the Absolute Uniqueness of Unconditioned Reality Itself

It was proved above that unconditioned reality itself must be the simplest reality (simpler than all other realities). The question now arises as to whether there can be multiple instantiations of this simplest reality. If not, then this simplest reality must be absolutely unique. The proof will proceed in six substeps.

Substep 1

As proved above in Step 2 (Section II.B), unconditioned reality itself (that is, *pure* unconditioned reality) must be the simplest reality because it must be simpler than any reality that will admit of a real (or really possible) excluding difference from itself on the *same* level of simplicity (e.g., electrons admit of non-electrons — protons, neutrons, etc. — on the same level of simplicity, which requires that pure unconditioned reality be higher on the tree of being than electrons and *everything* else that is like electrons in this respect). Therefore, if there were a multiplicity of pure unconditioned realities, they would *all* have to have the highest level of simplicity (i.e., stand at the top of the tree of being). This is represented in the following diagram by I_1, $I_2 \ldots$ where, for example, I_2 signifies the second instantiation of pure unconditioned reality.

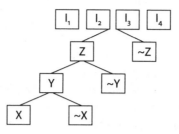

Substep 2

Let us suppose that there are multiple instantiations of pure unconditioned reality at the top of the tree of being (I_1, I_2, I_3, I_4 — see the chart above); then there would have to be some *difference* between these hypothetical instantiations. If there were not, the hypothetical instantiations would be the selfsame, and therefore one.

Substep 3

This *difference* implies the presence of some instantiating factor that is not identical with "pure unconditioned reality" (such as space, or some differentiating element within each hypothetical instantiation, or different thoughts in the divine mind, etc.). If there were no instantiating factor (which is *not* identical with pure unconditioned reality), there would be no difference between the various hypothetical instantiations of pure unconditioned reality, making these hypothetical instantiations the selfsame, and therefore one.

Substep 4

The presence of this instantiating factor means that every hypothetical instantiation of pure unconditioned reality cannot really be "*pure.*" It would have to be unconditioned reality *plus* an "instantiating factor which is not identical with *pure* unconditioned reality." Thus, the instantiation might be unconditioned reality *plus* positioning in a spatial manifold; or unconditioned reality *plus* an instantiating element in a particular instance of unconditioned reality (making a composite reality); or unconditioned reality *plus* a discrete thought in the mind of God, etc.

Substep 5

The instantiating *factor* must be less simple than pure unconditioned reality. Recall that pure unconditioned reality must be simpler than *every* "reality which will admit a real or really possible excluding difference from itself *on the same level of simplicity*" (e.g., an electron which admits of non-electrons such as protons, neutrons, etc.). This was proven above in Step 2 (Section II.B). Recall further from Substep 4 that a second (or more) instance of unconditioned reality requires an instantiating factor that is not identical with pure unconditioned reality. Now, this instantiating factor must be *less simple* than pure unconditioned reality, because it has to admit of real or really possible excluding differences on the same level of simplicity. Why? Because it is hypothesized to give rise to *different* instances of unconditioned reality on the highest level (same level) of simplicity. This means that the instantiating factor must be less simple than pure unconditioned reality.

Substep 6

An *instantiation* of unconditioned reality must also be less simple than *pure* unconditioned reality. Recall that an instantiation (say, I_2) must be pure unconditioned reality *plus* an instantiating factor (say, a position in a spatial manifold, or an element of individuation). Recall also that this instantiating factor must be less simple than pure unconditioned reality (proved in Substep 5). Now, since this "instantiating *factor* which is less simple than pure unconditioned reality" would have to be intrinsic to (or affect) every hypothetical instantiation of unconditioned reality (say, I_2), it would make that instantiation less simple than *pure* unconditioned reality (i.e., if the instantiating factor is less simple than pure unconditioned reality, the *composite* of "pure unconditioned reality *plus* the less simple instantiating factor" would also have to be less simple than pure unconditioned reality). Therefore, pure unconditioned reality would have to be simpler (higher on the tree of being) than every *instantiation* of it.

Conclusion

Therefore, any "second" or "third" (etc.) instance of unconditioned reality would always have to be less simple than *pure* unconditioned reality, making pure unconditioned reality absolutely unique as the simplest reality. It must stand alone on the highest level of simplicity — at the top of the tree of being (see the diagram below).[15] Recall that unconditioned reality itself signifies pure unconditioned reality; therefore, it is equivalent to conclude that unconditioned reality itself is absolutely unique at the highest level of simplicity.

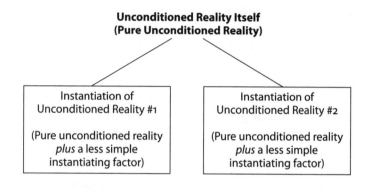

IV. Step Four: Proof That Unconditioned Reality Itself Is Unrestricted

We may now proceed to a proof of the unrestricted power of the unique, absolutely simple, unconditioned Reality. It is very closely connected to the proof for absolute simplicity (Section II), and so opens the way to formalize the proof for "an absence of intrinsic or extrinsic boundaries or restrictions in the one unconditioned Reality."

Recall from Section II.B that unconditioned Reality itself is at the highest level of simplicity, and that there can be no real or really possible alternative states of affairs on that highest level of simplicity. The implication of this is not only that unconditioned Reality itself is absolutely simple and unique, but also that it is unrestricted. A brief review of the notion of restrictedness, boundary, or finitude will bring this to light.

15. St. Thomas Aquinas states the above fundamental insight through the notion of an "absolutely perfect Being." Such a Being would be identical with an absolutely simple Being, because an absolutely simple Being has no intrinsic boundary or magnitude that would limit its perfection or power. If one substitutes "absolute simplicity" for "absolute perfection," one can see microcosmically the above six substeps in St. Thomas's proof: ". . . it has been shown that God is absolutely perfect, lacking no perfection. If, then, there are many gods, there must be many such perfect beings. But this is impossible. For, if none of these perfect beings lacks some perfection, and does not have any admixture of imperfection, which is demanded for an absolutely perfect being, nothing will be given in which to distinguish the perfect beings from one another. It is impossible, therefore, that there be many gods" (Aquinas 1955, p. 158, Bk. One, Ch. 42, paragraph 3).

The presence of real or really possible alternatives on the same level of simplicity reveals the presence of boundaries, because alternatives on the same level of simplicity are exclusionary and those exclusions arise out of restriction, finitude, or boundaries (see above, II.A). Viewed from the opposite perspective, boundaries, restrictions, and finitude "make room for" real or really possible alternative states of affairs on the same level of simplicity. By limiting X, restrictions, finitude, or boundaries make room for real and really possible not-X (on the same level of simplicity). For example, the boundaries of square create the conditions for really possible "*non*-squares" on the same level of simplicity (such as circles, triangles, trapezoids, parallelograms, etc.). The restrictions of electron behavior create the conditions for really possible *non*-electron behaviors on the same level of simplicity (such as protons, neutrons, positrons, etc.). Wherever there is restriction, finitude, or a boundary, there will be "room" for real or really possible alternative states of affairs on the same level of simplicity that will exclude one another and hence create the possibility of incompatible states of affairs.

This insight provides the major premise for the proof of the unrestricted power of the one "unconditioned Reality itself," which may be formalized in a *modus tollens* syllogism. Recall that a *modus tollens* syllogism is:

> If A, then B.
> Not-B.
> Therefore not-A.

We may now proceed to the syllogism:

> If any reality X has finitude, restriction, or a boundary, then there could be a real or really possible state of affairs on the same level of simplicity (a real or really possible not-X) which would be excluded by X, and so constitute an incompatible state of affairs. This major premise simply restates the insight given above.
>
> But, there can be no real or really possible states of affairs that are incompatible with (excluded by) unconditioned Reality itself, because that exclusion precludes those states of affairs from existing (since unconditioned Reality itself must ultimately ground the existence of everything real or really possible — see above, Sections I and II).
>
> Therefore, unconditioned Reality itself has no finitude, restriction, or boundary (*modus tollens*).

In order to clarify the *modus tollens* pattern in the above syllogism, it may be briefly restated as follows:

> If restriction, then really possible incompatible states of affairs.
>> But no really possible incompatible states of affairs with unconditioned Reality.
>
> Therefore, no restriction in unconditioned Reality.

Note that the denial of this conclusion leads to a most fundamental ontological contradiction. Why? Because if unconditioned Reality itself is restricted or finite, then there could be other real or really possible alternative states of affairs on the highest level of simplicity. But this is truly contradictory, because those alternative states of affairs would be incompatible with (excluded by) unconditioned Reality itself, making their conditions unfulfillable (in which case, they could not be real or really possible). Thus, the contention that "unconditioned Reality itself is restricted" is tantamount to asserting the contradiction that "impossible states of affairs are real or really possible."

What does "unrestricted" or "infinite" mean in the context of this proof? The kind of "unrestrictedness" referred to here cannot be imagined (a picture-thought with spatial and temporal magnitude), because unconditioned Reality itself is not an unrestricted *magnitude* (a divisible continuum such as space or time). Since unconditioned Reality itself is absolutely simple, it cannot be conditioned by any magnitude whatsoever because absolute simplicity has no intrinsic restrictions (such as magnitudes) or extrinsic restrictions (see above, Section II). Therefore, "unrestrictedness" does not refer to something like an unrestricted magnitude, but rather to "the complete absence of intrinsic or extrinsic boundary in unconditioned Reality itself." This "negative way" of viewing unrestrictedness (i.e., absence of restriction) has no imaginable magnitude, component parts, or conditions.

The closest one can come to expressing this notion of unrestricted existence is either:

1) to deny the existence of restrictions within such a reality (the *via negativa*),[16] or

---

16. This is known as the "*apophatic* way," or the "*via negativa*." It seems to have been recognized first by Pseudo-Dionysius the Areopagite in about A.D. 500. See Dionysius the Areopagite 1940, pp. 196-99.

2) to see the unrestricted Reality in relation to everything that is below it on the tree of being (i.e., everything that is less simple than it).[17]

At first glace it might seem that the *via negativa* has relegated us to a complete absence of knowledge about unconditioned Reality itself; but this is not the case because unconditioned Reality itself must be power or act (since it is the ultimate fulfillment of conditions of everything that exists). Thus, "unrestricted" here means "*un*restricted *power*" or "*un*restricted *act*" or "*no* extrinsic or intrinsic limit to *power*" or "*no* extrinsic or intrinsic limit to *act*," or "*no* magnitude conditioning *power*," or "*no* magnitude conditioning *act*," etc.[18] For this reason, Saint Thomas Aquinas and his followers refer to it as "pure power" or "power itself," or "pure act" or "act itself," or "pure existence" or "existence itself," or "pure being" or "being itself" (where the Latin infinitive "*esse*" is used to refer to "existence" or "being").

Though these concepts cannot be positively imagined (like picture-thinking), they are replete with content that cannot be tied down to the limited powers of our imagination. As such, they properly refer to a Reality which is likewise filled with unimaginable power and act — content.

---

17. As will be explained in Chapter 6, Section II, this is the hyperphatic way of understanding an unrestricted Reality.

18. St. Thomas Aquinas recognized this idea of infinity (i.e., infinite power), and carefully distinguished it from quantitative infinities and ongoing quantitative magnitudes. He refers to the magnitude of infinity as a "spiritual magnitude," which he references back to "power in a non-quantitative sense." This, of course, is corollary to the notion of absolute simplicity spoken of in Step Two of the proof above. The following quotation elucidates the difference between "infinities of things, magnitudes, or quantities" (which are only potential infinities) and "a Reality without any intrinsic restriction or magnitude" (which must be absolute simplicity): "Since, as the philosophers teach, 'the infinite accompanies quantity,' infinity cannot be attributed to God on the ground of multitude. For we have shown that there is only one God and that no composition of parts or accidents is found in Him. Nor, again, according to continuous quantity can God be called infinite, since we have shown that He is incorporeal. It remains, then, to investigate whether according to spiritual magnitude it befits God to be infinite. . . . ¶ We must therefore show that God is infinite according to the mode of this sort of magnitude. The infinite here will not be taken in the sense of privation, as in the case of dimensive or numerical quantity. For this quantity is of a nature to have a limit, so that such things are called infinites according as there is removed from them the limits they have by nature; which means that in their case the infinite designates an imperfection. But in God the infinite is understood only in a negative way, because there is no terminus or limit to His perfection: He is supremely perfect. It is thus that the infinite ought to be attributed to God" (Aquinas 1955, pp. 165-66, Bk. One, Ch. 43, paragraphs 1 and 3).

Conclusion to Steps One Through Four

Step One proved that at least one unconditioned reality must exist. The consequences of denying this are that nothing, including the reader, would be able to exist.

Step Two showed that "unconditioned reality itself" must be compatible with everything that is real or could be real (and therefore would have to be the simplest reality). A denial of this would argue a most fundamental ontological contradiction (if unconditioned reality itself were not absolutely simple, it would allow for real or really possible states of affairs that are incompatible with the very ground of their existence).

Step Three proved that this simplest reality would have to be simpler than multiple instantiations of it, and so any second, third, etc. instantiation would always have to be less simple than the first (unconditioned reality itself), making unconditioned reality itself absolutely unique as the simplest reality. The consequence of denying this is an intrinsic contradiction ("there is no difference or differentiating factor between the various instantiations," which makes them the selfsame one).

Step Four proved that this one "unconditioned Reality itself" had to be unrestricted power or act. The consequence of denying this is not only the denial of a valid *modus tollens* syllogism, but more importantly, it argues a most fundamental ontological contradiction (i.e., if the one unconditioned Reality itself had a boundary, it would leave room for real or really possible alternative states of affairs that are incompatible with the very ground of their existence).

If we are to avoid denying our own existence or arguing fundamental ontological contradictions or intrinsic contradictions, it would seem necessary to affirm the existence of a unique, absolutely simple, unrestricted, unconditioned Reality.[19]

---

19. During virtually every class I have taught on this subject, a student will inquire precisely at this point, "If there can only be one unrestricted, unconditioned reality, how can you explain the Trinity?" Just in case some readers are asking the same question, I will give a brief response. In Christian tradition, the "Trinity" does not refer to three instances of unrestricted, unconditioned reality (nor three instances of unrestricted power). As shown above, this is impossible (because any second or more instance would have to be a most fundamental ontological contradiction). The "Trinity" refers to three distinct self-consciousnesses (self-awarenesses — "awareness of awareness" — traditionally termed "Persons") making an unconditional *use* of the *one* unrestricted, unconditioned Reality. This does not argue a contradiction. This is what is meant by the doctrine "there are three Persons, but one Nature (i.e., unrestricted power) in God."

V. Step Five: Proof That the One Unconditioned Reality Is the Continuous Creator of All Else That Is

This argument may be broken down into two steps:

A) the unique, absolutely simple, unrestricted, unconditioned Reality itself must be the Creator of all else that is, and
B) this Creator must *continuously* create.

V.A. The Unique, Absolutely Simple, Unrestricted, Unconditioned Reality Itself Is the Creator of All Else That Is

Substep 1

Definitions:

a) "Creation" means the ultimate fulfillment of a conditioned reality's conditions. The word "ultimate" is used here to differentiate creation from a "*proximate* cause" (a proximate fulfillment of conditions). For example, the existence and proper structure of a cat's cells is a proximate fulfillment of the cat's conditions. Alternatively, "creation" refers to the ultimate fulfillment of the cat's conditions by the one unconditioned Reality itself. (Recall that every conditioned reality is ultimately dependent on an unconditioned reality for the fulfillment of its conditions; otherwise it would be nothing — see Step One.)
b) "Creator" means the source (power or act) which ultimately fulfills a conditioned reality's conditions. This source or power is unconditioned Reality itself (see below, Substep 2).

Substep 2

We begin by showing that everything in reality must be a conditioned reality except the one unconditioned Reality itself.

a) In all reality, realities must be either conditioned or unconditioned (complete disjunction).
b) There can be only *one* unconditioned Reality itself in "all reality" (proved in Step III).

c) Therefore, all other realities in "all reality" must be conditioned realities (by disjunctive syllogism).

Substep 3

As proved in Step One (Section I), conditioned realities cannot have their conditions ultimately fulfilled by conditioned realities alone. Even an infinite number of conditioned realities cannot ultimately fulfill the conditions of conditioned realities. Two conclusions can be drawn from this:

a) For any conditioned reality X, there must always be a most fundamental (*last*) condition to be fulfilled. Otherwise, a conditioned reality would be dependent for its existence on the fulfillment of an infinite (unfulfillable) number of conditions (see Hypothesis ~F in Step I.C, above).

b) This most fundamental (last) condition must be fulfilled by the one *unconditioned* Reality itself. If it were not, this last condition would depend on a "conditioned reality whose conditions were not fulfilled" (i.e., a nonexistent — nothing), meaning that all other conditions of contingent reality X would not be fulfilled, meaning, in turn, that conditioned reality X could not exist (see Hypothesis F in Step I.B, above).

Substep 4

Since there must be a last condition, and since this last condition must always be fulfilled by an unconditioned reality, and since there can only be one unconditioned Reality itself, and since everything in "all reality" besides the one, unconditioned Reality must be a conditioned reality, then *the one, unconditioned Reality must be the Creator (the source of the ultimate fulfillment of conditions) of all else that is real.*[20]

20. St. Thomas Aquinas argues this point in much the same way. He first demonstrates the simplicity of self-subsisting Being Itself (*ipsum suum esse subsistens* — what has been termed in this proof "unconditioned Reality itself"), then argues the uniqueness of self-subsisting Being itself, which implies that the rest of reality must be non-self-subsisting beings (which have been termed "conditioned realities" in this proof). This requires that the one, self-subsisting Being itself be the Creator of all else that is: ". . . it must be said that every being in any way existing is from God. For whatever is found in anything by participation, must be caused in it by that to which it belongs essentially, as iron becomes ignited by fire. Now it has been shown above when treating of the divine simplicity that God is the essen-

V.B. The Creator Must Continuously Create All Else That Is Real

This may at first appear confusing to those who interpret "creation" as "*creatio ex nihilo*" (a one-time creation of the universe out of nothing). Though this is a common meaning of "creation," *this* argument views "creation" in a broader way as "the ultimate fulfillment of conditions by the unconditioned Reality itself." Naturally this definition is not in conflict with "*creatio ex nihilo*"; it simply includes the possibility of the Creator (the source, power, or activity of the ultimate fulfillment of conditions) continuously fulfilling conditions ultimately, and, as it were, "holding or conserving" conditioned realities in being.

Substep 1

No conditioned reality can ever become unconditioned, because there can be only one unconditioned Reality itself (from Step III, above).

Substep 2

Therefore, every conditioned reality must be dependent on the unconditioned Reality itself for the ultimate fulfillment of its conditions at every moment that those conditions could cease to be fulfilled.

Substep 3

If the unconditioned Reality itself does not ultimately fulfill the conditions of every conditioned reality at every moment they are dependent on such fulfillment, they would cease to be real. This is sometimes referred to as "radical contingency," which reflects the radical and continuous dependence of all conditioned realities on the one unconditioned Reality itself.

---

tially self-subsisting Being; and also it was shown that subsisting being must be one; as, if whiteness were self-subsisting, it would be one, since whiteness is multiplied by its recipients. Therefore all beings apart from God are not their own being, but are beings by participation. Therefore it must be that all things which are diversified by the diverse participation of being, so as to be more or less perfect, are caused by one First Being, Who possesses being most perfectly" (Aquinas 1947, pp. 229-30, Q.44, Art. 1).

Substep 4

Therefore, the Creator (the unique, absolutely simple, unrestricted, unconditioned Reality itself) must be a *continuous* Creator (source of the ultimate fulfillment of conditions) of all else that is real at every moment it could cease to be real (i.e., at every moment of its reality).[21] Analogously speaking, if the Creator stopped "thinking" about us, we would literally lapse into nothingness.

Conclusion

In view of the above five steps, the "unique, absolutely simple, unrestricted, unconditioned Reality itself which is the continuous Creator of all else that is" must exist. This Reality corresponds to what is generally thought to be "God."[22] God, as defined, must exist.

As noted in the conclusion to Section IV, the denial of the existence of God (as defined) would entail the denial of one's own existence, or arguing a most fundamental ontological contradiction or an intrinsic contradiction (or all of the above). If these alternatives are considered to be unreasonable or irresponsible (or both), the existence of God should be considered rationally affirmed.

21. St. Thomas Aquinas gives an elaborate proof of the necessity for God to conserve all created things in being. In the *Summa Theologica*, Question 104, Art. 1, he begins the proof by noting: ". . . a thing is said to preserve another *per se* and directly, namely, when what is preserved depends on the preserver in such a way that it cannot exist without it. In this manner all creatures need to be preserved by God. For the being of every creature depends on God, so that not for a moment could it subsist, but would fall into nothingness were it not kept in being by the operation of the Divine power . . ." (Aquinas 1947, pp. 511-12).

22. The God of faith generally includes these characteristics, but goes beyond them in the areas of divine self-revelation, grace, redemption of suffering, redemption of sin, relationship to human beings, providence, and prayer (to name but a few areas).

CHAPTER FOUR

A Lonerganian Proof for God's Existence

Introduction

If Lonergan is correct, then the unconditioned Reality proven in the last chapter would have to be not only a unique, absolutely simple, unrestricted, unconditioned Reality, but also unconditioned Intelligibility, and therefore an unrestricted act of understanding — understanding itself. This advances our knowledge of the unconditioned Reality, and sheds further light on the Super-Intellect implied by the design of our universe (Chapter 2).

Lonergan's proof may be stated as follows:

If the real is completely intelligible, then God exists.
But the real is completely intelligible.
Therefore, God exists.[1]

Lonergan's proof proceeds along the following lines. He begins with a comprehensive diagnosis of human understanding, and then moves from understand*ing* to the correlate structure of what is understood and affirmed (correctly grasped intelligibility).[2] He then shows that partial intelligibility is always open to further questions which must have correct answers grounded in the real.[3] This means that reality can ground the complete set of correct

1. Lonergan 1992, p. 695.
2. See Lonergan 1992, Chapters 10, 11, 14, and 15.
3. ". . . [The pure, unrestricted desire to know] reaches its objective, which is being, only when every intelligent question has been given an intelligent answer and that answer has been found to be correct. Being, then, is intelligible, for it is what is to be known by

answers to the complete set of questions (complete intelligibility), which implies that the complete set of correct answers to the complete set of questions (complete intelligibility) exists. Now, complete intelligibility would have to include unrestricted intelligibility (an intelligible that leaves no further question to be asked because it has no restrictions to its intelligibility). Such unrestricted intelligibility would have to include the intelligibility of understanding as well as understanding's grasp of itself, and even unrestricted understanding and unrestricted understanding's grasp of itself. Therefore, if complete intelligibility exists, then an unrestricted act of understanding — understanding itself — must also exist.[4] Lonergan shows that this unrestricted act of understanding — understanding itself — must be unique, and therefore may be referred to as "God."

Since Lonergan's proof turns on his notion of causality,[5] there is an opportunity to reshuffle his premises so that the proof can begin with the necessity of an uncaused cause (which I have defined as an "unconditioned reality fulfilling the conditions of conditioned realities") which is subsequently revealed to be a unique unrestricted act of understanding — understanding itself. I would like to take advantage of this opportunity in order to provide an alternative version of Lonergan's proof that may appeal to those who prefer to proceed from an *ontological* rather than an epistemological base. As will be seen, the conclusion is the same, namely, that an "unrestricted act of understanding — understanding itself" must exist.

Though this approach may frustrate Lonergan's own designs, it reveals the veracity of the proof from its beginning and makes it more accessible to those unfamiliar with Lonergan and his approach to cognitional theory. Though Lonergan intended that his proof of God be a moment in the unfolding of his cognitional theory and subsequent epistemology and ontology, I believe there is a benefit of first considering his proof for the existence of God and then using it as a light to reveal the sig-

---

correct understanding; and it is *completely* intelligible, for being is known completely only when all intelligent questions are answered correctly" (Lonergan 1992, p. 695; italics mine).

4. "If the real is completely intelligible, then complete intelligibility exists. If complete intelligibility exists, the idea of being [what I term 'unrestricted intelligibility,' which includes 'unrestricted understanding — understanding itself'] exists. If the idea of being exists, then God exists. Therefore, if the real is completely intelligible, God exists" (Lonergan 1992, p. 696).

5. See Lonergan 1992, pp. 674-80.

nificance and mystery of human intelligence. This is my reason for writing this chapter.

If the reader will permit this indulgence, I will reorder Lonergan's proof accordingly, beginning with the notion of causality defined in the previous chapter as "a fulfillment of a conditioned reality's conditions." According to this definition, an uncaused cause would be the ultimate fulfillment of conditioned realities' conditions, which would have to be an unconditioned reality. Thus, I will begin with the proof for an unconditioned reality. The following four steps reflect the order of presentation:

1) There must be at least one unconditioned reality.
2) An unconditioned reality must be unrestricted intelligibility (intelligible content that leaves no further questions to be asked because it is sufficient to ground the correct answers to all questions about it).
3) Unrestricted intelligibility must be unique (one and only one).
4) Unique unrestricted intelligibility must be an unrestricted act of understanding — understanding itself.

This "unrestricted act of understanding — understanding itself" may be understood to be "God." Therefore, God, as defined, must exist.

The above four steps allow us to arrive at Lonergan's conclusion from a quite different (but elucidating) point of departure. I will give the proofs for these steps (in Sections II.A through II.D) after defining two central terms: "understanding" and "intelligibility" (in Section I).

I. Definitions of "Understanding" and "Intelligibility"

The contours of the forthcoming proof of God's existence are dependent on the definition of two terms: "understanding" and "intelligibility." They are best understood in their intrinsic relationship to one another.

For Lonergan, understanding is preceded by experience, which is the presence of data (givens) to consciousness.[6] These "givens" have intelligible content (information that can be accessed by intelligent consciousness). Prior to understanding, this intelligible content is not in a relationship with other intelligible contents, and so its significance has not yet come to light. Rather, the intelligible content stands, as it were, by itself, embedded in what

6. See Lonergan 1992, pp. 95-97.

Lonergan calls an "empirical residue"[7] (an individual reality at a particular place and time within a spatio-temporal manifold).

When intelligibility is in the empirical world (independent of experience and understanding), it is intrinsic to a reality's activities, powers, and characteristics (which characteristics include size, shape, color, magnitudes, frequencies, position, etc.). These activities, powers, and characteristics influence and affect one another, but beyond this they contain information that is accessible to an intelligent subject.[8] This accessible information exists whether or not an intelligent subject actually understands it. It is, as it were, a "to be understood." This information is *relatable* to other information, and when intelligent consciousness grasps a relationship among various kinds of information, it *understands.*

When intelligent consciousness appears on the scene, it not only experiences a given, it recognizes intelligible content in this given (despite the content's being tied down by its empirical residue). The intelligent consciousness then goes beyond this recognition and *desires* to bring this intelligible content into full light (that is, into its full intelligible significance). Intelligent consciousness does this not only because it sees a pragmatic value in fully illuminated and significant information (e.g., it could lead one to fish better), but also because it wants this information *for its own sake.*[9] Intelligent consciousness enjoys bringing intelligent content into full light. Lonergan calls this the *"pure,* unrestricted desire to know."

What is the source of intelligent consciousness' pure unrestricted desire to know? It must be its tacit awareness of the more illuminated, more significant state of the given's intelligible content. As we shall see, this tacit awareness gives rise to questions, and points to what Lonergan calls "the notion of being"[10] (a tacit awareness of complete intelligibility). But before this can be explained, we need to explore further what intelligent consciousness does to bring the intelligible content of data to full light and significance.

---

7. ". . . [P]articular places and particular times pertain to the empirical residue. They are positive aspects of experience. Each differs from every other" (Lonergan 1992, p. 51).

8. Lonergan 1992, pp. 100-101.

9. "This primordial drive, then, is the pure question. It is prior to any insights, any concepts, any words; for insights, concepts, words have to do with answers, and before we look for answers we want them; such wanting is the pure question. ¶ On the other hand, though the pure question is prior to insights, concepts, and words, it presupposes experiences and images. Just as insight is not the concretely given or imagined, so the pure question is about the concretely given or imagined" (Lonergan 1992, p. 34).

10. See Lonergan 1992, Chapter 12 (pp. 372-98).

So, what does intelligent consciousness do? It sets the intelligible content of the given into *relationship*[11] with the intelligible content of other givens within particular heuristic contexts.

A heuristic context is the generic idea that allows for a very broad interrelationship of intelligible contents. For example, the idea of a map is a way of organizing relative positions among givens; the idea of a clock is a way of organizing the relative sequences and occurrences of givens; the ideas of genus and species are ways of organizing similarities and differences among givens; the idea of causality is a way of organizing conditioneds and conditions among givens; and so forth.

Notice that each of these heuristic contexts corresponds to a question. For example, the map corresponds to the question "Where?"; a clock to the question "When?"; genus, species, similarity, and difference correspond to the question "What?"; and cause, conditioned, and condition correspond to the question "Why?" These questions represent the purest form of heuristic context because they are not limited to a particular *way* of organizing content. For example, the question "Where?" is not limited to a *particular* map or set of maps; it can bring to mind the organizing context for any kind of relative positioning. So also the question "When?" is not limited to a particular clock or calendar, or even to a particular way of measuring time; it can bring to mind the organizing context for any sequence, frequency, or relationship among occurrences. So also with the questions "What?" and "Why?" Thus, the major questions (reflecting the major heuristic contexts) make possible the broadest interrelationship among intelligible contents and are therefore the purest and highest ideas that we have.[12] As such, they enable intelligent consciousness to be aware of what it is looking for.

---

11. ". . . [I]nasmuch as it is the act of organizing intelligence, insight is an apprehension of relations. But among relations are meanings, for meaning seems to be a relation between sign and signified" (Lonergan 1992, pp. 4-5). Also: ". . . [The canon of relevance] notes that this intelligibility immanent in the immediate data of sense resides in the relations of things, not to our senses, but to one another. Thus, mechanics studies the relations of masses, not to our senses, but to one another . . ." (Lonergan 1992, p. 101).

12. There is a paradox associated with the presence of questions (highest heuristic contexts) in human consciousness. Though this paradox is neither the point of this chapter nor ingredient to the proof of God's existence presented in it, it is tangentially germane because it points to a mystery in the operation of human consciousness which may point to a notion (tacit awareness) of complete intelligibility as a horizon of thought within human consciousness (see below, Section III).

The paradox may be expressed as follows: If heuristic contexts are needed to put intelligible content into relationship with other intelligible content, and if these relationships,

So then, what is an act of understanding? As we have seen, it begins with an experience (a presence of a datum — a given — to consciousness). Intelligent consciousness recognizes intelligible content in this datum that can be brought to full light and significance. Since intelligent consciousness is at least tacitly aware of the major heuristic contexts, it desires to bring intelligible content to full light and significance through them. So intelligent consciousness calls a particular heuristic context (or contexts) to mind by asking a question, say, "What is it?" The mere asking of the question activates the heuristic context (because the question would not be intelligible without it). Once the heuristic context is called to mind, previously understood intelligible content is set within this context. It now remains for intelligent consciousness to find an "appropriate fit" for the intelligent content of the new datum.

For example, we might see an elephant (for the first time) walking down the road. Since we are aware of new intelligible content in this datum, we might be provoked to ask, "What is it?" The mere asking of the question reveals that we have already activated high-level organizing ideas such as "similarity" and "difference" within our consciousness. Our tacit awareness of these ideas will cause us to bring other previously understood intelligible contents into this heuristic context. These other intelligible contents would be germane to the intelligible content we are trying to understand. Thus we may have previously understood "dog," "cat," "hippopotamus," "tree," "rock," and "sun." Even if we have come to understand only these six intelligible contents in the past, they will be sufficient for us to have an initial understanding of the new intelligible content. Indeed, even if we have understood only two intelligible contents in the past, we may still see the new content in *relation* to them.

What does this mean about our *very first* act of understanding? It would seem that it would have to have been dyadic (a unity of two distinct

---

in turn, are necessary for ideas, then how did we learn the heuristic contexts (which are our highest ideas)? It would seem that we could not have learned these ideas from experience because we would have had to use them in order to have abstracted them from experience. In short, if heuristic contexts are needed to transform the intelligibility of experience into the intelligibility of ideas, and heuristic contexts are themselves ideas, then they could not have come from the intelligibility of experience (we would have had to use them in order to have learned them from experience). This suggests that heuristic contexts are present to intelligent consciousness prior to experience. As we shall see at the conclusion of this section and in Section III, the same holds true for the notion of complete intelligibility (what Lonergan terms the "notion of being").

contents). We would have to have seen the similarities and differences of two distinct intelligible contents in a single act (an act comparing, say, a bird and a rock). Once this first act of understanding is complete, we can continue to have dyadic acts of understanding; but this is not necessary, for after the first dyadic act of understanding is complete, we can set the intelligible content of new data into relationship with the intelligible content of previously understood data.

Now, let us continue with our example. Recall that by asking the question "What is it?" we have called to mind the heuristic context of similarities and differences, and also previous germane contents (such as dog, cat, hippopotamus, tree, rock, and sun). We may now look for an appropriate fit within these data. We may notice the new datum (the elephant) is similar to cat, dog, and hippopotamus in that it is living and capable of sensation; and we may concomitantly notice that it is dissimilar to rock and sun in these respects. We may notice it is similar to tree in that it is living, but different from tree in that it has sensation and desire, etc.

Notice that the recognition of similarities and differences brings the intelligibility of the elephant's activities, powers, and characteristics more fully to light. The intelligibility of sensation is certainly within the elephant, but it is brought fully to light only when an elephant is set into *relationship* with a non-sentient being (such as a tree) in an act of understanding (in the form of an idea). So also with the intelligibility of "life." The intelligibility of life exists within the elephant, but it comes fully to light only when set in relationship to a non-living being (such as a rock). The interrelationship of data within the heuristic context of similarity and difference can bring out the intelligibility of all the elephant's activities, powers, and characteristics.

Furthermore, intelligibility can be brought to light by relationships among relationships. For example, "bigger than" and "smaller than" could be set out more precisely by a standard of comparison, such as a man's foot; the man's foot, in turn, could be replaced by a very exact standard such as a ruler, and the ruler could be subdivided, and so forth. The subdivision of the ruler could give rise to the recognition of units of measurement, and the units of measurement in turn could give rise to the recognition of abstract numbers. Now, the intelligibility of *some* of these ideas is intrinsic to the elephant, for example, "larger than the cat," "ten human feet taller than the cat," "ten feet tall from head to foot," etc. Even though the intelligibility of these ideas cannot be brought fully to light without a context of relationships, the intelligibility is intrinsic to the elephant.

Yet, after a certain point, the relationship among relationships gives rise to abstract ideas that are *not* intrinsic to the elephant *per se*. They may have been derived from relationships among relationships that originally began with an elephant and a cat, but their intelligibility cannot be limited to the particular data from which they were derived. Here is where the intelligibility of ideas like "number" comes to light. The elephant does not possess the intelligibility of "ten"; it possesses the intelligibility of being ten feet tall or "being ten human feet taller than the cat." But the notion of ten itself is intelligible when relationships are set into relationship with other relationships. When the intelligibility of measured size is set into relationship with quantity (e.g., ten elephants) and frequencies (e.g., three appearances of the full moon), the similarity among measurements (e.g., units and aggregation of units) becomes more and more evident, and the kinds of measurement and the rote activity of counting become less important. At this juncture, the abstract ideas of "unit" and "aggregation" become more apparent.

The intelligibility of number may now be separated from any sentient data, and can be understood solely in relationship to other numbers and the idea of aggregation ("plus"). For example, 2 makes sense in relation to 1 through the idea of aggregation ("plus"); and 1 makes sense in relation to 2 through the idea of subtraction ("minus"); etc. Intelligent consciousness grasps all three abstract ideas as a triad; and without this triad — this three-fold relationship — none of the parts would be intelligible. The sentient datum from which these abstract concepts emerged is now in the background while the relationship of ideas is in the foreground.[13]

Notice that when intelligibility is in the form of an idea (i.e., within a relationship, within a heuristic context, within an act of understanding, within intelligent consciousness), it can be detached from the empirical residue from which it was derived (i.e., the datum's individual manifestation at a particular place and time within the empirical world), for the empirical residue is no longer needed as a repository for intelligibility (information). An idea has become the new repository. Now this new repository does not limit (and does not have to limit) intelligibility to a specific thing, or a specific place and time (a specific spatio-temporal juxtaposition). Therefore, the in-

---

13. Lonergan illustrates this in his classic example of the cartwheel, which provides a *clue* to the immanent intelligibility of a perfect circle. In order to move from the cartwheel to the perfect circle, intelligent consciousness must remove all irrelevant sentient data from the cartwheel. When this is done, three interrelated ideal concepts are revealed: "central point," "infinity of equidistant radii," and "circle." The intelligibility of each of these concepts comes to light in relationship to the other two. Thus, each part must be seen within the context of the interrelated whole. See Lonergan 1992, pp. 31-32.

telligibility in this new repository can be meaningfully applied to a *multiplicity* of individuals and a *multiplicity* of spatio-temporal juxtapositions; and more importantly, it does not have to be applied to any individuals or spatio-temporal juxtapositions at all. The idea is, as it were, a pure state of intelligibility (completely detached from empirical, spatio-temporal, and individual limitations) that can be related to other pure states of intelligibility (also detached from empirical, spatio-temporal, and individual limitations).

For example, when the intelligibility of "elephant" is detached from the old repository (its empirical residue) by being taken into the new repository (i.e., an idea within a relationship within a heuristic structure within an act of understanding within intelligent consciousness), it no longer has to be attached to the empirical residue of the specific elephant from which it came; it can now be applied to many elephants, and therefore can be a predicate as well as a subject. It can then be used as an organizational principle for comparisons among different individual elephants, different species of elephants, etc.; it can ground other corollary ideas, which may be applied to situations that have nothing to do with elephants ("Joe was positively elephantine").

We may now want to make a distinction between words and ideas. Words are symbolic expressions communicated through visual, auditory, or tactile cues, pointing to a referent. The power of the word is the power to point beyond itself to that referent. The referent could be a specific individual (e.g., "Bob Spitzer"), or an idea of an individual (e.g., "man"), or an idea interrelating ideas (e.g., "thirty-two"), or an idea interrelating "interrelated groups of ideas" (e.g., the tensor calculus). Ideas are not words — an idea is intelligibility detached from empirical residue within a relationship within a heuristic context within an act of understanding within intelligent consciousness. Inasmuch as words have the power to point to what is beyond themselves (to refer), they can refer to ideas. Learning a word does not mean learning an idea. A child can learn the word "thirty-two" and have a tacit awareness that it has something to do with counting, but not grasp the specific intelligibility of "thirty-two."

Words are invaluable not only in the communication of ideas, but also in the classification and organization of ideas. Their power to refer allows them to be used as "shorthand" in the assembling of complex ideas and also in the communication of those complex ideas. This is particularly true of words that do not refer to specific individuals or ideas of individuals — that is, words that refer to relationships among ideas and relationships among relationships of ideas; for these last two referents have no correlate that can be pointed to or "imagined" in "picture-thinking." Here, the only way of assembling and communicating these ideas is through the use of words.

Certain kinds of intelligibility can only exist within the domain of the new repository (i.e., ideas) because they require a relationship in order for their intelligibility to become apparent. This would be true for the ideas of "larger than" and "smaller than" that we saw above. Even though the proposition "the elephant is larger than the cat" may be derived from the intelligibility of the elephant and the cat (in the empirical domain), the intelligibility of "larger than" could only exist in an idea since it must exist within a relationship (in an act of comparing). The same holds true for the elephant being ten feet taller than the cat. Once again, the intelligibility of the elephant and the cat may be found within the empirical domain, but the intelligibility of "ten feet taller than" must be contained within an act of comparison that makes use of both a measurement system and numeric system which can only exist in an idea (an interrelationship within a heuristic structure within an act of understanding within intelligent consciousness).[14]

Why is this so important? Because when we get to the fourth step of the proof of God's existence (Section II.D) we will be showing that unrestricted intelligibility has to be an unrestricted act of understanding. We can now incipiently see why this must be so. Unrestricted intelligibility cannot be limited to an empirical residue, specific spatio-temporal juxtapositions, or even specific instances of an idea. Unrestricted intelligibility would have to be completely detachable from everything that would limit intelligibility, and therefore, it would have to be an idea — a very special idea — an idea that is not limited to even specific relationships within specific heuristic contexts; an idea without any *specific* heuristic context, an idea whose heuristic context is complete intelligibility itself. This will be explained in detail in Section II.D.

II. Proof of the Existence of God

In the introduction to this chapter, I noted that there is an opportunity to give an alternative version of Lonergan's proof that begins with an ontologi-

---

14. By now it will be clear that understanding is not memory. Memory is the "retrievable storage" of what is experienced, imagined, or understood. Understanding is the conversion of intelligibility from "intelligibility embedded in empirical residue" to "intelligibility freed from that residue within an interrelationship within a heuristic context within intelligent consciousness." One can memorize what is understood, but memory is not understanding.

cal rather than an epistemological base. Though this version does not reflect Lonergan's priorities, it does respect the centrality of causality in his proof.

I will define causality in the same way as in the previous chapter because the definition of "causality" as "a fulfillment of a conditioned reality's conditions" does not unduly limit the notion to a particular kind of physics (such as Newtonian physics) and can apply to every known intelligible structure (from quantum theory to inflationary cosmology and beyond).

This proof of an unconditioned reality presents a virtually unassailable ontological basis for the other four steps in the proof of God's existence because the denial of its conclusion requires that nothing exist, which is patently contrary to fact. The proof proceeds as follows:

A. There must be at least one unconditioned reality.
B. An unconditioned reality must be unrestricted intelligibility.
C. Unrestricted intelligibility must be unique — one and only one.
D. Unique unrestricted intelligibility must be an unrestricted act of understanding — understanding itself.
E. All other intelligibility besides the one unrestricted act of understanding must be restricted and be a thought content of the one unrestricted act of understanding.

II.A. There Must Be at Least One Unconditioned Reality

I will present a brief rendition of the proof for an unconditioned reality given in the previous chapter (Section I). Recall from that chapter that an infinite number of conditioned realities without an unconditioned reality is equivalent to absolutely nothing, because without an unconditioned reality, there would be only conditioned realities. This would mean that every conditioned reality, say, CR_1, would have to depend on some other *conditioned* reality, say, CR_2, in order to exist. Hence, it is *nothing* until CR_2 exists and fulfills its conditions. Similarly, CR_2 would also have to depend on some other *conditioned* reality, say, CR_3, for its existence, and it would likewise be *nothing* until CR_3 exists and fulfills *its* conditions. And so forth, *ad infinitum*. Since every hypothetical conditioned reality is dependent upon other *nonexistent* conditioned realities for its existence, it will never come into existence. It does not matter whether one posits an infinite number of them; for each one in the series of dependence is still equal to nothing without the reality of the others. But if the "others" are nothing without others, and those "others" are nothing without still others, it does not matter if one postulates an infinite number of others (or arranges the infinite number of others in a circle). They are all still nothing in their dependence upon nonexistent conditions. Therefore, the hypothesis that there are only conditioned realities in "all reality" will always result in all reality being *nothing*, which is patently contrary to fact (including the fact of the reader's existence). Therefore, there must be at least one unconditioned reality in all reality. Every conditioned reality would have to depend on such an unconditioned reality for the ultimate fulfillment of its conditions.[15]

Since an unconditioned reality is not dependent on the fulfillment of any conditions for its existence, it must exist through itself. This "existence through itself" does not mean being the cause of itself; for, as noted in the previous chapter, "*causa sui*" is intrinsically contradictory, for a self-causing being would never be able to come into existence. It would have to exist before it existed in order to cause itself to exist. Put into our definition of "causality" (the fulfillment of a conditioned reality's conditions), *causa sui* would entail that a reality's existence be dependent on the fulfillment of conditions within itself; but this means that the fulfillment of this reality's conditions be dependent on the existence of the reality (because the fulfillment of the conditions is intrinsic to it). But the reality cannot yet exist because its conditions (within it) have not yet been fulfilled, and these conditions cannot be fulfilled because they are within a nonexistent reality. In sum, there is vicious circularity of nonexistence — the fulfillment of conditions does not exist because the reality does not exist, and the reality does not exist because the fulfillment of conditions (within the reality) does not exist.

From the above it is clear that "existence through itself" implies no fulfillment of conditions, and therefore, no conditions of existence whatsoever. Inasmuch as this reality would have to be the ultimate fulfillment of any conditioned reality's conditions, it must have the power to fulfill such conditions. Therefore, at least one unconditioned reality (one power existing through itself) capable of fulfilling conditioned realities' conditions must exist.

---

15. Notice that this argument does not depend on showing the impossibility of an infinite *regression*. Rather, it depends solely on the recognition that an infinite *amount* of "dependency on the fulfillment of conditions" is equal to absolutely nothing without a reality that does *not* depend on the fulfillment of conditions. Zero × infinity = zero.

II.B. An Unconditioned Reality Must Be Unrestricted Intelligibility

This proof has four premises:

1) If any reality has restricted intelligibility, then it will leave coherent questions unanswered about itself.
2) If any reality leaves coherent questions unanswered about itself, then its intelligibility is grounded in reality beyond itself.
3) If any reality's intelligibility is grounded in reality beyond itself, then its existence is conditioned by that reality beyond itself.
4) But the existence of an unconditioned reality cannot be conditioned by anything.

Therefore, an unconditioned reality's intelligibility cannot be grounded in reality beyond itself (*modus tollens* with Premise #3).

Therefore, an unconditioned reality cannot leave any coherent questions about itself unanswered (*modus tollens* with Premise #2).

Therefore, an unconditioned reality cannot be restricted in its intelligibility (*modus tollens* with Premise #1).

Proof of Premise #1: If any reality has restricted intelligibility, then it will leave coherent questions[16] *unanswered about itself.* Any restricted intelligible must leave a question unanswered because the intelligibility (information) available to answer questions about it is restricted. Thus, there can always be more questions about a restricted reality than there will be intelligibility (information) available to answer them. Let us suppose, for example, that an intelligent subject is querying about a particular intelligible (questionable) reality, like a tree. Initially, one asks questions about it that are answerable by intelligibility (information) intrinsic to the tree. What makes its leaves green? Chlorophyll. What gives rise to chlorophyll? Molecular processes described by X, Y, Z. What gives rise to those molecular processes? Photosynthesis — its energy source. What gives rise to photosynthesis? Eventually,

---

16. A "coherent question" is one that does not ask a contradiction (e.g., "Why is the circle a square in the same respect at the same place and time?") or about an unreal state of affairs (e.g., "How does light travel through an ethereal medium?" — Einstein disproved the existence of an ethereal medium in the Theory of Relativity).

one will notice that the questions can no longer be answered by intelligibility (information) intrinsic to the tree *alone*. One has to begin examining electrochemical reactions and molecular structures, which are dependent upon atomic and subatomic processes, which give rise to questions about electrical fields, which, in turn, give rise to questions about fields and energy. At this juncture, the answers to the questions about the tree's intelligibility have gone far beyond the tree's intelligibility alone to answer.

In taking the vantage point of a questioning *person,* one reaches the point at which the answers derived from the intelligibility (information intrinsic to the tree) are subject to further questions. But the intelligibility (information) necessary to answer them must be found from intelligibility *outside* the tree. Why? Because the intelligible reality (the tree) has a *restricted* amount of intelligibility. Inasmuch as the *answers* from a restricted intelligible have an *intrinsic limit* (i.e., they *do not keep on going indefinitely*), they will eventually be open to further questions that cannot be answered by the restricted intelligible reality alone. Thus, we might say that every restricted intelligible reality is *more* questionable than answerable. There will always be a domain of answers that give rise to more questions than the intelligibility of the reality can answer by itself. This is the fate of all restricted intelligibility.

Notice that the "intelligibility sufficient to answer a question about a given reality" is not linked to an intelligent subject. It resides in the *reality* about which questions can be asked. Thus, every reality is a questionable — an "exhaustively questionable," irrespective of the intelligence or curiosity of any questioning subject.

Proof of Premise #2: If any reality leaves coherent questions unanswered about itself, then its intelligibility is grounded in reality beyond itself. For Lonergan, every coherent question must have a correct answer because every coherent question is open to the *entire range* of coherent answers (a coherent answer is one that is non-contradictory). Notice that any given question "Why?" or "What?" etc., is open to the whole range of X and really possible not-X, and the entire range of X and really possible not-X covers all possible coherent answers except absolute nothingness.[17]

For example, I may be looking at a datum having field-like characteristics and I may ask, "What is it?" It might be an electron, but then it might be

---

17. ". . . [W]hat is apart from being is nothing, and so what is apart from intelligibility is nothing. It follows that to talk about mere matters of fact that admit no explanation is to talk about nothing" (Lonergan 1992, p. 675; see also pp. 676-77).

something else (the whole range covered by "really possible non-electrons" — such as proton, neutron, undefined quantum field . . .). But "really possible non-electrons" not only includes electromagnetic fields and particles which are not electrons, but also all "non-electromagnetic" realities (e.g., space-time fields, gravitation, etc.). The only term that can adequately represent what is not covered by the intelligibility of electron and the entire range of "really possible non-electrons" is "nothing." But "nothing" cannot adequately respond to the question "What is it?" about a given questionable *reality;* for that would be tantamount to calling the intelligibility of a given *reality* "nothing," which is a contradiction.

For Lonergan, if every question about a reality has a correct answer, then the complete set of correct answers to the complete set of questions exists. What does he mean by this? He means that there must be sufficient intelligibility in reality to answer every question that can be asked about reality. Thus, the intelligibility necessary to correctly answer the complete set of coherent questions about reality must exist in reality.

How do the above points affect Premise #2? If a restricted intelligible is one that does not have sufficient intelligibility to answer all questions about itself, then the intelligibility sufficient to answer those questions must exist elsewhere in reality (beyond that specific questionable intelligible). If it did not, then the intelligibility (information) necessary to answer these coherent questions about reality would not exist at all. This would mean that the answer to the coherent question "What is it?" about a questionable reality, is "*Nothing.*" Which, in turn, would mean that the intelligibility of a questionable *reality* is *nothing,* which is a contradiction.

Let us suppose, for example, that I am examining data resembling electrons. I might ask the question, "What is it?" The answer may come, "An electron." I would then ask, "What makes electrons function in this way?" Now, the moment I ask this question, I notice that the intelligibility intrinsic to electrons alone cannot answer the question. I cannot give the answer "Nothing" (because the intelligibility of the real is not "nothing"). So I must make recourse to reality that is more fundamental than "electron," such as electromagnetic fields, which provokes the question, "What are electromagnetic fields?" But then I find that electromagnetic fields cannot fully answer the question "What?" about themselves, which provokes me to make recourse to even more fundamental realities, such as "energy" (the common element in all physical forces, actions, and interactions) and "space-time." These realities are themselves questionable (e.g., "What is energy?"), but they do not have sufficient intelligibility to answer the question "What?"

about themselves either. And so I am forced again to move to even more fundamental realities beyond energy and space-time, such as "being" or "existence," and so forth.[18]

What is the point here? If every coherent question must have a correct answer, and the intelligibility for that answer cannot be "Nothing," and does not reside in the questionable reality itself, then it must be grounded somewhere else *in reality* — that is, in reality that is beyond the questionable reality (e.g., a more fundamental reality, or a condition of the reality, or an ultimate fulfillment of a conditioned reality's conditions, etc.).

Notice again that we are not speaking about the capacity of human intellection or the intelligence of any particular consciousness. We are speaking about intelligibility (information) *in reality.* If every coherent question must have a correct answer in reality, then there exists intelligibility in reality sufficient to answer that question. If the intelligibility does not reside in a particular questionable reality alone, then it must be grounded in reality beyond a particular questionable reality, because the intelligibility of the real cannot be "nothing."

Proof of Premise #3: If any reality's intelligibility is grounded in reality beyond itself, then its existence is conditioned by that reality beyond itself. The key insight here is as follows. If the intelligibility of a particular questionable reality is grounded in a reality beyond itself, then the questionable reality could not exist without the existence and operation of the reality beyond itself.[19] This applies to all possible questions: "What?" "Why?" "Where?" "When?" "How many?" "How frequently?" "How much?" etc.

The above insight is most easily seen with respect to the question **"Why?"** because, as Lonergan notes, the question "Why?" is asking for an explanation (an intelligible reason) for *existence.*[20] That explanation could

18. See Lonergan 1992, Chapter 19, Section 8.

19. Notice that Lonergan links "dependence for intelligibility" to causality, and shows that different kinds of dependence for intelligibility are linked to different kinds of causality: "In general, causality denotes the objective and real counterpart of the questions and further questions raised by the detached, disinterested, and unrestricted desire to know. As such questions are of various kinds, distinctions are to be drawn between different types of causes . . ." (Lonergan 1992, p. 674). In this proof, I show that each kind of question (Why? What? etc.) manifests a different kind of intelligibility, and *every* "reliance on intelligibility beyond itself" entails conditionedness. Therefore, an unconditioned reality cannot be dependent on intelligibility beyond itself, and therefore must be unrestricted in its intelligibility.

20. "If nothing existed, there would be no one to ask questions and nothing to ask questions about. The most fundamental of all questions, then, asks about existence . . ." (Lonergan 1992, p. 676).

either be intrinsic to the questionable reality itself (implying that the reality *exists* through itself and is therefore unconditioned in its existence), or the answer could be grounded in something other than the questionable reality (i.e., it is a conditioned reality and therefore, its *existence* depends on the fulfillment of conditions beyond itself).[21] Now, if a particular questionable reality does not have sufficient intelligibility to answer the question "Why?" about itself, then it is *not* an unconditioned reality, and therefore, it must be dependent on the fulfillment of conditions beyond itself. Thus, any questionable reality that leaves open the question "Why?" must be dependent on some reality beyond itself for its existence. Restated in the terms of the premise, any reality that is *restricted in its intelligibility* to answer the question "Why?" about itself, must be *conditioned in its existence*.

The question **"How?"** (implying, "How does it act or operate?") is a corollary of the question "Why?" If the intelligibility of a questionable reality is sufficient to answer all questions "How?" about itself, then that questionable reality acts through itself; however, if the intelligibility of a questionable reality is *not* sufficient to answer all questions "How?" about itself, then that questionable reality does not act through itself, and therefore acts through another. Now activity and existence are commensurate. For example, if a cat can never *act* like a cat without various cells and structures of cells, etc., then the cat can't really *be* a cat without those cells and structures of cells. Similarly, if cells can never act like a cell without molecules and structures of molecules, then they cannot *be* cells without those molecules and structures of molecules. If a reality can never act in a way that makes it "to be what it is" without the fulfillment of certain conditions, then it cannot "*be* what it is" without the fulfillment of those conditions. If a reality is conditioned in its essential activity, it is also conditioned in its existence. Thus, if the intelligibility of a particular reality is not sufficient to answer all questions "How?" about itself, then it is conditioned in its existence. Once again we see that if a reality is restricted in intelligibility, then it is conditioned in its existence.

The same holds true for the question **"What?"** Let us return to the example used above about answering questions about data resembling electrons. Recall that electrons cannot completely answer the question "What is it?" about themselves. One must make recourse to more fundamental reali-

---

21. ". . . [E]very proportionate being that exists, exists conditionally; it exists inasmuch as the conditions of its existence happen to be fulfilled; and the contingency of that happening cannot be eliminated by appealing to another happening that equally is contingent" (Lonergan 1992, p. 677).

ties like electromagnetic fields. But notice that electrons are dependent on electromagnetic fields not only for their *intelligibility,* but also for their *existence.* If a questionable reality is not completely intelligible without a reality beyond it (e.g., more fundamental than it, such as electromagnetic fields), then it cannot *exist* without that reality beyond it. Electrons are not completely intelligible without electromagnetic fields, and they cannot *exist* without electromagnetic fields.

The same holds true for electromagnetic fields. Recall from above that electromagnetic fields are not completely intelligible without making recourse to energy and space-time; so they are dependent on energy and space-time not only for their intelligibility, but also for their existence. Electromagnetic fields cannot be real if energy and space-time are not simultaneously real. (Note that the intelligibility of energy and space-time go far beyond the intelligibility of electromagnetic fields.)

The same holds true for energy and space-time, which leads us to recognize more fundamental realities (such as "unconditioned reality itself" or "being itself") to ground *both* their intelligibility and their *existence.* Again we see *that what is restricted in intelligibility is conditioned in existence.*

All other questions, such as "Where?" "When?" "How much?" "How many?" "How frequently?" etc., imply even more conditions to existence than the questions "Why?" "How?" or "What?" For example, the question **"Where?"** implies a location; a location, in turn, implies that intelligibility is restricted to a relative position, which means it is conditioned by a spatial manifold (or some other contemporaneous manifold that can hold together distinct relative positions "here" and "there" simultaneously). If the spatial manifold does not exist, then the relative position does not exist; and if the relative position does not exist, then intelligibility in that relative position does not exist either. Once again we see that restriction of intelligibility implies a condition of existence.

The same holds true for the question **"When?"** Any questionable reality to which the question "When?" properly applies must be restricted (or restrictable) in its intelligibility to a particular span of time, which implies that it is conditioned by a temporal manifold (a non-contemporaneous manifold unifying "earlier" and "later"[22]). This implies that the questionable reality is not unconditioned in its existence.

The same holds true for all questions pertaining to the quantification of reality (e.g., How much? How many? How frequently? etc.). As will be shown,

22. See Chapter 5, Section II.C for a detailed explanation of this.

any reality that is quantifiable in its magnitude, spatio-temporal position, or frequency of appearance, must be restricted in its intelligibility, and if it is restricted in its intelligibility, then it must be dependent on a reality beyond it (e.g., more fundamental than it) for its intelligibility and existence.

The question **"How much?"** reveals a specific quantity. A specific quantity, in turn, must inhere in a quantifiable reality, and a quantifiable reality must be restricted. As restricted, it must depend on reality beyond itself. For example, the charge of an electron is $e = 1.6 \times 10^{-19}$ coulombs. But this particular quantity must inhere in some particular quantifiable reality (i.e., an electron); but inasmuch as this electron is quantifiable, it must also be restricted in its intelligibility, which means it must be dependent on a more fundamental reality for *both* its intelligibility and existence — electromagnetic energy. (The explanation for why it is dependent on a more fundamental reality for *both* its intelligibility and existence is given above in the explanation of the question "What?") Therefore, every reality about which the question "How much?" can be coherently asked must be dependent upon reality beyond itself for both its intelligibility and existence (i.e., it must be *conditioned* in its existence).

The question **"How many?"** implies distinct instances of realities within a group; and this group implies some kind of contemporaneous unification of the individuals in that group (such as a spatial manifold) which, in turn, implies dependency on this contemporaneously unifying manifold for both intelligibility and existence (for if a spatial manifold did not exist, the individuals within the group could not be contemporaneously unified, and therefore, there would be nothing about which to ask the question "How many?").

The question **"How frequently?"** implies a finite time of appearance, and a finite time of appearance implies being conditioned by time (a non-contemporaneous manifold). Being conditioned by time, in turn, implies dependency on a non-contemporaneous manifold for both intelligibility and "remaining in *existence*" (duration).

We may now summarize our results. If any reality is restricted in its intelligibility in any way (e.g., Why? What? How? Where? When? How much? How many? How frequently? etc.), then either (1) it does not exist or act through itself (incomplete answer to the questions "Why?" and "How?" respectively), in which case it will have to exist or act through another, implying that it is conditioned in its existence, or (2) its intelligibility is insufficient to answer the question "What?" or any of its correlates ("Where?" "When?" "How much?" "How many?" "How frequently?" etc.) about itself, which implies that it must be dependent for its intelligibility on a reality beyond it (e.g., more fundamental than it), which implies, in turn, that it is conditioned by this more fundamental reality for its existence. In either case, if a reality is restricted in its intelligibility, it must also be conditioned in its existence by something beyond it.

Proof of Premise #4: But the existence of an unconditioned reality cannot be conditioned by anything. This is obviously *a priori* true to avoid the contradiction that an unconditioned reality has conditions of its existence.

Conclusion:

Therefore, an unconditioned reality's intelligibility cannot be grounded in a reality beyond itself (*modus tollens* with Premise #3).

Therefore, an unconditioned reality cannot leave any coherent questions about itself unanswered (*modus tollens* with Premise #2).

Therefore, an unconditioned reality cannot be restricted in its intelligibility (*modus tollens* with Premise #1). This conclusion may be restated as follows: an unconditioned reality must be unrestricted intelligibility.

We may now proceed to the next step, which shows that unrestricted intelligibility must be unique (one and only one).

II.C. Unrestricted Intelligibility Must Be Unique — One and Only One

This argument has four premises:

1) If there are two or more of anything, then there must be some difference between them (for if there were no difference between them, then they would be the selfsame, and therefore one).
2) But if there is a difference between them, it would have to be either (a) a difference of formal intelligibility or (b) a difference of instantiation (or both).
3) But a difference of formal intelligibility among two unrestricted intelligibles is intrinsically contradictory (restricted unrestricted intelligibility).
4) And two or more instances of unrestricted intelligibility are also intrinsically contradictory (restricted unrestricted intelligibility).

Therefore, there cannot be a multiplicity of unrestricted intelligibles (*modus tollens*).

Therefore, unrestricted intelligibility must be one and only one.

Proof of Premise #1: If there are two or more of anything, then there must be some difference between them. This is *a priori* true, for if there is no difference of any kind (i.e., no difference as to intelligibility or instance), the two hypothetical realities are in fact the selfsame, and therefore one.

Proof of Premise #2: But if there is a difference between them, it would have to be either (a) a difference of formal intelligibility or (b) a difference of instantiation (or both). There are two ways in which realities can be differentiated — according to their formal intelligibility or their instantiation. Formal intelligibility means a difference of intelligibility irrespective of distinct instantiation. For example, two electrons are the same from the vantage point of formal intelligibility, but distinct in instantiation, while an electron and a proton have distinct formal intelligibilities *as well as* distinct instantiations.

Differences in formal intelligibility are differences in characteristics, qualities, kind of power, *way* of acting, or *way* or *kind* of being. If there is no difference in any of these, then there is no difference in formal intelligibility, but there could still be a difference in instantiation.

Differences in instantiation can occur extrinsically, intrinsically, or both. Examples of *extrinsic* instantiation would be instantiation through a continuum or a manifold, such as a spatial manifold where two intelligibles are separated through a difference of relative position within the continuum. Another (more metaphysical) extrinsic instantiation might be being two distinct thoughts in the mind of God (e.g., a thought of this universe and a thought of heaven, where the two thoughts are not linked together by a continuum or a manifold, but rather held together by *different instances* of divine mentation).

Intrinsic instantiation could occur through a principle of instantiation infused into formally intelligible content. Two distinct infusions of this principle could then constitute two distinct instances of identical intelligibility (without need of a continuum or manifold to separate them).

The distinction between extrinsic and intrinsic instantiation is not important for this proof. I make recourse to it only to show some examples of how two identical formal intelligibilities can be distinct from one another through instantiation. It is important to see only that if two or more realities are not differentiated according to their formal intelligibility, they must be differentiated according to instantiation, otherwise they are the selfsame one (and the multiplicity is merely hypothetical).

Proof of Premise #3: But a difference of formal intelligibility among two unrestricted intelligibles is intrinsically contradictory (restricted unrestricted intelligibility). As noted above, if there is a difference according to formal intelligibility, then one intelligible reality would have to have some formal intelligibility that the other one did *not* (that is, one reality would have to have formal intelligibility to answer some questions that the other one did not). Now this cannot be properly applied to the case of two hypothetical *unrestricted* intelligibles, because that would imply that one unrestricted intelligible had some formal intelligibility that the other one did not (i.e., had formal intelligibility sufficient to answer questions that the other one did not). But the intelligible reality that could *not* answer questions that the *other* intelligible reality *could* answer would have to be restricted in its formal intelligibility (*a priori*). This would give rise to an intrinsic contradiction, namely, the restricted intelligibility of a reality that is supposedly unrestricted in its intelligibility. For this reason, there cannot be a difference among unrestricted intelligibles according to formal intelligibility.

*Proof of Premise #4: And two or more **instances** of unrestricted intelligibility are also intrinsically contradictory (restricted unrestricted intelligibility).* The general argument for this premise is as follows: If there were two or more instances of unrestricted intelligibility (which are identical in their formal intelligibility, but not in their instantiation), then there would still have to be a restriction to their intelligibility implied by their distinct instantiation, because their intelligibility is restricted to their particular instance, which cannot completely extend into the other instance or instances if the difference between the instances is to be preserved.

The mere postulation of a second instance of unrestricted intelligibility presents an irresolvable dilemma. Either there will be no difference between the two instances of unrestricted intelligibility (in which case they are really the selfsame one), or there is a difference between the two instances, but one of the instances must be "restricted unrestricted intelligibility" (a contradiction). Let us examine this more closely. If one says that the intelligibility of Instance #1 extends completely into the intelligibility of Instance #2 (such that Instance #2 does not answer any questions about its particular instantiation that Instance #1 does not also identically answer, and Instance #1 does not answer any questions about its particular instantiation that Instance #2 does not also identically answer), then there is absolutely no difference between Instance #1 and Instance #2. The supposed instantiation is merely illusory.

Alternatively, if one says that the intelligibility of Instance #1 does *not* extend completely into the intelligibility of Instance #2 (or the intelligibility of Instance #2 does not extend completely into the intelligibility of Instance #1 — which means that Instance #1 or Instance #2 can answer some questions about its particular instantiation that the other one cannot answer — which preserves the difference between them), then at least one of the instances of unrestricted intelligibility would have to be *restricted* (because there are some questions that one of them can answer about its particular instantiation that the other one could *not*). We again see that the instance that can*not* answer some questions must be restricted, meaning that at least one of the instances of unrestricted intelligibility must be restricted in intelligibility — an obvious contradiction.

Therefore, one can either preserve the difference between the two instances (and get an intrinsic contradiction — "restricted unrestricted intelligibility"), or one can blend the intelligibility of the two supposed instances completely into one another (in which case there is only one reality, since there is no difference). In either case, one and only one unrestricted intelligibility is allowable.

Though the above argument needs no further support, there is another telling argument against a multiplicity of instances of unrestricted intelligibility. It arises out of the need for a reality beyond (more fundamental than) all *instances* of unrestricted intelligibility through which these multiple instances exist. Such a "reality beyond (more fundamental than) the instances that exist through it" would have to have intelligibility beyond that of any particular instance. It would have to answer questions that any particular instance of unrestricted intelligibility could not answer. This would once again imply that the *instances* of unrestricted intelligibility are restricted.

Recall from above that there are two ways through which instantiation can occur: extrinsically and intrinsically. Extrinsic instantiation occurs through a medium (such as space-time, where one instance of something has a different relative position than another instance within a continuum — a unity). Now, if there were two instances of unrestricted intelligibility separated by a spatio-temporal continuum, that spatio-temporal continuum (with its contents) would have to be able to answer questions that either of the instances of unrestricted intelligibility could not (because it has more content — two or three instances of unrestricted intelligibility as distinct from merely one). But if this were true, then all the instances of supposedly unrestricted intelligibility would have to be restricted (and therefore all of them would be intrinsically contradictory — restricted unrestricted intelligibility).

Now, extrinsic instantiation does not have to be through a spatio-temporal continuum. It could be through another medium that keeps the two instances of reality distinct (such as distinct thoughts in the mind of God). But again, one encounters the same problem, namely that the medium through which instances of unrestricted intelligibility are extrinsically instantiated (in this case, the mind of God) would have to be able to answer questions that each of the two distinct instances of unrestricted intelligibility (contents of the divine mind) would not be able to answer. Once again, this implies that all hypothetical *instances* of unrestricted intelligibility would have to be restricted — another intrinsic contradiction.

Well, what about *intrinsic* instantiation? An example of this might be a "principle of instantiation" infused within distinct realities. This would allow two realities with similar formal intelligibility to "have something" that the other one did not). Now this presents the same problem as extrinsic instantiation, for both instances of unrestricted intelligibility would have to be real, and therefore reality (the totality of all that is real) would have to be more intelligible than any of the intrinsic instantiations of unrestricted intelligibility it encompasses. But this implies that every instance of unrestricted intelligibility is restricted because reality must be able to answer questions that distinct instances of unrestricted intelligibility cannot. Again, we are confronted with every instance of unrestricted intelligibility in reality being restricted (meaning that all of them are intrinsically contradictory).[23]

---

23. Notice that reality (the totality of all that is) is not *more* than unrestricted intelligibility (i.e., unrestricted intelligibility *plus* restricted intelligibility), because all restricted intelligibility must exist through unrestricted intelligibility. It can never, as it were, lie outside of unrestricted intelligibility so as to add to it, because it is completely derivative upon unrestricted intelligibility — much like the contents of my thought are derivative upon my act of thinking. Thus, I do not say that my thoughts add to me, because they exist through me. Even though the contents of my thoughts are distinct from my act of thinking, they do not add anything more to me ontologically since they exist through me. Similarly, restricted intelligibility may be viewed as a thought-content of an unrestricted act of understanding. (We will show, in the next subsection, that unrestricted intelligibility is an unrestricted act of understanding.) As such, reality cannot be considered to be more than this unrestricted act of understanding, because the thought-contents of an unrestricted act of understanding do not add anything ontologically to the unrestricted act of understanding since they exist through it. Thus, reality is the one unrestricted act of understanding and all its thought-contents in one single whole. The restricted thought-contents are distinct from the unrestricted act of understanding, but they do not add anything to it ontologically. This will be explained in subsections II.D and II.E.

Therefore, it really does not matter whether instantiation occurs extrinsically or intrinsically, for reality (the totality of all that is) will be able to answer questions that any instance of reality cannot answer. But this cannot be the case if the instances of reality are unrestricted intelligibility, for this implies that each and every instance of supposedly unrestricted intelligibility is restricted (an obvious contradiction). Therefore, a multiplicity of instances of unrestricted intelligibility must in all cases be illusory, meaning that there can only be one unrestricted intelligibility.

All other intelligibility in reality must be restricted and must exist through the one unrestricted intelligibility, because the one unrestricted intelligibility must be its ground. (This will be explained in the next two subsections.)

Conclusion. We can now see why unrestricted intelligibility must be unique (one and only one). Recall that differentiation must occur through formal intelligibility or instantiation, or both; but any difference in formal intelligibility among two or more hypothetical unrestricted intelligibilities requires that the second (or more) "unrestricted intelligible(s)" be intrinsically contradictory (restricted unrestricted intelligibility); and any difference in instantiation among two or more hypothetical unrestricted intelligibles requires that the two intelligibles *not completely* extend into one another (to preserve the difference between them), which, in turn, requires that the second (or more) unrestricted intelligible(s) be an intrinsic contradiction (restricted unrestricted intelligibility). Therefore, unrestricted intelligibility must necessarily be unique — "one and only one" (*modus tollens*).[24]

II.D. Unique, Unrestricted Intelligibility Must Be an Unrestricted Act of Understanding — Understanding Itself

Up to this point, the following has been established: (1) there must be at least one unconditioned reality, (2) an unconditioned reality must be unrestricted intelligibility, and (3) unrestricted intelligibility must be unique. This triple conclusion may be rephrased as follows: a unique, unconditioned reality which is unrestricted intelligibility exists.

Can we get a further insight into this unique, unrestricted intelligibility? The exposition of understanding and intelligibility in Section I can help

---

24. Lonergan proceeds to the proof for uniqueness by showing that an unrestricted act of understanding must be one act, and that the idea of being must be one in that one unrestricted act of understanding. See Lonergan 1992, p. 668.

us to do so. Recall that intelligibility can be in the empirical world. When it is, it is intrinsic to the powers, activities, and characteristics of empirical reality, and so it is conditioned by individuation and a spatio-temporal manifold.

Recall further that intelligibility can be detached from the empirical domain and its empirical residue by an act of understanding that sets the intelligible content into a relationship within a heuristic context. This brings out the nuance and significance of the intelligible content (now seen in relation to other intelligible contents) and even allows ideas to be formed from relationships among ideas, and even relationships among relationships of ideas. This last insight helps to shed light on the nature of unique, unrestricted intelligibility.

Sections II.B and II.C make clear that unrestricted intelligibility cannot be conditioned by space and time; if it were, its intelligibility would be limited to that particular space and time. Likewise, unrestricted intelligibility cannot be limited to an instance that does not include other instances; if it were, its intelligibility would be restricted to that particular instance. Moreover, unrestricted intelligibility cannot be limited by an empirical residue for the same reason. But what, then, can unrestricted intelligibility be — if it cannot be in space or time, in empirical individuation, or even an instance that does not include other instances?

It must be the content of an act of understanding, for an act of understanding allows intelligibility to stand by itself, detached from any limiting spatio-temporal, empirical/material, individuating repository; it allows intelligibility to stand for and embrace a multitude of instances (as when an idea is used in predication); and it allows ideas to be formed from relationships among ideas. Now, if intelligibility is truly unrestricted, it would have to have *all* of these qualities, and therefore, it would have to be the content of an act of understanding.[25]

---

25. Lonergan summarizes this insight quite succinctly as follows: ". . . [I]ntelligibility either is material or spiritual or abstract: it is material in the objects of physics, chemistry, biology, and sensitive psychology; it is spiritual when it is identical with understanding; and it is abstract in concepts of unities, laws. . . . But abstract intelligibility necessarily is incomplete, for it arises only in the self-expression of spiritual intelligibility. Again, spiritual intelligibility is incomplete as long as it can inquire. Finally, material intelligibility necessarily is incomplete, for it is contingent in its existence and in its occurrences, in its genera and species . . . moreover, it includes a merely empirical residue of individuality, noncountable infinities, particular places and times. . . . It follows that the only possibility of complete intelligibility lies in a spiritual intelligibility that cannot inquire because it understands everything about everything" (Lonergan 1992, pp. 696-97).

Now, the act of understanding that enables unrestricted intelligibility to exist as an idea must itself be unrestricted, because the power that enables the unrestricted idea to exist cannot have any restrictions that the idea itself does not have. But what is an unrestricted act of understanding like? How can it be described or explained?

To begin with, we can eliminate two explanations from the outset. First, an unrestricted act of understanding cannot be an act of mentation through a material brain, because a material brain cannot accommodate unrestricted intelligibility since it is restricted in both its intelligibility and its material functioning. The same can be said for artificial intelligence, which also is restricted in its intelligibility and material (electromagnetic, electrochemical, or even biochemical) functioning. Indeed, we will have to eliminate any apparatus, power, or activity that is in any way material or restricted in its power to ground intelligibility.

This means we will have to begin our explanation with a power that is capable of bringing together, in a single act, the interrelationship among unrestricted intelligibility and all restricted intelligibility. What kind of power could this be? Our most promising clue may be found in the notion of absolute simplicity elucidated in the previous chapter (Section II). Recall from that chapter that when a power has less intrinsic or extrinsic restrictions or boundaries, it excludes less reality from itself; it is, as it were, *more inclusive* — more capable of being in unity with what is less simple (more restricted) than itself. Now, if it is capable of being in unity with more of reality, it is likewise capable of unifying that reality through itself.

Recall that an act of understanding sets intelligible content into relationship with other intelligible content. How does it do this? First and foremost, through an act of unification — an act that can bring together diverse intelligible contents so that they might be compared, and their intelligibility might be illumined, through other diverse intelligibility. This act of unification certainly does not have to occur through a brain or some other material apparatus or power. Indeed, as we saw above, it cannot occur through such a restricted apparatus. The power that is capable of unifying, in a single act, the interrelationship among unrestricted intelligibility and all restricted intelligibility would have to be absolutely *simple;* that is, it would have to be a power devoid of any intrinsic or extrinsic boundaries or restrictions. Recall that we cannot imagine such a power because our imaginations would improperly impose a spatio-temporal manifold upon it. Thus, we may only think about it as follows: a power without extrinsic or intrinsic restriction capable of unifying, in a single act, the interrelationship among unrestricted intelligibility and all restricted intelligibility.

Since this power has no extrinsic or intrinsic restrictions, it cannot be conditioned by a spatio-temporal manifold (which would impose such restrictions on it). This means that it would be completely transparent to itself (it can be, as it were, inside itself), which is the condition necessary for a perfect act of self-consciousness (being aware of awareness).

The problem of "consciousness being inside itself" may be understood through human acts of self-consciousness. When I am aware of my awareness, my awareness is at once the understanding and the understood. Now this cannot occur through a spatial manifold, for that would mean that one's awareness would have to traverse space to get inside itself, much like a dog not only nipping its tail, but swallowing its entire self. If the dog were to do such a thing, it would have to travel at an infinite velocity (meaning that no time could elapse to traverse the spatial magnitude). Thus, there are two ways of producing the effect of "being inside oneself": (1) traversing a spatial magnitude at an infinite velocity, or (2) not being conditioned by a spatial magnitude at all. The first would appear to be a violation of the canon of parsimony (Ockham's razor), while the second manifests simple, parsimonious elegance.

Now let us return to our acting power which is not conditioned by a spatial magnitude. By its very nature, it must be able to be inside itself. Indeed, it could be inside itself "inside itself." The absence of conditioning by a spatial magnitude makes it, by nature, perfect self-transparency, and as an act of understanding it is a perfectly self-transparent act of understanding — that is, an act of understanding understanding itself perfectly.

Inasmuch as this acting power is an unrestricted act of understanding — understanding itself, it can be at once both understanding and understood. The only difference between the *act* of understanding and its *content* (namely, itself) would be its *relationship* to itself. Furthermore, in its capacity to unify all restricted intelligibility (through an absence of restrictions, which would produce exclusionary properties), it can ground the interrelationship among all restricted intelligibility (in one unifying mentative act), and then set that interrelationship among all restricted intelligibility into relationship with itself as both understanding and understood.

Free from all intrinsic and extrinsic restrictions, this acting power, this unrestricted act of understanding, is able to be the ground of complete intelligibility. Its unification of the whole of restricted intelligibility with its transparency to itself leaves no question unanswered. All possible questions are answered in itself and through its grounding of all restricted intelligibility. This is why Lonergan refers to it as "God," and we must hasten to add, an "intelligent God" — a "perfectly intelligent God."

II.E. All Other Intelligibility Besides the One Unrestricted Act of Understanding Must Be Restricted and Be a Thought Content of the One Unrestricted Act of Understanding

We may now draw some obvious conclusions from the previous four steps of the proof. To begin, the one unrestricted act of understanding must be the ontological ground (Creator) of all restricted intelligibility. The following makes this clear:

1) Every conditioned reality is ultimately dependent on an unconditioned reality for its existence (see Step 1 in Section II.A).
2) There is only one unconditioned reality, because an unconditioned reality must be unrestricted intelligibility (see Step 2 in Section II.B) and unrestricted intelligibility must be unique — "one and only one" (see Step 3 in Section II.C).
3) Therefore, everything in reality (besides the one unconditioned reality) must be conditioned, and must therefore be ultimately dependent upon the one unconditioned reality for its existence. Therefore, the one unconditioned reality (unrestricted intelligibility) must be the ontological ground (Creator) of all else that is real (all restricted intelligibility).

Now the question arises about how this one unconditioned reality (unrestricted intelligibility) ontologically grounds (creates) all else in reality (all restricted intelligibility). As shown above, the one unconditioned reality is an unrestricted act of understanding — understanding itself (Step 4 in Section II.D). How would an unrestricted act of understanding ground the whole of restricted intelligibility?

As might by now be evident, the *whole* of restricted intelligibility (in all of its interrelationships) can only be grounded through an *idea*, because the *whole* of restricted intelligibility includes many dimensions that must be detached from the empirical residue, space-time juxtaposition, and individuation. These dimensions are intelligible only through *relationships* or "relationships among relationships" which require a new repository (other than the empirical residue or a principle of individuation). As explained above, this new repository is an idea (the content of an act of understanding — see Sections I and II.D).

Now since the *whole* of restricted intelligibility can only exist through this new repository (an idea) and since the *whole* of restricted intelligibility must be ontologically grounded in the one unrestricted act of understanding, then the whole of restricted intelligibility must be the content of the one unrestricted act of understanding. The *whole* of restricted intelligibility must be a "thought" in the "mind" of God.

Now since the *whole* of restricted intelligibility is the content of the unrestricted act of understanding (i.e., it exists through the unrestricted act of understanding, as an idea), reality (the totality of all that is real) is *not more* than the unrestricted act of understanding (i.e., it is not the unrestricted act of understanding *plus* restricted intelligibility). Restricted intelligibility can never, as it were, lie outside of the unrestricted act of understanding so as to add to it, because the whole of restricted intelligibility is completely derivative upon the unrestricted act of understanding. This is similar to human thinking wherein the contents of our thoughts are derivative upon our acts of thinking. Thus, I do not say that my thoughts add to me, because they exist through me. Even though the contents of my thought are distinct from my act of thinking, they do not add anything more to me ontologically[26] since they exist through me. Similarly, inasmuch as the whole of restricted intelligibility is a content of the unrestricted act of understanding, it does not add anything ontologically to the unrestricted act of understanding. Thus, reality (the totality of all that is real) is the one unrestricted act of understanding with all its thought-contents in one single whole.[27] The restricted thought-contents are distinct from the unrestricted act of understanding, but they do not add anything to it ontologically.[28]

---

26. "Adding to it ontologically," here, means "adding being" or "adding reality" to something. A thought does not add anything to my *power* to think or even my material being. It is simply a content, an effect of my act of thinking which is *intrinsic* to that act. If contents of thought were to *ontologically* add anything to me, I would be genuinely hesitant to think about cockroaches and spiders.

27. This is the opposite of pantheism and panentheism, which hold that restricted realities *constitute* God. In contrast to this, this proof holds that the unrestricted act of understanding creates all restricted intelligibility through *Its* mentative act. God can think of anything He wants, and it will not become — constitute — God.

28. Lonergan expresses this point as follows: ". . . [I]n the one idea there are to be grasped many beings; in the immaterial, nontemporal, nonspatial idea there are grasped the

II.F. Conclusion to the Proof

Therefore, a completely unique, unconditioned Reality, which is at once unrestricted intelligibility and an unrestricted act of understanding — understanding itself, must exist. This unique unrestricted act of understanding understands Itself through Its complete self-transparency, and is the ontological ground (Creator) of all restricted intelligibility which exists as a content (idea) through It.

In order to deny this conclusion, one will have to either deny the existence of an unconditioned reality (which entails denying one's own existence), or deny that an unconditioned reality is unrestricted intelligibility, and therefore, unique (which entails intrinsic contradictions). If these denials are thought to be either unreasonable or irresponsible (or both), then one should affirm the existence of an unrestricted act of understanding — understanding itself grounding the whole of restricted intelligibility as a content of Its understanding. This reality possesses the attributes of "God."

III. The Mystery of Human Understanding: The Notion of Being

The above proof for God's existence sheds light on the transcendentality of human intellection, which Lonergan points to in the parallelism between "the idea of being" (i.e., the idea of complete intelligibility) and "the notion of being" (i.e., the notion of complete intelligibility). As seen above, complete intelligibility can only exist as an idea in an unrestricted act of understanding which must be unique. Human beings cannot have such an idea, for human acts of understanding are restricted (open to further questions). Nevertheless, there seems to be a *derivative* of the *idea* of complete intelligibility in restricted acts of understanding. It seems to act as a "beyondness" that is not grasped by a human act of understanding but, rather, is present to a human act of understanding as a horizon. Lonergan calls this "the *notion* of being" (i.e., the *notion* of complete intelligibility).

The rationale for Lonergan's contention will be given in Chapter 8, Section I, so a brief list of the points to be argued there will be sufficient for our present purposes:

---

material, the temporal, and the spatial. There must be, then, a primary component grasped inasmuch as there is a single act of understanding, and a secondary component that is understood inasmuch as the primary component is grasped" (Lonergan 1992, p. 669).

1) The foundation of Lonergan's argument is his affirmation that he has the capacity to recognize incomplete intelligibility *whenever* it is manifest, and that this will incite a question such as "What is it?" "Why is it?" "How is it?" etc. Thus he believes he has a pure, *unrestricted* desire to know.[29]

2) The source of the pure unrestricted desire to know seems to be a desire to know "all that is to be known." This desire must have an accompanying *awareness* of "all that is to be known" sufficient to incite the desire. It does not have to be an explicit, discursive awareness (like an idea in an act of understanding), but merely an awareness sufficient to incite desire. Let us call this a *tacit* awareness of "all that is to be known."

3) Now, this tacit awareness of all that is to be known may be likened to a tacit awareness of "what would be sufficient for an explanation of everything about everything." Any time one experiences or understands intelligibility that falls short of "what would be sufficient for an explanation of everything about everything," a question is incited and the pure unrestricted desire to know continues on its path. It will not stop until it reaches its objective of explaining everything about everything; not even if it reaches the highest viewpoints in mathematics, physics, metaphysics, etc. — it will always reveal when something is not sufficient to explain everything about everything.[30]

4) The source of this tacit awareness of "what is sufficient for an explanation of everything about everything" cannot be a natural source (empirical data, finite data, or the contents of restricted acts of understanding) because the tacit awareness of "what is sufficient for an explanation of everything about everything" is always beyond *every*

---

29. "Immanent within [the process of understanding] and operative of it lies an intelligent and rational consciousness that unrestrictedly intends a correspondingly unrestricted objective named being, or the all, or everything about everything, or the concrete universe" (Lonergan 1992, p. 380).

30. Lonergan calls this the "notion of being," and describes it as follows: "[T]he notion of being penetrates *all* cognitional contents. It is the supreme heuristic notion. *Prior* to every content, it is the notion of the *to-be-known* through that content. As each content emerges, the 'to-be-known through that content' passes without residue into the 'known through that content.' Some blank in *universal anticipation* is filled in, not merely to end that element of anticipation, but also to make the filler a part of the anticipated. Hence, *prior* to all answers, the notion of being is the notion of the *totality* to be known through all answers" (Lonergan 1992, pp. 380-81; italics mine).

"intelligible reality that leaves a question unanswered," and every *restricted* intelligible always leaves a question unanswered.[31] Therefore, the tacit awareness of "what is sufficient for an explanation of everything about everything" is always beyond any *restricted* intelligible. Its source must therefore be an *unrestricted* intelligible — that is, the Idea of complete intelligibility, which is the content of an unrestricted act of understanding (see above, Sections II.B and II.D). The Idea of complete intelligibility, then, must be the source of our awareness of the explanation of everything about everything.

5) But the idea of complete intelligibility can only occur through an *unrestricted* act of understanding, and so human beings cannot have *understood* this *Idea*. They can only have a *notion* of it. Since human beings cannot understand it as an idea, they cannot hold it and control it on their own. It must be, as it were, held and controlled *by Its source,* and must act solely as an ungrasped horizon or backdrop to the content of any human act of understanding that reveals the "shortcomings" (the incompleteness) of that content and incites a further question.

This tacit awareness of the presence of complete intelligibility as horizon points to the presence of God to human intelligence, which implies a transcendental dimension of human self-consciousness. If human beings really do have an unrestricted desire to know, and if this unrestricted desire to know arises out of a tacit awareness of "what would be sufficient for an explanation of everything about everything," and this awareness can only have the "Idea of complete intelligibility" (which can only occur through an unrestricted act of understanding) as its source, then human beings have a tacit awareness of the unrestricted act of understanding ("God") as horizon.

This tacit awareness of the unrestricted act of understanding as horizon would be the impetus of all questioning, creativity, and striving for a better world. It transforms consciousness into intelligent, creative self-consciousness that strives toward a horizon beyond the empirical residue, beyond spatio-temporal juxtaposition, indeed, beyond any restriction whatsoever. Thus, it is at once the source of curiosity, creativity, and human transcendentality. This may give new meaning to the intrinsic relationship between divine and human consciousness (between God and human beings). This will be taken up in Chapter 8, Section I on the desire for perfect Truth.

31. See above, Section II.B, *Proof of Premise #1.*

CHAPTER FIVE

Proof of a Creator of Past Time

Introduction

The proof for a beginning (and Creator) of past time has been the source of considerable debate since its formulation by the Kalam philosophers, a school of medieval Arabic philosophers who promoted natural theism and advocated for the impossibility of an "actual infinite" being applied to a finite or aggregative structure.[1] The Kalam proof against the infinity of past time was not accepted in the Western medieval world because Saint Thomas Aquinas followed Aristotle in allowing for the *possibility* of infinite temporal regression.[2]

---

1. Craig 1979(b), p. 4.

2. Saint Thomas considered a version of the Kalam argument in *ST* I,Q46,6: "Further, if the world always was, the consequence is that infinite days preceded this present day. But it is impossible to pass through an infinite medium. Therefore we should never have arrived at this present day; which is manifestly false" (Aquinas 1947, pp. 242-43). Saint Thomas's statement of the Kalam argument is quite lucid, but his response does not disprove it: "Passage is always understood as being from term to term. Whatever bygone day we choose, from it to the present day there is a finite number of days which can be passed through. The objection is founded on the idea that, given two extremes, there is an infinite number of mean terms" (Aquinas 1947, p. 244). That any particular span within a hypothetical infinite span is finite does not prove that an infinite span is possible. Indeed, as David Hilbert (the father of finite mathematics) implies, the hypothesis of an infinite span undermines the mathematical coherency (and therefore the possibility) of all finite or aggregative spans within it. Therefore, ironically, Saint Thomas's response to the argument (when considered in light of Hilbert's prohibition) is really a proof of what he is trying to disprove. Of course, Saint Thomas did not have the benefit of the extensive development of mathematics between the thirteenth and twentieth centuries. A formal proof of the inapplicability of infinity to past time in any standard universe (including our own) will be given in Section IV.

Aristotle was unfamiliar with the Kalam proofs (which were developed a thousand years after him), and, in his view of "time," "causality," and mathematics, he was unable to definitively rule out the possibility of infinite past time. As a result, Saint Thomas Aquinas and the Christian world inherited a legacy that provided for the philosophical possibility of infinite past time.[3]

Saint Thomas did not need to prohibit infinite past time in order to conclusively prove the existence of God. Instead, he chose to do this by showing the impossibility of an infinite *essentially* subordinated series, and left open the possibility of an infinite *temporally* subordinated series.

An essentially subordinated series resembles the first step of the proofs given in Chapters 3 and 4, which show either that an infinity of conditioned realities is equal to nothing without at least one *un*conditioned reality, or that an infinite chain of dependents at a single moment is unfulfillable. These two kinds of arguments are unassailable, because if one does not admit to the existence of at least one unconditioned reality, one will have to deny one's own existence (see Chapter 3, Section I; and Chapter 4, Section II.A).

Saint Thomas seriously considered some ontological objections to infinite past time, but was unable to prove their veracity to his own satisfaction. For example, he speculated that if a soul had been created at every moment during infinite past time, there would have to be an infinity of

---

3. But we must hasten to add that Saint Thomas did not believe the contrary position could be proven either, namely, the eternity of past time. Indeed, he refutes the three arguments for the eternity of past time (derived from Aristotle) in his *Commentary on the Sentences of Peter the Lombard* (II Sent., d.1, q.1, a.5). A synopsis of these refutations may be found in Baldner 2007, pp. 3-6. The refutations are quite definitive.

Saint Thomas also implies that there is no inherent contradiction in "infinite past time" (II *Sent.* d.1, q.1, a.5) because past time cannot be considered an *actual* entity through which a contradiction could occur. But this argument proceeds from his definition of "time" ("the number/measure of motion") which, in turn, depends on his definition of "motion" ("the actuality of that which is in potency while it is in potency"). This would imply that "time" is merely accidental, and therefore is not a reality through which an ontological contradiction can occur. (For a fuller explanation of this argument, see Baldner 2007, pp. 8-9.) *However*, if "time" in contemporary physics is shown to be a real constituent of the nature of the physical world (as in General Relativity Theory and Quantum Theory), then the metaphysical notions of time offered by Bergson and other contemporary philosophers would be more appropriate than Saint Thomas's ("the number/measure of motion"). These more contemporary definitions of time are subject to Hilbert's prohibition of actual infinities in finite or aggregative structures. If Saint Thomas had been aware of the General Theory of Relativity and the developments in mathematics that led to Hilbert's prohibition, I am inclined to think that he would not have held on to the possibility of infinite past time.

individual souls existing today.[4] Nevertheless, he does not seem to have recognized the paradoxes intrinsic to what would today be called a Cantorian set,[5] and therefore, was not convinced that infinite past time could not be real.

Furthermore, he did not have a view of time corresponding to the notions of "real time" implied by contemporary physics (particularly the General Theory of Relativity) and in the philosophical theories of Peirce, Bergson, Whitehead, and many others who believed that time is a *real* aggregative structure. In contrast, Saint Thomas believed, as did Aristotle, that time was merely the measure of motion. It did not seem to have any more reality than being a measurable characteristic (an accident) of motion. Therefore, a prohibition of infinite time (as he understood it) did not seem earthshaking. Thus, he decided not to risk giving what might be viewed as a very "suspect" proof of the existence of God, and rested his case on the far more secure prohibition of an infinite *essentially* subordinated series.

In view of the above developments in physics and mathematics (and the philosophical response to them), I do not believe this proof is nearly as suspect as Saint Thomas considered it over 700 years ago. Indeed, I believe that a very probative version of this proof can be formulated if two theoretical developments are taken into serious consideration: (1) an ontological explanation of time as "a continuous succession of non-contemporaneous distension intrinsic to changeable reality" (which means time must be a real aggregative structure), and (2) the mathematical distinction between an actual and potential infinity (and the prohibition of *actual* infinities to finite or aggregative structures).

It is my intention to show contemporary audiences the veracity of these two postulates (Sections II and III), and then to formulate a proof for the impossibility of infinite past time in our universe or any other standard

---

4. Saint Thomas was not convinced that this argument presented a definitive problem, and in the end, he resolved, "But this argument is not to the point, for God could have made the world without making men or creatures with souls, or he could have made men when in fact he did make them, even if he had made the rest of the world from eternity. In either case, an infinite number of souls would not remain after the bodies had passed away. Furthermore, it has not yet been demonstrated that God cannot cause an infinite number of things to exist simultaneously" (*De Aeternitate Mundi,* trans. Miller 1997).

5. "Cantorian set" is named after Georg Cantor, who postulated sets with an actual infinite number of members. As will be seen in Section III of this chapter, David Hilbert believes such sets undermine the axioms of finite mathematics, and therefore finite mathematics itself.

universe (Section IV), and then to show the necessity of a creator of past time which is not, itself, conditioned by time (Section V). This will hopefully provide the additional data Saint Thomas would have needed to fill the speculative gaps that he believed made this proof quite suspect. I believe this proof is worth pursuing, not only because it has a different starting point from the previous two philosophical proofs, but also because it shows the need for a creator of time and of temporally conditioned universes. This leads us back to an extraordinary synergy with Chapter 1 (which showed the need for a beginning of past time in the mathematical modeling of any inflationary universe).

Before pursuing these objectives, I will discuss an analytical contradiction in the expression "infinite past time" which reveals the problematic character of this idea, and provides an initial clue to its inapplicability to our universe or any other changeable universe (Section I).

I. An Analytical Contradiction

The problematic character of infinite past time is revealed by a seemingly inescapable analytical contradiction in the very expression "infinite past time."

If one splits the expression into its two component parts: (1) "past time" and (2) "infinite," and attempts to find a common conceptual base that can apply to both terms (much as a lowest common denominator can apply to two different denominators in two fractions), one can immediately detect contradictory features. One such common conceptual base is the idea of "occurrence," another, the idea of "achievement," and still another, the idea of "actualizability." Let us begin with the expression "past time."

Past time can only be viewed as having occurred, or having been achieved, or having been actualized; otherwise, it would be analytically indistinguishable from present time and future time. In order to maintain the analytical distinction among these three interrelated ideas, present time must be viewed as "occurring," or "being achieved," or "being actualized"; and future time must be viewed as "not having occurred," "not achieved," and "not actualized." The notion of "past" loses its intelligibility with respect to present and future if its meaning were to include "occurring," "being achieved," or "being actualized" (pertaining to the present); or "not having occurred," "not achieved," or "not actualized" (pertaining to the future). If past time is to retain its distinct intelligibility, it can only be viewed as "having occurred," "achieved," and "actualized."

Now let us turn to the other side of the expression, namely, "infinite." Throughout this chapter, I will view "infinity" within the context of an aggregating succession because I will show that real time in changeable universes must be an "aggregating succession of non-contemporaneous distension" (see below, Sections II and IV). Now, infinities within an aggregating succession imply "unoccurrable," "unachievable," and "unactualizable," for an aggregating succession occurs one step at a time (that is, one step after another), and can therefore only be increased a finite amount. No matter how fast and how long the succession occurs, the "one step at a time" or "one step after another" character of the succession necessitates that only a finite amount is occurrable, achievable, or actualizable. Now, if "infinity" is applied to an aggregating succession, and it is to be kept analytically distinct from (indeed, contrary to) "finitude," then "infinity" must always be more than can ever occur, be achieved, or be actualized through an aggregating succession ("one step at a time" succession). Therefore, infinity would have to be unoccurrable, unachievable, and unactualizable when applied to an aggregating succession. Any other definition would make "infinity" analytically indistinguishable from "finitude" in its application to an aggregating succession. Therefore, in order to maintain the analytical distinction between "finitude" and "infinity" in an aggregating succession, "infinity" must be considered unoccurrable (as distinct from finitude which is occurrable), unachievable (as distinct from finitude which is achievable), and unactualizable (as distinct from finitude which is actualizable). We are now ready to combine the two parts of our expression through our three common conceptual bases:

"**Infinite**	**Past Time"**
"(The) unoccurrable	(has) occurred."
"(The) unachievable	(has been) achieved."
"(The) unactualizable	(has been) actualized."

Failures of human imagination may deceive one into thinking that the above analytical contradictions can be overcome, but further scrutiny reveals their inescapability. For example, it might be easier to detect the unachievability of an infinite series when one views an infinite succession as having a beginning point without an ending point, for if a series has no end, then, *a priori*, it can never be achieved. However, when one looks at the infinite series as having an ending point but no beginning point (as with infinite past time reaching the present), one is tempted to think that the presence of the ending point must signify achievement, and, therefore, the infinite series was achieved. This conjecture does not avoid the contradiction of "infinite past time" being "an achieved unachievable." It simply manifests a failure of our imagination. Since we conjecture that the ending point has been reached, we think that an infinite number of steps has really been traversed, but this does not help, because we are still contending that unachievability has been achieved, and are therefore still asserting an analytical contradiction.

Another failure of our imagination arises out of thinking about *relative* progress in a historical succession. Our common sense might say that infinite past history is impossible because an infinity is innumerable, immeasurable, and unquantifiable, making the expression "an infinite number" an oxymoron. But then we get to thinking that infinite history *seems* plausible because each step *relative* to the other steps is quantifiable in its progression; each step is subject to *relative* numeration. Therefore, it seems that history can really achieve an infinite number of steps.

However, as the above analysis reveals, this cannot be so because an infinity in a continuous succession must be unachievable or unactualizable as a *whole* (otherwise, it would be analytically indistinguishable from "finitude" in an aggregating succession). Since, as has been said, past time must be achieved or actualized (otherwise it would be analytically indistinguishable from "present" and "future"), "infinite past time" must be an "achieved unachievable" or an "actualized unactualizable" (an intrinsic contradiction). Moreover, the expression "an infinite number" is also an intrinsic contradiction because "number" implies a definite quantity, whereas "infinity" implies innumerability (more than can ever be numbered). Therefore, infinite history and its characterization as "a completion of infinite time" remain inescapably analytically contradictory.

This intrinsic analytical contradiction reveals the problematic character of the very idea of "infinite past time." It now remains for us to show the inapplicability of this problematic idea to our universe, and indeed, to any really possible changeable universe. This step will give ontological ("synthetic") significance to the analytical contradiction by showing that the condition of the *real* world (i.e., our real universe, or any really possible changeable universe) will contradict (and therefore resist) the application of this problematic idea to it. The result will be that no *real* universe could have had infinite past time (Section IV).

Before we can proceed to this proof, we must first give an ontological explanation of real time[6] (Section II), and then show that this real time must

---

6. "Real time" will be defined as "a continuous succession of non-contemporaneous

be intrinsic to any changeable universe (also Section II), and then explain Hilbert's distinction between actual and potential infinities so that it will be clear that "infinite past time" (as defined) must be an actual infinity, which Hilbert shows to be inapplicable to any reality to which the axioms of finite mathematics can be applied (Section III). The *ontological* proof against an infinity of past time will follow from this (Section IV).

II. An Ontological Explanation of Real Time

As noted above, ambiguities surrounding the ontological status of time seemed to make the proof of a creation of past time quite suspect to ancient and medieval philosophers, but subsequent developments in science revealed that time not only had *real* effects on motion, change, and energy emission, but also that motion, change, and energy emission had *real* effects on the measurement of time. Time could no longer be considered a mere accidental property of motion or a mere subjective quality imposed on motion by someone measuring it. Time was found to be ingredient to both change *and* existence. It is the necessary condition for change and motion *and* produces the effect of duration (endurance in existence, or "non-cessation" of existence).

So how did the ontological status of time move from the "measure of motion" (conceived as either the measurability of motion or a measurement imposed on motion by an intelligent subject) to a real non-contemporaneous distension of reality (into *earlier* and *later*), enabling contradictory states in the same reality (e.g., the cat alive and dead) to be non-simultaneous? It would seem to go back to the time of Newton and Leibniz, who tried to apply the infinitesimal calculus to Galileo's ΔT in the laws of motion. Galileo's formula ($\Delta D/\Delta T$) already implied that time had to have some distension (divisible magnitude) because the reduction of ΔT to zero would effectively require that the formula for velocity entail division by zero (which is mathematically prohibited). In order to formalize physics, Newton and Leibniz needed to calculate instantaneous velocity and instantaneous acceleration, but this presented a paradox because the "instant" upon which instantaneous velocity was based cannot be a real constitutive part of temporal distension (because an instant has zero mag-

---

distension." Each of these terms will be defined within the context of the explanation given in Section II.C, below.

nitude, and, as Euclid suggested long ago, points cannot be constitutive of lines because they have no magnitude — only position).

This led to a debate about whether time was real. On the one hand, it seemed to be real because ΔT could not be reduced to zero. On the other hand, it did not seem to be real because instantaneous velocity seemed to be a real building block of contemporary physics, and besides, it seemed ridiculous to have a present (existing) moment with non-contemporaneous magnitude (earlier and later).[7]

This debate continued for over a century until Albert Einstein's publication of the General Theory of Relativity (see Chapter 1, Section I). The Theory of Relativity is grounded in the invariant velocity of light in all reference frames. When this is combined with Planck's constant, it entails a finitely small minimum possible interval of time, termed "Planck time" ($t_p = 5.39 \times 10^{-44}$ s) and a finitely small minimum interval of space, termed "Planck length" ($l_p = 1.62 \times 10^{-33}$ cm). Once again, doubt was cast on the possibility of reducing the Δ of time to zero in physics and the physical universe.

In light of this, philosophers and physicists such as Henri Bergson, Alfred North Whitehead,[8] David Bohm,[9] Milic Capek,[10] and Ilya Prigogine[11] (among many others), began to reflect on how time could be real. They theorized that something like a non-contemporaneous distensive magnitude (earlier-later) has to condition reality, which is in a state of changing, becoming, and even enduring. Existence is not mere facticity at an instant, but rather a non-contemporaneous distension allowing for everything from continual transition (becoming) to continual enduring. This definition of time makes events into a real non-contemporaneously distended, interactive, asymmetrically related whole.

I will explain this requirement for real time below in five steps. Before proceeding, it will be helpful to make two preliminary distinctions: (1) the distinction between description, scientific explanation, and ontological explanation (since I will be employing the method of ontological explanation

7. This is the problem that Bergson wrestled with in *Duration and Simultaneity,* and caused him to postulate the existence of an elementary memory or consciousness to hold together before and after in a finitely small minimum interval of duration. See below, Section II.C.2.

8. See Whitehead 1978.

9. See Bohm 1986.

10. Capek 1976 and 1961.

11. See Prigogine 1986.

— Section II.A) and (2) the distinction between space — a *contemporaneous* manifold (Section II.B) — and time — a *non*-contemporaneous manifold (Section II.C).

II.A. Description, Scientific Explanation, and Ontological Explanation

Ontological explanations are different from descriptions and scientific explanations. Descriptions relate data to an observer (e.g., the sun is rising). Scientific explanations relate data to other data through qualitative and quantitative apparatuses (e.g., the earth is rotating on its own axis and is orbiting around the sun). Obviously, true descriptions can be false explanations. Ontological explanation is distinct from scientific explanation because it relates data to necessary conditions rather than relating data to data. Thus, the question for ontology is, "What are the conditions *necessary* for the *possibility* of . . . ?"[12]

This kind of explanation seeks more than scientific explanation, for it desires to go beyond the mere articulation of relationships among data in, say, the equations of physics. For example, it is not satisfied with the equations of gravitation or the velocity and direction of an orbiting body. It wants to know *what* gravitation is, *what* velocity is, and *what* the spatial context of position and direction is. This "what" seeks to explain a less fundamental reality in terms of more fundamental ones. In order to get at this deeper or more fundamental reality, we commonly make recourse to *necessity*, that is, the conditions necessary for the possibility of gravitation, velocity, and direction. This pulls us into realities such as fields, space, time, and even space-time. These more fundamental realities, in turn, are open to even more fundamental explanations, which again pull us into even more fundamental conditions necessary for the possibility of the previous fundamental realities. We then begin to look at the nature of unity itself (as distinct from aggregate), existence, real possibility, pure existence, and unconditioned existence. This kind of procedure will guide the five steps of our inquiry into real time, below.

12. See Spitzer 2000, pp. 261-64.

II.B. An Ontological Explanation of Space

Let us turn, for a moment, to an ontological explanation of space[13] (a contemporaneous manifold), for this will help to distinguish it from time (a *non*-contemporaneous manifold) and will show the possibility of time applying to an entire spatially (contemporaneously) unified group of realities (namely, a universe).

To begin, space is not nothing. There cannot be "more or less" of nothing as there can be "more or less" of space. Nothing is simply nothing. As will be seen below, nothing is not continuous, dimensional, connectable, or orientable. Yet space in the observable universe has all four of these characteristics.[14]

If space is not nothing, then what is it? Let us begin with locomotion. Locomotion entails displacement (i.e., a change in place). Displacement, in turn, entails distinct yet unified places. "Distinct yet unified places" entails: 1) contemporaneous separation of those places, and 2) intrinsic unity of those contemporaneously separated places. Were there no unity between contemporaneously separated places, there would be no possibility of moving from one to the other. Completely disunified places preclude motion.

This intrinsic unity of contemporaneously separated places constitutes the most fundamental quality of space, namely, continuity. Continuity, in turn, is the condition necessary for the possibility of the other three characteristics of space in our observable universe, namely, dimensionality, connectivity, and orientability.[15]

The main point to notice is that space is a divisible manifold which allows for continuity, dimensionality, connectivity, and orientability. As such, it is intrinsically unified contemporaneous separation which allows realities to be contemporaneously separated (in place — according to "here" and "there") while at the same time allowing locomotion from "here" to "there" through its intrinsic unity. Since space is an intrinsically unified *contemporaneous* separation, we do not encounter the problem of how non-contemporaneous parts can be held together (as we do with time), for all parts exist contemporaneously.

---

13. I have elsewhere given an extensive ontological explanation of space, so I will here be quite brief. See Spitzer 1989, pp. 109-58.

14. See Davies 1977, pp. 5-11.

15. See Davies 1977, pp. 1-27.

Now, this does not mean that all parts of the contemporaneously existing manifold can be *reached* from all other parts simultaneously. This would require an infinite velocity, which is a highly problematic, if not intrinsically contradictory, idea (and does not seem to be achievable in our universe anyway). According to the Theory of Relativity, any observer within the spatial continuum is subject to a maximum velocity (namely, c, the invariant velocity of light) and therefore cannot reach any spatially separated part of the universe at the moment it is contemporaneous with his own. Nevertheless, there is a part of the universe that is contemporaneous with his own (even though it is not reachable, and therefore not knowable to him contemporaneously). This intrinsically unified, contemporaneously separated manifold is what is meant by "space."

As will be seen below, time transforms reality (such as an electron) into a whole of real, continuous, interconnected, asymmetrically ordered events. But time is not restricted to doing this to *individual* realities (such as electrons). The presence of a contemporaneous manifold (i.e., space) allows time to do this to an entire group of realities unified through this manifold. Hence, time can condition a *universe* (as a whole) through space (the contemporaneous unification of that universe).

II.C. Real Time

We may now proceed to an ontological explanation of time, which will be taken up in five steps:

1) existential non-coincidence,
2) real time as a non-contemporaneous distensive manifold,
3) time as the limiting condition of existence,
4) the succession of time and the asymmetry of events, and
5) manifestations of real time.

II.C.1. Existential Non-Coincidence

It is perhaps best to begin our ontological analysis of time without making recourse to locomotion (which combines space and time). This may be done by looking at a non-spatial change such as death. Let us suppose a cat dies. One of the most apparent ontological truths about this occurrence is that "the state before" and "the state after" cannot be coincident. If they were, it would be an obvious contradiction (the cat simultaneously alive and dead). This, of course, is the problem with all history. Changed existential states cannot be coincident without contradiction. Therefore, wherever there is change, indeed, wherever there is changeability, there must also be some existential non-coincidence that allows differing states to occur within a single entity (e.g., a cat). Let us sum up this initial definition of time as "the existential non-coincidence necessary for the possibility of changed states within a single entity." If this existential non-coincidence were not objectively real, changeable beings and changeable states within the same being would have to be simultaneous, and therefore intrinsically contradictory, and therefore impossible. In view of this, time may also be defined as "that without which all history is a contradiction."

II.C.2. Real Time as a Non-Contemporaneous Distensive Manifold

At this point, one will want to ask, "What is 'existential non-coincidence'?" or "How does it manifest itself?" The temptation here is to spatialize it, by, for example, inserting a spatial continuum between "the cat alive" and "the cat dead." Though this may be very satisfying from the vantage point of human imagination, it leads to a host of problems. To begin with, our cat both alive and dead is in the same place, and the separation of its existential states is not describable by an extensive — spatial — separation. Yet, the cat's change does require a non-extensive separation (frequently termed "a distensive separation"). One must be careful here not to visualize distensive separation as a three-dimensional continuum, otherwise one will be imposing a quasi-spatial continuum between events.

Henri Bergson wrestled with this problem, and finally made recourse to a kind of "protomentalist unified separation of existential states" which he termed "elementary memory." He supposed that this elementary memory existed in the universe as a whole, as a kind of very "elementary cosmic consciousness." In a famous passage in *Duration and Simultaneity*, he noted:

> What we wish to establish is that we cannot speak of a reality which endures without inserting consciousness into it.[16]

In order to show this, he constructs a thought experiment in which he assumes the above existential non-coincidence of incompatible states:

16. Bergson 1965, p. 48. See also Spitzer 1989, pp. 12-14.

We shall have to consider a moment in the unfolding of the universe, that is, a snapshot that exists independently of any consciousness, then we shall try conjointly to summon another moment brought as close as possible to the first, and thus have a minimum amount of time enter into the world without allowing the faintest glimmer of memory to go with it. We shall see that this is impossible. Without an elementary memory that connects the two moments, there will be only one or the other, consequently a single instant, no before and after, no succession, no time.[17]

I do not wish here to affirm Bergson's protomentalist conclusions, but I do want to acknowledge the ontological conditions of change and time that Bergson recognized in reaching them, namely,

1) a real existential non-coincidence between changed states,
2) a fundamental unity within this separation that unifies the non-coincidence of earlier and later, and
3) the non-spatial (and hence, for Bergson, the "elementary memory" or "elementary consciousness") character of this "unity of existential non-coincidence."

These three ontological conditions now give a further refinement of our ontological explanation of time, namely, "a non-spatial unity intrinsic to existential non-coincidence necessary for changeability." Inasmuch as this unity is divisible into "earlier" and "later" (as Bergson correctly surmises) it is a non-contemporaneous manifold. This non-contemporaneous manifold is distinct from a spatial unity which is a contemporaneous manifold (see above, II.B). Since the transition from earlier to later is akin to a "stretching from within," I will refer to it as "distension" instead of "extension" which more properly applies to a contemporaneous (spatial) manifold. Hence, "real time" may now be defined as a "non-contemporaneous" distensive manifold intrinsic to changeable realities (or groups of changeable realities unified through a contemporaneous manifold, such as space).

II.C.3. Time as the Limiting Condition of Existence

The question now arises, "What is this non-contemporaneous distensive manifold intrinsic to changeable reality?" Ontological explanation tries to

17. Bergson 1965, p. 48.

answer this question by making recourse to more fundamental principles of reality. Bergson thinks he has located one such principle in his notion of "elementary memory" or "elementary consciousness." Whitehead believes he has done so through his notion of creativity (a super-mentative state imbuing process and reality): "Primitively time has the character of process, which has 'creativity' as its essence and reveals itself in the becoming of actual occasions (PR, 31f)."[18] Another approach has been to make recourse to "existence" or "being" (which is considered to be more fundamental than time). The constraints of this chapter do not permit me to go into a complete explanation of this most fundamental principle, so I will give only two points and refer the reader to quite lengthy explanations in my other works.[19]

1) Existence. Existence is not brute facticity. As noted in Chapter 3 (Sections I and V), it is the ultimate fulfillment of the conditions of a conditioned reality. A "conditioned reality" may be defined as "a reality whose existence is *dependent* on the fulfillment of conditions." These conditions could be states, fields, structures, positions, space-time configurations, quantum information — whatever is needed for the existence of another real condition or state.[20] A "cause" will be defined as "the *proximate* fulfillment of any conditioned reality's conditions" (e.g., the existence of cells and structures of cells required for the existence of a cat). "*Existence*," in contrast, signifies "the *ultimate* fulfillment of a conditioned reality's conditions by an *unconditioned* reality (a reality that does not depend on the fulfillment of any conditions for its existence).[21] This ultimate fulfillment of conditions could go through hundreds of thousands of steps (e.g., atoms → protons → quarks → . . . → unconditioned reality).

2) Ontological time. Since a conditioned reality can cease to exist, its conditions are not fulfilled unqualifiedly and absolutely. Thus, its existence (the ultimate fulfillment of its conditions by an unconditioned reality) must have a qualification or limiting condition intrinsic to it. I would submit that time is this intrinsic, limiting condition of a conditioned reality's existence.

18. Ashmore 1972, p. 194.

19. See Spitzer 2000, pp. 268-76, and 1989, pp. 60-90.

20. Recall the example of a conditioned reality given in Chapter 3 (Section I.A.1.) concerning cats, which are dependent on cells and structures of cells, etc.

21. Recall the proof of the necessity for an unconditioned reality given in Chapter 3, Sections I and V; and Chapter 4, Section II.A. — An infinity of conditioned realities (i.e., realities that are dependent on the fulfillment of conditions for their existence) is existentially equivalent to nothing (without a reality that is completely unconditioned).

Though time may at first seem to be "positive" (a non-contemporaneous distensive manifold intrinsic to changeable reality), it really emerges as a "negative," that is, a limiting condition of ultimate positivity (i.e., existence). Ontological time may now be defined as "the non-contemporaneous distensive manifold which intrinsically limits a conditioned reality's existence."

II.C.4. The Succession of Time and the Asymmetry of Events

Before discussing the succession of time, it should be noted that time's seeming flow cannot be a motion. Inasmuch as motion has not only spatial displacement, but also temporal displacement ($\Delta D/\Delta T$), ontological time cannot be a motion, for if it were, this motion would itself have to have a temporal component (its own $\Delta D/\Delta T$), which temporal component being considered a motion, would itself have to have its own temporal component . . . constituting an infinite regression. We must therefore avoid implying that time is a motion, and stay close to the above definition, namely, that time is a non-contemporaneous distensive manifold which limits a conditioned reality's existence.

Yet, if time is neither a motion nor a spatial (contemporaneous) manifold, then how do we account for its apparent aggregation or succession? Though we cannot say that time is moving or flowing, or that it is aggregating like a spatial continuum, we can say that it aggregates along with the continued existence of changeable realities. The fact that changeable realities can change in state (or even go out of existence) means that they do not simply exist; they exist over against the real possibility of changing or going out of existence. This means that they must continue or endure in existence. This "enduring in existence" must occur through the same kind of non-contemporaneous distensive manifold that prevents contradictory states in the same entity (e.g., the cat alive and *then* dead). Therefore, this non-contemporaneous distensive manifold (which is divisible into earlier and later) is responsible for both preventing contradictions in history and transforming existence into "enduring in existence." Inasmuch as a changeable reality's "enduring in existence" occurs through an aggregating succession of earlier and later, so also does the time (the non-contemporaneous distensive manifold) in which earlier-later is embedded. We may now integrate this successive and aggregative component into our definition of real time: "an aggregating succession of non-contemporaneous distension intrinsic to changeable reality which limits a conditioned reality's existence."

Bergson's "thought experiment" is perhaps the best way of imagining this aggregating succession without spatializing it or turning it into a motion — "an elementary memory/consciousness holding together the aggregating succession of non-contemporaneous distension (earlier and later) intrinsic to an enduring changeable reality." That Bergson's hypothesis is easy to imagine does not mean that it is correct. It is simply one possible metaphysical ground of the "aggregating succession of non-contemporaneous distension" that *could* be correct. Other conjectures that meet the above conditions also qualify as possible metaphysical grounds for real time.

In what sense, then, can we consider time to be asymmetrical (unidirectional)? Inasmuch as time is neither spatial nor a motion (with a particular direction) we cannot say that *time* is asymmetrical, but we can say that the transition of *contingent states of affairs* conditioned by time (i.e., events) is asymmetrical. Thus, once transitions have been made through time, one cannot go back to the earlier state as it *was*[22] because that earlier state no longer exists. It has been replaced by the later state. The only way of returning to the earlier state as it *was* (going back in time) is to subscribe to something akin to Bergson's cosmic elementary memory. If such a memory existed, and remembered all past states that have transitioned through the continuous succession of non-contemporaneous distension, and held all these states in a sequenced form exactly as they occurred prior to the transition, then that cosmic elementary memory might be able to take an entity from a later memory and put it back into an earlier memory. But paradoxes soon abound.

First, there is the problem of a later entity being put into an earlier moment "as it was." The moment the later entity arrives in the earlier, the earlier is no longer "as it was." Furthermore, this possibility gives rise to a host of irresolvable paradoxes. Davies gives one example:

> One could then construct a booby-trapped device which could destroy itself by a coded signal sent into the past, thereby removing the possibility of sending the signal in the first place — an obvious contradiction![23]

From an ontological point of view, it must be concluded that even though *time* is not asymmetrical, the condition that ontological time per-

22. One, of course, can move to a state similar to an earlier state, but this does not mean that one is going back in time, that is, returning to the earlier state itself, for that earlier state no longer exists.

23. Davies 1977, p. 47.

mits (namely, events — which pass out of existence and come into existence) *is* asymmetrical because past events no longer exist (unless there really is some kind of cosmic consciousness similar to the one mentioned above). We can therefore say that time is not asymmetrical, but the events made possible by time are asymmetrical.

II.C.5. Manifestations of Real Time

Real time (the continuous succession of non-contemporaneous distension) must be measurable, because it cannot be an instant (a dimensionless point) or an infinitesimal (which functions like a dimensionless point). As Bergson noticed, an instant will not suffice to explain temporal distension (earlier-later). I would hasten to add that a dimensionless instant cannot separate two existential states in the same reality (e.g., the cat alive and dead). Thus, the minimum unit of time must be *finitely* small. As such, it cannot be really infinitely divisible; for if it were, it would be composed of infinitely small — zero magnitude — parts. Such zero-magnitude parts cannot constitute a distensive manifold because the aggregation of an infinite number of zero-magnitude parts is still zero magnitude. (Recall that a zero-magnitude part cannot separate contradictory states in the same reality — e.g., the cat alive and dead).

Even though an intelligent subject could *theoretically* divide a magnitude of real time *ad infinitum,* the smallest possible unit of real time cannot be zero magnitude and therefore must be finitely small (and measurable). These finitely small minimum units of time aggregate within a whole of past time as any changeable reality endures in existence. The same holds true for any group of changeable realities that are contemporaneously unified through, say, a *spatial* manifold.

Some mathematicians attempted to get around this problem by postulating a notion of infinitesimals which were "infinitely small, but greater than zero." This was connected to "asymptotic approaches to zero" in the calculus where an interval was in a constant approach to zero (with continuously smaller intervals being traversed toward the limit) without the limit ever being reached.[24] However, as Greek mathematicians surmised long ago,

---

24. Leibniz attempted to justify this notion of infinitesimal as useful in *mathematics* because such a continuously vanishing quantity would always be less than any fixed amount, and would therefore allow for near-perfect mathematical derivations (Leibniz 1956, vol. 2, pp. 586-87).

such notions do not resolve the question of natural minimums, because they are problematic on two levels. First, the definition of infinitesimal is equivocal (it implies *both* zero magnitude and non-zero magnitude).[25] Second, this definition would make a finite magnitude infinite because if an infinitesimal has any non-zero magnitude whatsoever (even though one calls it "infinitely small"), it will aggregate to an infinite magnitude when it is multiplied by itself an infinity of times (which is implied by an infinity of parts resulting from infinite division). Now, inasmuch as this finite magnitude would have an infinity of parts from its infinite divisibility, and each of these parts is hypothesized to have a very small but nevertheless *non-zero* magnitude (attributable to an equivocal definition of "infinitesimal"), it must aggregate to an infinite magnitude (because a non-zero magnitude × infinity = an infinite magnitude). Therefore, an intrinsic contradiction (an infinite finite magnitude) is unavoidable. This gives rise to some predictable factors within any contingent universe (including ours).

1) A finitely small minimum interval of time. The above finitely small minimum intervals of time are necessary to allow for non-contemporaneous separation without reducing such separation to a dimensionless instant or an aggregate of dimensionless instants (which is still a dimensionless instant). This would suggest that change could not occur in any time interval less than this finitely small interval. From the vantage point of ontology, no particular *quantity* for minimum time is necessary (though a finitely small minimum interval of time *is* necessary). Hence, one cannot say that Planck time ($t_p = 5.39 \times 10^{-44}$ s), which is a minimum interval of time for certain kinds of change in the observable universe, would have to be such a minimum in regions beyond our observable universe (if, indeed, there are any). Furthermore, this minimum may only be applicable to certain kinds of change within the universe, while another number may be applicable to other kinds of change in the universe.[26]

2) A finitely small minimum interval of space. The above analysis of infinitesimals also applies to space. If contemporaneous separation is not to

25. This rejection was held by Euclid and Archimedes. It was also implied by Leibniz and Newton, though their vagueness on this caused Weierstrass to show that the infinitesimal could be completely ruled out of the calculus. In contemporary times, Abraham Robinson tried to revitalize the infinitesimal in non-standard analysis, but carefully distinguished between its formal validity in non-standard systems and its non-applicability in the standard (real) universe. See Spitzer 1989, pp. 90-102. See also Robinson 1966 and Davis and Hersh 1981, pp. 237-54.

26. Spitzer 1989, pp. 81-90.

be reduced to a dimensionless point or an aggregate of dimensionless points (which is still a dimensionless point), then there would also have to be a finitely small interval of space. Again, one need not associate this with the Planck interval of minimum space ($l_p = 1.62 \times 10^{-33}$ cm), because no quantity is *ontologically* necessary. However, it currently seems that physical activity cannot occur in a spatial interval less than this within our universe.

3) A finitely small minimum unit of energy emission. With respect to energy emission, finitely small minimums of space and time would have to delimit the way in which energy could be emitted because energy could not be emitted in a time less than its natural minimum (10^{-43} s), nor in a space less than its natural minimum (10^{-33} cm). This suggests that energy be manifested in finitely small minimum thresholds (whose parameters are determined by minimum space and minimum time). In our universe, these thresholds would seem to resemble Planck's quanta, which are emitted or absorbed in "lumps" of energy (finitely small minimum units) as determined by the frequency of radiation. Planck discovered that a single constant could convert any frequency of radiation to the minimum amount of energy required for emission or absorption ($E = h\nu$). This constant is equal to: $\hbar = 6.6 \times 10^{-34}$ joule seconds.

4) A maximum unit of velocity. There is yet another necessary constant, but it is a natural maximum instead of a natural minimum, namely, the constant of maximum velocity. A minimum interval of time predicts a maximum possible velocity (because no specific distance could be traversed in any less time than that minimum possible interval). Stated differently, since spatial displacement cannot take place in zero seconds, infinite velocity is impossible. Therefore, there must be a finite maximum velocity. In our universe, the upper limit to velocity seems to be equivalent to the speed of light: $c = 300,000$ km/s. Since this number can be determined only through empirical discovery, it might be superseded by velocities of yet undiscovered particles or radiation (e.g., tachyons). For the moment, however, it seems to be valid for virtually every manifest displacement of radiation.[27]

If the above conclusions are correct, then any changeable state of affairs would have to exist through real time (a finitely small minimum of non-contemporaneous distension). This limiting condition of contingent existence necessitates an asymmetry of change, a minimum unit of duration,

---

27. There may be some instances in which maximum velocity does not apply, such as the transfer of "information" within a quantum system. "Information," however, is quite distinct from mass energy which is subject to change and contemporaneous separation.

a maximum allowable frequency or velocity of change, and a minimum threshold of the manifestation of energy. The quantities of such minimums and maximums are arbitrary from the vantage point of ontology, but their existence along with that of real time would have to be present wherever changeable realities exist.

The use of necessity and the lack of empirical measurement in the above analysis may seem quite incomplete to physicists, but it does predict the presence of real time and asymmetrical transitions in any hypothetical conception of a changeable universe. This ontological explanation of time is important for applying the Hilbertian prohibition of actual infinities to past time, for as will be seen, Hilbert's prohibition of actual infinities applies to any finite or aggregative structure. From the above, we can see that past time (the whole of the aggregating succession of non-contemporaneous distension intrinsic to changeable reality — or a contemporaneously unified group of changeable realities) is such an aggregative structure. This means that an infinity cannot be applied to it without undermining it and its aggregative structure.

We are now in a position to set out an ontological explanation of events. Recall that real time is intrinsic to all changeable reality, and when changeable reality is conditioned by time, it is distended into an aggregating succession of asymmetrically connected events. Each event occurs through the temporalization of a reality (or a contemporaneously unified group of realities — like a universe). This temporalization (intrinsically unified distensive separation) not only allows contradictory states to exist within the same reality (e.g., the cat alive and *then* dead), it also transforms existence into a "continuing in existence" or an "enduring in existence," which would have to last at least one minimum interval of duration (e.g., 5.39×10^{-44} s in this universe, if the Planck minimum time represents the minimum interval of duration).

Thus, every event (whether it be for a single reality or an entire universe) is constituted by a distensive manifold (earlier $\rightarrow$ later) which is not reducible to a zero magnitude instant or an infinitesimal (which is functionally equivalent to a zero magnitude instant). The source of this distensive manifold is unknown (i.e., we do not know whether it is akin to Bergson's "elementary memory/consciousness" or to some other metaphysical ground), but it must be intrinsic to every changeable reality (otherwise contradictory states in that reality would have to be simultaneous).

These events are actual, continuous, and asymmetrical, and so they form a real, continuous, asymmetrical succession (even though past events no longer exist). Past events *were* real, *were* related to proximate present events, *did* have real effects on proximate present events, and cannot be arbitrarily removed from their place in past *reality* without creating contradictions in that past history (the simultaneous occurrence of contradictory states within a particular reality or spatially unified group of realities). This means that past history (the continuous succession of past events) is a real non-contemporaneously distended, interactive, asymmetrically related *whole*.

One last point must now be considered, namely, a *universe*. Recall that real time is not only intrinsic to particular changeable realities, but also to groups of realities unified through a *contemporaneous* manifold, such as space. One such contemporaneously unified group of realities is a universe. Inasmuch as the realities of a universe are contemporaneously unified, they can share a single temporal (non-contemporaneous) manifold which is intrinsic to their contemporaneous manifold (say, space). Thus, a universe is not only *extrinsically* measurable as a whole (e.g., our observable universe is 13.7 billion years old), but also possesses a single *intrinsic* temporal (non-contemporaneous) manifold through its contemporaneous (e.g., spatial) unification. This means that a universe can have a single intrinsic temporal manifold and an extrinsically measurable age *as a whole*.

We may now proceed to an explanation of Hilbert's distinction between potential and actual infinities and the prohibition of the application of *actual* infinities to finite or aggregative structures.

III. Hilbert's Prohibition of Actual Infinities

In order to expedite the explanation of Hilbert's prohibition, it will be helpful to draw a distinction between three kinds of infinity that are genuinely distinct from one another and cannot be used as analogies for one another (Section III.A). This will show why Hilbert's prohibition only applies to C infinities (infinities hypothesized to be within finite or aggregative structures — Section III.B).

III.A. Three Kinds of Infinity

For the sake of convenience, I will term these three kinds of infinity A, B, and C:

1) "A-infinity." "Infinite" frequently has the meaning of "unrestricted," (e.g., "infinite power" means "unrestricted power"). It can only be conceived through the "*via negativa*," that is, by disallowing or negating any magnitude, characteristic, quality, way of acting, or way of being that could be restricted or introduce restriction into an infinite (unrestricted) power. Therefore, "infinite," here, is *not* a mathematical concept. It is the negation of any restriction (or any condition that could introduce restriction) into power, act, or being.

2) "B-infinity." "Infinite" is also used to signify indefinite progression or indefinite ongoingness. An indefinite progression is never truly actualized. It is one that *can* (potentially) progress *ad infinitum*. Examples of this might be an interminably ongoing series, or an ever-expanding Euclidean plane. The series or the plane never *reaches* infinity; it simply can (potentially) keep on going *ad infinitum*. Thus, Hilbert calls this kind of infinity a "potential infinity."

3) "C-infinity." "Infinite" is sometimes used to signify "infinity *actualized* within a finite or aggregative structure." Mathematicians such as Georg Cantor hypothesized a set with an actual infinite number of members (a Cantorian set) which would not be a set with an ever-increasing number of members or an algorithm which could generate a *potential* infinity of members. Examples might be an existing infinite number line, or an existing infinite spatial manifold, or the achievement of an infinite continuous succession of asymmetrical events (i.e., infinite past history).

The Hilbertian prohibition applies to the C-infinity alone, for, as will be seen, it is not concerned with non-mathematical infinities (i.e., an A-infinity), and it permits indefinitely ongoing (continually potential) successions through finite or aggregative structures (i.e., B-infinities). Before showing Hilbert's and others' prohibition of C-infinities, the two permissible kinds of infinities will be discussed.

An **A-infinity** has long been recognized by the Scholastic tradition. As noted above, it is not a mathematical infinity (such as infinite sets, infinite number lines, infinite successions, etc.) and it is not applied to finite or aggregative structures (such as spatial magnitudes, temporal magnitudes, fields, forces, etc.). Hence, it does not postulate an infinite Euclidean plane, infinite past time, an infinite number line, infinite space, infinite history, infinite thermometers, infinite density, or an infinite physical force. An A-infinity is simply the recognition of "non-restrictedness" in power. It is, therefore, a negation of anything that has restriction or could imply restriction of infinite power.

As Scholastic philosophers have long recognized,[28] one can only speak about "infinite power" or "infinite being" by *negating* any restriction (or structure giving rise to a restriction such as a divisible magnitude) to the power itself. Thus, one can say that "infinite power" is *not* restricted as to form, way of acting, space-time point, or even to spatiality itself (which is a divisible magnitude having intrinsically finite parts).

Such negative statements are not equivalent to "no knowledge" or unintelligibility; for one *does* know that infinite power does *not* have a restriction. Yet, at the same time, one cannot positively *imagine* (through, say, picture-thinking) what such unrestricted power would be. Every image we have is likely to restrict the entity we are conceiving either intrinsically or extrinsically.

Our inability to conceive or imagine this entity does not in any way rule out its possibility, for our inability to conceive of it does not reveal an intrinsic contradiction or "an extrinsic contradiction with some existing reality"; it merely admits the limits of our spatializing, temporalizing, finitizing imagination and conception. Thus, as we shall see, Hilbert's prohibition of an "actual infinity" does not extend to an A-infinity, for an A-infinity is neither a mathematical infinity nor an application of infinity to a *finite* or aggregative structure. Interestingly enough, Hilbert's prohibition of a C-infinity could actually constitute a proof for an A-infinity (see below, Section V).

A **B-infinity** is quite distinct from an A-infinity because it is both a mathematical infinity and an application of infinity to a finite or aggregative structure. Unlike the prohibited C-infinity, the B-infinity applies a mathematical infinity to a finite or aggregative structure in only a *potential* way. Therefore, the B-infinity acknowledges only the *possibility* that a finite or aggregative structure *could continue* to progress *indefinitely*. Thus, the B-infinity does not imply that a Cantorian set (with an infinite number of members) actually exists. It implies that a particular algorithm (sufficient to define the set) can *continue* to generate members *indefinitely*. Furthermore, it does not hold that an infinite number line actually exists, but rather that one can continue to generate numbers on the line indefinitely. The existence (completion or achievement) of an infinite number line is never advocated, but only the *potential* to continue to generate numbers indefinitely.

---

28. Beginning with Pseudo-Dionysius the Areopagite. See Dionysius the Areopagite 1940. See also the discussion in Chapter 3, Section IV, and the forthcoming discussion in Chapter 6, Section II.

The same holds true for magnitudes such as space (a contemporaneous magnitude) and time (a non-contemporaneous aggregative magnitude). A potential infinity implies that a spatial magnitude has the *potential* to continue expanding indefinitely. Similarly, it holds that a non-contemporaneous succession of events has the potential to continue indefinitely (into the *future*). It does not imply that an infinite spatial magnitude really exists or that an infinity of continuously successive historical events actually occurred.

The Hilbertian prohibition does not apply to a B-infinity because one is not advocating the existence (actuality) of a mathematical infinity within a finite or aggregative structure. As we shall see momentarily, infinity applied to the succession of *future* events will not give rise to a Hilbertian paradox because future events are only potential. An infinity never exists. Future time can only be an *indefinitely* increasing succession of events; never the existence (actuality) of a mathematical infinity. As will be seen, such is not the case with past time, which explains why infinite past time falls under the Hilbertian prohibition.

A **C-infinity,** like a B-infinity, is both a mathematical infinity and an application of infinity to a finite or aggregative structure. The important difference, however, between the B and C-infinities is that the C-infinity implies the *existence* (actuality) of a mathematical infinity within a finite or aggregative structure. As noted above, examples of a C-infinity would be an actual Cantorian set with an actual infinite number of members, or an infinite number line with an actual infinite number of positions, or an actually existing infinite spatial magnitude, or an actual occurrence of an infinite number of events in the past. Thus, if C-infinities could really exist, there could be infinite space, infinity degrees Fahrenheit, infinite mass density, infinite physical force, and infinite past time. These notions seem irresolvably paradoxical *prima facie,* because the mathematical infinity applied to them destroys their intelligibility as finite or aggregative structures. The proof for this goes beyond *prima facie* intuition. It extends to the requirements for mathematical intelligibility itself. Thus, as Hilbert shows, a mathematical infinity existing within a finite or aggregative structure undermines the very possibility of finite mathematics, and therefore the very possibility of quantifying those finite or aggregative structures. Therefore, a C-infinity must, in all cases, be illusory.

Now, it was shown above that the succession of past events is a real, non-contemporaneously distended, interactive, asymmetrically related, continuously successive *whole*. As such, it must be an *actual* asymmetrical progression. It does not matter that past events no longer exist, because all past events did exist and affected, and were related to, present events as they passed out of existence. Thus, they constitute a real past progression. This is sufficient to qualify "a past succession of events" for Hilbert's prohibition, because the application of an infinity to it *must* be a C-infinity (not a B-infinity).

If a C-infinity must in all cases be rejected (because it entails the undermining of finite mathematics and the quantification of finite or aggregative structures), then an infinite past succession of events must also be rejected. This will be shown first by summarizing Hilbert's (and others') prohibition of C-infinities (Section III.B), and second through a formal proof that illustrates the contradictory and incoherent nature of the C-infinity applied to past time (Section IV).

It is important not only to distinguish among these three kinds of infinity, but also to avoid analogizing one with the other. Thus, infinite future time cannot be a proper analogy for infinite past time. As can be seen, they are quite distinct (a B-infinity versus a C-infinity, respectively). Furthermore, infinite future time cannot be used as an analogy for infinite power (a B-infinity versus an A-infinity, respectively). The rules for each kind of infinity do not apply meaningfully to the other kinds.

III.B. The Mathematical Prohibition of C-Infinities

The above discussion was brought to the attention of philosophers of mathematics by David Hilbert, who attempted to clarify the notion of an infinite numeric series which was thought to exist as a completed totality:

> Just as in the limit processes of the infinitesimal calculus, the infinite in the sense of the infinitely large and the infinitely small proved to be merely a figure of speech, so too we must realize that the infinite in the sense of an infinite *totality,* where we still find it used in deductive methods, is an *illusion.*[29]

Hilbert is proposing here that, even though a B-infinity (one with the potential to continue indefinitely without being actual) is mathematically admissible, a C-infinity (the existence of a mathematical infinity within a finite or aggregative structure) is not mathematically admissible because it presents irresolvable paradoxes and contradicts the very axioms of finite mathematics.

29. Hilbert 1964, p. 135.

In recounting the history of the "actual infinite" (Hilbert's designation of a C-infinity from Georg Cantor's actual infinite set of numbers) Hilbert notes that the Russell-Zermelo paradox presents so many devastating contradictions that it nearly undermined deductive procedure in mathematics:

> These contradictions, the so-called paradoxes of set theory, though at first scattered, became progressively more acute and more serious. In particular, a contradiction discovered by Zermelo and Russell had a downright catastrophic effect when it became known throughout the world of mathematics. Confronted by these paradoxes, Dedekind and Frege completely abandoned their point of view [belief in the coherency of an infinite set as proposed by Cantor] and retreated.[30]

Hilbert then concludes that the technique of ideal elements (which can imply infinities) cannot be used *if they change the fundamental axioms of finite numbers to which they have been applied.* Since this does not occur with potential infinities (B-infinities), but *always* occurs with actual infinities (C-infinities), Hilbert rejects the use of the latter in any way that could apply to the real world (i.e., real magnitudes, real counting, real series, etc.):

> In summary, let us return to our main theme and draw some conclusions from all our thinking about the infinite. Our principal result is that the infinite is nowhere to be found in reality. It neither exists in nature nor provides a legitimate basis for rational thought — a remarkable harmony between being and thought. . . . The role that remains for the infinite to play is solely that of an idea — if one means by an idea, in Kant's terminology, a concept of reason which transcends all experience and which completes the concrete as a totality [a B-infinity]. . . .[31]

Hilbert's analysis shows that the existence of a mathematical infinity in a finite or aggregative structure results not only in a contradiction, but also in the undermining of the axioms of finite numbers which it was intended to complete. If devastating consequences for the whole of mathematical reasoning are to be avoided, C-infinities must *not* be applied to real magnitudes, successions, series, or any finite or aggregative structure that could be considered real (such as past time).

30. Hilbert 1964, p. 141.
31. Hilbert 1964, p. 151.

Hilbert's prohibition of C-infinities continues to be widely held by contemporary mathematicians. As William Lane Craig notes:

> According to Robinson, "Cantor's infinities are abstract and divorced from the physical world [Robinson 1969, p. 163]." This judgment is echoed by Fraenkel, who concludes that among the various branches of mathematics, set theory is "the branch which least of all is connected with external experience and most genuinely originates from free intellectual creation [Fraenkel 1973, p. 240]." As a creation of the human mind, state Rotman and Kneebone . . . when one selects from an infinite set an infinite subset, the actual possibility of such an operation is not implied. "The conception of an infinite sequence of choices (or of any other acts) . . . is a mathematical fiction — an idealization of what is imaginable only in finite cases [Rotman and Kneebone 1966, p. 60]."[32]

Of course, infinities can be applied to sets in merely theoretical or abstract ways (e.g., Cantorian sets or the Zermelo-Fraenkel universe of sets), but this cannot be thought to have applicability to the real world:

> [T]he Zermelo-Fraenkel universe of sets exists *only* in a realm of abstract thought. . . . [T]he "universe" of sets to which the . . . theory refers is in no way intended as an abstract model of an existing Universe, but serves merely as the postulated universe of discourse for a certain kind of abstract inquiry.[33]

In sum, Hilbert's, Fraenkel's, Rotman's, Kneebone's, Zermelo's, Robinson's, and many others' analysis shows that the existence of a mathematical infinity in a finite or aggregative structure results not only in a contradiction, but also in the undermining of the axioms of finite numbers which it was intended to complete. If devastating consequences for the whole of mathematical reasoning (and also the applicability of mathematics to the finite universe) are to be avoided, C-infinities must not be applied to real magnitudes, successions, series, or any finite or aggregative structure that could be considered real (such as past time).

---

32. Craig 1993(a), p. 10. Many other mathematicians and philosophers have recognized this as well. See, for example, Whitrow 1954-55, pp. 215-25; 1967, pp. 422-42; 1968; and 1970, pp. 224-33.

33. Rotman and Kneebone 1966, p. 61. Italics mine.

At this juncture, the reader will probably notice the invalidity of the hypothesis "infinite past history" or "infinite past time." The ontological explanation of time, which shows that history must be a continuous succession of events (each of which has real distensive separation and real power to aggregate the whole of the continuous succession) reveals that when infinity is applied to it, it must imply "infinity within an *actual* finite or aggregative structure," which implies an actual infinity (a C-infinity). As noted above, this C-infinity must be considered illusory (nonexistent within a standard universe) because it undermines the axioms of finite mathematics which ground the quantifiable intelligibility of the realities in that universe (and also the applicability of mathematics to the finite universe). This deduction alone is sufficient to show that infinite history (implying infinite past time) cannot exist through any possible reality (or contemporaneously unified group of realities) in any possible universe. Therefore, there will have to be a beginning (and a creator) of past time wherever past time exists.

C-infinities not only undermine the axioms of finite mathematics, but also the intelligibility of the finite or aggregative *realities* to which they have been applied. For example, the existence of an infinity in the whole of past history would undermine the distensive separation of every part of that past history (reducing its aggregative effect within the whole to nothing — a dimensionless point), because an infinite distension minus any finite part, or any infinite part which is a subset of the whole, is still infinity. But this cannot be the case in real history, because every part of past time must maintain its distensive separation and its power to aggregate the whole. If it did not, then history would be fraught with irresolvable contradictions (e.g., the cat alive and dead simultaneously).

We will now proceed to a formal demonstration of how infinity applied to past time undermines its real distensive separation and its capacity to aggregate the whole. The undermining of these two real characteristics of time requires that history be fraught with contradictions that obviously could not and did not occur. This will formalize the above conclusion that infinite past time cannot be applied to our universe or any other standard universe.

IV. A Formal Argument Against the Infinity of Past Time in Any Changeable Universe

The proof of finite past time in any changeable universe is dependent on the above definition of time ("an aggregating succession of non-contemporaneous distension intrinsic to changeable reality"). This proof may be set out in a complex syllogism as follows.

>Premise #1: If there is no real time (as defined above) intrinsic to a changeable universe, then that universe's history would be a complete contradiction.

>Premise #2: If real time is intrinsic to any changeable universe, then *every part* of its non-contemporaneous distension would have to be integrally constitutive of the whole of past time in that universe (i.e., no part of the whole of past time could be functionally equivalent to zero magnitude in that universe).

>Premise #3: If the total magnitude of real past time in a particular universe is hypothesized to be infinite, then no part (not even an infinite part) can be an integral constitutive part (e.g., "a building block") of the whole of past time (i.e., every part, including infinite parts, would be functionally equivalent to zero magnitude in constituting the whole of past time).

>Premise #4: But no universe's history (including our universe's history) can be a complete contradiction (*a priori*, and contrary to fact).

>Conclusion #1: Therefore, there must be real time intrinsic to every changeable universe (*modus tollens* — Premise #1).

>Conclusion #2: Therefore, *every part* of real time must be integrally constitutive of the whole of past time in any particular universe (*modus ponens* — Premise #2).

>Conclusion #3: Therefore, the total magnitude of real past time (past non-contemporaneous distension) in any changeable universe cannot be infinite (*modus tollens* — Premise #3).

>Conclusion #4: Therefore, the total magnitude of past time in any changeable universe must be finite (restatement of Conclusion #3).

Proof of Premise #1:

If there is no real time (an aggregating succession of non-contemporaneous distension) intrinsic to a changeable universe, then that universe's history would be a complete contradiction.

Recall that real time is an aggregating succession of non-contemporaneous distension intrinsic to reality, which allows realities to avoid contradictory states (such as the cat alive and dead simultaneously). Recall further that non-contemporaneity is a manifold which can be divided into *earlier* and *later*.[34] This manifold cannot be constituted by dimensionless instants or infinitesimals, because dimensionless points cannot constitute any magnitude, and more importantly, they cannot separate contradictory states within the same entity.

Now, given that there is non-contemporaneous distension intrinsic to changeable reality, it not only separates non-contradictory states, but also produces duration (i.e., remaining in existence over against the possibility of changing or going out of existence). Once reality is "temporalized," it does not simply exist, it *remains* in existence, or *endures* in existence. Now, this remaining or enduring in existence is extrinsically measurable and intrinsically divisible. It is extrinsically measurable because its distension can be compared to any regular motion used as a standard (e.g., one rotation of the earth on its own axis — a 24-hour day).[35] It is intrinsically divisible because it is not a dimensionless point, and inasmuch as it has magnitude (i.e., non-contemporaneous distension), it can be divided until one reaches some *non-zero* (finitely small) minimum interval.[36]

Thus, we can know of the reality of time (intrinsically divisible, non-contemporaneous distension in changeable realities) in two ways: (1) through its separation of contradictory states in particular realities (e.g., the cat alive and then dead), and (2) in the measurable duration (remaining in existence) of changeable realities. In the second way, we not only know *that* time is real, but also *the aggregated amount* of real time intrinsic to changeable reality. Notice that this "amount" is not merely a *subjective* measurement, but real time's measur*ability*.

Recall further that real time is not only intrinsic to particular changeable realities, but also to groups of realities unified through a *contemporaneous* manifold, such as space. One such contemporaneously unified group of

34. Many ontological grounds have been proposed for this earlier-later manifold, such as Bergson's cosmic memory (see above), Whitehead's creativity (Whitehead 1978), David Bohm's implicate order (Bohm 1986), and Capek's non-spatialized temporal ground (Capek 1976). See also Spitzer 1989.

35. This contention is not affected by the special and general theories of relativity (which account for the differences in clocks in reference frames with different relative velocities), because those differences arise out of the invariant velocity of light. These differences can be reconciled through the Lorentz-Einstein transformation — Radical 1 minus (v^2/c^2). In any case, no matter what measuring device is used in whatever reconcilable reference frame, the amount of non-contemporaneous distension intrinsic to temporalized reality is measurable.

36. The reasons for the necessity of a *finitely* small (non-zero) minimum interval of non-contemporaneous distension are given above in Section II.C.5.

realities is a universe, whose age is extrinsically measurable as a whole. Inasmuch as the realities of a universe are contemporaneously unified, they can share a single temporal (non-contemporaneous) manifold which is intrinsic to their contemporaneous manifold (say, space). This single "non-contemporaneous distensive manifold" enables a universe's accumulated duration to be measured as a whole (e.g., our observable universe is 13.7 billion years old).

This means that time not only prevents the simultaneity of contradictory states in single realities, but also in groups of realities within a contemporaneously unified universe. Hence, it prevents Mars from being in two different spatial positions relative to the Earth simultaneously. Furthermore, it prevents contradictions among collective realities, such as "no one having been killed in the Battle of the Bulge" and "many people having been killed in the Battle of the Bulge" occurring simultaneously.

We may now proceed to the proof of Premise #1. If there were no non-contemporaneous distension intrinsic to a universe, the entire history of that universe would be collapsed into a single instant, which would effectively make the history of every change in that universe (changes in individual realities, changes in relative position, changes in groups of realities, etc.) a complete contradiction.

Proof of Premise #2:

If real time is intrinsic to any changeable universe, then every part of its non-contemporaneous distension would have to be integrally constitutive of the whole of past time in that universe (i.e., no part of the whole of past time could be functionally equivalent to zero magnitude in that universe).

Every part of real time in any universe not only separates contradictory states within that universe, but also separates earlier and later parts of real time in that universe. Imagine, for a moment, three finitely small magnitudes of real time with Magnitude #1 being the earliest and Magnitude #3 being the latest. Magnitude #2 would separate Magnitude #1 from Magnitude #3. If Magnitude #2 were the functional equivalent of a dimensionless point (of zero magnitude), then Magnitude #1 and Magnitude #3 would collapse into one another (and would, as it were, be continuous). But if a contradictory state exists between Magnitude #1 and Magnitude #3 (which is separated by Magnitude #2), then making Magnitude #2 the functional equivalent of a dimensionless point makes that contradiction simultaneous. For example, say the cat were alive at the *end* of Magnitude #1, died during magnitude #2, and was dead at the *beginning* of Magnitude #3. The reduction of Magnitude #2 to the functional equivalent of a dimensionless point would make the cat alive and dead simultaneously (an obvious contradiction). Similarly, in any changing universe, the reduction of any magnitude of time to the functional equivalent of a dimensionless point would produce contradictions wherever change occurred in that universe.

If such contradictions are to be avoided, then every part of real time in any universe cannot be the functional equivalent of a dimensionless point; and if it is not the functional equivalent of a dimensionless point, then it must *really* non-contemporaneously separate earlier parts (e.g., Magnitude #1) from later parts (e.g., Magnitude #3); and if it *really* non-contemporaneously separates earlier and later parts of the whole of past time, then it must be aggregately constitutive (e.g., "a building block") of the whole of past time in that universe.

Working backwards, then, if every part of past time is not really aggregately constitutive (i.e., "an aggregate building block") of the whole of past time in a particular universe, then it really does not non-contemporaneously separate earlier moments from later moments of past time in that universe; and if it really does not non-contemporaneously separate earlier from later moments of past time in that universe, then it is the functional equivalent of a dimensionless point; and if it is the functional equivalent of a dimensionless point, then it would not non-contemporaneously separate contradictory states in that universe (again, an obvious contradiction).

Proof of Premise #3:
If the total magnitude of real past time in a particular universe is hypothesized to be infinite, then no part (not even an infinite part) can be an aggregate constitutive part (e.g., "an aggregate building block") of the whole of past time (i.e., every part, including infinite parts, would be functionally equivalent to zero magnitude in aggregately constituting the whole of past time).

The postulation of an infinite magnitude of past time has the effect of reducing each and every finite and infinite part within it to a *non*-aggregative, *non*-constitutive status (i.e., a non–"aggregate building block" status), because an infinite whole minus a finite interval is still an infinite whole (undifferentiatable from its original state). An infinite whole minus an infinite part of the whole (there are an infinite number of infinite parts within an infinite whole) is still equal to the infinite whole (undifferentiatable from its original state). Finally, an infinite whole minus an infinity of infinite parts of itself is still an infinite whole (undifferentiatable from its original state). Therefore, every part of the whole (including an infinite part and an infinity of infinite parts) is the functional equivalent of a dimensionless point (of zero magnitude) *in aggregately constituting* the whole. Now, if every part of an infinite magnitude is the functional equivalent of a dimensionless point (of zero magnitude) in aggregately constituting the whole, then no part can be really aggregately constitutive of that whole. Therefore, an infinite magnitude makes all finite and infinite parts of that magnitude non-aggregative, non-constitutive (i.e., non–"aggregate building blocks") of the whole.

Now this conclusion is in direct conflict with the requirements of real time in a changing universe elucidated in Premise #2 (i.e., that every part of real time non-contemporaneously separates earlier and later parts of the whole of past time, making every part of past time really aggregately constitutive — a "building block" — of the whole of past time). This requirement of real time in a changing universe is necessary for the prevention of contradictory states within that universe. Therefore, the hypothesis of infinite past time in any changeable universe must be false, and therefore, past time in any changeable universe must be finite.

This result arises out of the incoherency of applying a C-infinity to finite or aggregative reality (recognized by Hilbert and other mathematicians — see above, Section III.B). The C-infinity not only undermines the axioms of finite mathematics; it also undermines the applicability of finite mathematics to the real world. In this particular case, the application of a C-infinity to the whole of past time in a universe, i.e., a C-infinity, makes every part of the total magnitude of past time non-aggregative, and non-constitutive (i.e., a "non–building block") of the whole. But in the real world described by finite mathematics, every part of past time must not only non-contemporaneously separate contradictory states within a universe, but also non-contemporaneously separate earlier magnitudes from later magnitudes of past time. This means that in the real world described by finite mathematics, every part of real past time must really be aggregative and constitutive (i.e., a "building block") of the whole of past time. Once again, the C-infinity has undermined real relationships in the finite world, and undermined the applicability of finite mathematics to that real world.

The following premise and conclusions are a formal restatement of the incoherency of applying an infinity to past time (a C-infinity) in a real universe:

Premise #4:

But no universe's history (including our universe's history) can be a complete contradiction (*a priori,* and contrary to fact).

Conclusion #1: Therefore, there must be real time intrinsic to every change-able universe (*modus tollens* — Premise #1).

Conclusion #2: Therefore, *every part* of real time must be aggregately con-stitutive of the whole of past time in any particular universe (*modus ponens* — Premise #2).

Conclusion #3: Therefore, the total magnitude of real past time (past non-contemporaneous distension) in any changeable universe cannot be infinite (*modus tollens* — Premise #3).

Conclusion #4: Therefore, the total magnitude of past time in any change-able universe must be **finite** (restatement of Conclusion #3). This conclusion is confirmed by several well-known astrophysicists.[37]

*   *   *

Clarification of Future Time. At this point, the reader might wonder, "Well, what about future time?" The answer is, quite simply, that future time is a *B-infinity,* for future time never exists (it is always an incomplete horizon). Infinite future time only implies that non-contemporaneous distension can continue to increase indefinitely in total magnitude. It does not imply the existence of infin-ity in a finite or aggregative structure (a C-infinity). Therefore, Hilbert's prohi-bition does not apply to future time any more than it does to an ever-expanding universe, an ever-expanding Euclidean plane, an ever-growing number line, or an ever-growing generation of members of a set. That is why infinite future time cannot be an analogy for infinite past time, and vice versa.

V. Proof of a Creator of Past Time Which Is Not Itself Conditioned by Time

The following proof arises out of three sets of deductions grounded in the necessary finitude of past time:

> First Set of Deductions: Every universe must be caused by a reality transcending that universe.

37. Ellis, Kirchner, and Stoeger 2003, p. 14.

Second Set of Deductions: There must be a beginning cause (a first cause) of every aggregative succession of temporally conditioned causes of past time.

Third Set of Deductions: The first cause (beginning cause) of any aggregative succession of temporally conditioned causes of past time cannot itself be conditioned by time.

First Set of Deductions: Every universe must be caused by a reality transcending that universe.

If the application of infinity to past time is a C-infinity, and a C-infinity is inapplicable to real time, then past time must be finite in our universe and any universe to which the axioms of finite mathematics apply. This implies that past time has a beginning (a *terminus a quo* — a terminus from which) in any universe. Three consequent deductions follow:

1) *Therefore, any universe must have a beginning.* As shown above, the *past time* of any universe must have a beginning (a *terminus a quo*). This beginning is applicable not only to the *past time* of any universe, but also to the *universe itself*; for if a universe is intrinsically conditioned by real time, then the beginning of time would have to represent the beginning of everything conditioned by time, namely, the universe itself.

2) *Therefore, any universe could not have caused itself to exist.* Inasmuch as any universe must have a beginning, that beginning constitutes the point prior to which it did not exist (it was literally nothing). As implied in (1) above, if our universe's past time did not exist prior to its beginning, neither did the universe itself, for the existence of the universe is coincident with the real time that conditions it. Now, if the universe was nonexistent, it could not have brought itself into existence, for from nothing, only nothing comes (*a priori*).

3) *Therefore, something transcending every universe must cause that universe to exist.* If every universe must have been nothing prior to its beginning, and nothing can only produce nothing, something other than that universe must cause it to exist. This cause must transcend the universe it creates, because the universe it causes did not yet exist prior to causation.[38]

---

38. The above three deductions are a restatement of what William Lane Craig terms the Kalam argument, which goes as follows: (1) Everything that begins to exist has a cause of

Second Set of Deductions: There must be a beginning cause (a first cause) of every aggregative succession of temporally conditioned causes of past time.

The question now arises about whether the *cause* of any universe is itself conditioned by time. It was shown above that the cause of any changeable universe must transcend that universe and *its* past time. But this "*cause*" might itself be conditioned by time, and therefore have its own past time quite independent of the past time of the universe it creates.

Now, if the cause of any universe were itself conditioned by time, then its past time would have to be finite (because past time in *any* reality or universe cannot be infinite without undermining the real aggregately constitutive character of every part of the whole of past time). Hilbert's prohibition of C-infinities applies to past time in "*causes* of temporally conditioned universes" as much as it does to temporally conditioned universes themselves, because it does not matter *what* reality is conditioned by past time; past time must be finite in every reality that is conditioned by time.

Now, if the cause of our universe's past time is also conditioned by time, and its past time is finite, then it too must have a beginning (a *terminus a quo*) "before" which it was nonexistent, and if it were nonexistent, it would not have been able to cause itself, and therefore, it would also have to have a cause of its past time. Let us call this hypothetical "cause of the cause of our universe" Cause #2.

Of course, the question will again arise, "Is Cause #2 conditioned by time?" If it is, the same set of deductions will again apply and Cause #2 will have to have still another cause (call it "Cause #3").

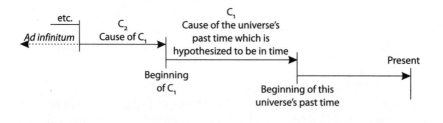

---

its existence. (2) The universe began to exist. (3) Therefore, the universe has a cause of its existence (Craig 1993, p. 4).

The question now arises about whether we can proceed to an infinity of causes of causes. The following argument will show that this cannot occur in any aggregative succession of temporally conditioned causes of past time.

(1) An infinity of temporally conditioned causes is equivalent to an infinite magnitude of past time. Inasmuch as each hypothetical cause is conditioned by time, and all of these causes are arranged in an infinite aggregative succession, the total magnitude of the aggregative succession is expressed by the equation "infinity × a non-zero magnitude = an infinite magnitude." It does not matter that a finite amount of past time is hypothesized in *each* of the causes; the infinity of aggregately successive causes makes these finite magnitudes into an infinite total magnitude. There is really no difference between postulating an infinity of microseconds, an infinity of seconds, an infinity of years, and an infinite aggregative succession of temporally conditioned causes; all of these hypotheses equal an infinite temporal magnitude because infinity times any non-zero magnitude equals infinity.

(2) Hilbert's prohibition of C-infinities applies to this hypothesis as much as it does to infinite past time in one universe. If past time is hypothesized to be infinite (in any arrangement, in any reality, or in any aggregate combination of realities), then none of its parts, not even an infinity of infinite parts, can be really aggregately constitutive of the whole of past time in that reality or combination of realities. But as has been shown many times above, every part of real time must be aggregately constitutive of the whole of past time in any reality or aggregative succession of temporally conditioned realities (otherwise, contradictions would abound in the histories of those changeable realities or universes).

(3) Therefore, an infinite aggregative succession of temporally conditioned *causes* of past time cannot exist.

(4) Therefore, there must be a finite number of temporally conditioned *causes* of past time (one or more, but not an infinity).

(5) Therefore, there must be a beginning cause (a first cause) of every aggregative succession of temporally conditioned causes of past time.

Third Set of Deductions: The first cause (beginning cause) of any aggregative succession of temporally conditioned causes of past time cannot itself be conditioned by time.
If the first cause were conditioned by time, then its past time would have to be finite. If its past time were finite, then it would have to have a beginning.

And if it had a beginning, it would be nonexistent "before" that beginning. And if it were nonexistent "before" its beginning, it would have to be caused by a transcendent reality, meaning that it could *not* be the *first* cause.

The only way in which the first cause can be truly first is if it is not conditioned by time, for this would mean that it does not have to have a past time which would have to have a beginning, which, in turn, would have to have a transcendent cause.

Therefore, there must ultimately exist a first cause of every universe, which first cause is not itself conditioned by time.

Now, it may be asked, what does it mean for a reality "not to be conditioned by time"? I have attempted a response to this question in this book and elsewhere.[39] For the moment, suffice it to say that such a reality resembles an A-infinity (one that recognizes "non-restrictedness" in power or being by prohibiting the application of finite or aggregative structures to it). Why view this reality as an A-infinity? Because the absence of temporal conditioning (an aggregative structure) suggests that it is not subject to spatio-temporal magnitude, not changeable, not changing, not moving in space-time, and not caused.

The reality in question, then, seems to resemble "absolute simplicity" (see Chapter 3, Section II). Recall that "simplicity" means "less intrinsic and extrinsic restriction." Though this proof is not concerned with an absence of *extrinsic* restrictions in the first cause, it is certainly concerned with an absence of *intrinsic* restrictions (inasmuch as it denies the possibility of temporal conditioning — an aggregative structure — in the first cause).

Now, recall that intrinsic restrictions cause beings to be divisible into parts (through a contemporaneous manifold like space, or a non-contemporaneous manifold like time). But a purely simple being would have no such intrinsic restrictions, and therefore would have absolutely no parts. It would be completely transparent to itself — purely inclusive to itself, like a pure act of self-consciousness grasping itself grasping itself, without "circling back," indeed, without motion, displacement, or spatio-temporal transference of any kind (see Chapter 4, Section II.D).

This reality supersedes the capacity of the human imagination, which experiences reality as fundamentally temporalized. Nevertheless, the limits of human imagination do not represent the limits of reality or even the limits of what reason can prove.

---

39. See Chapter 4, Section II.D (the Lonerganian argument on the unrestricted act of understanding — understanding itself). See also Spitzer 1989 and 2000.

Conclusion

The prohibition of a C-infinity (infinite past time) points us to an A-infinity, that is, a Reality which transcends the axioms of finite mathematics because It is unrestricted in its power. The conclusion that there must exist a first cause of all temporally conditioned causes which is not itself conditioned by time is similar to such a Reality because it lacks intrinsic restriction and is a First Cause of temporally conditioned realities. These qualities are frequently attributed to God.

This conclusion corresponds quite neatly with the one reached in Chapter 1, which showed the virtual inevitability of an initial singularity in any inflationary model universe. This initial singularity requires a causative force outside of universal space-time asymmetry to bring it into being. We might conclude this chapter with the same words used to conclude Chapter 1, from the physicist Paul Davies:

> The [initial] singularity must be regarded as a temporal boundary of all things. Consequently, the question does not arise of what happened *before* [the singularity]. The word "before" implies a temporal order, and this ceases to exist at the [initial] singularity. The same is true of the question of causation. It is often asked what caused the creation event. The whole identification of cause and effect with time *order* (cause always preceding effect) is in any case dubious, so that to require the creation to have a cause which *precedes* it is not in fact necessary. Moreover, the notion of a preceding causation is clearly meaningless here because temporal considerations cannot be extended beyond the [initial] singularity.[40]

What kind of cause does not have to act in time? It would seem to be the kind of Creator indicated in the above proof — a Creator which is not Itself conditioned by time.

---

40. Davies 1977, pp. 159-61.

Methodological Considerations and the Impossibility of Disproving God

Introduction

Four areas germane to the philosophical proofs of God's existence merit closer inspection:

   I) common methodological elements,
  II) three approaches to the notion of "God,"
 III) the impossibility of disproving the existence of God, and
  IV) the tenuous rationality of atheism.

They merit closer inspection because they respond to problematic considerations raised within the history of philosophy. Though the foregoing proofs stand on their own logical and evidential merits, clarification of these issues might help to put some of these historical problematic concerns to rest.

I. Common Methodological Elements

The foregoing philosophical proofs for the existence of God have three foundational methodological constituents: (A) complete disjunction within metaphysical assertions, (B) the notion of "infinity," and (C) causality.

I.A. Complete Disjunction Within Metaphysical Assertions

Hypothetical-deductive reasoning can be of two sorts:

(1) metaphysical, where one sets up a hypothesis, and then *dis*proves it in order to show that the state of affairs *contrary* to the hypothesis must be true, and

(2) scientific, where one sets up a hypothesis, and then develops an experimental apparatus that will test for that one particular hypothesis in order to show that it is true.

One might ask why *dis*proving is used in metaphysics while experimental *proving* is used in science. The answer lies in the nature of the objects being proved. Metaphysics is concerned with categories that are completely disjunctive (i.e., finite-infinite, conditioned-unconditioned, caused-uncaused, material-immaterial, etc.). Notice that completely disjunctive categories exhaust the whole range of possibility. Therefore, one of the categories must be true for any given reality at any given place or time. Likewise, one of them must be false for any given reality at any place and time. Therefore, if one *dis*proves an object's being finite, it *must* be infinite, and if one *dis*proves an object's being infinite, it *must* be finite. Similarly, if one *dis*proves an object's being caused, it *must* be uncaused; and if one *dis*proves an object's being uncaused, it *must* be caused. Notice also that both sides of the disjunction refer to a specific, meaningful, *positive* characteristic about an object. For example, finite and infinite both refer to meaningful, positive characteristics about an object; so do caused and uncaused, conditioned and unconditioned, material and immaterial, and so forth.

Such is not the case with objects proved in science, for science is not concerned with completely disjunctive, positive characteristics (which exhaust the whole range of possibilities). Physics, for example, is not concerned with *whether* an object is finite, but with what kind of finitude it has (e.g., proton-like, neutron-like, electron-like, etc.). It is concerned with the *parameters* or the *degree* of finitude relative to other objects in the physical universe. Again, physics is not concerned with whether an object is caused or uncaused, but with the parameters surrounding its causation. Science's interest in the detail of finitude, conditions, qualities, relations, and causation renders disproof almost meaningless. For example, to disprove that an object in the laboratory is a proton does not give rise to knowledge about a *specific* positive characteristic about the object (such as its being uncaused or infinite). Rather, it indicates only that the object could be any one of a virtually infinite number of possible alternatives (e.g., an electron, a neutron, or any other possible atomic or subatomic particle).

In short, metaphysics is concerned with completely disjunctive categories. These categories refer to specific, meaningful, positive characteristics of reality. Hence, when one *dis*proves one side of the disjunction (say, the finitude of an object), one immediately *proves* the other side of the disjunction (i.e., the infinity of the object).

In contrast to this, science does not investigate completely disjunctive characteristics. It investigates the "details" within one side of the disjunction (e.g., finitude, causation, conditionedness). Thus, science does not have access to the whole range of possibilities for any given object. Its interest in detail prohibits it from drawing metaphysical conclusions (i.e., being able to prove the existence of something by disproving its opposite). Since a negation in science (e.g., "object X is not a proton") refers to a virtually infinite range of possible alternatives, science is forced to prove a specific characteristic about an object through experimentation.

We may now examine how this completely disjunctive character was involved in our previous proofs. In Chapter 3, we began with the hypothesis that all reality is composed of only conditioned realities. We then showed that this hypothesis is false. If any reality were dependent upon an infinite number of conditions, it could not exist. And if it were dependent upon a finite number of conditions, it would depend on a last condition whose conditions were not fulfilled. In either case, nothing, including the writer, would exist. But the writer is a rigorously corroborated existing state of affairs, and therefore, it had to be contended that the proposition "all reality is composed of only conditioned realities" is false. Since "conditionedness" is completely disjunctive, it follows that there must be at least one unconditioned reality in all reality.

Chapter 5 began with the hypothesis that past time is infinite. Notice that "infinite" is a completely disjunctive characteristic (i.e., it can be combined with its opposite to give the entire range of possibilities for any given object X — finite-infinite). When it was shown that infinite past time contradicts the nature of any possible changeable universe (including our own universe), it necessarily followed (by complete disjunction) that past time *must be finite*. Since the whole range of possibilities is captured by the disjunction of finite-infinite, then if past time is not infinite, it *must* be finite.

Metaphysics should not be summarily rejected because it does not correspond to the experimental or empirical grounding of science. As we saw above, science has to ground itself in this experimental/empirical procedure because it cannot effectively use "disproof" as a means of proving the opposite. It is compelled to make use of empirical grounding because it does not avail itself of completely disjunctive categories. Metaphysics, however, has the good fortune of using such categories, and therefore can reasonably and responsibly prove the existence of particular realities by disproving their disjunctive counterparts.

It would be unduly limiting to insist that every discipline use the same methodology, for metaphysical method can stand on its own apart from scientific method. If intrinsic and ontological contradictions are universally false, and negations of rigorously corroborated existing states of affairs are factually false, then metaphysics (with its use of completely disjunctive categories) should be considered both reasonable and responsible.

I.B. The Notion of "Infinity"

It is frequently contended that proofs for the existence of God rely on an *assumption* of the impossibility of infinite regression. This is certainly *not* the case with the proofs presented in the foregoing chapters.

The metaphysical/ontological proofs for the existence of God given in Chapters 3 and 4 do not rest on the *assumption* of the impossibility of infinite regression; but rather on the verifiable assertion that without an unconditioned reality, nothing can exist. The notion of infinity appeared in these proofs only to prove the hypothesis that "an infinity of conditioned realities without an unconditioned reality is equal to absolutely nothing."

Recall from Chapter 3 (Section I.F) and Chapter 4 (Section II.A) that the hypothesis of *only* conditioned realities in the set of "all reality" entails that every conditioned reality, say, CR_1, depends on some other conditioned reality, say, CR_2, in order to exist. Hence, it is nothing until CR_2 exists and fulfills its conditions. Similarly, CR_2 would also have to depend on some other conditioned reality, say, CR_3, for its existence, and it would likewise be nothing until CR_3 exists and fulfills its conditions. And so forth, *ad infinitum*. Since every hypothetical conditioned reality is dependent upon other *non*existent conditioned realities for its existence, it will never come into existence. It does not matter if one postulates an infinite number of others (or arranges the infinite number of others in a circle), they are all still nothing in their dependence upon nonexistent conditions. Therefore, the hypothesis that there are only conditioned realities in "all reality" will always result in all reality being nothing, which is obviously contrary to fact. Evidently, there was no assumption made about the impossibility of infinite regression in this proof in Chapters 3 and 4.

Recourse to a prohibition of infinite regression was made only in Chapter 5 with respect to an infinite *temporally* subordinated series in the past (i.e., infinite past time). Indeed, this is the only kind of proof that requires a consideration of the impossibility of infinite regression. Notice that an infinite regression was not *assumed* to be false in the proof in Chapter 5. Rather, it was shown that the hypothesis of an infinite amount of past time would contradict the aggregately constitutive nature of every part of past time. Since this "constitutive nature of every part of past time" is necessary to prevent historical contradictions in our universe (and any other universe), infinite past time contradicts the facts of our universe and the conditions necessary for any other changeable universe.

Furthermore, Hilbert's analysis showed that the use of a C-infinity would not only undermine the axioms of finite mathematics, but would also contradict the nature of any reality to which finite mathematics could be applied. Past time is no exception to this. As shown in the ontological explanation of time given in Chapter 5 (Section II), past time is a reality to which finite mathematics can be applied.

In sum, no assumption about the impossibility of infinite regression need be made in any proof for the existence of God. Metaphysical/ontological proofs (such as those given in Chapters 3 and 4) do not need to make recourse to infinite regression. Proofs resting on the hypothesis of an infinite temporally subordinated series (such as the one given in Chapter 5) can demonstrate irresolvable ontological contradictions when infinities are applied to past time.

I.C. Causality

The notion of causation has led to a myriad of objections to traditional proofs of God's existence throughout the last four centuries. Three criticisms have been leveled against the use of causation in the past:

1) the assumed universality of the causal principle in proofs for God's existence,
2) inadequate definitions of causality, and
3) an inability to prove conclusively the existence of causal relationships.

These three objections are summed up by Bertrand Russell's rather dismissive treatment of the First Cause argument:

> It is maintained that everything we see in this world has a cause, and as you go back in the chain of causes further and further you must come to a First Cause, and to that First Cause you give the name of God. That argument, I suppose, does not carry very much weight nowadays, because, in the first place, cause is not quite what it used to be. The philosophers and men of science have got going on cause, and it has not anything like the vitality it used to have; but, apart from that, you can see that the argument that there must be a First Cause is one that cannot have any validity. I may say that when I was a young man and was debating these questions very seriously in my mind, I for a long time accepted the argument of the First Cause, until one day, at the age of eighteen, I read John Stuart Mill's Autobiography, and I there found this sentence: "My father taught me that the question 'Who made me?' cannot be answered, since it immediately suggests the further question 'Who made God?'" That very simple sentence showed me, as I still think, the fallacy in the argument of the First Cause. If everything must have a cause, then God must have a cause. If there can be anything without a cause, it may just as well be the world as God, so that there cannot be any validity in that argument.[1]

The major thrust of Russell's argument concerns the **first of the above problems,** namely, the assumed universality of the causal principle. Russell believes that "First Cause arguments" are based on the *assumption* that "*everything* must have a cause." If any metaphysician seriously assumed this, then he would be liable to Russell's judgment that his argument is (stupidly) open to the question, "What caused God?" Fortunately, I can attest that very few metaphysicians in history were stupid enough to argue Russell's "universality of causation," making his rendition of "First Cause arguments" a straw man. It should be noted that in the three philosophical proofs given above, it was never assumed that "*everything* has a cause." Indeed, the assumption was quite the contrary.

In the metaphysical proof (given in Chapter 3), a complete disjunction was given: In all reality there is either only conditioned (caused) realities or there is at least one unconditioned (uncaused) reality. This proof does not

1. Russell 1957, pp. 6-7.

assume that *everything* has a cause, but rather demonstrates that an unconditioned reality (i.e., an uncaused reality) would have to exist if the hypothesis that "all reality is conditioned" entails that nothing exist. It does entail this. And hence, the proof does not fall prey to the question, "What caused God?" because this question, within the context of the proof, would be "What caused the unconditioned (uncaused) reality?" which is, of course, absurd. The Lonerganian argument rests on grounds similar to the metaphysical one (see Chapter 4, Section II.A), and so does not fall prey to Russell's objection for the same reasons.

In the third proof (given in Chapter 5), it was not assumed that everything had to have a cause, and a first uncaused cause was likewise not assumed. Rather, it was shown that a first cause of past time had to exist because the hypothesis of infinite past time contradicted the aggregately constitutive nature of time necessary to prevent contradictions in history. Thus, a first uncaused cause was shown to be necessary, and further, to transcend temporality altogether.

In sum, all three proofs never assumed the universality of the causal principle (*"everything* must have a cause"). Indeed, every proof assumed the hypothetical possibility of the contrary (i.e., that an uncaused reality could exist).

Russell's statement also includes an implication of the **second of the above-mentioned objections to causation,** namely, inadequate definitions of causation: "The philosophers and the men of science have got going on cause, and it has not anything like the vitality it used to have. . . ."[2] Since the days of Hume[3] and Kant,[4] the objection has been raised that we do not know precisely what a cause is. In recent years in the areas of quantum mechanics and Relativity Theory, the notion of causation has expanded enormously to include information in quantum fields, changes in space-time geometry, non-aggregative motion in plasmas, and a host of other non-linear, non-experienceable, seeming causal relationships. Most philosophers and scientists do not believe they understand one one-hundredth of the possible manifestations of causes. But one does not have to understand or experience the

2. Russell 1957, pp. 6-7.

3. Hume 1969, pp. 58-60.

4. Kant 1965, pp. 205, 230, and 253. He uses his problematic notion of causality to show "problems" in the First Cause argument. See, for example, pp. 389-90, 409ff., 415ff., 464ff. Notice that Kant defines causality according to the linear dynamics of seventeenth- and eighteenth-century (Newtonian) physics, limiting its usefulness in contemporary physics and ontology.

full range of causation in order to use some general principles of causation within the arguments for God's existence.

Recall for a moment that science is quite different from metaphysics. Science seeks to understand the *particulars* of *data* (say, causation within a quantum field), while metaphysics uses completely disjunctive categories with the most general definition possible. Thus, the only definition of causation with which the above three proofs are concerned is what is completely disjunctive to "an unconditioned reality" (first and second proofs), and "a creator of past time outside of this universe" (third proof). These proofs do not require an experience or understanding of every possible manifestation of the above three references to the "caused." Indeed, they do not have to make recourse to the notion of "causation" (with all of its historical baggage) at all.

Recourse was made to three categories that could adequately cover the entire range of action, interaction, interrelationship, and energy emission in the General Theory of Relativity, Quantum Theory, quantum cosmology, string theory, etc. — namely, "conditioned realities" (realities that *depend* on the fulfillment of conditions of *any* kind for their existence) and "conditions" (*any* reality upon which a conditioned reality depends for its existence) and "unconditioned reality" (a reality that does not depend on conditions of *any* kind for its existence). Conditioned realities and conditions can include space-time manifolds, electromagnetic fields, quantum fields, plasma fields, positions in the space-time manifold, structures of complexes, magnetic monopoles — literally *any* reality that is *not unconditioned*.

Dependence on conditions is all that needs to be known in order for the proof to function. The *kind* of condition is absolutely irrelevant to the *functioning* of the proof. No doubt, in the future, the meaning of causation will be enhanced and changed with respect to the *kinds* of conditions and conditioned realities. But what will remain unchanged is that there will be conditioned realities, and that these realities will not, by themselves, be able to exist without an unconditioned reality. Furthermore, what will remain unchanged is that an unconditioned reality must be absolutely simple (proved in Chapter 3, Section II.B) and unrestricted intelligibility (proved in Chapter 4, Section II.B); and that absolute simplicity and unrestricted intelligibility must be **unique**; which means that *everything else* in reality must be *conditioned*. This puts to rest Russell's further criticism that "if there can be anything without a cause, it may just as well be the world as God."

By now it will be clear that the first two proofs do not *assume* that realities need a cause. Far from it — they actually *demonstrate* that all realities that are not absolutely simple and unrestrictedly intelligible must be conditioned (caused) realities. So long as the proofs require nothing more than these most generic, completely disjunctive definitions of "causation," philosophers and scientists can keep changing and expanding their views of causation without affecting the intelligibility or the validity of the three abovementioned proofs.

The third objection to causality (our inability to know definitively of the existence of causal relationships) dates back to the time of David Hume.[5] But as was shown, this objection does not apply to the above three philosophical proofs, because it is not necessary to know of the existence of *particular* causal relationships at the *beginning* of any of the proofs. The first and second proofs, for example, begin only with the disjunction of two *hypotheses:* either (1) reality is composed of only conditioned (caused) realities, or (2) it has at least one unconditioned (uncaused) reality in it.

At the *end* of the proof, two conclusions are adduced: (a) that there must exist one and *only* one unconditioned (uncaused) Reality in all reality, and (b) that *everything else,* as a consequence, must be a conditioned (caused) reality (by complete disjunction). Thus, these two proofs do not depend on or assume any knowledge of any particular causal relationship in order to function. Rather, they prove that everything in all reality besides God is subject to conditions and therefore causal relationships. The third objection to causation, then, is not only irrelevant to the first two proofs; the two proofs clarify the very ambiguity that is raised against them as an objection.

In conclusion, the notion of causation does not undermine the above three proofs for God's existence. Rather, the three proofs add clarity, veracity, and universality to the notion of causation. They add *clarity* by defining "causation" in the most generic (i.e., completely disjunctive) way. These completely disjunctive definitions embrace all particular manifestations of causality that science may adduce both now and in the future. The proofs add *veracity* to the notion of causality because they *demonstrate* (without assuming) that *all reality,* except the one, unconditioned Reality, must be conditioned (caused). They add *universality* to the notion of causality for the same reason.

The proofs do even more in their *interrelationship.* They show an interconnection among three kinds of causation, namely, that the cause of finite reality is also the cause of finite intelligibility and the cause of temporal-

5. Hume 1969, pp. 58-60.

ity. If the ultimate source of causation is at once an absolutely simple Reality, an unrestricted act of understanding, and a transtemporal Creator, then this might suggest a connection between the three kinds of causation themselves. These connections are better explored in a work on metaphysics. For the moment, suffice it to say that a unity of the above three characteristics of causation in their source suggests a unity in their manifestation. If such unities are taken seriously (instead of being ignored because of their implications for the existence of God), they could produce significant clarity in the concepts used by the physical sciences.

II. Three Approaches to the Notion of "God"

We may now move from the methodological principles for *proving* God's existence, to the methodological principles for *understanding* the proofs' conclusions. By now the reader will have noticed that the three proofs conclude to the existence of a similar reality: a unique, absolutely simple, infinite, perfectly intelligible, unrestricted act of understanding which is the continuous Creator of all else that is.

One important point bears repeating about this "infinite Reality" in all three proofs; namely, that "infinite" does not mean a B-infinity (indefinite ongoingness) or a C-infinity (an infinity falsely hypothesized to be actual within a finite or aggregative structure, such as space or time). "Infinite," here, means an A-infinity; that is, not being conditioned or restricted by any intrinsically or extrinsically limiting substructure or superstructure (such as spatial continua, temporal continua, fields, and forces). It therefore refers to "absolute simplicity" as defined in the first proof (Chapter 3), "unrestricted intelligibility" as defined in the second proof (Chapter 4), and "transtemporality" as defined in the third proof (Chapter 5).

Since the structure of our imagination is spatio-temporal, and our understanding is both finite and relational (see Chapter 4, Section I), we will not be able to comprehend this "infinite Reality" *as It is in Itself.* The limits of our imagination and understanding will impose restrictions on the infinite Reality which are really not there. Philosophical tradition, beginning with Pseudo-Dionysius the Areopagite,[6] refers to this way of imagining and understanding as kataphatic knowledge (the *via positiva,* or the "positive way"). Since we cannot comprehend the infinite Reality in a positive way, we

---

6. See Dionysius the Areopagite 1940, pp. 196-99.

have to make recourse to three imperfect approaches to understanding, namely:

1) apophatic knowledge (commonly called the "*via negativa*" or the "negative way"),
2) hyperphatic knowledge (looking down the tree of being), and
3) analogy.

The *via negativa* understands what the Infinite is not; the *via negativa* is not an absence of knowledge, but knowledge of what the Infinite cannot be. Though to say that the Infinite "has *no* intrinsic or extrinsic boundaries or boundary conditions" is the most accurate way of speaking and thinking about the infinite One, its purely negative content is quite dissatisfying.

If I were to answer the question, "What is an apple?" by saying that it is *not* an orange or any other citrus fruit, that it is *not* a banana, an avocado, etc., you might soon grow frustrated with the purely negative content of my answers. Though negative content is meaningful content, it fails to satisfy. Are we left completely bereft? Recall from Chapter 3, Section IV that the infinite One is the one unconditioned Reality, and that this one unconditioned Reality must be power or act (since it is the ultimate fulfillment of conditions of everything that exists). Thus, "infinite" here means "*un*restricted power" or "*un*restricted act" or "*no* extrinsic or intrinsic limit to power" or "*no* extrinsic or intrinsic limit to act," or "*no* magnitude conditioning power," or "*no* magnitude conditioning act," etc. Though these concepts cannot be positively imagined (like picture-thinking), they are replete with content that cannot be tied down to the limited powers of our imagination. As such, they properly refer to a Reality which is likewise filled with unimaginable power and act — content.

The *via negativa* does not exhaust the possible approaches to the infinite Reality. There is also a **hyperphatic approach** (understanding from above). Essentially, the hyperphatic approach moves down the tree of being and tries to see the absolutely simple, super-unifying power that stands at the top of the tree of being in relation to everything below It. By looking down from the top of the tree of being, one gets a "sense" of absolute simplicity by noticing all the other kinds of simplicity transcended by It and unified through It. Thus, one sees absolute simplicity as simpler (less restricted and more self-transparent) than a human act of self-consciousness, which is simpler than a universal unified field, which is simpler than a space-time field, which is simpler than an electromagnetic field. . . . Of course, one does not get a positive idea of what this super-unifying simplicity really is, but one gets a *sense* of Its power from all the intrinsic and extrinsic restrictions that are left behind as one goes up the tree of being. One gets a sense of Its power by seeing the power of what is below It on the tree of being; a sense of Its self-transparency by seeing the transparency of what is below It on the tree of being; a sense of Its inclusivity and capacity for unification by seeing the inclusivity and capacity for unification of what is below It on the tree of being, etc.

Another hyperphatic approach may be taken from the Lonerganian proof, that is, through the notion of an unrestricted act of understanding unifying the whole of finite intelligibility through Its completely transparent understanding of Itself. When one reflects on the capacity of understanding to abstract from the empirical residue and "produce" an idea that can be used predicatively, and then to unify ideas into systems, and even unify systems into super-systems (through higher and higher viewpoints), one gets a *sense* of the capacity of the unrestricted act of understanding to unify and understand the whole of finite intelligibility in relation to Itself. Again, when one reflects on the higher viewpoints represented by higher and higher systems of mathematics (moving from arithmetic to geometry and algebra, to analytic geometry and trigonometry, to the calculus and non-standard geometries, and even to the tensor), one gets a sense of the capacity of an unrestricted act of understanding. Though one has no positive idea of the unrestricted content of an unrestricted act of understanding, one has a *sense* of the absolutely highest viewpoint that this super-unifying super-intellection achieves. It may not be ultimately satisfying, but it is something — a *positive sense.*

There is yet another approach to understanding the infinite Reality which was proposed by the Scholastic tradition, particularly Saint Thomas Aquinas — namely **analogy.** I begin with an essential insight addressed in the second proof with respect to the notion of simplicity. Recall that boundaries (restrictions) exclude. The less intrinsic or extrinsic boundaries, the less exclusion. Absolute simplicity would be the absence of all intrinsic and extrinsic boundaries, which would therefore imply a completely *inclusive* Reality. Proper analogies of this Reality would have to be capable of being completely inclusive by their very nature. As will be explained in Chapter 7, there are five possible "candidates" for such complete inclusivity manifest in the world and accessible to human consciousness: truth, love, goodness/justice, beauty, and unity/being.[7]

---

7. These are termed "the transcendentals" by neo-Platonists and Thomists.

An apprehension of *truth* entails seeing *unity* amidst difference, for any act of understanding involves comparison, and comparison involves bringing together distinct images or ideas. As noted in Chapter 4 (Section I), if I wished to go beyond the mere imaginary experience of a giraffe, I will need to compare it to non-animals and to other animals. Each such comparison requires bringing together objects that exclude one another in their difference. This "bringing together of excluding objects" constitutes an overcoming of the boundaries producing their exclusion. Thus, mentation, by its very nature, unifies what excludes in an extra-mental state. If this "holding together" of intrinsically opposed objects requires a substrate that is more inclusive than either of the objects held together, then the substrate of mentation must be more inclusive than the contents of any of its ideas.

The act of unification in mentation might provide a suitable *analogy* for a *purely* inclusive Reality (a Reality without intrinsic or extrinsic boundaries). If one could take one's own mentative experience and apply it to a Reality which is capable not only of being an underlying unity for images and ideas, but also for all finite reality, and also between Itself and the entire scope of finite reality It unifies, then one might have an analogous "notion" of what this Reality might be (see Chapter 4, Section II.D). But, of course, such an analogy will fall far short of the mark, because our mentative acts are not capable of unifying realities, let alone all finite reality and the unity between absolute simplicity and all finite reality. Nevertheless, one can get a *positive entryway,* though vague, to the mentation of a purely inclusive Reality.

The same might be said of *love.* Inasmuch as egocentricity psychologically separates human beings from one another, it turns the separation of embodiment into a separation of inner worlds. Love (through an act of empathy) overcomes this psychological separation, and thereby overcomes the exclusionary properties of egocentricity and allows the inner world of the other to blend with one's own. Like mentation, this empathetic act suggests an underlying substrate that can hold together two opposed egocentric conditions. Some have argued that one could not even recognize the opposition between one's own inner world and that of another without such an underlying unity; for the very recognition of opposition requires bringing together the two opposed elements so that the opposition can be revealed. In any case, this underlying unity which brings together opposed consciousnesses and then overcomes the opposition must be more inclusive than the acts of consciousness it brings together. Perhaps this act could also be an analogy for a purely inclusive Reality.

Such an analogy would once again be vague because it could not begin to capture a reality capable of entering into unity with all finite consciousnesses and capable of overcoming the animosity and egocentricity that might arise out of these created consciousnesses. Even though our acts of love (and the feelings intrinsic to them) do not begin to approach the unconditional act of love intrinsic to a purely inclusive Reality, they might provide a glimmer of positivity, though inadequate, about that Reality.

Thus, we could get a sense of what God's empathy might be *like* through our own acts of empathy, particularly if we are aware of the regions of dissimilarity. So also, we might get a sense of what God's care might be *like* by analogy to our own; and even what His compassion might be like, etc.

As will be shown in Chapter 7, other analogies might be made through *goodness/justice*, which overcomes the intrinsic enmity among people; or *beauty*, which is the refulgence of the unity underlying diverse forms. Indeed, all unity and the apprehension of unity could provide analogies for a purely inclusive Reality. For the moment, suffice it to say that these acts of unification give a foundational cognitive base from which an analogy of complete inclusivity can be extrapolated.

Thus, we could get a sense of what God's goodness might be *like* through the goodness of, say, Mother Teresa (being careful to note the regions of dissimilarity). We could get a sense of what God's justice might be like by looking at a naturally fair and just person (like Aristotle's *spoudaios*). Furthermore, we could get a sense of what God's beauty might be like by noting the refulgence and majesty of Bach's Mass in B minor played in a magnificent cathedral; and so forth. Though the dissimilarities may be constantly before us, the sense of continuity between the analogate and God does give an incipient positive awareness of what God might be *like*.

III. The Impossibility of Disproving the Existence of God

It may be thought that the existence of God can be disproved. One obvious difficulty with this contention is that it would entail the denial of the three aforementioned proofs, which, in turn, would entail a myriad of intrinsic contradictions and denials of fact (including the denial of one's own existence). But there is a more sweeping problem with this contention, namely, it cannot be accomplished *in principle* because the unrestricted nature of God renders all methods of disproof fruitless. This can be shown by referring back to the three ways of proving the truth or falsity of claims. Recall from the introduction to Part Two that a claim may be considered reasonable and responsible if:

1) it can be affirmed by rigorous public corroboration, *or*
2) its denial leads to an intrinsic contradiction, *or*
3) its denial leads to a contradiction of fact (a rigorously corroborated state of affairs).

None of these methods can be used to prove the nonexistence of God. The following will make this clear.

The first method (rigorous public corroboration) is quite useful for proving the *existence* of a reality, but useless for proving the *nonexistence* of a reality. If, for example, I wish to prove the *existence* of dogs, I need only experience one, and have other people corroborate that experience. However, if I wish to prove the *nonexistence* of, say, phoenixes, I would have to experience everything that there is to experience, be certain that I had exhausted the entire range of possible experiences, and notice that phoenixes are not there. This would seem to be a rather daunting prospect.

Proving the nonexistence of *God* by this method is even more daunting, for God, as defined (the absence of intrinsic or extrinsic parameters which make realities accessible to human sensation, imagination, and understanding), is, in principle, beyond human experience. If God were to be experienceable, *God* would have to make an *aspect* of Himself accessible to us (such as an experience of His love or beauty — as in mystical or religious experience).[8] Therefore, the first method of disproof cannot be applied to an unconditioned, unrestricted being (God).

The second method (proving falsity through intrinsic contradiction), is equally fruitless. As noted above, contradictions arise out of the *exclusionary* properties of boundaries or restrictions (e.g., the boundaries of square exclude the boundaries of circle, or the boundaries of proton exclude the boundaries of electron, such that one cannot have a square-circle or a proton-electron in the same respect at the same place and time). An entity

---

8. It should be noted that not even God can make his *entire* essence — an unrestricted act of understanding — understandable to a subject without the capacity to understand it (e.g., one capable of only restricted acts of understanding). As with the square-circle (see above, Chapter 3, Section II), this is not a deficiency of God's power, but rather a deficiency solely attributable to the excluding boundaries of a partially simple being. Since humans are capable only of conditioned acts of understanding, God cannot force us to understand what we are in principle incapable of understanding (i.e., unrestricted understanding).

without *any* intrinsic or extrinsic boundaries or restrictions (i.e., an absolutely simple Reality — see Chapter 3, Sections II and IV) would be purely inclusive, and therefore, would not exclude anything *extrinsically* (from Itself) or *intrinsically* ("within" Itself). If there are no exclusionary properties *intrinsic* to "absolutely simple, unrestricted, unconditioned Reality," then there can *never* be a basis for *intrinsic* contradiction. If there is no boundary or restriction, there is no basis for contradiction.

The third method (proving nonexistence through a contradiction of fact) is also fruitless for a similar reason. If a reality is to be proven contradictory to fact (i.e., to be a contradiction of a publicly corroborated state of affairs), it must be capable of being contradicted. For example, if I am to prove that an electron does not exist at a particular coordinate (x, y, z), then all I need to do is prove that there is a proton (or some other contradictory particle or state of affairs) at that coordinate (x, y, z) in the same respect at the same time. The contradictory properties of electron and proton make this kind of disproof possible.

However, as noted above, contradiction is based on the exclusionary property of boundaries or restrictions. Now, if an entity has *no* intrinsic or extrinsic boundaries or restrictions (as has been defined of God), it does not exclude any bounded or restricted being *from itself*; it does not extrinsically exclude anything. Therefore it cannot be contradicted by *any* bounded or restricted being. Thus, one cannot say, "If protons exist, God cannot exist," for the boundaries of protons will never exclude the boundarylessness of God. Similarly, one cannot say, "If squares exist, God cannot exist," for the boundaries of square do not exclude the boundarylessness of God. The same holds true for all finite realities. The boundaries of a finite thing cannot exclude the boundarylessness of God. Therefore, nothing finite can ever be used to contradict the existence of God. This means that nothing finite (and therefore nothing in our world) could ever be the basis for disproving "God" (as defined).

Inasmuch as these three methods exhaust the scope of formal proof or disproof, it follows that the existence of God cannot be disproved in principle. Thus, given the above definition of "God" (i.e., as absolutely simple — without intrinsic or extrinsic boundaries or restrictions), it would seem that atheism could not be a rational enterprise in the same way as theism.

IV. The Tenuous Rationality of Atheism

At this juncture, the reader might ask, "If the existence of God cannot be disproved, what is the foundation of atheism?" The *brief* answer is that it can*not* be grounded in a formal argument based upon the definition of "God" given above ("absolutely simple" or "unrestricted," or "infinite" — in the sense of an A-infinity). If a proof against the existence of God is to be formulated, it would have to have an alternative *definition* of God that introduces exclusionary properties, restrictions, or finitude into the definition.

For example, if one defines "God" as a being which would necessarily interfere with **human freedom** (which would be contrary to the purely inclusive properties of perfect love and perfect goodness/justice, etc.), then one might be able to formulate an argument which says, "If human beings are absolutely free,[9] then 'god' (defined as necessarily interfering with freedom) cannot exist."

But the definition of God in this argument is arbitrarily restrictive (and contradicts the absolute simplicity and unrestrictedness of the unconditioned Reality proven in Chapters 3 and 4). Furthermore, if one understands a purely inclusive God to be perfectly loving and good, one would have to say that God helps human freedom in every way possible to be complete and perfect, and therefore, would not undermine human freedom.

Again, one might have had a terrible experience of **suffering or grief,** and think to oneself, "How could God allow this to happen? My grief is incompatible with a perfectly loving God!" One might go on to think that this is a disproof of the perfect love of God which might suggest that God is not purely inclusive or that pure inclusivity does not include love; and if pure inclusivity does not include love, and God is not perfectly loving, then there is no point in affirming His existence.

There can be little doubt that the primary reason for atheism is the inability to answer the question of human suffering. The importance of this question has led me to write yet another volume entitled *Suffering and the God of Love.* For the moment, I will endeavor a brief answer, though this is quite dangerous because the superficiality intrinsic to brevity may cause resentment on the part of readers who have suffered greatly. Nevertheless, I will proceed in the hopes that the reader will forgive this un-

---

9. The notion of absolute human freedom implied in Jean-Paul Sartre's *Being and Nothingness* is a very disputable claim, but this is not the point of our discussion, which is concerned with the definition of "God."

avoidable flaw, and direct attention to my other volume on suffering for a lengthier treatment.

Once again, atheism arises out of an assumed *definition* — but this time it does not arise out of a definition of "God"; it arises out of a definition of "love" which is attributed to God. The effect is essentially the same because when the inadequate definition of love is attributed to God, it seems to mitigate the perfect inclusivity of God. So, what is this so-called inadequate definition of "love"? It is one that holds that love is incompatible with suffering. In my view, this definition is overly simplistic for several reasons. I will mention only two of them here.

First, the above definition does not consider the interrelationship between freedom and love. If our love is to be our own, then we must be free to do acts of unlove (which could cause great harm, suffering, or evil). Stated conversely, if we are not free to do anything but love, then our love is not our own. It is merely a program of behavior that has nothing to do with our choice. Our love would not be *self*-initiated. Thus, if God wants to create *loving* creatures (in imitation of his perfect love), God has to create *free* beings who can cause suffering and evil in the world by their choices. The dynamics of love and freedom require that God allow us the latitude to grow in love through our human freedom. God's only alternative to allowing free beings to choose unloving acts is to completely refrain from creating loving creatures. Is that something that perfect Love would do?

The second problem with defining love as incompatible with suffering is that it does not allow for suffering to purify freedom toward love. I will speak solely for myself, here; but often I have contented myself with an incredibly superficial view of life's meaning (e.g., material well-being, ego-satisfactions, status, etc.) and incredibly superficial views of human beings (as material beings instead of transcendental beings; as problems instead of mysteries) during the "good" times. It was only when I was challenged by real suffering that I began to ask more probative questions, to search for deeper purpose in life, and to let go of what was then manifestly superficial (underliving my life).

These moments of suffering led me to the discovery of love as the purpose of life — to the enjoyment of others' companionship and friendship, to the recognition of the goodness and lovability of others, to the depth of empathy and compassion; indeed, to the discovery of my heart. I do not think I could have let go of my more superficial, materialistic, egocentric views of happiness and meaning without having experienced suffering, deprivation, and need for others.

233

Furthermore, I do not believe that I would have discovered my own *transcendental* identity without this same deprivation and need. Much like Saint Augustine, my contentment with material and ego-satisfactions distracted me from noticing that I had desires for *perfect* and *unconditional* Truth, Love, Goodness/Justice, Beauty, and Home (see the extensive treatment in Chapter 8). Though I went to church and had some religious sensibility, I tended to live life on a material-ego level. Suffering not only led to a discovery of my heart, but also of my transcendental desires; and this discovery, in turn, led not only to a discovery of my transmaterial being (what might be termed my "soul"), but also of my yearning for unconditional Love — my yearning for God.

In retrospect, I am grateful for the suffering that led me to the discovery of love, my heart, my soul, and the loving God. I did not like my suffering while I was experiencing it, but the journey — the journey in *freedom* — that led to the discovery of what is truly pervasive, enduring, and deep, made the suffering worthwhile; for it led to an eternity's worth of purpose, a true respect for the transcendent other, and the discovery not merely of my heart, but of my transcendent heart and my call to unconditional Love. No, for me, suffering was not incompatible with love. Suffering was the instrument of Love.[10]

A third issue has recurrently emerged throughout the history of philosophy, namely, **the problem of evil.** It would seem that if God is perfect Goodness and Love, He would not permit evil in the world; and furthermore, it would seem that anything evil should be *excluded* by God (who was defined above to be a perfectly *inclusive* Reality). Again, the seeming incompatibility between a perfectly good God (a perfectly inclusive God) and evil arises out of an assumed *definition*. This time, the definition of "evil" seems incompatible with perfect Goodness and inclusivity. Since evil seems to be evident, it seems to mean either that God is not perfectly good or that a perfectly good (perfectly inclusive) God does not exist.

Let us consider the first point, namely, that if God is perfectly good, He would not allow evil in the world. This contention has already been addressed above with respect to the definition of "love," so I will only briefly repeat the germane point: if God were to disallow all human evil, then God would have to disallow the free choice to act in an evil way; and if God disal-

10. In *Suffering and the God of Love,* I have adduced several deeper correlations between suffering and love. Hopefully, the above is sufficient to reveal the superficiality of a definition of "love" that is incompatible with suffering.

lowed the free choice to act in an evil way, He would not allow our good actions to be self-initiated. He would essentially have programmed us for good behaviors, but not allowed us to choose good behaviors over against the option of choosing evil ones; therefore, He would have foreclosed the possibility of our good actions truly being *self*-initiated, and therefore truly being our own.

Furthermore, acts of human evil can purify our freedom toward perfect Love, for when evil actions are perpetrated against us, we are challenged to respond with a gift of self (love) in forgiveness, mercy, and compassion. These selfless actions (which are frequently undeserved by the perpetrators) are the highest manifestations of human generosity and love. Ironically, they are elicited by evil. The story of my life, as well as world history and literature, are replete with examples of how forgiveness of evil has led to the intensification of goodness and love. Would Europe be the same without the Marshall Plan in which America forgave the debt (and built up the economies) of the nations with whom it had been at war?[11] Would Victor Hugo's hero, Jean Valjean, have existed without the forgiveness of the priest from whom he had stolen the candles?[12] Would the great ideas of human rights and economic rights have occurred without the forgiveness of centuries of oppression? The list goes on and on.

Evil elicits vengeance, and vengeance begets vengeance, *unless* a free agent intervenes and lets go of the just offense in a recognizable act of compassion. This act not only stops the cycle of vengeance begetting vengeance, but also calls collective human consciousness to a higher ideal, a higher sense of collective self, which is at once intrinsically beautiful, while allowing the real possibility of peace. Ironically, this greatest of human choices can be induced by evil.

We may now proceed to the second point of tension between God and evil, namely, that if God is perfectly good, He must *exclude* evil (which seems to contradict His pure *inclusivity*). Again, the problem is definitional, for the definition of "evil" seems to get in the way of God being *both* perfect goodness and perfect inclusivity. However, the definition of "evil" that does this views "evil" as something positive — as something existing in itself.

---

11. This was done in contradistinction to the Treaty of Versailles, which left Germany destitute amidst its war reparations after the First World War. Many believe that this act of "justice" (or perhaps better, retribution) led to the rise of National Socialism (the Nazi Party) in Germany, and eventually to the Second World War.

12. *Les Misérables.*

A brief summary of the volumes that have been written on this since the time of Plato shows a more comprehensive view of "evil" that does not view it as something positive or existing in itself. In this view, evil is seen to be a *negation* of a free being's power to love. Obviously, the free being exists, and his power to love exists (and is positive). But evil does not exist apart from this free being and his positive capacity to love. Evil occurs when the existing free agent negates (ignores or undermines) his positive power to love.

Now, these evil actions could have, say, angry feelings embedded in them. But these feelings are not identifiable with evil itself; they are the *result* of evil (that is, a free agent's choice to ignore or undermine his capacity for love). Furthermore, destructive (evil) behaviors may come from this free agent, but these behaviors are also not identifiable with evil itself; they are the result of evil (i.e., a free agent's choice to ignore or undermine his capacity for love). Thus, the occurrence of evil is not something that exists in itself; rather, it is the result of a free agent's choice to ignore or undermine the capacity for affection, empathy, compassion — love.

In sum, evil can occur through an existing free agent, and it arises out of the ignoring or undermining of an existing capacity for love. It can give rise to feelings and destructive behaviors that have ontological status. However, the evil *of* the free agent, *of* the feelings, and *of* the destructive behaviors does not exist of itself. It occurs *through* the negating of the positive power to love in the free agent. If this definition of evil is correct, then it is not excluded by God; for it has no existence that can be excluded. God's perfect goodness and perfect inclusivity remain completely compatible.

There are other kinds of atheism not connected to the notion of "God," and therefore not concerned with incompatibility between God and a particular phenomenon (say suffering or evil). For example, socio-political atheism generally tends to be more *irreligious* than atheistic. It objects to religion because it is, say, an "opium of the people"[13] (a distraction from needed socio-political change). Philosophers who proffer these claims frequently do not offer any argument against the existence of God, but rest their case on their sense of religion as antithetical to human progress.

Many such philosophers frequently ignore the fact that religion is responsible for social progress in many arenas, such as the initiation and advancement of laws, legal systems, social welfare systems (through, say, prophets who exhorted the populace to care for widows and orphans),

13. Marx 1970.

236

schools and educational systems, hospitals and health care systems, etc. This makes those philosophers' selective view of history quite suspect.

I would like to conclude this section by returning to an important point made earlier — namely, that I do not want my brief treatment of suffering and evil to convey in any way a disregard for the true suffering that so many have endured in their lives. Grief at the loss of a loved one, debilitation at the loss of one's faculties, indignity at the hands of callous individuals, should never be underestimated. My sole purpose in treating the above topics was to show how careful we must be in our definitions of "love," "evil," and "God." As we attempt to translate our deepest emotions and experiences into concepts, we will want to remember that the more nuanced and complete the definitions, the more they will correspond to the truth; and the more they correspond to the truth, the more they will present the path to healing and deliverance within the horizon of unrestricted Love, Goodness, Justice, Beauty, and Home. This leads us to the topic of our next two chapters.

The Transcendentals:
The Divine and Human Mysteries

INTRODUCTION TO PART THREE

Part Two of this book used three philosophical proofs to ground reasonable and responsible belief in the one, unconditioned, absolutely simple, infinite, unrestrictedly intelligible, unrestricted act of understanding which is the continuous Creator of all else that is. Chapter 3 showed that an unconditioned Reality had to be a *unique,* absolutely simple Reality, and Chapter 4 showed that an unconditioned Reality had to be a *unique,* unrestrictedly intelligible, unrestricted act of understanding. We are now in a position to assemble these two conclusions. Since an unconditioned Reality must be unique, this one Reality must possess the attributes of both absolute simplicity *and* unrestricted intelligibility (an unrestricted act of understanding). We must conclude from this that absolute simplicity is unrestricted intelligibility and unrestricted understanding in one and the same Reality.

This combined conclusion gives rise to a further question, namely: If absolute Simplicity (in Its perfectly unifying and self-transparent nature) is unrestricted Intelligibility and unrestricted Understanding, can anything more be said about It? Can the combined conclusion of both proofs reveal a deeper truth about absolute Simplicity/ perfect Unity/ perfect Self-transparency/ unrestricted Understanding? If the neo-Platonists are correct, it can.

In **Chapter 7** we will discuss the neo-Platonic contention that there are at least three other dimensions of absolute Simplicity (to which human beings have access), namely, Love itself,[1] Goodness itself, and Beauty itself.

1. Love itself, though important to Christianity and Christian neo-Platonism, does not appear in the list of transcendentals in the medieval period, but as will be seen, it pos-

When these are combined with Being itself (the one unconditioned Reality), Unity itself (the One — absolute Simplicity), and Truth itself (unrestricted Intelligibility or the unrestricted act of understanding), one arrives at what medieval philosophers refer to as "the transcendentals."

Though there are obvious similarities between the characteristics of the medieval view of the transcendentals and what I am about to espouse, I am here not concerned with defending the idea that the transcendentals are present in everything that exists (though I do believe this to be so). Rather, I am interested in showing that the one unconditioned Reality, which is an unrestricted act of understanding, is also Goodness itself, Love itself, and Beauty itself in Its absolute simplicity. This not only gives a deeper insight into the divine mystery, but also into the human one, for there is remarkable parallelism between the five dimensions of absolute Simplicity (Being itself, Truth itself, Love itself, Goodness itself, and Beauty itself) and the five human aspirations for the perfect and unconditioned.

In **Chapter 8,** I will show that human consciousness seems to possess five aspirations or desires that can be satisfied only by the above-mentioned transcendentals, namely, the desire for ultimate Home, ultimate Truth, ultimate Love, ultimate Goodness, and ultimate Beauty. Any conditioned or restricted satisfaction of these five aspirations or desires results in unfulfillment, want, or even frustration. It seems as though the five manifestations of absolute Simplicity form a confluence with the five human desires for ultimacy, leading one to suspect not only a connection between the divine mystery and the human mystery, but also a presence of the divine mystery to human consciousness.

If God is present to human consciousness as its fulfillment in truth, love, goodness, beauty, and being (home), then human reason can go beyond confirming the *existence* of God as a unique, unconditioned, absolutely simple, unrestricted Creator, to unveiling the nature of this God as perfectly truth-filled, loving, good, and beautiful. Augustine stated this connection clearly when he exclaimed: "For Thou hast made us for Thyself and our hearts are restless until they rest in Thee."[2]

Such a God would not be disinterested in us, but intensely interested in fulfilling us through the highest use of our freedom. It would seem that such a good and loving God would not be interested in undermining human

---

sesses the attribute of absolute Simplicity and absolute Unity that the other four transcendentals apparently possess.

2. Augustine 1991, Book I, Chapter 1.1.

freedom, but rather, in bringing it to fruition, for, as will be seen, truth, love, and goodness have no real significance in us apart from our freedom. As noted in the previous chapter, if we do not *choose* truth, love, and goodness (over against the possibility of inauthenticity, egocentricity, and evil) then *we* would not have been true, loving, or good; we would only be acting according to preprogrammed behaviors that were not our own, but those of the "programmer."

If we are interested in being truly free and fulfilled, we will have to explore our desires for perfect, unconditioned, and unrestricted Truth, Love, Goodness, and Beauty; and if these desires correspond with the nature of the one unconditioned Reality, then we will want to pursue that unconditioned Reality. Or perhaps better, we will want to allow that one unconditioned Reality to pursue us.

CHAPTER SEVEN

The Divine Mystery: Five Transcendentals

Introduction

This chapter will be divided into two parts. The first (concerned with the unconditioned Reality, absolute Simplicity, and unrestricted Intelligibility — Being itself, Unity itself, and Truth itself, respectively) will consist in a review of points that have been made in Chapters 3 and 4. The second part (concerned with Love itself, Goodness itself, and Beauty itself) is new material revealing other possible manifestations of absolute Simplicity (perfect Unity). If there can be only one absolute Simplicity (perfect Unity), then the one unconditioned Reality would not only be perfect Simplicity and unrestricted Intelligibility, but also perfect Love, Goodness, and Beauty. The unconditioned Reality would then hold out hope for the fulfillment of all human beings through the perfection of their freedom. It would seem incumbent upon us, therefore, to closely examine these manifestations of perfect Unity in the hopes of beholding ourselves and others in our foremost dignity and destiny.

I. The Interrelationship Among Absolute Simplicity, Perfect Unity, and Unrestricted Understanding

The reader might have noticed the interrelationship among three conclusions given in Chapters 3 and 4:

1) simplicity is related to unity,
2) unity is related to understanding, and therefore
3) perfect simplicity is both perfect unity and unrestricted understanding.

I will review the above three conclusions as preparation for an examination of the connection between the divine and human mysteries.

Recall from Chapter 3 that the unconditioned Reality cannot exclude any conditioned reality because *all* conditioned realities are ultimately and radically dependent on It. Given that boundaries, restrictions, parameters, and anything that gives rise to boundaries, restrictions, and parameters (such as space, time, formal qualities, magnitudes, etc.) give rise to exclusion, the unconditioned Reality must be free from any of these restrictions, formalities, and magnitudes. It must, therefore, be purely inclusive of and compatible with all other beings which have boundaries, restrictions, and parameters (and hence, It has been referred to by many philosophers as "Being itself" or "pure Being"[3]).

The above absence of boundaries, restrictions, parameters, etc. is termed "absolute simplicity." Conditioned realities have *relative* simplicity. The fewer boundaries, restrictions, and parameters they have, the simpler and more inclusive they are.[4] The unconditioned Reality's lack of *extrinsic* boundaries and restrictions allows for causation of and unity among conditioned beings. Its lack of *intrinsic* boundaries and restrictions allows for self-transparency like self-consciousness.

We are now in a position to understand the intrinsic relationship among absolute Simplicity, perfect Unity, and unrestricted Understanding. A brief examination of the points made in Chapter 4 (Section II.D) will reveal this intrinsic relationship in seven steps.

---

3. St. Thomas Aquinas refers to the uncaused Cause of Aristotle (God) as essentially "*ipsum esse subsistens*" (subsisting Being Itself) — Summa Theologica I, Q3, A4, and also I, Q4, A1. This terminology has deep roots in the neo-Platonic tradition with which Saint Thomas was familiar.

4. Medieval philosophers recognized this in the so-called "great chain of being" or the "tree of being," which was discussed, in part, in Chapter 3, through the notion of simplicity. Some forms of physical reductionism in the late eighteenth and nineteenth centuries questioned this notion of simplicity, and implicitly attempted to explain levels of being solely by means of *complexities* among simple material elements. The discovery of quantum systems and other fields (including plasma fields and space-time fields) has led to a reconsideration of the notion of simplicity in the contemporary age. For the medieval viewpoint on what I termed "relative simplicity," see Lovejoy 1970. For an explanation of quantum systems and fields, see Chapter 3, Sections II.A and II.B.

1) Unrestricted Intelligibility (the existence of which is proved in Step 2 of the Lonerganian argument) must be the content of an act of understanding, for an act of understanding allows intelligibility to stand by itself, detached from any limiting spatio-temporal, empirical/material, individuating repository; it allows intelligibility to stand for and embrace a multitude of instances (as when an idea is used in predication); and it allows ideas to be formed from relationships among ideas. Now, if intelligibility is truly unrestricted, it would have to have all of these qualities, and therefore, it would have to be the content of an act of understanding.

2) Now, the act of understanding which enables unrestricted intelligibility to exist as an idea must itself be unrestricted, because the power which enables the unrestricted idea to exist cannot have any restrictions that the idea itself does not have.

3) An unrestricted act of understanding cannot occur through a material brain, because a material brain cannot accommodate unrestricted intelligibility, since it is restricted in both its intelligibility and its material functioning. The same can be said for artificial intelligence, which also is restricted in its intelligibility and material functioning (electromagnetic, electrochemical, or biochemical functioning). Indeed, we will have to eliminate any apparatus, power, or activity that is in any way material or restricted in its power to ground intelligibility.

4) Now, if unrestricted Intelligibility must include the relationship between itself and the whole of finite intelligibility, then an unrestricted act of understanding must be a power which is capable of *bringing together*, in a single act, the interrelationship between unrestricted Intelligibility and the whole of restricted intelligibility.

5) The explanation for how such a power could operate is revealed in the convergence of the first and second proofs (in Chapters 3 and 4, respectively). Recall that both proofs begin with the same first step, namely, that at least one unconditioned reality must exist (otherwise, nothing would exist). The first proof subsequently showed that this unconditioned Reality is absolutely simple, and therefore unique; the second (Lonerganian) proof showed that an unconditioned Reality had to be unrestricted Intelligibility, and therefore unique. Thus, the *same* unique unconditioned Reality must be at once absolutely simple and unrestricted intelligibility. This corresponds neatly to the requirement for our unrestricted act of understanding, namely, that it bring together, in a single act, the interrelationship between unrestricted In-

telligibility and the whole of restricted intelligibility. Unrestricted Intelligibility must be absolute Simplicity, and absolute Simplicity provides the explanation of how an unrestricted act of understanding could bring unrestricted and restricted intelligibility together in a single act.

6) Recall that less restriction entails less exclusion, which entails more inclusion, which entails greater capacity for being in *unity* with what is less restricted. Therefore, absolute Simplicity is the perfect capacity to unify — which would allow it to unify the whole of finite intelligibility.

7) Furthermore, an unrestricted act of understanding (which is absolute Simplicity) cannot be conditioned by a spatio-temporal manifold (which would impose such restrictions on it). This means that it would be completely transparent to itself (it can be, as it were, inside itself), which is the condition necessary for a perfect act of self-consciousness.

Therefore, the notion of absolute simplicity can explain how an unrestricted act of understanding can unify and ground the whole of finite intelligibility, and also how it can be perfectly aware of itself, and therefore how it can ground the whole of finite intelligibility through its understanding of itself. Therefore, absolute Simplicity, perfect Unity, and unrestricted Understanding are intrinsically interrelated through the same power in the selfsame Being.

Set in the terminology of neo-Platonism and Thomism: Being itself (the one unconditioned Reality) is the One (perfect unity through absolute simplicity) and also Truth itself (unrestricted intelligibility through an unrestricted act of understanding). They are interrelated through the same power in one and the same Reality — showing forth the richness of Being.

II. The Ontological Status of Love, the Good, and the Beautiful

My purpose here is to show that Love itself, Goodness itself, and Beauty itself exemplify the characteristics of perfect unity (absolute simplicity) identified with the unconditioned Reality (Being itself) and unrestricted intelligibility (Truth itself). As will be seen, each of these qualities is a kind of *unity* which is simple enough to hold together excluding realities. In their pure form, they appear to be absolutely simple, and therefore seem to be the same as the one, absolutely simple, unconditioned Reality which is unrestricted intelligibility through an unrestricted act of understanding. Thus, in their seeming absolute simplicity, Love itself, Goodness itself, and Beauty itself seem to be coincident with Being itself, perfect Unity, and Truth itself. The following will help to elucidate this.

II.A. The Ontological Status of Love

This discussion of love begins with the experience of empathy and moves to the actualization of *agapē*. This will manifest the unifying activity of love (that is, the unification of *autonomous*, self-conscious beings into empathetic, caring, self-giving *interpersonal* beings).

Empathy (in-feeling; in Greek, *en-pathos*; in German, *ein-Fühlung*, coined by Rudolf Lotze in 1858) begins with a deep awareness of and connection to the other as both given and uniquely good. When one allows this awareness of and connection to the other to affect one, it produces an acceptance of the other and a consequent unity of feeling with the other, which opens upon an identification with the other tantamount to a sympathetic vibration. Though this unity with the feelings and being of another does not cause a loss of one's self or self-consciousness, it does cause a break in the radical autonomy one can effect when one focuses on oneself as the center of one's personal universe (egocentricity). Were it not for the capacity to be radically open to the unique goodness of the other, human beings might be inexorably caught up in egocentricity and radical autonomy, making them the equivalent of "personal Leibnitzean monads." However, empathy does not allow self-consciousness to become radically autonomous and absolute; it presents the possibility of relational personhood whenever one chooses to accept one's "unity of feeling with the other," and to identify with the being of the other.[5]

This acceptance and identification of the feelings and being of the other give rise to concern for the other, which evolves into care for the other as the relationship grows. This care, in its turn, can completely reverse the human tendency toward autonomy (over against the other), and give rise to a self-giving that can become self-sacrificial (*agapē*). Through empathy, then, love goes beyond itself, and initiates a unity with the other whereby doing the good for the other is just as easy as, if not easier than, doing the

---

5. Edith Stein has written a powerful essay on this phenomenon in *On the Problem of Empathy.* See Stein 1989.

good for oneself. Through free choice, self-sacrifice can become as natural as self-interest.

The forthcoming ontological explanation will show empathy's power to overcome self-consciousness' propensity toward radical autonomy and its consequent power to initiate a caring bond capable of self-sacrifice. Here, we may see a similarity between Love itself, Being itself, and Truth itself. Just as Being itself (the one unconditioned Reality) unifies all conditioned realities as the ultimate fulfillment of their conditions, and just as unrestricted Intelligibility (the unrestricted act of understanding) grounds and unifies the intelligibility of the whole of restricted intelligibility, so the power of empathy giving rise to the power of care unifies self-conscious identities amidst their propensity for radical autonomy. The absolute simplicity of the unconditioned Reality and unrestricted Intelligibility allows them[6] to effect this act of total unification. Inasmuch as empathy is able to overcome the natural propensity of self-consciousness to greater and greater autonomy through its seeming capacity to unify self-consciousnesses, it would also seem to be simpler than self-consciousness, which suggests a simplicity similar to the unconditioned Reality and to unrestricted Intelligibility.

I do not intend to assert the last proposition above as proven, for I am not able to prove the absolute simplicity of perfect Love in the same way as proving the absolute simplicity of the unconditioned Reality (Chapter 3) and unrestricted Intelligibility (Chapter 4). Nevertheless, I do assert it as more than an interesting aside. The propensity of self-consciousness to turn in on itself and to become radically, and even completely, autonomous is quite real. Everyone who has reflectively lived through an egocentric moment has experienced it. Similarly, the power of empathy (a radical openness to the other allowing for a unity of feeling with the other, leading to concern, care, and *agapē*) really does overcome this propensity toward radical and even complete autonomy. Though this datum is not as demonstrable as the absolute simplicity of the unconditioned Reality and unrestricted Intelligibility, it should give one pause, for it reveals another dimension of unity and simplicity that may find its perfection in absolute simplicity itself (in the one, unconditioned, unrestrictedly intelligible Reality).

The simplicity and unity of love does not seem to have any intrinsic or extrinsic limit. If love (empathy → concern → care → *agapē*) can unify the

---

6. Even though these are two different acts of unification, they occur through the same Reality because the unconditioned Reality is unrestricted intelligibility (the unrestricted act of understanding).

radical autonomy of *two* human beings, why would it not be able to overcome the autonomy of hundreds or thousands, or millions of human beings? Why would it not be able to unify all human self-consciousnesses throughout all history? Indeed, why would it not be able to unify this totality of humanity with perfect self-consciousness (the perfect, self-transparent, mentating activity of the unrestricted act of understanding)?

If there is no intrinsic limit to the simplicity (unifying power) of love, then perfect Love is capable of perfect unification. This would seem to suggest that Love itself once again resembles absolute simplicity. Recall that there can be only *one* absolute simplicity; therefore, if Love itself really is absolutely simple, it would have to be the same as Being itself and Truth itself (the same Reality). Thus, there is warrant to believe that the one unconditioned Reality is not only unrestricted Intelligibility, but also perfect Empathy; indeed, perfect Love.

II.B. The Ontological Status of the Good

This brief ontological study of the good will be restricted to the common good (with its correlates of justice and the natural law). Any complete ontology of the good would begin with "the good" considered as an object of desire, and would look at the universality of such desirability in being. It would also view the good from the vantage point of purposefulness (final causation) and the goodness of everything fulfilling its own purpose.[7] I do not mean to diminish the importance of an ontology of *natural* goods, but am more interested here in the unifying property of the good as it manifests itself in human society, community, and culture.

Human beings are more than empathetic interpersonal consciousnesses. They are, as Aristotle suggested long ago, social animals. Though empathy can overcome self-consciousness' propensity for radical autonomy by establishing relationships based on unity of feeling, care, and self-sacrifice, it does not necessarily preserve civil society or community, for civil society is more than a collection of empathetic relationships; more than a collection of families and friends; civil societies seek common purpose and ideals amidst neighbors *and strangers,* stakeholders *and competitors,* those

---

7. See, for example, Aristotle's *Nicomachean Ethics* 1173a 4: "But perhaps even in inferior creatures there is some natural good stronger than themselves which aims at their proper good" (Aristotle 1942).

with similar interests *and those with divergent interests.* Civil societies seek common purpose, common cause, and the common good amidst individuals having little or no empathy for one another.

Of course, societies seek nothing; human beings within societies seek common purpose and common cause amidst diverse interests. What is it within human beings that seeks commonality amidst strangers, competitors, and even potential enemies? Many philosophers have theorized that it is nothing more than a pragmatic urge, that is, a desire to keep civil society organized enough to allow for internal and external protection, a marketplace, the development of infrastructure and social goods, etc. I do not wish to debate these pragmatists here, but only to suggest that such narrow views of the drive toward civil society might omit a very important part of the human spirit, namely, the tendency to be ennobled and inspired by the ideals of civil society and the love of justice, rights, the law, the common good, and civil peace.

Throughout history, we have not generally viewed justice or the common good dispassionately. We symbolize them with flames, eagles, and deities. The ideals of civil society have made the human heart soar. So too have the two primary principles that have animated civil society from its inception: justice and the common good. Wherever there has been a community, there have been judges or chiefs with judicial authority. Wherever there has been a complex society, there have been legal codes and juridical administrations. But we must go beyond the mere presence of these legal codes and juridical systems, and see the dignity, nobility, and even deity with which they are frequently enshrined. Human beings not only love other human beings in empathy, they also love justice and the common good, and the civil society that operates through these two principles.

In the previous subsection, it was noted that self-consciousness had a propensity toward radical autonomy and egocentricity (which empathy can overcome). There is yet another propensity of self-consciousness which is related to the drive for radical autonomy, but more serious in its consequences, namely, the propensity to negate or undermine other human beings for personal advantage. This is what justice and the law seek to prevent. It occupies the majority of the content of every legal code dating back to the Ten Commandments, the Code of Hammurabi, and earlier: "Do not bear false witness," "Do not kill," "Do not steal," "Do not covet another's property," etc. One can sense egocentricity and pride underlying these acts, and a desire to take from another or to negate another in order to achieve that egocentric advantage. It is precisely this propensity that justice and the common good counteract. Justice overcomes not only a barrier between human beings, it overcomes the *negation* of other human beings for selfish self-interest.

As implied above, the notions of justice and the common good overcome these invasive, negating propensities not merely through a pragmatic urge, but through genuine *love* of the ideals these terms represent. The love of justice, law, and the common good strikes an uplifting apollonian note within us. We seem to instinctively sense nobility not only behind the power of the law, but behind the notion of justice that the law and its power seek to preserve.

Aristotle recognized that some human beings have a sense of the good that forms the ground for the voluntary pursuit of virtue. Notice that he believed that all people were not equally endowed with this sense of the good:

> . . . but one must be born with an eye, as it were, by which to judge rightly and choose what is *truly good,* and he is well endowed by nature who is well endowed with this. For it is what is greatest and most noble, and what we cannot get or learn from another, but must have just such as it was when given us *at birth,* and to be well and nobly endowed with this will be *perfect and true excellence* of natural endowment.[8]

Saint Thomas Aquinas goes further and ascribes the first principles of natural law (*synderesis*) to *all* human beings:

> . . . [I]t is fitting that we have bestowed on us *by nature* not only speculative principles but also practical principles. . . . [T]he first practical principles bestowed on us by nature, do not belong to a special power but to a special *natural* habit, which we call *synderesis.* Thus *synderesis* is said to incite to good and to murmur at evil, inasmuch as we proceed from first principles to discover and judge of what we have discovered.[9]

If the reader has experienced within him or herself this power of being "incited toward good and murmuring (expressing discontent) toward evil," and if this power has guided his or her practical reason and has even incited a love of justice itself and the good itself, then one will have discovered a power[10] as important (though not the same) as empathy; a power that unites

8. Aristotle 1942, 1114b5-10. Italics mine.
9. Aquinas 1947, p. 407 (Pt. 1, Q.79, Art. 12). Italics mine.
10. Even though Saint Thomas does not view conscience as a *separate* power apart

strangers for the common good; a power that resists taking advantage of superiority of social power (e.g., social status, intelligence, wealth, and birthright); a power inciting preference for fairness and rectitude of relationship over personal and social advantage and aggrandizement.

This natural power to love good and shun evil, to love justice and the common good, and to shun injustice and the undermining of society, is essentially a *unifying* power. It transforms self-consciousness' propensity to be over-against others and in conflict with others, into a sense of shared good, common cause, and "*esprit de corps.*" Henceforth I will refer to it as the "love of justice and the good."

The "love of justice and the good" is a natural unifier, for it overcomes the natural barriers and enmity arising out of competition for scarce resources, fear of strangers, natural animosity, survival of the fittest, and suspicion of others' potential injustice. It overcomes the natural barriers and enmity of irresponsibility (responsibility to myself alone, or the complete abdication of responsibility) by calling individuals to a higher duty to the just society. It can also lead to self-sacrifice (the sacrifice not only of one's advantage and aggrandizement, but also of one's very self) for the sake of the good of society or for goodness and justice within society. These unifying powers of the "love of justice and the good" appear to have the qualities of simplicity.

Before considering the simplicity of the good's unifying power, we may do well to pause for a moment and consider the complementarity between love and the good in human self-consciousness. Three of these complementarities are described in the history of philosophy by the "love-justice dialectic": (1) Love tends to look first toward care for the *individual,* and through this lens, to move toward care and co-responsibility for the *group,* or even civil society. Conversely, the good has the connotation of looking first toward the *common good,* that is, the good of civil society, the culture, and the group, and then moving from this to the good of the *individual.* (2) Love begins with care and empathy, and from this moves toward co-responsibility and duty. Conversely, the good tends to move from co-responsibility and duty to empathy and care. (3) Love proceeds from compassion and mercy, and then moves to justice and the need for the law, whereas the good proceeds from justice and respect for the law and then

---

from reason, he nonetheless views it as a part of (a habit of) the power of reason. When reason is animated by the desire for good and the revulsion of evil, it may be termed "the power of conscience." That is the way I am using "power of conscience" in this section.

moves to a specific application of the natural law, and then to respect for the individual protected by the law, and then to compassion and mercy under the law. In sum, love and goodness must eventually overlap, but they overlap each other from opposite directions. As will be seen below, in their pure form, Love itself is Goodness itself, and Goodness itself is Love itself.

We may now return to the matter of the simplicity inherent in the good's unifying power. Recall that the simplicity of the unconditioned Reality enables It to unify beings with excluding boundaries, and that the simplicity of the unrestricted act of understanding enables It to unite ideas with excluding boundaries into a single idea of all finite intelligibility, and that the simplicity of empathy unites autonomous self-consciousnesses through a single shared feeling. So also, the first principle of the natural law (to love good and shun evil) suggests simplicity by uniting strangers, competitors, and even potential enemies through a natural love of goodness, justice, and the common good. Even if one cannot feel empathy for a stranger, competitor, or enemy, one can still be united with them through the love of goodness, justice, and the common good. This unity is more than an abstraction, for it overcomes a natural propensity to take advantage of strength, extinguish enemies, and pursue, at all costs, "survival of the fittest." The "love of justice and the good" creates community amidst not only divergent but also antagonistic interests.

The unifying power and simplicity of the "love of justice and the good," like the simplicity and unity of love, seem to have no intrinsic or extrinsic limit. Though appropriate social structures must be formed to avert the actions of people who ignore their internal sense of justice and goodness, the "love of justice and the good" *itself* does not seem to have any intrinsic or extrinsic limit to its power to unify.

If the "love of justice and the good" can unify a community of strangers, why would it not be able, through appropriate education and social structures, to unify a society? Or one society with another? And another? Indeed, why would it not be able to unify an entire world? The only limits to its power to unify seems to be either culpable ignorance of it or the choice not to follow it. Since these alternatives do not speak to the "love of justice and the good" *itself*, but only to its *use* by human beings, it would seem that the "love of justice and the good" might qualify as another manifestation of simplicity, and that the "love of justice and the good" *itself* might qualify as another manifestation of *absolute* Simplicity.

If there is no intrinsic or extrinsic limit to the unifying power of the "love of justice and the good" *itself*, then *perfect* "love of justice and the good" would seem to be perfect unity. This means that the "love of justice and the good" itself resembles Being itself, Truth itself, and Love itself. Recall that there can be only *one* absolute simplicity. If Being itself, Truth itself, Love itself, and the "love of justice and the good" itself are *all* absolutely simple, then they must *all be* the same unique Reality. Though the absolute simplicity of the "love of justice and the good" itself cannot be proved in the same way as that of the unconditioned Reality or unrestricted Intelligibility, the implication of its seemingly unlimited power to unify does again give one pause. It is difficult to resist seeing the similarity underlying the unifying power of Being, Truth, Love, and Goodness/Justice. Bernard Lonergan recognized this confluence of the transcendentals when he noted:

> . . . the primary intelligible also is the primary truth and the primary good; and so in a completely perfect spiritual being the primary intelligible is identical not only with an unrestricted act of understanding . . . [but also] a completely perfect act of loving the primary good.[11]

II.C. The Ontological Status of the Beautiful

I do not intend to develop an aesthetic philosophy here, for I am concerned mostly with the unifying, or perhaps better, the harmonizing property of *beauty*. Aesthetic philosophy, in its concern for art, goes far beyond the phenomenon of beauty or aesthetic emotions (e.g., the repose, reveling, and enjoyment arising out of harmony and resplendence) to the communication of the range of human relational emotions (e.g., love, hate, fear, joy, anger, trust, and suspicion). Though beauty is frequently a part of art, art need not be beautiful. Furthermore, art frequently uses symbolic expression to point to human or social purpose, whereas beauty by itself (without the artist's intentions) can do this only implicitly and indirectly.

Beauty and art can also evoke sublime, glorious, and exalted emotions, and can, therefore, communicate the glorious itself, sublimity itself, and ultimate home itself. As will be noted below, beauty does this by exemplifying perfection within its proper form, while art can do this through both "perfection of form" and symbolic expression (e.g., using images to point beyond themselves to mystical or spiritual realities). I would not want to create too sharp a distinction between beauty and art, but only to suggest that there is

11. Lonergan 1992, p. 681.

something in beautiful objects themselves (independent of an artist's intention) that can give rise not only to feelings of delight, repose, reveling, and enjoyment, but also to feelings of *sublime* repose, home, reveling, and joy. This is reflected in the aesthetic philosophy of Roger Fry who, in the last paragraph of his essay "Retrospect," attempted to detach "the aesthetic quality" from all other practical and ethical concerns in order to appreciate it for itself:

> One can only say that those who experience [the purely aesthetic quality of significant form, which is something other than agreeable arrangements of form, harmonious patterns, and the like] feel it to have a peculiar quality of "reality" which makes it a matter of infinite importance in their lives. Any attempt I might make to explain this would probably land me in the depths of mysticism. On the edge of that gulf I stop.[12]

What does Fry mean by this pure aesthetic quality which will land him "in the depths of mysticism"? It may do well to begin with a more basic question, namely, "What is it about beautiful objects that evokes delight, repose, reveling, enjoyment, and even sublimity?" Johannes Lotz, going back to Albert the Great, suggests that three characteristics give rise to the above aesthetic emotions: perfection of a particular form (essence), harmonious resonance, and "shining forth" (luster or splendor) pointing beyond itself.[13]

The first characteristic refers to what we enjoy in "natural objects coming to perfection." When something reaches its *"to ti ēn einai"* ("what it was supposed to be" — the perfection of its form), it is a delight to see. We not only revel in something coming to perfection in essence, but also in proportion and appearance. When things are disordered, dysfunctional, or flawed, they either evoke no emotion, or cause a sense of disturbance or revulsion. In a sense, then, individual form brought to perfection is intrinsically beautiful.

The second quality of beauty, harmonious resonance, is perhaps the best-recognized quality of beautiful objects. When different forms blend together (i.e., do not conflict with one another), each form brings out hidden aspects of the other. In music, for example, the harmony of two notes brings out aspects of the individual notes that are unrecognized in their isolation. What note #1 does to note #2 is not recognized when note #1 stands by itself.

12. Fry 1998.
13. Lotz 1972, p. 30.

The same holds true for the visual arts. When one form blends "harmoniously" with another, the two forms bring out aspects of each other that remain hidden when they are in isolation. The same holds true for architecture and poetry, and any other manifestation of beauty. Harmony (a complementary blending), then, is more than an absence of conflict or disorder. It is also a revealing of hidden beauty within individual forms.

Yet there is more to harmony than the evoking of deeper delight, repose, reveling, and enjoyment. Certain harmonies reach to the deepest emotions (the sublime emotions) within us. In the glory of a Brahms symphony (complex harmonies amidst complex melodies), breathtaking architecture (having large scale amidst minute proportionality), and Eliot's *Four Quartets* (filled with metaphysical ideas, dense metaphors, and beautiful poetic form), beauty points beyond mere delight, repose, reveling, and enjoyment, to a kind of ecstasy, a sublime reveling, a "*mysterium tremendum*," or a sense of being at home with the Divine. The more complex, grand, and sustained the harmony, the more it evokes the sublime or exalted emotions, and the more it seems to connect us with the glorious, the beautiful, and the Sublime Itself. We are now beginning to approach Roger Fry's "matter of infinite importance" whose explanation lies in the "depths of mysticism."

The third quality of beauty, "shining forth," splendor, and luster, refers to "access to perfection of form or harmony." The less hidden the first two qualities of beauty are, the more we delight, repose, or revel in it. But "shining forth" is much more than this. As suggested above, complex, grand, and sustained beauties point beyond their complementary unified forms to unity, perfection, and sublimity itself. One might say that simple objects of beauty point to the perfection of the form through which it exists, but complex beauties tend to point beyond the perfection of a particular form to *Perfection itself.* When one hears Mozart's *Requiem,* one recognizes and then reposes and revels in more than music brought to its perfection, more than the human emotions evoked by the harmonies and melodies. One enjoys the more perfect manifestation of unity, and then reposes and revels in it, feeling a deep and abiding sense of exaltation and glory. Now, when the *Requiem* is performed within a magnificent church with magnificent art, and the music, art, and architecture are unified as a whole, one feels drawn into a perfection bigger than all the forms combined. One is drawn into the perfection of complex unification to which one appends the name "glorious" or "magnificent."

Again, when one beholds not only a beautiful ocean, but a beautiful mountain and waterfall and sky forming a single contiguous whole, with the motion of the sea and the waterfall, and the flight of birds, and the movement of wind rustling through vegetation, the harmonious totality shines forth and points not only to a unity amidst complexity, but a taste of unity itself, a taste of repose itself; perhaps stated best, a taste of ultimate Home itself. Again, we find another manifestation of *simplicity;* a blending of forms that not only demonstrates unity, but gives the felt perception of unity. It not only points to the perfection of a form, but points beyond any form to Perfection itself.

This kind of unity seems to have no intrinsic limit. The susceptibility of form to intrinsic unification (as if the forms were created to be unified; created to complement one another; created as radically incomplete anticipating a home in their highest unifications — like mathematics), this kind of anticipatory completion, this perfect anticipatory unity of incomplete form, seems to have as its base Unity itself or Beauty itself. As the notes are combined with other notes, as musical forms are combined with architectural, artistic, and natural forms, the origin of these partial manifestations of perfection is revealed, and so, at once, we resonate with (we say "we feel") Unity itself, Perfection itself, and Beauty itself. When we resonate with Perfection itself, we feel at once in ecstasy and at home, in a flurry of activity and at a still point.

It seems that *all* forms have an ideal complementarity with *all* other forms, revealing yet another kind of ideal or perfect unification within the phenomenon of beauty. This ideal or perfect complementarity and perfect unity among diverse forms suggests yet another manifestation of ideal or perfect simplicity (in addition to perfect Truth, Goodness, and Love).

As another manifestation of perfect simplicity, Beauty itself would seem to be associated with Love itself and Goodness itself, which is Truth itself and Being itself. Furthermore, inasmuch as there can only be one perfect Simplicity, it would seem that Beauty itself would have to be *identical* with Love itself, Goodness itself, Truth itself, and Being itself. As such, each manifestation of absolute Simplicity manifests and evokes the others. Thus, Truth itself, Goodness itself, and Love itself evoke the purest form of exultation, nobility, and glory (Beauty itself); and Beauty itself, in its perfect complementarity and unity of form, evokes the perfect complementarity and unity of unrestricted Intelligibility, perfect Empathy, and perfect Goodness.[14]

Plato speaks powerfully of this insight in the *Symposium* by means of a hyperphatic[15] approach through the many levels of Beauty's manifestation:

14. See Balthasar 1982, p. 18.
15. See Chapter 6, Section II.

He who would proceed aright in this matter should begin in youth to visit beautiful forms; and first . . . to love one such form only. . . . [S]oon he will of himself perceive . . . that the beauty in every form is one and the same . . . and will become a lover of all beautiful forms; in the next stage he will consider that the beauty of the mind is more honorable than the beauty of the outward form . . . until he is compelled to contemplate and see the beauty of institutions and laws [the Good/Justice], and to understand that the beauty of them all is of one family, and that personal beauty is a trifle; and after laws and institutions he will go on to the sciences, that he may see their beauty [the Truth], . . . and at last the vision is revealed to him of a single science, which is the science of beauty everywhere. . . . He who has been instructed thus far in the things of love [Love itself], and who has learned to see the beautiful in due order and succession, when he comes towards the end will suddenly perceive a nature of wondrous beauty . . . a nature which in the first place is everlasting, not growing and decaying . . . secondly, not fair in one point of view and foul in another . . . as if fair to some and foul to others, or in the likeness of a face or hands or any other part of the bodily frame, or in any form of speech or knowledge, or existing in any other being . . . but beauty *absolute, separate, simple* [i.e., absolutely simple], and *everlasting* [i.e., Beauty itself], which without diminution and without increase, or any change, is imparted to the ever-growing and perishing beauties of all other things.[16]

For Plato, Beauty itself is inextricably linked to Truth itself, Justice/ Goodness itself, and Love itself, which is perhaps the most fundamental insight of this chapter. Inasmuch as all of these transcendentals are absolutely simple, they must be unique, and therefore the same Reality.

Conclusion to the Chapter

The unity among all manifestations of absolute Simplicity would seem to be at once a unique unconditioned Reality, unrestricted Intelligibility, perfect Empathy, perfect "love of justice and the good," and perfect Beauty (complementarity of *all* form). And this is what many refer to as "God."

The reader may now want to return to the treatment of *analogy* in the

16. Plato 1993, 210a-211b. Italics mine.

previous chapter (Section II). Recall that analogies are not identities — they have similarities to and dissimilarities from that to which they point. In this case, any analogy of God we might take from our experience will always fall short of the mark because our experience is both finite and conditioned. Thus, for example, the experience of compassion from a true friend (who is, nevertheless, finite and conditioned) can point to (yet fall short of) the perfect love of God; the experience of an incredibly fair person points to (yet falls short of) the perfect justice/goodness of God; and the experience of breathtaking natural beauty (a sunset over an ocean, a scene from a mountain lake, etc.) points to (yet falls short of) the perfect beauty and glory of God.

As will be seen in the next chapter, God is not only perfect Truth, Love, Justice/Goodness, Beauty, and Being; God is also the fulfillment of our transcendental desire for perfect Truth, Love, Goodness, Beauty, and Home. The confluence between the five manifestations of perfect Simplicity and the five human yearnings for the ultimate reveals not only the presence of God to human consciousness, but also the care of the loving, good, and glorious God in bestowing this sublime dignity upon humankind.

CHAPTER EIGHT

The Human Mystery:
Five Yearnings for the Ultimate

Introduction

As noted in Chapter 7, the five manifestations of perfect simplicity correspond to the five human yearnings for the ultimate (the desire for perfect Truth, Love, Goodness, Beauty, and Home). In order to understand the profound dignity of human beings entailed by this correspondence (i.e., that human beings are made in the image of God), it may do well to briefly investigate the evidence and implications of these five desires for the ultimate.

I. The Desire for Perfect Truth

Let us begin with a clue that is manifest every day in the conduct of children who persistently query, "Why is *that*?" One gives an answer, and they ask the further question, "Well, why is *that*?" This seems to go on indefinitely until an adult brings it to an end. This process reveals that children (indeed, all of us) recognize the inadequacy of partially intelligible answers, and that true satisfaction will only occur when complete intelligibility has been achieved.

Another clue concerning this desire for complete intelligibility may be found in some intellectuals' "despair of the truth." History is replete with examples of brilliant men and women trying to find the perfect and unconditioned in philosophy, science, and mathematics, but there always seems to be some unanswered question that gets in the way of perfect intelligibility being fully manifest — a flaw in what could otherwise have been a perfect system. These disenchantments have, on many occasions, brought the brilliant from the heights of complete self-confidence, to the depths of protecting invalid ideas and systems beyond their time. Again, the problem is not with the thirst for truth and knowledge, or love of the process of inquiry, but rather with trying to extract perfect and unconditional Truth from an imperfect and partially intelligible world.

Human beings are not seeking merely pragmatic knowledge (e.g., "How can I get more food with which to live?"), they seem to want to know just for the sake of knowing, and seem to be endowed with a desire for *complete* explanation. They recognize when they have not arrived at this point, indicating that they are already beyond the answer at which they have arrived. Human beings have the remarkable capacity of knowing that they do not know, yet one must ask, "How is this possible unless they have some awareness of what is beyond what they already know?"

The reader may recall a discussion of this point after the Lonerganian proof for the existence of God (in Chapter 4, Section III). Lonergan contends that he (and any others who could affirm it for themselves) have a "pure unrestricted desire to know" that arises out of what he terms "the notion of being." The reasoning for this may be summarized in eight steps:

1) In the process of human cognition and understanding (see Chapter 4, Section I), one major question seems to evade a *natural* explanation (an explanation from the natural world — the world of empirical data, finite data, and finite acts of understanding), namely: "Since every question reveals an awareness of the incompleteness of what we understand, and since this, in turn, entails an awareness of intelligibility beyond what we understand, and since we ask questions about everything we understand, how can this 'awareness of intelligibility beyond everything we understand' be explained?" How can we be aware of something beyond everything we understand? Lonergan might phrase this question as: "How do we have a sufficient awareness of what we do not know in order to have a pure unrestricted desire to know?" That is, how do we have an ongoing knowledge of the incomplete intelligibility of every restricted act of understanding (which grasps only restricted intelligibility) sufficient to ask questions unceasingly until complete intelligibility has been reached?

2) The only seeming explanation is that we know our understanding is incomplete, and if we did not know that it was incomplete, we would not ask any further questions ("What?" "Why?" "How?" etc.). We would be very content to know our names, and to respond to biological opportunities and dangers — nothing more. It is the awareness of

"something more to be known" at the very moment when something is known that drives the further question.

3) Lonergan affirms that he has a pure *unrestricted* desire to know, that is, he desires to know *all* that is to be known; and that he has the capacity to ask further questions when he has not yet grasped "all that is to be known." The same holds true for myself, and I will speak only for myself at this juncture, because I would like the reader to affirm for him or herself the same judgments that I have made in the process of coming to know the pure unrestricted desire to know, and the notion of being, within myself.

4) Now, the question arises, how could I have the power to ask a question every time I understand something that does not meet the expectation of "all that is to be known"? It would seem that I would have to have some awareness (at least a tacit awareness) of "all that is to be known" sufficient to know that whatever I have grasped has not yet met this objective. Thus, I might move from analytical geometry, to the calculus, to non-Euclidean geometries, to the tensor, and know that the tensor does not adequately describe the whole of mathematical intelligibility — and it truly does not. Similarly, I can attain an understanding of space-time fields, electromagnetic fields, quantum fields, the grand unified field, etc., and realize that the grand unified field still does not exhaust all that is to be known — and it truly doesn't. This applies to every area of inquiry and every field of knowledge, and I would know if my idea did not *explain everything about everything* — I would know.

5) The question again arises, how would I always know that there is more to be known when I have grasped even the highest ideas through the highest viewpoints? How would I know that those ideas and viewpoints did not explain everything about everything? How do I know what qualifies for an explanation of everything about everything? How can I have a "pre-knowledge" (an awareness) of the explanation of everything about everything sufficient to keep on asking questions, and to know what will fail to meet the objective of an explanation of everything about everything? This last question contains the clue to how I could have a pre-knowledge of "everything to be known." I must have a tacit awareness of "what is sufficient to qualify for an explanation of everything about everything." Obviously, I cannot explicitly know all the contents that I do not know; but I could have a *tacit* awareness of what would be sufficient for an explanation of everything about everything. This would explain how I could reach very high viewpoints of

mathematics, physics, and metaphysics, and still know that I did not have an explanation of everything about everything — and even have a sense of where to turn to find such an explanation.

6) What could be the origin of this awareness? It cannot be a natural source (empirical data, finite data, or the contents of restricted acts of understanding) because the tacit awareness of "what is sufficient for an explanation of everything about everything" is always *beyond* every "intelligible reality *which leaves a question unanswered*," and every re-stricted intelligible always leaves a question unanswered.[1] Therefore, the tacit awareness of "what is sufficient for an explanation of every-thing about everything" is always beyond any *restricted* intelligible. Its source must therefore be an *unrestricted* intelligible — that is, the Idea of complete intelligibility, which is the content of an unrestricted act of understanding. The Idea of complete intelligibility, then, would seem to be the source of my tacit awareness of "what is sufficient for an ex-planation of everything about everything."

7) Even though the Idea of complete intelligibility is the *source* of my tacit awareness of "what is sufficient for an explanation of everything about everything," I cannot say that I *understand* this Idea, because, as is clear from the Lonerganian proof (Chapter 4, Section II.D), the Idea of complete intelligibility is the Idea of "unrestricted intelligibility in rela-tion to the whole of finite intelligibility." Now, the understanding of this Idea can only occur through an *unrestricted* act of understanding which I, evidently, do not have. (Aside from the fact that I can affirm this for myself, an unrestricted act of understanding must be unique — see Chapter 4, Section II.C — and I would not be that unique Real-

---

1. Recall from Chapter 4, Section II.B that any restricted intelligible must leave a question unanswered because the intelligibility (information) available to answer questions about it is restricted. Thus, there can always be more questions about a restricted reality than there will be intelligibility (information within the restricted reality) available to answer them. Seen from the vantage point of a questioning *person*, one reaches the point at which the answers derived from the intelligibility (information intrinsic to a reality) are subject to further questions. But the intelligibility (information) necessary to answer them must be found from intelligibility outside that reality. Why? Because the intelligible reality has a *re-stricted* amount of intelligibility. Inasmuch as the *answers* from a restricted intelligible have an intrinsic limit (i.e., they do not keep on going indefinitely), they will eventually be open to further questions that cannot be answered by the restricted intelligible itself. Thus, we might say that every restricted intelligible is *more* questionable than answerable. There will always be a domain of answers that give rise to more questions than the intelligibility of the reality can answer.

ity.) Therefore, even though the Idea of complete intelligibility would seem to be the *source* of my tacit awareness of "what is sufficient for an explanation of everything about everything," I cannot have understood It (because It is understandable only by an unrestricted act of understanding).

But how can this be? Lonergan uses the terminology of "notion" ("the notion of being," or what I would term "the notion of complete intelligibility"). What is a notion if it is not an understood idea? It is a presence to consciousness — not a presence that is held or controlled by my consciousness, but one that is held or controlled outside of my consciousness while still being present to it. Now if I don't understand this presence, then how am I aware of it? I must be aware of it as something on the *horizon;* as something beyond my understanding, but, nevertheless, something that can act as a *backdrop* over against which I compare the ideas that I *have* understood. This would explain how I would know that there is more to be known at the very moment I have understood something new, and would explain how I would know that the tensor is not the complete explanation of mathematics, and that mathematics is not the complete explanation of intelligibility itself. I am comparing it to a backdrop that is so much more than the highest possible viewpoints, so much more than any restricted intelligible, so much more than any content of a *restricted* act of understanding (no matter how high the viewpoint).[2]

Now, as I said, I do not understand, hold, or control this Idea; it is, as it were, held and controlled for me as a backdrop to compare the intelligibility of the ideas that I *have* understood. But what is holding and controlling this Idea for me as a backdrop? I must adduce that It would be Its source, namely, the unrestricted act of understanding.

8) But this would mean that the Idea of complete intelligibility, that is, the content of an unrestricted act of understanding, that is, the divine essence, is present to me as a horizon, that is, as a backdrop that can be compared to every intelligible content I grasp through my restricted acts of understanding. The presence of the divine essence, therefore, must be the impetus for my awareness of incomplete intelligibility, the impetus for every question, the impetus for every act of creativity.

2. Lonergan 1992, pp. 380-81. A complete quotation may be found in Note 30 in Chapter 4 of this book.

If the divine essence were not present to me, I would only be capable of recognizing objects of biological opportunity and danger, such as food, snakes, my name, affection, etc., but nothing more, for I would not ask questions about intelligibility (such as "What?" "Why?" "How?" — which penetrate the nature of reality). My curiosity would be limited to biological opportunities and dangers, to discerning the mood of my master, to detecting whether an herb might be poisonous or a creature dangerous. Intelligibility (the nature of things, heuristic contexts, "What?" "Why?" "How?") would be quite beyond me — totally unrecognized by me. Therefore, I would not have a *pure* desire to understand — let alone a pure, *unrestricted* desire to understand. Without the notion of complete intelligibility (the presence of the Idea of complete intelligibility, the presence of the divine essence), I would find fulfillment through a fine piece of meat and ignore the tensor.

9) Yet the presence of the divine essence does not ask the question for me; it does not create for me. It provides the crucial datum of incomplete intelligibility that incites me to ask the question — but I do not have to answer this question, I do not have to seek an answer; I don't even have to ask the question. I can behold incomplete intelligibility, and instead of pursuing its invitation, eat a bon-bon and watch a rerun on television. If I let myself ask the question and freely pursue the answer to it, then I will truly detach data from the empirical residue and truly situate its intelligibility within the new repository of understanding in *my* consciousness, and thereby create and understand ideas that are lovely to behold in themselves and also may have application to the world for some good end. The presence of the divine essence does not do this for me; it simply incites and invites. The question, the seeking, the understanding, the creation, and the freedom intrinsic to it all — God allows that to belong properly to me — a co-creator, as it were, in His image.

A particularly powerful demonstration of the *notion* of complete intelligibility was given in the domain of mathematics by Kurt Gödel in 1931,[3] and was revised by John R. Lucas in 1961,[4] and by the eminent physicist Roger Penrose in 1989.[5] In brief, Gödel showed that there will always be unprovable propositions within any set of axiomatic statements in arithmetic.

3. Gödel 1931, pp. 173-98.
4. Lucas 1961, p. 120.
5. Penrose 1989(a).

Human beings are able not only to show that consistent, unprovable statements exist, but also to prove that they are consistent by making recourse to axioms beyond those used to generate these statements. This reveals that human thinking is not based on a set of prescribed axioms, rules, or programs, and is, by nature, *beyond* any program. A deeper explanation of Gödel's theorem may prove to be helpful. Stephen Barr, summing up the Lucas version of Gödel's argument, notes:

> First, imagine that someone shows me a computer program, P, that has built into it the ability to do simple arithmetic and logic. And imagine that I know this program to be consistent in its operations, and that I know all the rules by which it operates. Then, as proven by Gödel, I can find a statement in arithmetic that the program P cannot prove (or disprove) but which I, following Gödel's reasoning, can show to be a true statement of arithmetic. Call this statement G(P). This means that I have done something that that computer program cannot do. I can show that G(P) is a true statement, whereas the program P cannot do so using the rules built into it.
>
> Now, so far, this is no big deal. A programmer could easily add a few things to the program — more axioms or more rules of inference — so that in its modified form it can prove G(P). (The easiest thing to do would be simply to add G(P) itself to the program as a new axiom.) Let us call the new and improved program P'. Now P' is able to prove the statement G(P), just as I can.
>
> At this point, however, we are dealing with a new and different program, P', and not the old P. Consequently, assuming I know that P' is still a consistent program, I can find a Gödel proposition for *it*. That is, I can find a statement, which we may call G(P'), that the program P' can neither prove nor disprove, but which I can show to be a true statement of arithmetic. So, I am again ahead of the game. . . . This race could be continued *forever.*[6]

Since human beings can *indefinitely* prove propositions that are not provable through the axioms from which they were derived, it would seem that human intelligence is *indefinitely beyond* any axiomatic or program-induced intellection.

Gödel's proof shows that human thinking is not only *always* beyond

6. Barr 2003, p. 214. Italics mine.

axioms, rules, and programs (to which artificial intelligence is limited), but also capable of *genuinely originative creativity* (that is, capable of thinking without deriving from or making recourse to any prior axioms, rules, or programs). If hardwiring and programming cannot produce such originative creativity, what can? Lonergan's notion of being may prove to be the only tenable explanation — that is, a notion of complete intelligibility that stands as a horizon or backdrop to human understanding, inviting it, as it were, to go beyond what it understands, to the goal of complete intelligibility.

Since, as was said above, the source of the notion of complete intelligibility would seem to be the Idea of complete intelligibility (which can only occur through an unrestricted act of understanding), Lonergan and other philosophers[7] have implied or asserted the presence of the divine essence (God) to human consciousness. For them (and for me), God not only exists, but is present to each and every one of us in every act of originative creativity. Even though God does not create for us, He is the invitation to and the condition necessary for originative creativity. This grounds the belief in human transcendentality (the presence of a "soul").

II. The Desire for Perfect Love

As implied in Chapter 7, human beings also appear to have a "sense" of *perfect and unconditional Love.* Not only do we have the power to love (i.e., the power to be naturally connected to another human being in profound empathy, emotion, care, self-gift, concern, and acceptance), we have a "sense" of what this profound interpersonal connection would be like if it were perfect. This sense of perfect Love has the positive effect of inciting us to pursue ever more perfect forms of love. However, it has the drawback of inciting us to *expect* ever more perfect love from other human beings. This generally leads to frustrated expectations of others and consequently to a decline of relation-

---

7. Other contemporary philosophers, such as Karl Rahner (1968, pp. 163-230, 387-406) and Emerich Coreth (1968, pp. 103-97), have adduced the same conclusion as Lonergan from their own experiences and reflections. Physicists such as Sir Arthur Eddington have tried to capture this insight in less formal ways through metaphors like "light beckoning us ahead" (Eddington 1928, pp. 327-28 — see the first quotation in the Introduction to this book). As this light (the divine essence) reveals the inadequacy of partially intelligible answers (by pointing beyond them), it incites a desire within us to ask further questions and to creatively construct an ever-greater repository of human knowledge.

ships that can never grow fast enough to match this expectation of perfect and unconditional love.

This phenomenon gradually manifests itself. For example, as the first signs of imperfection, conditionedness, and finitude begin to emerge in my beloved, I may show slight irritation, but have hopes that the ideal will soon be recaptured (as if it were ever captured to begin with). But as the fallibility of the beloved begins to be more acutely manifest (the other is not perfectly humble, gentle, kind, forgiving, self-giving, and concerned with me in all my interests) the irritation becomes frustration, which, in turn, becomes dashed expectation: "I can't believe I thought she was really the *One*." Of course, she wasn't the *One*, because she is not perfect and unconditioned. Nevertheless, the dashed expectation becomes either quiet hurt or overt demands, both aimed at extracting a higher level of performance from the beloved. When she does not comply, thoughts of terminating the relationship may arise.

The root problem was not with the authenticity of this couple's love for one another. It did not arise out of a lack of concern, care, and responsiveness, a desire to be self-giving, responsible, self-disciplined, and true. Rather, it arose out of a false expectation that they could be *perfect* and *unconditional* love, truth, goodness, fairness, meaning, and home for one another.

Why do we fall prey to what seems to be such an obvious error? Because our *desire* for love and to love is unconditional, but our *actuality* is conditioned. Our desire is for the perfect, but our actuality is imperfect. We, as human beings, therefore, cannot satisfy one another's desire for the unconditional and the perfect. If we do not have a *real* unconditional and perfect being to satisfy this desire, we start looking around us to find a surrogate. Other human beings at first seem like a very good surrogate, because they display qualities of self-transcendence. Hence, we confuse one another for the perfect and unconditioned, and undermine the very relationships that hold out opportunities for growth, depth, joy, common cause, and mutual bondedness.

What is the origin of this desire for unconditional love? Just as the unrestricted desire to know must include a notional awareness of complete intelligibility to give rise to an awareness of and dissatisfaction with every manifestation of incomplete intelligibility, so also the desire for unconditional love must include a notional awareness of unconditional Love to give rise to the awareness of and dissatisfaction with every manifestation of conditioned and imperfect love. This notional awareness of unconditional Love seems to be beyond any specifically known or concretely experienced love, for it seems to cause dissatisfaction with every conditioned love we have known or experienced.

Thus, our dissatisfaction would seem to arise out of an ideal of unconditional Love that has neither been experienced nor actualized. How can we have an awareness of love that we have neither known nor experienced? How can we even extrapolate to it if we do not know where we are going? The inability to give a logical answer to these questions has led some philosophers to associate the desire for unconditional love with "the notion of unconditional Love within us," which would seem to have its origin in unconditional Love itself.

Lonergan believes that when we fulfill our desire for unconditional Love by authentically loving God, we simultaneously fulfill our capacity for self-transcendence, which includes our desire for perfect Truth, Goodness, and Beauty:

> I have conceived being in love with God as an ultimate fulfillment of man's capacity for self-transcendence; and this view of religion is sustained when God is conceived as the supreme fulfillment of the transcendental notions, as supreme intelligence, truth, reality, righteousness, goodness.[8]

It would seem that any other way of fulfilling our desire for unconditional Love will fail to satisfy, because such "fulfillments" will be finite and conditioned (given the uniqueness of the unconditioned Reality and Its unconditional Love).[9]

III. The Desire for Perfect Justice/Goodness

As with the "sense" of perfect and unconditional truth and love, philosophers have long recognized the human desire for *perfect justice or goodness*. Not only do human beings have a sense of good and evil, a capacity for moral reflection, a profoundly negative felt awareness of cooperation with evil (guilt), and a profoundly positive felt awareness of cooperation with goodness (nobility); they also have a "sense" of what perfect, unconditioned justice/goodness would be like. Human beings are not content to simply act in accordance with their conscience now, they are constantly striving for ways to achieve the more noble, the greater good, the higher ideal. They even go so far as to pursue the perfectly good or just order.

8. Lonergan 1972, p. 111.
9. See Chapter 3, Section III; and Chapter 7, Section II.A.

A clue to this desire for perfect justice/goodness may be gleaned from children. An imperfect manifestation of justice from parents will get the immediate retort, "That's not fair!" Adults do the same thing. We have a sense of what perfect justice ought to be, and we believe others ought to know this. When this sense of perfect justice has been violated, we are likely to respond with, "That's not fair!" A violation of this sort always seems particularly acute. We seem to be in a state of shock. We really expect that perfect justice ought to happen, and when it doesn't, it so profoundly disappoints us that it can consume us. We can feel the same outrage towards groups, social structures, and even God.

One need only look at last year's newspapers to find a host of well-meaning, dedicated, and generous men and women who have tried to extract the perfect and unconditioned from the legal system, the ideals of social justice, and institutions dedicated to the common good. The despairing rhetoric of dashed idealism and cynicism does not belong solely to early Marxism; it can be found in public defenders who decry the legal system for prosecuting the innocent, and victims who vilify the very same system for letting the guilty go free. It can also be found in educators who criticize the educational system for not setting high enough standards, and in community advocates who tear down the very same system for making the standards too high and too exclusive. But our imperfect world will not allow either side to be *perfectly* correct.

As with our "sense" of perfect and unconditional love, our sense of perfect and unconditional justice/goodness has both a positive and negative side. The positive side is its ability to fuel all our strivings for an ever more perfect social order, a more just legal system, greater equity and equality, and even our Promethean idealism to bring the justice of God to earth. The negative side of this "sense" of perfect or unconditional justice is that it incites our expectations for *perfect* justice in a *finite* and conditioned world, meaning that our Promethean ideals are likely to be frustrated. This causes disappointments with the culture, the legal system, our organizations, and even our families. We seem to always expect more justice and goodness than the finite world can deliver, and it causes outrage, impatience, judgment of others, and even cynicism when it does not come to pass.

What is the source of this "sense" (notion) of perfect justice/goodness, even the Promethean desire to save the world, and to be the "ultimate hero"? As with the desire for complete intelligibility and unconditional love, the desire for perfect justice/goodness seems to go beyond any experience or knowledge of justice we could possibly have. Our frustrated idealism reveals that we continually see the limits of any current manifestation of justice and goodness which, in turn, reveals that we are already beyond those limits. Given that our desire for justice/goodness will only be satisfied when we reach perfect, unconditional Justice/Goodness, it would seem that our desire is guided by a notional awareness of perfect, unconditional Justice/Goodness; and, given that such a notion of perfect, unconditional Justice/Goodness cannot be obtained from a conditioned and imperfect world, it would seem that its origin is from perfect, unconditional Justice/Goodness itself. For this reason, philosophers have associated this notion of perfect, unconditional Justice/Goodness with the presence of God to human consciousness.[10]

Some philosophers recognize the presence of God to human consciousness not only in the desire for perfect Justice/Goodness, but also in the experience of *conscience.* Immanuel Kant and John Henry Newman are the best-known expositors of this view. Kant set the stage for this approach to God by disclosing his awareness of absolute duty through a categorical imperative (a duty and command to action without exception, condition, or qualification).

> Through the idea of the supreme good as object and final end of the pure practical reason the moral law leads to religion, that is, to the recognition of all duties as divine commands, not as sanctions, that is, as ar-

10. Plato associated "Goodness itself" with the author of light in his famous allegory of the cave in the *Republic:* "But, at any rate, my dream [of the cave and the sun] as it appears to me is that in the region of the known the last thing to be seen and hardly seen is *the idea of good,* and that when seen it must needs point us to the conclusion that this is indeed the cause of all that is right and beautiful, giving birth in the visible world to light, and the author of light and itself in the intelligible world being the authentic source of truth and reason, and that anyone who is to act wisely in private or public must have caught sight of this . . . their souls ever feel the upward urge and the yearning for that sojourn above" (Plato 1961(b), 517c-d).

Other neo-Platonists, such as Saint Augustine, also identify the desire for goodness and happiness with an awareness of the highest good (God): "Just as the objects which men see in the sunlight and choose to enjoy are many and varied, yet the light in which the sight of each man watching sees and holds what he enjoys is one; so even if the goods are many and varied from which each man may choose what he wishes, determining to discern, grasp, and enjoy the *highest good* rightly and truly, nevertheless it is possible that the very light of wisdom, in which these goods can be discerned and grasped, is one wisdom common to all wise men" (Augustine 1964, pp. 59-60).

Contemporary philosophers, such as Bernard Lonergan, have made formal associations between being, truth, and the good. See, for example, Lonergan 1992, p. 681. See the quotation on p. 253 of this book.

bitrary commands of an alien will which are contingent in themselves, but as essential laws of every free will in itself, which, however, must be looked on as commands of the supreme Being, because it is only from a morally perfect (holy and good) and at the same time all-powerful will, and consequently only through harmony with this will, that we can hope to attain the highest good, which the moral law makes it our duty to take as the object of our endeavour.[11]

The essence of Kant's thought here may be summarized in two statements in his *Opus Postumum:* "In the moral-practical reason lies the categorical imperative to regard all human duties as divine commands";[12] which causes him to view God as follows: "the concept of God is the concept of an obligation-imposing subject outside myself."[13] Kant moves from an intrinsic awareness of an absolute moral duty (categorical imperative) to an awareness of a morally perfect will which is the source of that absolute duty, and then to an awareness of the supreme Being who is an "obligation-imposing subject outside [himself]." Notice that this transition of awareness is not a formal set of inferences, but rather an unfolding of the meaning of the absolute duty which is central to Kant's existence. Copleston cites J. H. Bernard's translation of the *Critique of Judgment* as follows:

> [The moral argument] does not supply any objectively-valid proof of the existence of God; it does not prove to the sceptic that there is a God, but that, if he wishes to think in a way consonant with morality, he must admit the assumption of this proposition under the maxims of this practical reason.[14]

This unfolding of the awareness of God through an appreciation of absolute duty bears a remarkable resemblance to John Henry Newman's rational approach to theism. I will present these texts so that the reader will be able to relate the internal experience and conclusions of Newman to his or her own personal experience. If the reader does resonate with the experience of Newman, then it will be yet another example of God's presence as a hori-

11. Kant 2004, §233.
12. *Opus Postumum* (Berlin critical edition), vol. 21, p. 12. Rendered in English by Copleston in 1960, p. 179.
13. *Opus Postumum* (Berlin critical edition), vol. 21, p. 15. Rendered in English by Copleston in 1960, p. 179.
14. J. H. Bernard, trans. 1931, p. 381; cited in Copleston 1960, p. 170.

zon in human consciousness. We concluded to the "presence of God to human consciousness" in Section I with respect to the notion of complete intelligibility (the notion of being). We may now see it in another form, though this time not as a conclusion to a set of inferences, but rather as an unfolding of the meaning of interpersonal divine authority within human consciousness.

Adrian J. Boekraad and Henry Tristram have published an edition of one of the more important unpublished papers of John Henry Newman titled *Proof of Theism*.[15] Since Newman presents his points quite systematically, I will here present only the main movements of the argument with a brief interpretation of his texts. His general argument proceeds as follows. He begins with an overview of his main contention:

> Ward thinks I hold that moral obligation is, because there is a God. But I hold just the reverse, viz. there is a God, because there is a moral obligation. I have a certain feeling on my mind, which I call conscience. When I analyse this, I feel it involves the idea of a Father and a Judge, — of one who sees my heart, etc.[16]

Newman then proceeds to a rather Cartesian assessment of the unity of his consciousness and his existence, which shows that his consciousness is as undeniable as his existence (since one cannot be aware of the latter without being aware of the former). He further shows that he has an *immediate* awareness of his consciousness, and therefore he does not have to deduce it or believe in it. Belief occurs when one is not certain, but Newman is as aware of his consciousness as he is of his existence. He intends to show later that if conscience is intrinsic to his consciousness, then he can be just as immediately aware of his conscience as he is of his consciousness and existence. He then proceeds to a definition of conscience:

> Man has within his breast a certain commanding dictate, not a mere sentiment, not a mere opinion, or impression, or view of things, but a law, an authoritative voice, bidding him do certain things and avoid others. I do not say that its particular injunctions are always clear, or that

15. I will cite the texts of Newman from the work of Boekraad and Tristram 1961 titled *The Argument from Conscience to the Existence of God,* and then cite the page numbers from Newman's unpublished paper as given by Boekraad and Tristram.

16. Boekraad and Tristram 1961, p. 103; citing Newman (unpublished), p. 1.

they are always consistent with each other; but what I am insisting on here is this, that it commands, that it praises, it blames, it promises, it threatens, it implies a future, and it witnesses the unseen. It is more than a man's own self. The man himself has no power over it, or only with extreme difficulty; he did not make it, he cannot destroy it.[17]

Though Newman is speaking about conscience in a more universal way here, it does reflect his experience of his own conscience, and therefore may be fit into the *personal* self-diagnosis and argument he is offering in *Proof of Theism*. For Newman, conscience "commands" (just as for Kant, the categorical imperative imposes duty). He is not so much concerned with whether the specific dictates of the command are always consistent from person to person or from culture to culture, but is impressed by the seeming universality of what is ingredient to conscience's dictates, namely, "command, praise, blame, promise, a future, and the unseen." These characteristics intrinsic to conscience's dictates imply something more than a mere standard or authority. They seem to have an origin outside the self; an origin that is not a matter of human learning (which is controlled by the curious subject), but rather one that is uncontrolled by the self. The more we recognize, listen to, and obey this uncontrollable authority, the clearer it and its *dictates* become:

> Conscience implies a relation between the soul and something exterior, and that moreover, superior to itself; a relation to an excellence which it does not possess, and to a tribunal over which it has no power. And since the more closely this inward monitor is respected and followed, the clearer, the more exalted, and the more varied its dictates become, and the standard of excellence is ever outstripping, while it guides, our obedience, a moral conviction is thus at length obtained of the unapproachable nature as well as the supreme authority of that, whatever it is, which is the object of the mind's contemplation.[18]

It seems that the dictates of conscience and the presence of its authority are somewhat dim in the unpracticed moral agent; but as one listens to and follows these dictates, the dictates themselves and the presence of their source become clearer and clearer to the point of being virtually undeniable.

---

17. Newman 1908, Sermon #64. See also Boekraad and Tristram 1961, p. 114; citing Newman (unpublished), pp. 11-12.
18. Boekraad and Tristram 1961, p. 113; citing Newman (unpublished), pp. 10-11.

The presence of this authority is so strong that Newman is impelled to make his first inference:

> This is Conscience, and, from the nature of the case, its very existence carries on our minds to a Being exterior to ourselves; for else, whence did it come? and to a being superior to ourselves; else whence its strange, troublesome peremptoriness? . . . [Its] very existence throws us out of ourselves and beyond ourselves, to go and seek for Him in the height and depth, whose voice it is.[19]

This passage is not merely an *inference* of God from the presence of an uncontrollable authority; Newman is relating yet another part of his *experience* of conscience. Namely, a presence which not only invites us out of ourselves, but draws us and even throws us out of ourselves. It is a presence which calls us to itself — sets us seeking "for Him in the height and depth, whose voice it is." If we respond to this invitation; if we follow the call of the "voice," then its *personal* presence will become apparent. Newman uses the voice of Callista (the protagonist in his 1855 novel of the same name) to make this point:

> [God] says to me, Do this, don't do that. You may tell me that this dictate is a mere law of my nature, as is to joy or to grieve. I cannot understand this. No, it is the echo of a person speaking to me. Nothing shall persuade me that it does not ultimately proceed from a person external to us. It carries with it its proof of its divine origin. My nature feels towards it as towards a person. When I obey it, I feel a satisfaction; when I disobey a soreness, — just like that which I feel in pleasing or offending some revered friend. . . . The echo implies a voice; a voice a speaker. That speaker I love and I fear.[20]

In order to clarify and validate this experience, Newman contrasts the experience of conscience to the experience of what he calls "taste" (aesthetic experience), and shows that aesthetic experiences do not call me out of myself in an interpersonal way as does the experience of conscience. If conscience were only intrapersonal (private), it would resemble aesthetic experience, but it is so much more:

19. Boekraad and Tristram 1961, pp. 114-15; citing Newman (unpublished), p. 12.
20. Boekraad and Tristram 1961, p. 116; citing Newman (unpublished), p. 13.

Now I can best explain what I mean by this peculiarity of feeling [intrinsic to conscience], by contrasting it with the rules of taste. As we have a notion of wrong and right, so we have of beautiful and ugly; but the latter set of notions is attended by no sanction. No hope or fear, no misgiving of the future, no feeling of being hurt, no tender sorrow, no sunny self-satisfaction, no lightness of heart attends on the acting with beauty or deformity. It is these feelings, which carry the mind out of itself and beyond itself, which imply a tribunal in future, and reward and punishment which are so special.[21]

He then focuses on these special feelings to distill the *interpersonal* nature of them, revealing that these feelings could not be experienced were it not through a relationship with another person — a person like a father:

[T]he feeling is one analogous or similar to that which we feel in human matters towards a *person* whom we have offended; there is a tenderness almost tearful on going wrong, and a grateful cheerfulness when we go right which is just what we feel in pleasing or displeasing a father or revered superior. So that contemplating and revolving on this feeling the mind will reasonably conclude that it is an unseen father who is the object of the feeling. And this father has necessarily some of those special attributes which belong to the notion of God. He is invisible — He is the searcher of hearts — He is omniscient as far as man is concerned — He is (to our notions) omnipotent. . . .[22]

We may now summarize Newman's thought on this matter. First, he claims that he does not *believe* in conscience any more than he *believes* in his consciousness; he is *directly aware* of them, for consciousness is intrinsic to his awareness of everything — including his own existence, and conscience is intrinsic to his consciousness, presenting him with an awareness of interpersonal relationship and authority. He then describes in five steps how conscience is an *immediate* awareness or experience of a personal God:

1. He observes that conscience commands him, and that this command includes praise, blame, promise, a future, and the unseen (and is in *immediate* relationship with his consciousness when it does so).

21. Boekraad and Tristram 1961, pp. 117-18; citing Newman (unpublished), p. 14.
22. Boekraad and Tristram 1961, pp. 118-19; citing Newman (unpublished), pp. 14-15.

2. He then observes that intrinsic to this "praise, blame, promise, etc." is a concomitant awareness of an *external source* ("Its very existence throws us out of ourselves and beyond ourselves, to go and seek for Him in the height and depth, whose voice it is").

3. He then shows that these feelings are not reducible to other kinds of feelings within human consciousness (such as aesthetic feelings): "[The feeling of beauty or ugliness] is attended by no sanction. No hope or fear, no misgiving of the future, no feeling of being hurt, no tender sorrow, no sunny self-satisfaction, no lightness of heart. . . ."

4. He then shows that there is a *personal* dimension intrinsic to these special qualities of the feelings of conscience: "[T]he feeling is one analogous or similar to that which we feel in human matters towards a *person* whom we have offended; there is a tenderness almost tearful on going wrong, and a grateful cheerfulness when we go right which is just what we feel in pleasing or displeasing a father. . . ."

5. He then reveals that this personal dimension is not completely similar to those experienced with human beings, but has a divine dimension which is implicit in its supreme authority ("an authoritative voice, bidding him do certain things and avoid others. . . . The man himself has no power over it, or only with extreme difficulty; he did not make it, he cannot destroy it."). When this *supreme* authority is considered within the context of "the voice of a father," it manifests divine attributes ("So that contemplating and revolving on this feeling the mind will reasonably conclude that it is an unseen father who is the object of the feeling. And this father has necessarily some of those special attributes that belong to the notion of God. He is invisible — He is the searcher of hearts — He is omniscient . . .").

The more we recognize, listen to, and follow the urgings of conscience, the more clear and evident both the dictates of conscience and its personal, external, divine source become.

Newman has not formulated an *inferential* argument here; rather, he has rationally unfolded the fivefold dimension of his immediate experience of God in his conscience. He reveals, as it were, a dimension within a dimension within a dimension within the feelings and experience of conscience. What are these dimensions? A divine dimension (invisible, searcher of hearts, omniscient . . .) *within* a personal dimension (a tenderness almost tearful on going wrong, and a grateful cheerfulness when we go right) *within* special qualities (sanction, hope, fear, misgiving of the future, feelings of being hurt, tender sorrow) *within* the feelings and experience of conscience (praise, blame, promise, etc.). This total experience of conscience ("the divine dimension within the personal dimension within the special qualities within the feelings and experience of conscience") is intrinsic to his consciousness, and therefore, he is *immediately* aware of it.

Thus, Newman is not making an inferential argument; he is unfolding his own immediate experience of God through his conscience. If readers resonate with this, they may also be able to experience the personal God through conscience. Newman assures us that the more we listen to and follow our conscience, the more deeply and clearly we will experience the God who both guides and invites us to His life of transcendent and perfect goodness.

IV. The Desire for Perfect Beauty

One need not read the nineteenth-century Romantic poets or listen to the great Romantic composers, or view the works of Romantic artists to see the human capacity to idolize *beauty*. One only need look at the examples of simple dissatisfaction with beauty in our everyday life. We don't look good enough and neither do other people. The house is not perfect enough, the painting can never achieve perfection, and the musical composition, though beautiful beyond belief, could always be better. Once in a great while, we think we have arrived at consummate beauty. This might occur while looking at a scene of natural beauty: a sunset over the water, majestic green and brown mountains against a horizon of blue sky; but even there, despite our desire to elevate it to the quasi-divine, we get bored and strive for a different or an even more perfect manifestation of natural beauty — a *little* better sunset, another vantage point of the Alps that's a *little* more perfect.

As with the desire for the other three transcendentals (perfect Truth, perfect Love, and perfect Justice/Goodness), human beings seem to have an awareness of what is more beautiful. It incites them to the desire for this more perfect ideal. This desire has both a positive and a negative effect. The positive effect is that it incites the continuous human striving for artistic, musical, and literary perfection. We do not passively desire to create, we passionately desire to create, to express in ever more beautiful forms, the perfection of beauty that we seem to carry within our consciousness. We do not simply want to *say* an idea, we want to express it beautifully, indeed, more beautifully, indeed, perfectly beautifully. We do not simply want to express a mood in music, we want to express it perfectly beautifully. This striving has left a legacy of architecture and art, music and drama, and every form of high culture.

The negative effect is that we will always grow bored or frustrated with any imperfect manifestation of beauty. This causes us to try to make perfectly beautiful what is imperfect by nature. It is true that a garden can achieve a certain perfection of beauty, but our continuous desire to improve it can make us grow terribly dissatisfied when we cannot perfect it indefinitely.

This is evidenced quite strongly in the artistic community. When one reads the biographies of great artists, musicians, and poets, one senses the tragedy with which art is frequently imbued. What causes these extraordinarily gifted men and women to abuse themselves, to judge themselves so harshly, to so totally pour themselves into their art? Perhaps it's when art becomes a "god," when one tries to extract perfect and unconditional beauty from imperfect and conditioned minds and forms.

Where does this sense of perfect beauty come from? As with the other three yearnings for the ultimate, we are led to the Beautiful itself, for dissatisfaction with even the most beautiful objects of our experience reveals our ability to indefinitely perceive the limits of worldly beauty, which, in turn, reveals our ability to be beyond those limits, which, in turn, reveals a notional awareness of what perfect beauty might be (a notional awareness of a beauty without imperfection or limit).

Now this movement toward perfect beauty seems to occur in stages. First we focus upon the beauty of sensation (worldly beauty or, for Plato, the beauty of appearances or images), but as noted above, we seem to be perpetually beyond all worldly beauty; and so we turn to a less sensation-based (image-based) notion of beauty and focus on the beauty of *ideals* (such as justice, the common good, law, rights, civil peace, and the persons and institutions that attempt to make these ideals real). But as noted above, the finitude and conditionedness of these forms of beauty cause us to search still elsewhere for the fulfillment of our yearning for more. It seems that many here turn to the beauty of *ideas*, particularly the beauty of higher viewpoints in philosophy, mathematics, the equations of physics, and other disciplines. These ideas not only have an intrinsic beauty (such as the symmetry, elegance, and unifying power of the equations of physics), but also the beauty of nobility and ideal. They speak of human achievement, self-sacrifice, and even human transcendentality. Yet, even the beauty of the good and the true in their interrelationship is still not enough, and once again we begin the search for something more.

These stages resemble those in Plato's ascent to perfect Beauty in the *Symposium*. This ascent reveals not only our desire for perfect Beauty, but also a hyperphatic approach[23] to the object of our desire:

> He who from these ascending under the influence of true *love,* begins to perceive that [perfect, absolutely simple, eternal] beauty, is not far from the end. And the true order of going, or being led by another, to the things of *love,* is to begin from the beauties of earth and mount upwards for the sake of that other beauty, using these as steps only, and from one going on to two, and from two to all fair [beautiful] forms, and from fair forms to fair practices [beautiful institutions], and from fair practices to fair notions, until from fair notions he arrives at the notion of absolute beauty, and at last knows what the essence of beauty is [the hyperphatic way]. . . . [W]hat if man had eyes to see the true beauty, the *divine* beauty, I mean, pure and dear and unalloyed, not clogged with the pollutions of *mortality* and all the colors and vanities of human life, thither looking, and holding converse with the true beauty *simple and divine?* Remember how in that communion only, beholding beauty with the eye of the mind [soul], he will be enabled to bring forth, not images of beauty, but realities (for he has hold not of an image but of a reality), and bringing forth and nourishing true virtue to become the friend of God and be *immortal,* if mortal man may. . . . I try to persuade others, that in the attainment of this end human nature will not easily find a helper better than *love.*[24]

As noted in the last chapter, Plato was convinced of the divine character of Beauty itself, and believed that human beings not only had a desire for it, but also had the capacity to behold it and be fulfilled through it. He believed that this required proper instruction so that neophytes would not fix upon the lower orders of beauty, but instead move progressively toward higher ones. He intimates that the achievement of "beholding absolute Beauty" betokens immortality and points to human transcendentality (a "soul").

We may now return to our main point. Recall that dissatisfaction with even the most beautiful objects of our experience reveals our ability to indefinitely perceive the limits of *imperfect* beauty, which, in turn, reveals our ability to be beyond those limits, which, in turn, reveals a notional awareness of what perfect beauty might be (a notional awareness of a beauty with-

---

23. See Chapter 6, Section II.
24. Plato 1993, 211c-212b. Italics mine.

out imperfection or limit). Since it seems that the notion of perfect Beauty cannot be obtained or abstracted from a world of sensorial (imperfect) beauty, or even from the beauty of great ideals, goods, and truths (because they too are conditioned and imperfect), one is led to the conjecture that its origin arises out of perfect Beauty itself. For this reason, philosophers have associated the notion of perfect beauty with the notional presence of perfect Beauty (i.e., God) to human consciousness.

We may now conclude with another observation about the *unity* of the transcendentals. Notice in the above passage from Plato that the beholding of perfect Beauty includes the notional awareness and use of the good, the true, and love. For Plato, love is not only the desire for beauty but an awareness of its goodness, and the good is beautiful, true, and lovable.[25] When all four work together they help the soul to ascend to the state of its proper fulfillment. This proper fulfillment has an ecstatic dimension that points to the unity of the transcendentals — God. For this reason, Roger Fry connects it with mysticism:

> One can only say that those who experience [the purely aesthetic quality of significant form, which is something other than agreeable arrangements of form, harmonious patterns, and the like] feel it to have a peculiar quality of "reality" which makes it a matter of *infinite* importance in their lives. Any attempt I might make to explain this would probably land me in the depths of mysticism.[26]

---

25. Hans Urs von Balthasar not only associates the notion of perfect beauty with God; he sees it as the unifying element between perfect truth and perfect goodness. This quality of perfect beauty is what makes the truth and the good wholly attractive to us and reveals that beauty must be more than mere appearance. In volume 1 of *The Glory of the Lord,* he establishes the basis for his theological aesthetics by noting: "Beauty is the word that shall be our first. Beauty is the last thing which the thinking intellect dares to approach, since only it dances as an uncontained splendour around the double constellation of the true and the good and their inseparable relation to one another. Beauty is the disinterested one, without which the ancient world refused to understand itself, a world which both imperceptibly and yet unmistakably has bid farewell to our new world, a world of interests, leaving it to its own avarice and sadness.... We no longer dare to believe in beauty and we make of it a mere appearance in order the more easily to dispose of it. Our situation today shows that beauty demands for itself at least as much courage and decision as do truth and goodness, and she will not allow herself to be separated and banned from her two sisters without taking them along with herself in an act of mysterious vengeance. We can be sure that whoever sneers at her name as if she were the ornament of a bourgeois past — whether he admits it or not — can no longer pray and soon will no longer be able to love" (Balthasar 1982, p. 18).

26. Fry 1998, italics mine.

V. The Desire for Perfect Home

Human beings also seek a perfect sense of harmony with all that is. They not only want to be at home in a particular environment, they want to be at home with the totality, at home in the cosmos. Have you ever felt, either as a child or an adult, a sense of alienation or discord — a deep sense of not belonging? You ask yourself, "What could be the source?" and you look around and see that at this particular time you have a good relationship with your friends and your family. Your work relationships seem to be going fairly well; community involvements have produced some interesting friends and contexts in which to work. Yet, something's missing. You don't quite feel at home in a *general* sense. Yet you do feel at home with family, friends, organization, etc. You feel like you are out of kilter with, and don't belong to, the *totality*. And yet, all the *specific* contexts you look at seem just fine. You feel an emptiness, a lack of peace, yet there is absolutely nothing you can put your finger on.

Many philosophers and theologians connect this feeling with a human being's yearning to be at home with the totality; not merely to be in harmony with the totality, but to be perfectly at home (without any hint of alienation).

This desire for home with the totality also has both a positive side and a negative side. The positive side is that it presents a call to seek ever greater and deeper forms of harmony (peace within the world). It induces us to remove any form of alienation from our lives, the lives of others, and from our relationships with one another.

The negative side is the confusion and discontent that it brings. I may say to myself, "I do not understand why I feel this lack of peace, this emptiness, this sense of not belonging," and so I may tend to feel animosity towards individuals who can do nothing for me when I'm feeling it. One may look at one's wife and think, "Although I feel at home with her, she can do nothing for this peculiar sense of emptiness." Her helplessness induces frustration, and she is baffled by this seemingly inexplicable frustration. Again, I realize that my best friend, who seems to bring comfort in so many human situations, cannot help me to belong, to fit in, to feel at home in this *universal* sense. And so I display my frustration and restlessness at his powerlessness. Relationships have a way of taking a downward turn in these circumstances because we are trying to extract from them what they cannot give. The only way out, seemingly, is to find perfect home and harmony with *all that is*.

What gives rise to this "sense" of perfect home within the totality? It would seem to be linked to perfect Home, perfect Peace, or perfect Harmony *itself*; for our perception of incompleteness in every concrete manifestation of home reveals that we anticipate more home than any concrete manifestation can deliver; and this, in turn, reveals that we have a notional awareness of perfect home that would not seem to be derivable or abstractable from any concrete experience of home. Thus, the origin of this notional awareness would seem to be traceable to "perfect Home" itself. For this reason, philosophers and theologians have associated it with the presence of God to human consciousness.

When the desire for perfect home is even partially fulfilled, philosophers, theologians, and mystics variously refer to it as *joy — love — awe — unity — holiness — quiet.*

C. S. Lewis tried to describe the transcendent **joy** connected with perfect Home in his book *Surprised by Joy.* He compares it to the kind of joy that takes one over and adds a new intensity, awareness, and significance to life. He calls it a "stab of joy," which includes elements of awe and desire:

> It is difficult to find words strong enough for the sensation which came over me; Milton's "enormous bliss" of Eden (giving the full, ancient meaning to "enormous") comes somewhere near it. It was a sensation, of course, of desire; but desire for what? Not, certainly, for a biscuit tin filled with moss, nor even (though that came into it) for my own past. *Ioulianpotho* [Oh, I desire too much.] — and before I knew what I desired, the desire itself was gone, the whole glimpse withdrawn, the world turned commonplace again, or only stirred by a longing for the longing that had just ceased.[27]

Saint Teresa of Avila (the sixteenth-century mystic who founded the discalced Carmelites) wrote extensively about the spiritual and mystical life — particularly about the **love**-joy-ecstasy toward which she was drawn. Unlike C. S. Lewis, who wrote about being *"surprised* by joy" (i.e., being invited by God more deeply into the divine home), Saint Teresa speaks about the experience she frequently had in prayer in the Carmelite monastery. She speaks of an intrinsic connection between divine love and joy:

> The *loving* exchange that takes place between the soul and God is so sweet that I beg Him in His goodness to give a taste of this love to any-

27. Lewis 1955, pp. 16-18.

one who thinks I am lying. On the days this lasted I went about as though stupefied. I desired neither to see nor to speak. . . . [I]t seems the Lord carries the soul away and places it in *ecstasy*; thus there is no room for pain or suffering, because *joy* soon enters in.[28]

In his classic work, *The Idea of the Holy*, Rudolf Otto describes one kind of **awe** in his notion of the "numinous experience":

The feeling of [*mysterium tremendum*] may at times come sweeping like a gentle tide, pervading the mind with a tranquil mood of deepest worship. It may pass over into a more set and lasting attitude of the soul, continuing, as it were, thrillingly vibrant and resonant, until at last it dies away and the soul resumes its "profane," non-religious mood of everyday experience. It may burst in sudden eruption up from the depths of the soul. . . . It may become the hushed, trembling, and speechless humility of the creature in the presence of — whom or what? In the presence of that which is a mystery inexpressible and above all creatures.[29]

Evelyn Underhill, one of the foremost authorities on mysticism, spoke of "**unity** with the totality" (or "unity with all creation") as central to the mystical experience:

. . . and seeing with purged sight all things and creatures as they are in that transcendent order, [the self] detects in them too that striving of Creation to return to its centre which is the secret of the Universe.

A harmony is thus set up between the mystic and Life in all its forms. Undistracted by appearance, he sees, feels, and knows it in one piercing act of loving comprehension.[30]

Underhill was a mystic herself (in the Christian tradition), and wrote the following fragment in her spiritual diary (*Green Book*):

Today my God and Joy I felt and knew Thee, Eternal, Unchanging, transfusing all things, and most wholly and perfectly given to us in Christ — our indwelling with Him a Total Surrender to Thee — Thyself in all, the

28. Teresa of Avila 1976, p. 194.
29. Otto 1958, pp. 12-13.
30. Underhill 1930, p. 258.

one medium of our union — at Communion to find and love Thee in each soul to which Thou hast given Thyself. To know and find Thee, actually and substantially, in all nations and races and persons — this nourishes. . . . "Not grace alone, nor us alone, but Thy Grace in us." To use and cultivate it. . . . How far beyond anything one conceived the mysteries seem to stretch now. The more vivid the vision of Christ grows and the more insistent the demand for dedication, the more one can escape by this path from the maze of self-occupation. He draws and we run after.[31]

Rudolf Otto describes the experience of **holiness** as an experience of complete otherness; yet it is not an experience of alienation from this holy otherness, but rather an invitation into it. The awareness causes a profound sense of being "creature" — and being at home with one's creatureliness before the holy Other who is our home:

[A person's encounter with the Numinous Reality produces] the feeling of absolute "profaneness." . . . And at the same moment he passes upon the numen a judgement of *appreciation* of a unique kind by the category diametrically contrary to "the profane," the category "holy," which is proper to the numen alone. . . .[32]

The final quality of divine home connects the experience of "union with God" to **quiet**. This quiet is not an empty silence, but rather a silence filled with love that stills every aspect of alienation in the human heart. Evelyn Underhill describes this experience as follows:

In "Quiet" the eager will is silenced, the "wheel of imagination" is stilled. In Contemplation, the heart at last comes to its own — *Cor ad cor loquitur*. In their simplest forms, these three states [in which there is an element of quiet — recollective, quiet, and contemplative] involve the deliberate concentration upon, the meek resting in, the joyous communing with, the ineffable Object of man's quest.[33]

As the above quotations reveal, the experiences of joy — love — awe — unity — holiness — quiet dynamically interact through their divine source.

31. Underhill 1993, pp. 39-40.
32. Otto 1958, p. 51.
33. Underhill 1930, pp. 310-11.

Joy is not simply joy; it is God's joy, and God's joy is also God's love and majesty and unity and holiness and quiet. God's signature is contained in both His presence and the overlapping of the above experiences.

One might think that the experience of God would lead to fear of the immense, uncontrollable Creator-Other; but in fact the experience of the divine seems to be quite different. Despite the immensity and uncontrollable otherness of God, there seem to be a joy, love, and quieting of the human heart so profound that they transform what might have been an alienating otherness into a sense of perfect Home. Throughout the experience, there appears to be a sense of invitation — an invitation to go more deeply into the Holy Other — an invitation to come Home. When the experience is completed, one is left, as C. S. Lewis says, with a longing; or perhaps better, "a longing for the longing."

Thus, God seems to be present to human consciousness not only as the "Idea of complete intelligibility," not only as the "ideal of perfect Empathy," not only as the "ideal of perfect Justice/Goodness," not only as the "quality of perfect Beauty," but above all as the "invitation to perfect Home."

CONCLUSION TO PART THREE:
THE DIVINE AND HUMAN MYSTERIES

By now it will be apparent that the five human desires for the perfect and unconditioned match the five manifestations of absolute simplicity. We may now see the fulfillment of our deepest desires in greater perspective.

The fulfillment of our desire for perfect truth is *Truth* itself (the idea of complete intelligibility intrinsic to the unrestricted act of understanding — understanding itself).

The fulfillment of our desire for perfect love is *Love* itself, that is, the absolute simplicity and unity of perfect empathy-care-*agapē*, which breaks through the radical autonomy of self-consciousness and allows for a perfect communion of feeling, acceptance, and self-gift among all self-conscious beings.

The fulfillment of our desire for perfect justice/goodness is *Justice/ Goodness* itself, with its unlimited capacity to unify all divergent elements of a community through its unmitigated love of the good.

The fulfillment of our desire for perfect beauty is *Beauty* itself, which is the unity underlying perfect harmony, complementarity of diverse forms, and the glorious refulgence evoked by it.

This sheds greater light on the fulfillment of our desire for perfect

Home, for the perfect home we seek (perfect fulfillment, peace, freedom from alienation, and perfect expression of our freedom within the perfect expression of the whole community's freedom) entails and is actualized by perfect Truth, perfect Love, perfect Goodness, and perfect Beauty.

This should come as no surprise, for, if Truth itself, Love itself, Goodness itself, and Beauty itself are absolutely simple, then they are the self-same entity (because absolute simplicity is absolutely unique). Though human consciousness seems to separate these five desires for the ultimate, their satisfaction is attained through the same absolutely simple Reality. Thus, God is at once our ultimate Home, the ultimate fulfillment of our desires for perfect Truth, Love, Goodness, and Beauty, and is, therefore, our perfect fulfillment, peace, and freedom. For this reason, Saint Augustine begins his *Confessions* as follows: "For Thou hast made us for Thyself, and our hearts are restless until they rest in Thee."[34]

We may now return to the fundamental insight of Sir Arthur Eddington with which we began this book — an insight that recognizes not only the human desire for the Transcendent, but also Its impelling horizon which induces creativity within us:

> We all know that there are regions of the human spirit untrammeled by the world of physics. In the mystic sense of the creation around us, in the expression of art, in a yearning towards God, the soul grows upward and finds the fulfillment of something implanted in its nature. The sanction for this development is within us, a striving born with our consciousness or an Inner Light proceeding from a greater power than ours. Science can scarcely question this sanction, for the pursuit of science springs from a striving that the mind is impelled to follow, a questioning that will not be suppressed. Whether in the intellectual pursuits of science or in the mystical pursuits of the spirit, the light beckons ahead and the purpose surging in our nature responds.[35]

---

34. Augustine 1991, Book I, Chapter 1.1.
35. Eddington 1928, pp. 327-28.

Five Questions Toward the Unconditional Love of God

If it is true that "the heart has reasons that reason knows not of,"[1] then we will probably not be satisfied with only *reasons* for the existence and presence of God. As implied at the end of the previous chapter, we will also want to discover and even experience God's love. Perhaps the best way to provoke reflection on this love is to ask some questions that incite not only our minds but also our hearts. The following five questions may serve this purpose.

1) What is the most positive and creative power or capacity within me?
At first glance, one might want to respond that this power is intellect or creativity, but further reflection may show that the capacity to apprehend truth or knowledge, or to create, *in and of itself,* is not necessarily positive. Knowledge and creativity can be misused, and therefore be negative, destructive, manipulative, inauthentic, and thus undermine both the individual and common good. There is but one human power that contains its own end of "positivity" within itself, one power that is directed toward the positive by itself, and therefore one power that directs intellect and creativity to its proper, positive end. As may by now be evident, that power is love (*agapē*). Love's capacity for empathy, its ability to enter into a unity with others leading to a natural "giving of self," forms the fabric of the common good and the human community, and so seeks as its end the good of both individuals and that community.

Love, by its very nature, unifies, seeks the positive, orders things to their proper end, finds a harmony amidst diversity, and gives of itself in order to initiate and actualize this unifying purpose. This implies that love is naturally oriented toward perfect positivity and perfect fulfillment.

---

1. Pascal 1958, #277.

Furthermore, love would seem to be the one *virtue* that can be an end in itself. Other virtues do not *necessarily* culminate in a unity with others whereby doing the good for the other is just as easy if not easier than doing the good for oneself. Thus, courage, left to itself, might be mere bravado or might lead to the persecution of the weak. Self-discipline, left to itself, might lead to a disdain for the weak or a sense of self-sufficiency which is antithetical to empathy. Even humility can be overbearing and disdainful if it is not done out of love. Even though these virtues are necessary means for the actualization of love (i.e., authentic love cannot occur without courage, self-discipline, and humility), they cannot be ends in themselves, for they can be the instruments of unlove when they are not guided by the intrinsic goodness of love. Love seems to be the only virtue that can be an end in itself and therefore can stand by itself.

Now, if you, the reader, affirm the existence of this power within yourself and further affirm that it is the guiding light of both intellect and creativity, that its successful operation is the only way in which all your other powers can be guided to a positive end, that it is therefore the only way of guaranteeing positivity for both yourself and others, and that it therefore holds out the promise of authentic fulfillment, purpose in life, and happiness, then you will have acknowledged love to be the highest of all powers. You will then want to proceed to the next question.

2) If love is the one power that seeks the positive in itself, and we are made to find our purpose in life through love, could God (perfect Being), who created us with this loving nature, be devoid of love?
As implied in Chapter 7 (Section II.A), the seeming absolute simplicity of perfect Love points to its presence within the absolutely simple, unconditioned, unrestricted act of understanding who is the Creator of all else that is. The following questions may reinforce this inference.

If the Creator were devoid of love, why would that Creator create human beings not only with the capacity for love, but to be fulfilled only when they are loving? If the Creator is devoid of love, why make love the actualization of all human powers and desires, and therefore of human nature? If the Creator is not loving, then the creation of "beings meant for love" seems absurd. However, if the Creator *is* love, then creating a loving creature (i.e., sharing His loving nature) would seem to be both intrinsically and extrinsically consistent with what (or perhaps better, "who") He is. Could the Creator be any less loving than the "loving nature" He has created? Furthermore, if a Creator were perfect Being, wouldn't that perfect Being also be capable of the one power and virtue which can be an end in itself, that is, Love?

If you, the reader, can reasonably affirm the love of the Creator from the above, then you may want to proceed to the third question.

3) Is my desire to love and to be loved merely conditional, or unconditional?

As implied in Chapter 8 (Section II), human beings seem to have a desire not only for love, but also for perfect and unconditional love. We sometimes (mistakenly) expect our human beloveds to fulfill this desire for perfect and unconditional love, which clearly frustrates both us and them when their finitude does not allow it. This desire also drives us to seek further perfection in empathy and love, which can, in some individuals (say, Mother Teresa), be quite authentic and universal. Thus, there seems to be significant warrant for the belief that human beings will never be satisfied until they are able to give and receive perfect "empathy and unity with others whereby doing the good for the other is just as easy, if not easier, than doing the good for oneself."

The reader must now judge this contention for him or herself. If you did not have a desire for perfect and unconditional Love, why would you be so dissatisfied with imperfect and conditioned manifestations of love in others and in yourself (even from the time of childhood)? If you sense within yourself an inability to be ultimately satisfied by any form of conditioned or finite love, then you will have also affirmed within yourself the intrinsic desire for *unconditional* Love, which leads to the next question.

4) If my desire for love can only be ultimately satisfied by unconditional Love, then could the Creator of this desire be anything less than unconditional Love?

A simple response to this question might run as follows: If we assume that the Creator does not intend to frustrate this desire for unconditional Love within all of us, it would seem that His creation of the desire would imply an intention to fulfill it, which would, in turn, imply the very presence of this quality within Him. This would mean that the Creator of the desire for unconditional Love is (as the only possible fulfillment of that desire) Himself unconditional Love. The reader here is only affirming the inconsistency of a "Creator incapable of unconditional Love" creating a being with the desire for perfect and unconditional Love. This is sufficient for affirming the presence of unconditional Love in the Creator.

A more complete explanation might begin with the *origin* of the desire for perfect and unconditional Love. As implied in Chapter 8 (Section II), the awareness of unconditional Love (which arouses the desire for unconditional Love) seems to be beyond any specifically known or concretely experienced love, for it seems to cause dissatisfaction with *every* conditioned love we have known or experienced. How can we have an awareness of love that we have neither known nor experienced? How can we even extrapolate to it if we do not know where we are going? The inability of some philosophers to give a purely naturalistic answer to these questions has led them to associate the "tacit awareness of unconditional Love" with the "presence of unconditional Love itself to human consciousness." Unconditional Love itself would therefore seem to be the cause of our awareness of It and also our desire for It. Inasmuch as unconditional Love itself transcends all conditioned (and human) manifestations of love, it might fairly be associated with the Creator. The Creator would then be associated with our human awareness of and desire for unconditional Love. Therefore, it seems that the Creator would have to be at least capable of unconditional Love. If you, the reader, concur with this explanation of your desire for unconditional Love, you may want to proceed to the next question.

5) If the Creator is unconditional Love, would He want to enter into a relationship with us of intense empathy?
If one did not attribute unconditional Love to God, then the idea of God wanting to be in empathetic relationship with us might seem preposterous. A God of stoic indifference would not want to bother with creatures, let alone actually enter into empathetic relationship with them. However, in the logic of love, or rather, in the logic of unconditional Love, all this changes.

If we attribute the various parts of the definition of *agapē* to an unconditionally loving Creator, we might obtain the following result: God (as unconditional *Agapē*) would be unconditional empathy and care for others (even to the point of self-sacrificial care). As such, God would expect neither repayment for this care, nor any of the affective benefits of other kinds of love (such as affection, delight, the romantic feelings of *eros,* or the reciprocity of friendship — *philia*). Hence, God would not *need* affectionate feelings in order to love us, though He would have unconditional affection for us; He would not *need* the reciprocal commitment and caring of *philia*, though He would be unconditionally committed to us in friendship; and He would not have *need* of our romantic feelings, even though He would grace such feelings in the human endeavor toward exclusive love. God would seek to unconditionally protect, defend, maintain, and enhance the *intrinsic* dignity, worth, lovability, unique goodness, transcendental mystery, and eternity of every one of us.

Recall that love is empathizing with the other and entering into a unity with that other whereby doing the good for the other is just as easy as, if not easier than, doing the good for oneself. This kind of love has the non-egocentricity, humility, self-gift, deep affection, and care that would make infinite power into infinite gentleness, and would incite an unconditionally loving Being to enter into the deepest possible empathy with beloveds created in His image. This might characterize the way that unconditional Love would act — not being egocentrically conscious of the infinite distance between Creator and creature, but rather being infinitely desirous of bridging this gap in a perfect unity of perfect empathy and perfect care. It would be just like the unconditionally loving God to love like this.

If this is the case, then the unconditionally loving God would make Himself accessible to us in this kind of empathetic relationship, and so be present to us not merely as a horizon of understanding, an ideal of love and goodness, a quality of beauty, and an invitation to Home, but also as an *interpersonal* Being *relating* to us in unconditional empathy and love.

But you, the reader, will have to affirm these contentions through your own heart and mind. If you believe that God would relate to us in unconditional empathy and love, then it will be incumbent upon you to seek that God in revelation, others, the depths of the heart, and the movements of history. It will be incumbent upon you to seek the God of patience, kindness, mercy, empathy, affection, humility, gentleness, and peace through faith and prayer. This search is powerfully manifest by Augustine's prayer near the end of his *Confessions:*

> Late have I loved you, beauty so old and so new: late have I loved you. And see, you were within and I was in the external world and sought you there, and in my unlovely state I plunged into those lovely created things which you made. You were with me, and I was not with you. The lovely things kept me far from you, though if they did not have their existence in you, they had no existence at all. You called and cried out loud and shattered my deafness. You were radiant and resplendent, you put to flight my blindness. You were fragrant, and I drew in my breath and now pant after you. I tasted you, and I feel but hunger and thirst for you. You touched me, and I am set on fire to attain the peace which is yours.[2]

2. Augustine 1991, p. 201.

References

Adelberger, E., Heckel, B., and Nelson, A. 2003. "Test of the Gravitational Inverse-Square Law" *Nucl. Phys.* **B**672 87-100 (hep-th/0307284).

Adelberger, E., Heckel, B., and Hoyle, C. 2005. "Testing the Gravitational Inverse-Square Law," http://physicsworld.com/cws/article/print/21822.

Adler, Mortimer. 1980. *How to Think About God: A Guide for the 20th-Century Pagan.* New York: Macmillan.

Aguirre, Anthony, and Gratton, Steven. 2002. "Steady State Eternal Inflation." *Physical Review D* 65, 083507.

Alabidi, Laila, and Lyth, David. 2006. "Inflation Models and Observation," *Journal of Cosmology and Astroparticle Physics. JCAP* 0605:016.doi:10.1088-1475-7516/2006/05016.

Albrecht, A., and Sorbo, L. 2004. "Can the universe afford inflation?" *J. Phys.* **A**38 1345-70 (hep-th/0405272).

Aquinas, St. Thomas. 1947. *The Summa Theologica of St. Thomas Aquinas I.* Translated by Fathers of the English Dominican Province. New York: Benziger Brothers, Inc.

————. 1955. *Summa Contra Gentiles — Book One.* Translated by Anton C. Pegis. New York: Doubleday.

————. 1956. *Summa Contra Gentiles — Book Three.* Translated by Vernon J. Bourke. Garden City, NY: Image.

————. 1964. *Treatise on Happiness.* Translated by John A. Oesterle. Notre Dame: University of Notre Dame Press.

————. 1965. *Aquinas on Being and Essence.* Translated and commentated by Joseph Bobik. Notre Dame: University of Notre Dame Press.

————. 1968. *On Being and Essence.* Translated by Armand Maurer. 2nd revised edition. Toronto: The Pontifical Institute of Mediaeval Studies.

Aristotle. 1941. *The Basic Works of Aristotle.* Edited by Richard McKeon. New York: Random House.

————. 1942. *Nicomachean Ethics.* Translated by W. D. Ross in *The Student's Oxford Aristotle.* New York: Oxford University Press.

————. 1980. *Aristotle's Physics.* Translated by Hippocrates G. Apostle. Grinnell, IA: The Peripatetic Press.

————. 1984(a). *Metaphysics.* Translated by W. D. Ross in *The Complete Works of Aristotle,* vol. 2. Edited by Jonathan Barnes. Princeton: Princeton University Press.

————. 1984(b). *Nicomachean Ethics.* Translated by W. D. Ross in *The Complete Works of Aristotle,* vol. 2. Edited by Jonathan Barnes. Princeton: Princeton University Press.

————. 1991. *Aristotle: Selected Works,* 3rd Edition. Translated by Hippocrates G. Apostle and Lloyd P. Gerson. Grinnell, IA: The Peripatetic Press.

Arkani-Hamed, N., Dimopoulos, S., and Dvali, G. 1998. "The Hierarchy Problem and New Dimemsions at a Millimeter," *Phys. Lett.* **B**429 263-72 (hep-ph/9803315).

Ashmore, Jerome. 1972. "Diverse Currents in Whitehead's View of Time," *Process Studies* 2, no. 3 (Fall 1972): 193-200.

Ashok, S., and Douglas, M. 2004. "Counting Flux Vacua," *JHEP* 0401 060 (hep-th/0307049).

Aspect, Alain, Dalibard, J., and Roger, G. 1982. "Experimental Test of Bell's Inequalities Using Time-Varying Analyzers," *Physical Review Letters,* vol. 49, iss. 25, pp. 1804-7.

Augustine, St. 1955. *Confessions and Enchiridion.* Translated by Albert C. Outler. Philadelphia: Westminster Press.

————. 1964. *On Free Choice of the Will.* Translated by Anna S. Benjamin and L. H. Hackstaff. New York: Bobbs-Merrill.

————. 1991. *Confessions.* Translated by Henry Chadwick. New York: Oxford University Press.

Baldner, Steven. 2007. "Mediaeval Views of Creation: St. Albert, St. Bonaventure, and St. Thomas." A paper delivered at Gonzaga University, April 17, 2007 (http://www.gonzagafaithreason.org/links.asp).

Balthasar, Hans Urs von. 1982. *The Glory of the Lord: A Theological Aesthetics.* Translated by Erasmo Leiva-Merikakis. Edinburgh: T. & T. Clark.

Banks, T. 2007. "Entropy and initial conditions in cosmology," hep-th/0701146.

Banks, T., Dine, M. and Gorbatov, E. 2003. "Is There a String Theory Landscape?" *JHEP* 0408 058 (hep-th/0309170).

Banks, Thomas, and Fischler, Willy. 2002. "Black Crunch." http://arXiv.org/abs/hep-th/0212113v.

Barr, Stephen M. 2003. *Modern Physics and Ancient Faith.* Notre Dame: University of Notre Dame Press.

Barrow, J., and Dabrowski, M. 1998. "Is There Chaos in Low-Energy String Cosmology?" *Phys. Rev.* **D**57 7204-22 (hep-th/9711049).

Barrow, J., and Kunze, D. 1997. "Spherical Curvature Inhomogeneities in String Cosmology," hep-th/9710018.

Barrow, J., and Tipler, F. 1986. *The Anthropic Cosmological Principle.* New York: Oxford University Press.

Barvinsky, A., and Kamenshchik, A. 2006. "Cosmological Landscape from Nothing: Some Like It Hot," *JCAP* 0609 014 (hep-th/0605132).

References

Bassett, B. 1997. "The Preheating-Gravitational Wave Correspondence: I," *Phys. Rev.* **D**56 3439 (hep-ph/9704399).

Bassett, B., and Viniegra, F. 2000. "Massless metric preheating," *Phys. Rev.* **D**62 043507 (hep-ph/9909353).

Bergson, Henri. 1965. *Duration and Simultaneity*. Translated by Leon Jacobson. Indianapolis: Bobbs-Merrill.

Boekraad, Adrian J., and Tristram, Henry. 1961. *The Argument from Conscience to the Existence of God*. London: Mill Hill.

Bohm, David. 1986. "Time, the Implicate Order, and Pre-Space," in *Physics and the Ultimate Significance of Time*. Edited by David Ray Griffin. Albany, NY: SUNY Press, pp. 177-208.

Bojowald, Martin. 2007. "What Happened Before the Big Bang?" *Nature Physics* (July 1, 2007): 523-25.

————. 2008. "Following the Bouncing Universe," *Scientific American*, October 2008. http:www.sciamdigital.com/index.cfm?374-3048.

Borde, Arvind, Guth, Alan, and Vilenkin, Alexander. 2003. "Inflationary spacetimes are not past-complete," *Physical Review Letters*, vol. 90, no. 15, pp. 151301-1 — 151301-4.

Borde, Arvind, and Vilenkin, Alexander. 1994. "Eternal inflation and the initial singularity," *Physical Review Letters*, vol. 72, no. 21, pp. 3305-8.

————. 1997. "Violation of the weak energy condition in inflating spacetimes," *Physical Review* D, pp. 717-23.

Bousso, R., and Freivogel, B. 2006. "A paradox in the global description of the multiverse," hep-th/0610132.

Bousso, R., and Polchinski, J. 2000. "Quantization of Four-form Fluxes and Dynamical Neutralization of the Cosmological Constant," *JHEP* 0006 006 (hep-th/0004134).

————. 2004. "The String Theory Landscape," *Scientific American*, **291**, pp. 60-69.

Boyanovsky, D., Cormier, D., de Vega, H., Holman, R., and Kumar, S. 1998. "Out of Equilibrium Fields in Inflationary Dynamics: Density Fluctuations" (hep-ph/9801453).

Boyanovsky, D., Cormier, D., de Vega, H., Holman, R., Singh, A., and Srednicki, M. 1997. "Scalar Field Dynamics in Friedman Robertson Walker Spacetimes," *Phys. Rev.* **D**56 1939-57 (hep-ph/9703327).

Bozza, V. 2005. "General solution for scalar perturbations in bouncing cosmologies," *JCAP* 0602 009 (hep-th/0512066).

Bozza, V., and Veneziano, G. 2005(a). "Scalar Perturbations in Regular Two-Component Bouncing Cosmologies," *Phys. Lett.* **B**625 177-83 (hep-th/0502047).

————. 2005(b). "Regular two-component bouncing cosmologies and perturbations therein," *JCAP* 0509 007 (gr-qc/0506040).

Bradley, Walter L. 1998. "Designed or Designoid?" in *Mere Creation: Science, Faith & Intelligent Design*. Edited by William A. Dembski. Downers Grove, IL: InterVarsity Press.

Brandenberger, R., Easther, R., and Maia, J. 1998. "Nonsingular Dilaton Cosmology," *JHEP* 9808 007 (gr-qc/9806111).

Brandenberger, R., Frey, A., and Lorenz, L. 2008. "Entropy Fluctuations in Brane Inflation Models," arXiv:0712.2178.

Breuer, R. 1991. *The Anthropic Principle: Man as the Focal Point of Nature*. Boston: Birkhäuser.

Brock, D. L. 1992. *Our Universe: Accident or Design?* Wits, South Africa: Star Watch.

Brustein, R., and Veneziano, G. 1994. "The Graceful Exit Problem in String Cosmology," *Phys. Lett.* **B**329 429-34 (hep-th/9403060).

Buonanno, A., Meissner, K., Ungarelli, C., and Veneziano, G. 1998. "Classical Inhomogeneities in String Cosmology," *Phys. Rev.* **D**57 2543-56 (hep-th/9706221).

Buchbinder, I. L. 1998. *Ideas and Methods of Supersymmetry and Supergravity, or, A Walk through Superspace*. Philadelphia: Institute of Physics Publications.

Callender, Craig, and Huggett, Nick, editors. 2001. *Physics Meets Philosophy at the Planck Scale: Contemporary Theories in Quantum Gravity*. Cambridge: Cambridge University Press.

Cantor, Georg. 1915. *Contributions to the Founding of the Theory of Transfinite Numbers*. Translated and introduced by Philip E. B. Jourdain. New York: Dover.

Capek, Milic. 1961. *Philosophical Impact of Contemporary Physics*. Princeton: Van Nostrand.

———. 1976. *Concepts of Space and Time: Their Structure and Their Development*. Boston: Reidel.

Carlip, S. 2007. "Transient Observers and Variable Constants *or* Repelling the Invasion of the Boltzmann Brains," hep-th/0703115.

Carr, B., editor. 2007. *Universe or Multiverse?* Cambridge: Cambridge University Press.

Carr, B. and Rees, M. 1979. "The Anthropic Cosmological Principle and the Structure of the Physical World," *Nature* **278,** 605-12.

Carroll, Sean. 2007. "Against a Bounce." www. discovermagazine.com/cosmicvariance 2007/07/02/Against-Bounce.

Carter, Brandon. 1967. "The Significance of Numerical Coincidences in Nature," http://arxiv.org/abs/0710.3543.

———. 1974. *Confrontation of Cosmological Theories with Observational Data: Symposium*. Edited by M. S. Longair. Boston: Reidel.

Castelvecchi, Davide. 2004-5. "The Growth of Inflation," *Symmetry*. Batavia, IL. Vol. 1, Issue 02, pp. 1-6.

Ceresole, A., Dall'Agata, G., Giryavets, A., Kallosh, R., and Linde, A. 2006. "Domain walls, near-BPS bubbles and probabilities in the landscape," *Phys. Rev.* **D**74 086010 (hep-th/0605266).

Cleaver, G. 2006. "Before the Big Bang, String Theory, God, and the Origin of the Universe," unpublished manuscript, http://www.metanexus.net/conferences/pdf/conference2006/Cleaver.pdf.

———. 2008. "In Search of the (Minimal Supersymmetric) Standard Model String," in

References

F. Balogh, editor, *String Theory Research Progress*. Nova Science Publishers, Inc., chapter 2 (hep-ph/0703027).

Cleaver, G., Faraggi, A., and Nanopoulos, D. 1999. "String Derived MSSM and M-Theory Unification," *Physics Letters* **B** 455, Issues 1-4, 135-46 (hep-ph/9811427).

Cohn, J. 1998. "Living with Lambda," *Astrophys. J. Suppl.* 259 213 (astro-ph/9807128).

Coleman, S., and De Luccia, F. 1980. "Gravitational Effects on and of Vacuum Decay," *Phys. Rev.* **D**21, 3305.

Collins, James. 1947. *The Thomistic Philosophy of the Angels*. Washington, DC: Catholic University of America Press.

————. 1959. *God in Modern Philosophy*. Chicago: Regnery.

Collins, R. 2003. "Evidence for Fine-Tuning," in N. Manson, editor, *God and Design: The Teleological Argument and Modern Science*. New York: Routledge, pp. 178-99.

————. 2007. "How to Rigorously Define Fine-Tuning," http://home.messiah.edu/~rcollins/FINETUNE/chapter%203%20how%20to%20rigorously%20define%20fine-tuning.htm#TOC2_1

————. 2009. "The Fine-Tuning Argument for Theism," forthcoming in W. Craig, editor, *The Blackwell Companion to Natural Theology*. Oxford: Blackwell.

————. (forthcoming) *The Well-Tempered Universe*.

Copan, P., and Craig, W. 2004. *Creation Out of Nothing: A Biblical, Philosophical and Scientific Exploration*. Grand Rapids: Baker Academic.

Copleston, Frederick. 1960. *Modern Philosophy Part II — Kant,* vol. 6 in *A History of Philosophy*. New York: Doubleday.

Coreth, Emerich. 1968. *Metaphysics*. Translated by Joseph Donceel. New York: Herder & Herder.

Craig, William Lane. 1979(a). *The Existence of God and the Beginning of the Universe*. San Bernardino, CA: Here's Life Publishers, Inc.

————. 1979(b). *The Kalam Cosmological Argument*. New York: Barnes & Noble.

————. 1993(a). "The Finitude of the Past and the Existence of God," in *Theism, Atheism, and Big Bang Cosmology*. New York: Clarendon Press, pp. 3-76.

————. 1993(b). "The Caused Beginning of the Universe," in *Theism, Atheism, and Big Bang Cosmology*. New York: Clarendon Press, pp. 141-60.

————. 1993(c). "'What Place, Then, for a Creator?': Hawking on God and Creation," in *Theism, Atheism, and Big Bang Cosmology*. New York: Clarendon Press, pp. 279-300.

———— and Smith, Quentin. 1993. *Theism, Atheism, and Big Bang Cosmology*. New York: Oxford University Press.

Craig, W. L., and Moreland, J. P., eds. 2009. *The Blackwell Companion to Natural Theology.,* Malden, MA: Wiley-Blackwell.

Craig, W. L., and Sinclair, J. 2009. "The Kalam Cosmological Argument." In *The Blackwell Companion to Natural Theology*. Edited by W. L. Craig and J. P. Moreland. Malden, MA: Wiley-Blackwell.

Davies, Paul. 1977. *Space and Time in the Modern Universe*. New York: Cambridge University Press.

————. 1978. *The Runaway Universe*. New York: Penguin Books.

————. 1982. *The Accidental Universe.* New York: Cambridge University Press.

————. 1983. *God and the New Physics.* New York: Simon & Schuster.

———— and Brown, J. R. 1986. *The Ghost in the Atom.* New York: Cambridge University Press.

———— and Brown, Julian. 1988. *Superstrings: A Theory of Everything?* Cambridge: Cambridge University Press.

Davis, Philip J., and Hersh, Reuben. 1981. *The Mathematical Experience.* Boston: Houghton Mifflin.

Dawkins, Richard. 1986. *The Blind Watchmaker.* New York: W. W. Norton.

————. 1996. *Climbing Mount Improbable.* New York: W. W. Norton.

Denef, F., and Douglas, M. 2004. "Distributions of Flux Vacua," *JHEP* 0405 072 (hep-th/0404116).

————. 2006. "Computational Complexity of the Landscape," hep-th/0602072.

Descartes, René. 1931. "Meditations on First Philosophy," in *The Philosophical Works of Descartes.* Edited and translated by Elizabeth S. Haldane and G. R. T. Ross. Cambridge: Cambridge University Press.

Dine, M. 2004. "Is There a String Theory Landscape: Some Cautionary Remarks," hep-th/0402101.

Dionysius the Areopagite. 1940. *On the Divine Names.* Translated by C. E. Rolt. London: The Trustees of the Society for Promoting Christian Knowledge.

Donagi, R., Khoury, J., Ovrut, B., Steinhardt, P., and Turok, N. 2001. "Visible Branes with Negative Tension in Heterotic M-Theory," *JHEP* 0111 041 (hep-th/0105199).

Douglas, M. 2004(a). "The statistics of string/M-theory vacua," *JHEP* 0305 046 (hep-th/0303194).

————. 2004(b). "Statistical analysis of the supersymmetry breaking scale," hep-th/0405279.

Dyson, L., Kleban, M., and Susskind, L. 2002. "Disturbing Implications of a Cosmological Constant," *JHEP* 0210 011 (hep-th/0208013).

Earman, J., and Mosterin, J. 1999. "A Critical Look at Inflationary Cosmology," *Philosophy of Science* **66,** 1-49.

Eddington, Sir Arthur. 1928.*The Nature of the Physical World.* Cambridge: Cambridge University Press.

Einstein, Albert. 1945. *The Meaning of Relativity.* Princeton: Princeton University Press.

————. 1956. *Lettres à Maurice Solovine.* Paris: Gauthier-Villars.

————. 1961. *Relativity: The Special and the General Theory.* Translated by Robert W. Lawson. New York: Crown.

————. 1998. *The Collected Papers of Albert Einstein.* Translated by Anna Beck; Peter Havas, consultant. Princeton: Princeton University Press.

Ellis, G. F. R., Kirchner, U., and Stoeger, W. R. 2003. "Multiverses and Physical Cosmology," *Journal of the Royal Astronomical Society* 3 (August 28, 2003): 14. www:http://arXiv:astro-ph/0305292.

Erickson, J., Gratton, S., Steinhardt, P., and Turok, N. 2006. "Cosmic Perturbations through the Cyclic Ages," hep-th/0607164.

References

Feinstein, A., Lazkoz, R., and Vazquez-Mozo, M. 1997. "Closed Inhomogeneous String Cosmologies," *Phys. Rev.* **D**56 5166 (hep-th9704173).

Felder, G., García-Bellido, J., Greene, P., Kofman, L., Linde, A., and Tkachev, I. 2000 "Dynamics of Symmetry Breaking and Tachyonic Preheating," *Phys. Rev. Lett.* 87 011601 (hep-ph/0012142).

Felder, G., Frolov, A., Kofman, L., and Linde, A. 2002. "Cosmology with Negative Potentials," *Phys. Rev.* **D**66 023507 (hep-th/0202017).

Felder, G., Kofman, L., and Linde, A. 2001. "Tachyonic Instability and Dynamics of Spontaneous Symmetry Breaking," *Phys. Rev.* **D**64 123517 (hep-th/0106179).

Feynman, Richard. 1967. *The Character of Physical Law.* Cambridge, MA: MIT Press.

Foffa, S. 2003. "Bouncing Pre-Big Bang on the Brane," *Phys. Rev.* **D**68 043511 (hep-th/0304004).

Fraenkel, Abraham Adolf; Bar-Hillel, Yehoshua; and Levy, Azriel. 1973. *Abstract Set Theory.* Amsterdam: North-Holland Publishing Co.

Freivogel, B. and Susskind, L. 2004. "A Framework for the Landscape," *Phys. Rev.* **D**70 126007 (hep-th/0408133).

Fry, Roger. 1998. "Retrospect," in *Vision and Design.* Edited by J. B. Bullen. Mineola, NY: Dover.

Garriga, J., and Vilenkin, A. 2008. "Prediction and Explanation in the Multiverse," *Phys. Rev.* **D**77, 043526 (hep-th/0711.2559).

Gasperini, M. 1999. "Looking back in time beyond the big bang," *Mod. Phys. Lett.* **A**14 1059-66 (gr-qc/9905062).

———. 2000. "Inflation and Initial Conditions in the Pre-Big Bang Scenario," *Phys. Rev.* **D**61 087301 (gr-qc/9902060).

———. 2007. "Dilaton Cosmology and Phenomenology," hep-th/0702166.

———. 2008. "The Pre-Big Bang Scenario Bibliography," http://www.ba.infn.it/~gasperin/.

Gasperini, M., Maggiore, M., and Veneziano, G. 1997. "Towards a Non-Singular Pre-Big Bang Cosmology," *Nucl. Phys.* **B**494 315-30 (hep-th/9611039).

Gasperini, M., Maharana, J., and Veneziano, G. 1996. "Graceful exit in quantum string cosmology," *Nucl. Phys.* **B**472 349-60 (hep-th/9602087).

Gasperini, M., and Veneziano, G. 2003. "The Pre-Big Bang Scenario in String Cosmology," *Phys. Rept.* 373 1-212 (hep-th/0207130).

Gibbons, G. W., and Hawking, S. W. 1993. *Euclidean Quantum Gravity.* River Edge, NJ: World Scientific.

Giddings, S., and Marolf, D. 2007. "A global picture of quantum de Sitter space," hep-th/0705.1178.

Giddings, S., and Thomas, S. 2002. "High Energy Colliders as Black Hole Factories: The End of Short Distance Physics," *Phys. Rev.* **D**65 056010 (hep-ph/0106219).

Gilson, Etienne. 1956. *The Christian Philosophy of St. Thomas Aquinas.* New York: Random House.

———. 1960. *The Christian Philosophy of Saint Augustine.* New York: Random House.

Gingerich, Owen. 2000. "Do the Heavens Declare?" in *The Book of the Cosmos.* Edited by Dennis Richard Danielson. Cambridge, MA: Perseus Publishing.

Gödel, Kurt. 1931. "Über formal unentscheidbare Sätze der Principia Mathematica und verwandter Systeme I." *Monatshefte für Mathematik und Physik* 38, pp. 173-98.

Gonzalez, G., and Richards, J. 2004. *The Privileged Planet: How Our Place in the Cosmos Is Designed for Discovery.* Lanham, MD: Regnery.

Gott III, J. Richard, Gunn, James E., Schramm, David N., and Tinsley, Beatrice M. 1974. "An Unbound Universe?" *Astrophysical Journal* 194, pp. 543-53.

Gratton, S., Khoury, J., Steinhardt, P., and Turok, N. 2004. "Conditions for Generating Scale Invariant Density Perturbations," *Phys. Rev.* $D69$ 103505 (astro-ph/0301395).

Green, A., and Malik, K. 2001. "Primordial black hole production due to preheating," *Phys. Rev.* $D64$ 021301 (hep-ph/0008113).

Green, M., and Schwarz, J. 1985. "The Hexagon Gauge Anomaly in Type I Superstring Theory," *Nucl. Phys.* **255**, 93-114.

Green, M., Schwarz, J., and Witten, E. 1987. *Superstring Theory* (2 volumes). Cambridge: Cambridge University Press.

Greene, Brian. 2000. *The Elegant Universe: Superstrings, Hidden Dimensions, and the Quest for the Ultimate Theory.* New York: Vintage Books.

Gribbin, John. 1984. *In Search of Schrödinger's Cat.* New York: Bantam Books.

Griffin, David Ray. 1986. *Physics and the Ultimate Significance of Time: Bohm, Prigogine, and Process Philosophy.* Albany: State University of New York Press.

Guth, Alan H. 1997. *The Inflationary Universe: The Quest for a New Theory of Cosmic Origins.* Reading, MA: Addison-Wesley.

———. 1999. "Eternal Inflation," *Cosmic Questions,* April 14-16, 1999, National Museum of Natural History, Washington, DC, pp. 1-15.

———. 2001(a). "Time Since the Beginning." *Astrophysical Ages and Time Scales,* MIT-CTP-3285, ASP Conference Series, vol. 245. http://arxiv.org/abs/astro-ph/0301199.

———. 2001(b). "Interview of the Week." http://www.daystarcom.org/interview/06interview.htm.

———. 2003. "Looking Backward: Inflation and the Beginning of the Universe." The Universe from the Ground Up 2003 Symposium. http://www.nsf.gov/od/lpa/events/ground_astro/webcast/508slides/guth_508/sld001.htm.

Guth, A., and Weinberg, E. 1983. "Could the Universe Have Recovered from a Slow First Order Phase Transition?" *Nucl. Phys.* **B**212, 321.

Hartle, J., and Hawking, S. 1983. "Wave function of the universe," *Phys. Rev.* $D28$ 2960-75.

Hartle, J., and Srednicki, M. 2007. "Are We Typical?" hep-th/0704.2630.

Hawking, Stephen. 1980. "Theoretical Advances in General Relativity," in H. Woolf, editor, *Some Strangeness in the Proportion.* Reading, MA: Addison-Wesley.

———. 1988. *A Brief History of Time: From the Big Bang to Black Holes.* New York: Bantam Books.

———. 1993. *Black Holes and Baby Universes, and Other Essays.* New York: Bantam Books.

References

Hawking, S., and Page, D. 1987. "How Probable Is Inflation?" *Nucl. Phys.* **B 298,** 789-809.

Hawking, S., and Penrose, R. 1970. "The singularities of gravitational collapse and cosmology," *Proceedings of the Royal Society, London* **A 314,** 529-48.

Herbert, Nick. 1985. *Quantum Reality: Beyond the New Physics.* New York: Anchor Books.

Herdeiro, Carlos. 1996. "M-Theory, the Theory Formally Known as Strings," in Cambridge Relativity and Cosmology website. Edited by Paul Shellard. Cambridge: University of Cambridge.

Hertog, Thomas. 1996. "Quantum Cosmology," in Cambridge Relativity and Cosmology website. Edited by Paul Shellard. Cambridge: University of Cambridge.

Heyl, J., and Loeb, A. 2002. "Vacuum Decay Constraints on a Cosmological Scalar Field," *Phys. Rev. Lett.* 88 121302 (astro-ph/0111570).

Hilbert, David. 1964. "On the Infinite," in *Philosophy of Mathematics.* Edited by Paul Benacerraf and Hilary Putnam. Englewood Cliffs, NJ: Prentice-Hall, pp. 134-51.

Hogan, C. 2000. "Why the Universe Is Just So," *Rev. Mod. Phys.* 72 1149-61 (astro-ph/9909295).

Holder, R. 2004. *God, the Multiverse, and Everything.* Burlington, VT: Ashgate.

Hollands, S., and Wald, R. 2002. "An Alternative to Inflation," *Gen. Rel. Grav.* **34** 2043-55 (gr-qc/0205058).

Hoyle, Fred. 1951. *The Nature of the Universe.* New York: Harper.

———. 1981. *Engineering and Science.* Pasadena, CA: California Institute of Technology, pp. 8-12.

———. 1983. *The Intelligent Universe.* New York: Holt, Rinehart & Winston.

Hoyle, Fred, and Fowler, William A. 1973. "On the Origin of Deuterium," *Nature* 241, pp. 384-86.

Hoyle, Fred, and Wickramasinghe, C. 1981. *Evolution from Space.* London: J. M. Dent & Sons.

Hubble, Edwin. 1929. "A Relation between Distance and Radial Velocity among Extragalactic Nebulae," *Proceedings of the National Academy of Sciences* 15, pp. 168-73.

Hume, David. 1969. *A Treatise of Human Nature.* New York: Viking Penguin, Inc.

Jastrow, Robert. 1977. *Astronomy Fundamentals and Frontiers.* New York: Wiley.

———. 1978. *God and the Astronomers.* New York: W. W. Norton.

Kachru, S., Kallosh, R. Linde, A., and Trivedi, S. 2003. "de Sitter Vacua in String Theory," *Phys. Rev.* **D68** 046005 (hep-th/0301240).

Kachru, S., Kallosh, R., Linde, A., Maldecena, J., McAllister, L., and Trivedi, S. 2003. "Towards Inflation in String Theory," *JCAP* 0310 013 (hep-th/0308055).

Kallosh, R., Kofman, L., and Linde, A. 2001. "Pyrotechnic Universe," *Phys. Rev.* **D64** 123523 (hep-th/0104073).

Kaloper, N., Linde, A. and Bousso, R. 1999. "Pre-Big Bang Requires the Universe to Be Exponentially Large from the Beginning," *Phys. Rev.* **D59** 043508 (hep-th/9801073).

Kant, Immanuel. 1965. *Critique of Pure Reason.* Translated by Norman Kemp Smith. New York: St. Martin's Press.

———. 2004. *Kant's Critique of Practical Reason and Other Works on the Theory of Ethics.* Translated by T. K. Abbott. New York: Barnes & Noble.

Kapner, D., Cook, T., Adelberger, E., Gundlach, J., Heckel, B., Hoyle, C., and Swanson, H. 2007. "Tests of the Gravitational Inverse-Square Law Below the Dark-Energy Length Scale," *Phys. Rev. Lett.* **98** 021101 (hep-ph/0611184).

Kauffman, Stuart A. 1993. *Origins of Order: Self-organization and Selection in Evolution.* New York: Oxford University Press.

———. 1995. *At Home in the Universe: The Search for Laws of Self-organization and Complexity.* New York: Oxford University Press.

Khoury, J., Ovrut, B., Steinhardt, P., and Turok, N. 2001(a). "The Ekpyrotic Universe: Colliding Branes and the Origin of the Hot Big Bang," *Phys. Rev.* **D64** 123522 (hep-th/0103239).

———. 2001(b). "A Brief Comment on 'The Pyrotechnic Universe,'" hep-th/0105212.

———. 2002. "Density Perturbations in the Ekpyrotic Scenario," *Phys. Rev.* **D66** 046005 (hep-th/0109050).

Khoury, J., Ovrut, B., Seiberg, N., Steinhardt, P., and Turok, N. 2002. "From Big Crunch to Big Bang," *Phys. Rev.* **D65** 086007 (hep-th/0108187).

Khoury, J., Steinhardt, P., and Turok, N. 2003. "Inflation versus Cyclic Predictions for Spectral Tilt," *Phys. Rev. Lett.* 91 161301 (astro-ph/0302012).

———. 2004. "Designing Cyclic Universe Models," *Phys. Rev. Lett.* 92 031302 (hep-th/0307132).

Kim, H., and Hwang, J. 2007. "Evolution of linear perturbations through a bouncing world model: Is the near Harrison-Zel'dovich spectrum possible via a bounce?" *Phys. Rev.* **D75** 043501 (astro-ph/0607464).

Kirk, G. S., Raven, J. E., and Schofield, M. 1983. *The Presocratic Philosophers,* 2nd ed. New York: Cambridge University Press.

Kobakhidze, A., and Mersini-Houghton, L. 2007. "Birth of the Universe from the Landscape of String Theory," *Eur. Phys. J.* **C49** 869-73 (hep-th/0410213).

Kofman, L. 1996. "The Origin of Matter in the Universe: Reheating after Inflation," astro-ph/9605155.

Koonin, E. 2007. "The cosmological model of eternal inflation and the transition from chance to biological evolution in the history of life," *Biology Direct:* http://www.biology-direct.com/content/2/1/15.

Krauss, L. 2005. *Hiding in the Mirror: The Mysterious Allure of Extra Dimensions, from Plato to String Theory and Beyond.* New York: Viking.

Kuhnen, K. 1977. "Combinatorics," in *Handbook of Mathematical Logic.* Edited by Jon Barwise. Amsterdam: North Holland Press, pp. 371-401.

Kumar, J. 2006. "A Review of Distributions on the String Landscape," *Int. J. Mod. Phys.* **A21** 3441-72 (hep-th/0601053).

Land, K., and Magueijo, J. 2005. "The Axis of Evil," *Phys. Rev. Lett.* **95** 071301 (astro-ph/0502237).

———. 2007. "The Axis of Evil Revisited," astro-ph/0611518.

Leibniz, Gottfried Wilhelm. 1956. *Philosophical Papers and Letters,* vol. 2. Edited and translated by R. Latta. Oxford: Oxford University Press.

References

Leslie, J. 1989. *Universes*. New York: Routledge.

Lewis, C. S. 1955. *Surprised by Joy: The Shape of My Early Life*. New York: Harcourt, Brace & World, Inc.

Liddle, Andrew R. 2000. *Cosmological Inflation and Large-Scale Structure*. Cambridge: Cambridge University Press.

Liddle, A., and Mazumdar, A. 1998. "Inflation during oscillations of the inflaton," *Phys. Rev.* **D**58 083508 (astro-ph/9806127).

Linde, Andrei. 1986(a). "Eternal Chaotic Inflation," *Mod. Phys. Lett.*, A1, 81.

———. 1986(b). "Eternally Existing Self-Reproducing Chaotic Inflationary Universe," *Phys. Lett.*, B175, 395.

———. 1994. "The Self-Reproducing Inflationary Universe," *Scientific American*. November, pp. 48-56.

———. 1998. "The Self-Reproducing Inflationary Universe," *Scientific American*. Special issue on cosmology, Spring, pp. 98-104.

———. 2001. "Inflation and String Cosmology," *Int. J. Mod. Phys.* **A**17S1 89-104 (hep-th/0107176).

———. 2006. "Sinks in the Landscape, Boltzmann Brains, and the Cosmological Constant Problem," *JCAP* 0701 022 (hep-th/0611043).

Lonergan, Bernard. 1972. *Method in Theology*. New York: Herder & Herder.

———. 1974. *A Second Collection by Bernard J. F. Lonergan*. Edited by William F. J. Ryan and Bernard J. Tyrrell. Philadelphia: Westminster Press.

———. 1992. *Insight: A Study of Human Understanding*. In *Collected Works of Bernard Lonergan* 3, edited by Frederick E. Crowe and Robert M. Doran. Toronto: University of Toronto Press.

Lotz, Johannes B. 1972. "Beauty," in *Philosophical Dictionary*. Translated and edited by Kenneth Baker. Spokane, WA: Gonzaga University Press, p. 30.

Lovejoy, Arthur. 1970. *The Great Chain of Being*. Cambridge, MA: Harvard University Press.

Lucas, John R. 1961. "Minds, Machines, and Gödel," *Philosophy* 36, p. 120.

Lyth, D. 2002. "The primordial curvature perturbation in the ekpyrotic universe," *Phys. Lett.* **B**524 1-4 (hep-ph/0106153).

Maggiore, M., and Sturani, R. 1997. "The fine-tuning problem in pre-big bang inflation," *Phys. Lett.* **B**415 335-43 (gr-qc/9706053).

Martin, J., and Brandenberger, R. 2001. "The Trans-Planckian Problem of Inflationary Cosmology," *Phys. Rev.* **D**63 123501 (hep-th/0005209).

Marx, Karl. 1970. *Critique of Hegel's 'Philosophy of Right.'* Cambridge: Cambridge University Press.

McFadden, P., Turok, N., and Steinhardt, P. 2007. "Solution of a Braneworld Big Crunch/Big Bang Cosmology," *Phys. Rev.* **D**76, 104038 (hep-th/0512123).

Messiah, A. 1999. *Quantum Mechanics* (Two volumes bound as one). Mineola, NY: Dover Publications.

Miller, Robert T., translator. 1997. *De Aeternitate Mundi* (*On the Eternity of the World*) by Saint Thomas Aquinas. In *Medieval Sourcebook* (Fordham University). http://www.fordham.edu/halsall/basis/aquinas-eternity.html

Moss, Ian G. 1996. *Quantum Theory, Black Holes, and Inflation*. New York: Wiley.

Newman, John Henry. 1908. *Sermons on Various Occasions* in the uniform edition of the works of John Henry Newman. London: Longmans, Green & Company.

———. 1961. Unpublished manuscript entitled "Proof of Theism." Edited by Adrian Boekraad and Henry Tristram in *The Argument from Conscience to the Existence of God*. London: Mill Hill.

———. 1979. *An Essay in Aid of a Grammar of Assent*. Notre Dame: University of Notre Dame Press.

Newton, Sir Isaac. 1756. *Four Letters from Sir Isaac Newton to Doctor Bentley, Containing Some Arguments in Proof of a Deity*. London: R. & J. Dodsley.

———. 1999. *Isaac Newton's Observations on the Prophecies of Daniel and the Apocalypse of St. John*. Edited by S. J. Barnett. Lewiston, NY: E. Mellen Press.

Oberhummer, H., Csótó, A., and Schlattl, H. 2000. "Fine-tuning of carbon-based life in the universe by triple-alpha process in red giants," *Science* 289 (July): 88-90.

Ooguri, H., and Vafa, C. 2006. "On the Geometry of the String Landscape and the Swampland," hep-th/0605264.

Otto, Rudolf. 1958. *The Idea of the Holy: An Inquiry into the Non-Rational Factor in the Idea of the Divine and Its Relation to the Rational*. New York: Oxford University Press.

Overbye, D. 2008. "Big Brain Theory: Have Cosmologists Lost Theirs?" *The New York Times*, Science Section, January 15th.

Page, D. 2000. "Is Our Universe Likely to Decay within 20 Billion Years?" hep-th/0610079.

———. 2006. "Return of the Boltzmann Brains," hep-th/0611158.

———. 2007(a). "Typicality Defended," arXiv:0707.4169.

———. 2007(b). "Predictions and Tests of Multiverse Theories," in B. Carr, editor, *Universe or Multiverse?* Cambridge: Cambridge University Press, pp. 411-30.

Paley, William. 1831. *Natural Theology: Or, Evidences of the Existence and Attributes of the Deity*. Boston: Lincoln & Edmonds.

Pasachoff, J. M., and Fowler, William A. 1974. "Deuterium in the Universe," *Scientific American*. May.

Pascal, Blaise. *Pensées*. 1958. Translated by W. F. Trotter. New York: E. P. Dutton & Co., Inc.

Penrose, Roger. 1965. "Gravitational Collapse and Space-Time Singularities," *Physical Review Letters* 14, pp. 57-59.

———. 1974. "Singularities in Cosmology," in M. S. Longair, editor, *Confrontation of Cosmological Theories with Observational Data*. Boston: D. Reidel.

———. 1979. "Singularities and Time-asymmetry," in *General Relativity: An Einstein Centenary Survey*, edited by Stephen Hawking and W. Israel. Cambridge: Cambridge University Press.

———. 1981. "Time-asymmetry and quantum gravity," in C. Isham, R. Penrose, and D. Sciama, *Quantum Gravity 2*. Oxford: Clarendon Press, pp. 245-72.

———. 1989(a). *The Emperor's New Mind*. Oxford: Oxford University Press.

———. 1989(b). "Difficulties with Inflationary Cosmology," in E. Fergus, editor, *Pro-*

ceedings of the 14th Texas Symposium on Relativistic Astrophysics, Ann. NY Acad. Sci. **571,** 249-64.

————. 2005. *The Road to Reality: A Complete Guide to the Laws of the Universe.* New York: Alfred A. Knopf.

Penzias, Arno A., and Wilson, Robert W. 1965. "A Measurement of Excess Antenna Temperature at 4080 Mc/s," *Astrophysical Journal* 142, pp. 419-21.

Plantinga, Alvin. 1964. *Faith and Philosophy.* Grand Rapids: Eerdmans.

Plato. 1961(a). *The Collected Dialogues of Plato.* Edited by Edith Hamilton and Huntington Cairns. Princeton: Princeton University Press.

————. 1961(b). *The Republic.* Translated by Paul Shorey. In *The Collected Dialogues of Plato.* Edited by Edith Hamilton and Huntington Cairns. Princeton: Princeton University Press.

————. 1961(c). *Timaeus.* Translated by Benjamin Jowett. In *The Collected Dialogues of Plato.* Edited by Edith Hamilton and Huntington Cairns. Princeton: Princeton University Press.

————. 1993. *Symposium and Phaedrus.* Translated by Benjamin Jowett. New York: Dover.

Polchinski, J. 2006. "The Cosmological Constant and the String Landscape," hep-th/0603249.

Polkinghorne, John P. 1996. *The Faith of a Physicist: Reflections of a Bottom-Up Thinker.* Minneapolis: Fortress.

————. 1998. *Belief in God in an Age of Science.* New Haven: Yale University Press.

Prigogine, Ilya. 1980. *From Being to Becoming.* New York: W. H. Freeman.

————. 1986. "Irreversibility and Space-Time Structure," in *Physics and the Ultimate Significance of Time.* Edited by David Ray Griffin. Albany: State University of New York Press, pp. 232-50.

Räsänen, S. 2002. "On ekpyrotic brane collisions," *Nucl. Phys.* **B**626 183-206 (hep-th/0111279).

Rees, M. 1997. *Before the Beginning: Our Universe and Others.* Reading, MA: Addison-Wesley, p. 185.

————. 2000. *Just Six Numbers: The Deep Forces That Shape the Universe.* New York: Basic Books.

Rey, S. J. 1996. "Back Reaction and Graceful Exit in String Inflationary Cosmology," *Phys. Rev. Lett.* 77 1929-32 (hep-th/9605176).

Riddle, A., and Urena-Lopez, L. 2006. "Inflation, dark matter and dark energy in the string landscape," *Phys. Rev. Lett.* **97** 161301 (astro-ph/0605205).

Robbins, D., and Sethi, S. 2005. "A Barren Landscape?" *Phys. Rev.* **D**71 046008 (hep-th/0405011).

Robinson, Abraham. 1966. *Non-Standard Analysis.* Amsterdam: North Holland Press.

————. 1969. "The Metaphysics of the Calculus," in *The Philosophy of Mathematics: Oxford Readings in Philosophy.* Edited by Jaakko Hintikka. London: Oxford University Press.

Ross, James F. 1969. *Philosophical Theology.* New York: Bobbs-Merrill.

Rotman, B., and Kneebone, G. T. 1966. *The Theory of Sets and Transfinite Numbers.* London: Oldbourne.

Russell, Bertrand. 1957. *Why I Am Not a Christian, and Other Essays on Religion and Related Subjects.* New York: Simon & Schuster.

Sahni, V., and Starobinsky, A. 2000. "The Case for a Positive Cosmological Lambda-term," *Int. J. Mod. Phys.* **D9** 373-444 (astro-ph/9904398).

Sandage, Allan R. 1970. "Cosmology: A Search for Two Numbers," *Physics Today.* February.

Sandage, A. R., and Tammann, G. A. "Steps Toward the Hubble Constant," *Astrophysical Journal* in multiple parts — i: 190 (1974), pp. 525-38; ii: 191 (1974), pp. 603-21; iii: 194 (1974), pp. 223-43; iv: 194 (1974), pp. 559-68; v: 196 (1975), pp. 313-28; vi: 197 (1975), pp. 265-80.

Saygili, K. 1999. "Hamilton-Jacobi Approach to Pre-Big Bang Cosmology at Long Wavelengths," *Int. J. Mod. Phys.* **A**14 225-40 (hep-th/9710070).

Silk, Joseph. 1980. *The Big Bang.* San Francisco: W. H. Freeman.

Smith, Quentin. 1993(a). "The Uncaused Beginning of the Universe," in *Theism, Atheism, and Big Bang Cosmology.* New York: Clarendon Press, pp. 108-39.

————. 1993(b). "Atheism, Theism, and Big Bang Cosmology," in *Theism, Atheism, and Big Bang Cosmology.* New York: Clarendon Press, pp. 195-217.

Smolin, L. 2006. *The Trouble with Physics: The Rise of String Theory, the Fall of a Science, and What Comes Next.* New York: Houghton Mifflin.

Spitzer, Robert J. 1989. *A Study of the Nature of Objectively Real Time.* Ann Arbor, MI: U.M.I.

————. 2000. "Definitions of Real Time and Ultimate Reality," in *Ultimate Reality and Meaning: Interdisciplinary Studies in the Philosophy of Understanding* 23:3, pp. 260-67.

————. 2001(a). "Proofs for the Existence of God, Part I: A Metaphysical Argument," *International Philosophical Quarterly* 41:2, June, pp. 161-81.

————. 2001(b). "Proofs for the Existence of God, Part II," *International Philosophical Quarterly* 41:3, September, pp. 305-31.

————. 2003. "Indications of Creation in Contemporary Big Bang Cosmology," *Philosophy in Science,* vol. 10. Tucson: Pachart Publishing.

Stein, Edith. 1989. *On the Problem of Empathy.* Translated by Waltraut Stein. Washington, DC: Institute of Carmelite Studies Publications.

Steinhardt, P. J. 1983. "In the Very Early Universe," *Proceedings of the Nuffield Workshop, Cambridge,* 21 June–9 July, 1982. Edited by G. W. Gibbons, S. W. Hawking, and S. T. C. Siklos. Cambridge: Cambridge University Press, p. 251.

————. 2004. "Has the cyclic model been cycling forever?" http://www.physics.princeton.edu/~steinh/cyclicFAQS/index.html#eternal

Steinhardt, P., and Turok, N. 2002(a). "Cosmic Evolution in a Cyclic Universe," *Phys. Rev.* **D**65 126003 (hep-th/0111098).

————. 2002(b). "A Cyclic Model of the Universe," hep-th/0111030.

————. 2002(c). "Is Vacuum Decay Significant in Ekpyrotic and Cyclic Models?" *Phys. Rev.* **D**66 101302 (astro-ph/0112537).

————. 2005. "The Cyclic Model Simplified," *New Astronomy Reviews* **49,** 43-7, www.physics.princeton.edu/~steinh/dm2004.pdf.

————. 2006. "Why the cosmological constant is small and positive," *Science* **312** 1180-82 (astro-ph/0605173).

————. 2007. *Endless Universe: Beyond the Big Bang.* New York: Random House.

Steinmetz, Charles Proteus. 1967. *Four Lectures on Relativity and Space.* New York: Dover.

Susskind, L. 2003. "The Anthropic Landscape of String Theory," hep-th/0302219.

————. 2004. "Supersymmetry Breaking in the Anthropic Landscape," hep-th/0405189.

————. 2005. As quoted in *New Scientist,* December 17, 2005.

————. 2006. *The Cosmic Landscape: String Theory and the Illusion of Intelligent Design.* New York: Little, Brown & Company.

Teresa of Avila, Saint. 1976. "The Book of Her Life," in *The Collected Works of St. Teresa of Avila,* vol. 1. Translated by Kieran Kavanaugh and Otilio Rodriguez. Washington, DC: ICS Publications, pp. 31-308.

Tolley, A., Turok, N., and Steinhardt, P. 2004. "Cosmological Perturbations in a Big Crunch/Big Bang Spacetime," *Phys. Rev.* **D69** 106005 (hep-th/0306109).

Tolman, Richard C. 1987 [1934]. *Relativity, Thermodynamics, and Cosmology.* New York: Dover.

Tryon, E. P. 1973. "Is the Universe a Vacuum Fluctuation?" *Nature* 246.

Tsujikawa, S., Bassett, B., and Viniegra, F. 2000. "Multi-field fermionic preheating," *JHEP* 0008 019 (hep-ph/0006354).

Turner, M., and Weinberg, E. 1997. "Pre-Big Bang Inflation Requires Fine-Tuning," *Phys. Rev.* **D56** 4604-9 (hep-th/9705035).

Turok, N., Perry, M., and Steinhardt, P. 2004. "M Theory of a Big Crunch/Big Bang Transition," *Phys. Rev.* **D70** 106004 (hep-th/0408083).

Underhill, Evelyn. 1930. *Mysticism: A Study in the Nature and Development of Man's Spiritual Consciousness.* London: Methuen.

————. 1993. "Entry on Passion Sunday, March 18, 1923," in *Fragments from an Inner Life.* Harrisburg, PA: Morehouse Publishing.

Unruh, W. 1996. As quoted in *Science,* August 30, 1996.

Vanchurin, V., and Vilenkin, A. 2006. "Eternal Observers and Bubble Abundances in the Landscape," *Phys. Rev.* **D74** 043520 (hep-th/0605015).

van Elst, H. 2008. "Inflationary Cosmological Models/Scalar Field Solutions," http://www.maths.qmul.ac.uk/~hve/ref_dir/chinfl.html (bibliography).

Veneziano, G. 1995. "String Cosmology: Basic Ideas and General Results," hep-th/9510027.

————. 1997. "Inhomogeneous Pre-Big Bang String Cosmology," Phys. Lett. **B** 406, 297-303 (hep-th/9703150).

————. 1998. "A Simple/Short Introduction to Pre-Big Bang Physics/Cosmology," hep-th/9802057.

————. 1999. "Pre-bangian origin of our entropy and time arrow," *Phys. Lett.* **B454** 22-26 (hep-th/9902126).

Vilenkin, Alexander. 1982. "Creation of Universes from Nothing," *Physical Letters* 117B.

———. 1983. "Birth of Inflationary Universes," *Physics Review* D27, 2848.

———. 2006(a). *Many Worlds in One: The Search for Other Universes.* New York: Hill & Wang.

———. 2006(b). "The vacuum energy crisis," *Science* **312** 1148-49 (astro-ph/0605242).

von Neumann, John. 1955. *Mathematical Foundations of Quantum Mechanics.* Translated by Robert T. Beyer. Princeton: Princeton University Press.

Watanabe, Y., and Komatsu, E. 2008. "Gravitational inflaton decay and the hierarchy problem," *Phys. Rev.* **D77** 043514 (arXiv:0711.3442).

Whitehead, Alfred North. 1978. *Process and Reality: An Essay in Cosmology.* Edited by David Ray Griffin and Donald W. Sherburne. New York: Macmillan.

Whitrow, G. J. 1954-55. "The Age of the Universe," *British Journal for the Philosophy of Science,* 5, pp. 215-25.

———. 1961. *The Natural Philosophy of Time.* London: Thomas Nelson & Sons.

———. 1967. "Reflections on the Natural Philosophy of Time," *Annals of the New York Academy of Sciences* 138, pp. 422-32.

———. 1968. "Time and the Universe," *The Voices of Time.* Edited by J. T. Fraser. London: Penguin Press.

———. 1970. "Time and Cosmical Physics," *Studium Generale* 23, pp. 224-33.

———. 1978. "On the Impossibility of Infinite Past Time," *British Journal for the Philosophy of Science,* pp. 39-45.

Witten, E. 1995. "Some Comments on String Dynamics," hep-th/9507121.

Woit, P. 2006. *Not Even Wrong: The Failure of String Theory and the Search for Unity in Physical Law.* New York: Basic Books.

Zippin, Leo. 1962. *Uses of Infinity.* Washington, DC: Mathematical Association of America.

Index